The Odyssey of Woolly Mammoth Boy

One Man's Journey through Autism, Racism, Grief, and Surviving the American Dream

R. Vicente Rubio

The Odyssey of Woolly Mammoth Boy

One Man's Journey through Autism, Racism, Grief, and Surviving the American Dream

R. Vicente Rubio

Copyright © 2014 R. Vicente Rubio

All rights reserved. Except as permitted under U.S. Copyright Act of 1976, no part of this publication may be reproduced, distributed, or transmitted in any form or by any means, or stored in a database or retrieval system, without the prior written permission of the publisher.

Published by Together Editing Press
570 El Camino Real #150-365, Redwood City, CA 94063 United States
www.togetherediting.com

Cover artwork by Sebastian Smith.

Library of Congress Control Number: 2014935733
ISBN-13: 978-1-939698-00-1
Printed in the United States of America
First Edition: January 2014
9 8 7 6 5 4 3 2 1

Acknowledgements

I STARTED THIS BOOK IN BAD Endorf, Germany in July 2010, and finished it in a sunny home on a Hawaiian island on November 21, 2013. With great gratitude, I wish to offer a deep bow to the following people.

I would like to extend my sincere thanks to my editor, Anna Doherty, and the team at Together Editing & Design, Leslie Peters and Laura Neil. You not only afforded me your professional expertise, you also supported me through the challenging and emotional roadbumps I faced along the way. I could not have made it without your generous and loving support. Thank you.

Thank you, Adam Robbert, for tackling the initial proofreading and providing your kind and sensitive support.

Thank you, Sebastian Smith, for offering your creative artistic ideas and concepts for the cover art. You have been a great friend for many years, and I look forward to many more times together with you and your family.

I also wish to thank the following public libraries for the wonderful spaces to write: the Long Beach Public Library, Long Island, New York; the California State libraries of Los Gatos, Saratoga, and Los Altos; and the Town of Atherton Pubic Library.

A Note to My Mother

THIS BOOK RELATES MY MEMORIES, and mine alone. At the same time that I hold the truth of my own experience, I also know you did your best by us under very difficult circumstances and loved us as best you could.

You will undoubtedly remember many of these events differently. I pray that you can hear my story, and know that my own memories do not devalue yours—even where our stories are quite different, we are always joined by love.

Dedicated to my *dakini*
of Pure Emptiness and Pure Pleasure!

Irene Bell Brody

Beloved to many as Dr. Brody, Ph.D.

Contents

Acknowledgements i

Author's Note 1

Part 1: The Yearling 7

1. Ferdinand Magellan's Good Fortune 8
2. The United States Navy and My Dada 11
3. The Beginnings of Woolly Mammoth Boy 13
4. An Immigrant's Son Born to Two Colliding Shooting Stars from the Deepest Heavens 16
5. Woolly Mammoth Boy Discovers Tears 20
6. Tying Shoes and Other Early Lessons of Survival 22
7. Woolly Mammoth Boy with Hungry Hunters and the Ice Age 29
8. Dragons on the Wall 32

Part 2: Little Big Man 37

9. Woolly Mammoth Boy Is Reborn 38
10. "President Kennedy has been shot in Dallas!" 40
11. Woolly Mammoth Seagull Boy 44
12. Trouble at Paul Revere 45
13. Why Humans Love and Hate, According to Thought 49
14. The Altar Boy and His Fall from Grace 52
15. Learning Gentleman's Manners and Fire on Witch's Mountain 59
16. Abandonment Issues and Mom Dates Hank Williams 64
17. Across the Bridge and Back 68
18. Laundry, Doughnuts, and Racism 75
19. Fast Feet Bilbo Baggins, and a Rite of Passage 82

Part 3: Far Away Places 103

20. Over the Hills and Far Away 104
21. Love Letters and the .22 Caliber Rifle..................111
22. The Rudgear Estates Boys 118
23. Bolinas and *In Watermelon Sugar*..................129
24. Croissants and Vampires: The Journey North to Oregon 135
25. Mushroom Heaven and Nijinsky 140

Part 4: Dance, Woolly Mammoth Boy, Dance!.................. 149

26. Two Suitcases: "Go East, Young Man!" 150
27. Year One in NYC 156
28. "Once a Dancer, Always a Dancer." 174
29. Elevators and Bagels: NYC..................187

Part 5: Life Dancing 213

30. Boston Tea Party..................214
31. Rajada Falls and the Sacred Circle..................247
32. Return to the West..................269
33. San Francisco—Again 281

Part 6: In the Land of the Mountain Lion 299

34. The Catskill Mountains 300
35. The House of Yin..................310
36. Mind–Body and the Ground..................329
37. In the Land of the Woolly Mammoths..................346

Part 7: The Fury of Fire and Ice.................. 355

38. The Journey of Irene Bell Blue Pele Old Turtle..................356
39. December 30, 2010: Shokan, New York..................388
40. Poems by the Great Ocean..................397

41. Into the Haven of Pirates 414
42. Hurricane Irene: August 28, 2011 428

Part 8: Shugyosha Samurai 443
43. Vicente 444
44. The Path of the Warrior 450

Epilogue 455

About the Author 457

List of Image Attributions

Where noted, images are the author's.

Images used through public license:

p. 3, Woolly Mammoth image from Wikimedia Commons: in the Royal BC Museum in Victoria, Canada, display from 1979 using musk ox hair. Public License material, available at http://commons.wikimedia.org/wiki/File:Woolly_mammoth.jpg.

p. 154, Nijinsky image from Wikimedia Commons by way of the National Library of France: photo by Leon Bakst, 1911, Vaslav Nijinsky (1890–1950) in Le Spectre de la Rose by Michel Fokine (1880-1942). Costume by Leon Bakst (1867-1924). Image is in the Public Domain according to U.S. law (as of this publishing, 80 years have passed since the death of the original copyright holder). Available at http://commons.wikimedia.org/wiki/File:Nijinsky,_Le_Spectre_de_la_Rose,_1911.jpg.

p. 334, Kuka'ilimoku idol image from Wikimedia Commons: Kuka'ilimoku, Memoirs Bishop Museum, Vol. I, Fig. 22., prior to 1899. Photographed originally by Russell & Co., part of Memoirs by the Bernice Pauahi Bishop Museum (original publication date unknown). Image is in the Public Domain according to U.S. law. Available at http://commons.wikimedia.org/wiki/File:Kukailimoku,_Memoirs_Bishop_Museum,_Vol._I,_Fig._22.jpg.

p. 353, Mammoths in snow image from Wikimedia Commons: Woolly mammoths (Mammuthus primigenius) in a late Pleistocene landscape in northern Spain, by Mauricio Antón, (c) 2008 Public Library of Science, Creative Commons license. Available at http://commons.wikimedia.org/wiki/File:Woolly_mammoth_%28Mammuthus_primigenius%29_-_Mauricio_Ant%C3%B3n.jpg.

p. 429 Hurricane Irene image from Wikimedia Commons: Image of Hurricane Irene as seen by NASA's GOES-13 satellite on August 27, 2011 at 10:10 am EDT, about two hours after it made landfall at Cape Lookout, North Carolina, at 8 am, by the NASA/NOAA GOES Project. Image is in the Public Domain because all NASA images are public domain unless otherwise noted. Available at http://commons.wikimedia.org/wiki/File:Hurricane_Irene_landfall_NASA.jpg.

Images for which a license was purchased:

p. 30, Woolly Mammoth image

Author's Note

Stories about real events sometimes seem so outrageous that they border on the realm of fairytales. Fantastical, mythical, sacred, terrible, and dire, tales have been passed down throughout the history of humankind, one human being to another, one generation to the next. These verbal and written tales were used to teach, mentor, and convey the passage of time, and of living a life gone by. They speak of moments when it's possible to believe in magic—the unexplainable joy of the present, the innocence of holding hands with your first love, of not desiring anything else...ever. Tales tell of a time when all was not as it is today. They recall brief flashes where we experience things in a full register with all our senses—our entire self—and then they are gone forever.

In the early 2000s, I was in a very low place and felt like everything was falling apart in my life. My friend, mentor, and shaman Christina Stack guided me on a journey to the Lower World so I could meet my animal allies and get some assistance from them. She was a mentor who recognized my spiritual and healing strengths. She saw the powerful teacher I was, so when I called her in dismay about everything that seemed to be going down the drain, she asked me to come in and see her.

"Ron, I know you have experienced Native American sweat lodges and spiritual beliefs. I want you to journey to meet your animal allies. You are in need of their support. They reside in the Lower World. The Middle World is this plane, and the Upper World is where your teachers reside."

"I know that Puma is an animal power I have resonated with for many years," I said to her.

"Yes, that may be so, but descending into the Lower World is where your true animal ally will present itself to you."

With that, she began the journey.

I wore a pair of comfortable eye nightshades—the ones you wear to block out all light. A tape recorder was turned on, and I was asked to speak out loud about all I experienced. Christina drummed on a large round drum, beating out a steady trance rhythm. With the drumming I was sent into an "awake" trance, where I was quite aware of what I was doing, but at the same time my inner consciousness descended into the Lower World. Christina was there to guide me through the process so I would return whole when it was time to end the journey. She would be there to make sure I did not leave parts of myself behind.

Before the drumming started I was asked to see clearly a path of descent. I had to remember the exact path of my descent, because I would have to retrace my way back up. Christina started recording the journey; I began speaking out loud. The journey began…

The path started in my childhood home in San Francisco. I descended down the stairs from the upper floor of my home to the ground floor. I opened the door that led down into the basement. I could not see an opening to the Lower World until I discovered a large hole under the stair landing. I knew damn well that hole did not exist there when I was a child.

"Jump down the hole," Christina instructed.

I lowered myself into the hole and then dropped. It was a short slide down and then I landed on soft ground—like a jungle floor.

"Walk around now."

As I walked around in the lush vegetation, a large puma appeared and stared at me. I knew it would be puma that would meet me!

"No. Continue to walk around."

I continued to walk around. Large banana-like leaves surrounded me now. Suddenly, a large head parted the leaves above me. It was a large, white woolly mammoth!

"Follow it!"

I was amazed by its size and strength. It picked me up with its trunk and placed me on its back. A very young, small, white woolly mammoth tagged behind, holding the tail of the mammoth I was riding. A third white woolly mammoth was nearby. I was so happy!

"This is your power animal!"

Yes! We strolled through the jungle and neared a large swimming hole. They entered and we played in the water. I sat on the woolly mammoth's belly. We all got up and left the water. The white woolly mammoth lowered me onto the ground before it and stared into my eyes with its large, soft gaze. They began to walk away, back into the thick jungle.

"It is time for you to come back. Please retrace your path now."

I began to walk back through the jungle. I saw an opening—the end of the slide. I crawled up. I entered the basement. I walked up the stairs, opened the door, and left the basement. I walked up the stairs to the upper floor of my childhood home.

"You are back. Slowly take some breaths and open your eyes very slowly."

That was how I was introduced to my animal ally—the woolly mammoth. Christina told me the white woolly mammoth was communicating to me my

strength and solidity. I was reminded to be strong and grounded through the trying times I was experiencing. The white woolly mammoth was also showing me to be playful and joyful. With such strength I was reminded to be gentle and lighthearted.

I soon felt quite familiar with the woolly mammoth. Weeks later, while sitting in my backyard in Shokan, New York, I would "see" a small group of them strolling and grazing on our large open field. I found out that the mastodon—a cousin of the woolly mammoth—had inhabited the Hudson Valley in ancient times.

Woolly mammoths had fascinated me as a child, and through reflection and meditation, I came to see my life's journey in connection to these wild, primitive, powerful, mystical creatures.

Woolly Mammoth Boy is a survivor's tale. It is a story of how I filled a void in my life with creative and awkward perseverance. It is a tale of my dedication to living life with meaning and integrity, to flourishing through times of chaos wrapped in the bewilderment of self-doubt, and a tale of moving on when all around me did not make any sense. This is a tale of things that were and are no more—times that go blasting by like an icy Nor'easter wind rattling your bones, leaving you thankful you are still here to feel the next experience come along. This is my tale.

This is also my voice and my dreamtime vision. It is a tale of magic and the darkness of the soul exposed in the glare of the Sun's revealing brightness. This is the tale of a person transitioning between centuries of time, between the places I was supposed to be in, the places I chose to be in, and the places I was forced to fit in. Every chapter is framed through the Woolly Mammoth Boy lens, as I layer together what I experienced at the time and what I know now—this mystical approach is a metaphorical way to capture some of the profound differences in my experiences of life as a person with Asperger syndrome. (Asperger's was an official diagnosis from 1994 until 2013, when the American Psychological Association chose Autism Spectrum Disorder as an umbrella term. In this book, I use the term "Asperger's" and describe myself as an "Aspie" because that is the language I slowly came to understand. However, I hope my story will appeal to people on all parts of the autism spectrum, and to those who love and care for them.)

This book is for my clients, my students, and their parents and caregivers—all those I have had the privilege to teach and befriend in the last thirty years of my professional career as a dance teacher, martial arts instructor, and mentor. This is also a story for all the young people who are at risk and dealing with life transitions, divorce, family violence, or single parenting, and are challenged by drug addictions, running away, or suicidal mentalities.

Woolly Mammoth Boy is a book for neuro-typicals, people on the autism spectrum, and those with Post Traumatic Stress Disorder (PTSD) and Traumatic Brain Injury (TBI). People with PTSD and TBI display numerous behaviors and symptoms that are detrimental to both personal and social health. Many of these symptoms include sleep deprivation, eating disorders, and memory loss; dark, suicidal depressions; uncontrollable "zero-to-100-mile-an-hour" anger rages; and low tolerance for social and sensory stimulation. They also experience low energy, being spooked easily, and addiction, and process the world through the lens of a rigid, on-edge thinker. As a person recently diagnosed on the autism spectrum, I found many of these symptoms present in my own life, and as a victim of severe physical abuse during childhood, I sustained a TBI at a very early age while my tender brain was still developing. The physical violence and beatings, the yelling and screaming, and the demeaning psychological violence later manifested in PTSD behaviors that I expressed throughout my entire life.

I wrote this story for my daughters, nephews, and nieces, so they could know of a time and place they did not have to experience. Growing up in a tumultuous America during the '60s and '70s, I was also exposed to—and a recipient of—the blatant and degrading racism that flowed so easily in the society in which I was born a first-generation Filipino-American.

My experiences of being bullied and beaten, laughed at, passed over, segregated, ignored, and ridiculed because of the color of my skin, shape of my eyes, color of my hair, skinny, short stature, and the way I spoke, led me to developing a "Social PTSD." I played out my own racism and aggression against the white powers that had allowed racism to stay alive and well. The preciousness of my experience growing up was robbed by the vacancy of love and social connection.

    As for the people in my story—my family, friends, and foes—they may have another perspective on my accounts. What is written here are my recollections, void of blame or retribution. For right or wrong, this is how I experienced my life.

    I wrote this autobiography in my sometimes "salty" language, as my Marine vet buddies would say. This is the way I speak, and though I am politically correct most of the time, I still am who I am, so please forgive me if my language offends you in any way. Here then, my friends, are tales of great questing for valor and good deeds, of glorious failings into dark crevices in the deep Earth, and of surviving. This is a survivor's tale. Peace now my friends, and be comforted for these tales are true.

Part 1: The Yearling

1. Ferdinand Magellan's Good Fortune

When one wields the sword to conquer and rule...bittersweet will his reign be, and eventually he will fall by the sword.

–The Observations of Woolly Mammoth Boy

On April, 27, 1521, Captain-General Ferdinand Magellan, the head honcho of a Spanish naval expedition searching for a Pacific trade passage that would make Spain a world power, landed with his *conquistador* cronies on the small island of Mactan, which lies off the main island of Cebu, near a bigger island that would later be known as Bohol, Philippines. Magellan, the seafaring and greedy fool, really thought he had all the pieces in place. "Damn those dark native heathens!" he must have thought. "We enjoy the use of black powder and guns, superior body armor, and *mucho cojones*, and sail unknown waters halfway around the known world! How dare those brown-skinned barbarians, to whom we offer our friendship and holy guidance and salvation, defy our will! Our Spanish valor and steel will show these godless heathens to take heed when Spain says to yield...we are going to kick some serious heathen ass...God, Our Father be praised!"

He was wrong.

As Magellan waded ashore with his heavily armored, loaded down Spanish soldiers at low tide, they were immediately bogged down in the foot-grabbing, mudlike sand. In a moment of strategic brilliance and simplicity, the local Moro tribal chief, Lapu-Lapu, unleashed his warriors upon Magellan. Lapu-Lapu had waited patiently and safely on the shoreline watching these invaders fall into his trap. For you see, even the youngest Mactan village child—and even the village idiot—knew that the low tide always created impassable conditions to the shoreline. In the ensuing battle, the Moro warriors wounded Magellan with a spear thrust and a cut to his left leg. As Magellan bent over in pain, Lapu-Lapu swooped in. In his mighty hands he held a large cutlass that resembled a scimitar, and he gloriously lopped Magellan's Spanish head—a head so packed with dreams of power, women, and fine wine—clean off his body.

Magellan's head splashed into the salty water, freed from its fat, rich, European body, which now drifted into the lapping waters of the Cebu Straits and the Camotes Sea. For a microsecond in time and space, there was still brain activity in his dismembered head; his amazed, fluttering eyes saw the Moro chief Lapu-Lapu looking down, smiling, and finally spitting in his Spanish, black-bearded face.

Part of a mural at the Mactan Island Battle site, Cebu Island, Philippines. Photo by author.

Magellan's last thought as all brain activity ceased was, "Why that dirty bastard son-of-an-uncivilized-bitch!"

Tough beans, Ferdinand. *Silent weeping...*

The Spanish survivors returned to their boats and left without their captain's body. The Battle of Mactan Island was over.

Needless to say, the Spanish came back in great numbers and conquered the island natives. They promptly introduced Catholicism—*the* religion of religions—to the natives, and began an almost 400-year stranglehold on the 10,000-island archipelago the Spanish would name the Philippines, after their Spanish King Philip, who was living far away in bustling Madrid.

Ah, the sweet beginnings of a nation that would be the whipping boy for the Spanish, Americans, Japanese, and then the Americans again. The Philippines became a story of "love at first sight" for the small minority of rich Filipinos and their Spanish overlords. The Spanish, with their white skin, installed a toxic, Eurocentric, and internalized racism within the indigenous people—much as they did in Mexico, South America, and Central America. The Spanish kept the wealthy natives, who already had power and influence over their fellow countrymen, happy by establishing a landowner monopoly that still basks in the warm light of the Pacific Ocean sun today.

Ah, the sweet smell of success! Say it out loud, "I am brown and I think I am proud! (As long as my nose is long and straight rather than flat and wide, and my skin lighter than my dark brown servant boy!)."

Oh, thank the Great Spirit above Magellan never made it home alive! He would have never lived it down that some native bush-monkey kicked his Spanish ass!

In 2007, I made a pilgrimage to the Philippines to honor my grandfather, "Dada." He was a prisoner of the Japanese during the outbreak of World War II, and was forced on the Bataan Death March with the other Allied prisoners. Thousands of men died on the march, but Dada survived. During my pilgrimage, I retraced the Death March step-by-step starting at Kilometer Marker One. Later, I had the privilege to teach aikido on the island of Cebu. There, I also took up study of the Filipino fighting art *Lapunti Arnis*. My arnis teacher took me to visit the Mactan battle site on the island of Mactan not far away. In a moment of great delight, I fulfilled a lifelong dream. I spat upon the very place, marked by a stone, where that fool of a man Magellan lost his head! Dreams do come true!

Me at the stone that marks where Magellan lost his head. Photo by author.

2. The United States Navy and My Dada

Treasure your ancestors always for they went before you. They felt the stinging whip and the harsh salty seas. You sit now pretty on green grass twinkling your toes, smiling as you play with your toys and distractions.

–Woolly Mammoth Boy Remembers

TRADITIONALLY, IN THE UNITED STATES Navy before 1945, Filipinos were allowed to serve only as stewards, kitchen help, or clean-up boys, but by 1949 my maternal grandfather was a Chief Warrant officer, the first Filipino officer in the United Sates Navy. He was a US Navy man of World War I and World War II. Shortly before the outbreak of World War II in the Pacific Theater, "Dada"—Geraldo Vicente Ponciano—was serving in the US Navy in Manila, Philippines. Dada had moved his family to the provinces outside of Manila well before the December 7, 1941 attack on Pearl Harbor and the December 8, 1941 invasion by Japanese troops of the Philippines. After bitter fighting, my Dada was made a prisoner of war, as were all Allies forced to surrender to the victorious Japanese in April 1942. He was already in his late thirties.

All Allied prisoners of war taken in the battles for the island of Corrigidor and the Bataan mainland were gathered together to begin a special hell that came to be known as the Bataan Death March. This was a sixty-odd-mile march, in which thousands of Allied prisoners were killed if they fell, stumbled, grew too sick to continue, or looked at their Japanese guards the wrong way. Some were butchered by their Japanese captors for the pure joy of killing, and this proved to be only the first phase of the hell to come once the survivors reached their destination. Some were destined to die in labor camps on the mainland of Japan. Most of the deaths came from the hundreds of Filipinos who served in the Allied ranks; there is no love lost between Japanese and Filipinos from that generation today—but Dada survived. He survived the hell, the beatings, and the incredible horror of seeing comrades-in-arms beaten to death, starved, or fallen behind, never to be seen again.

Twenty years later, as I sat on the floor looking up into his aged face as a young five-year-old, he told me how, once he was freed, he went back to fight, and he killed the Japanese with a vengeance. His oldest son, an uncle whom I would never meet, was killed in guerilla action behind enemy lines. Dada would show me the physical scars on his body, and told me war stories that left deep wounds in his heart. In the early 1960s Dada would take me along with him to the Hunter's Point Naval Shipyard in San Francisco to do the family shopping for food at the base commissary. I would sit in the passenger seat of one of the cool cars he drove, and we would make the drive to Hunter's Point in style. We would ride up to the base gate, which was always manned by a real sturdy and smartly dressed United States Marine sentry.

As we pulled up to the gate, I watched with pure joy and pride as the Marine would stand tall and snap a real sharp salute to Dada; Dada would respond in kind, and then we would pass through the gate and into the base. Here it was, 1962, in a very white man's California, and a big, strong, white US Marine was saluting a shortly cropped white-haired Filipino man—all of five-foot-one-inch—a retired US Naval officer and my grandfather. Damn! I thought to myself. This was the coolest shit I had ever seen in my young life.

To this day I still draw much strength and pride from the vision of the hard-earned respect and service that my Dada gave to this country, the United States of America. No one was going to take that away. My Dada met presidents, admirals, and generals. He was the *MAN*. I was, and still am, so damn proud of my Dada. He died in 1985 and I could not come back for the funeral. I was stuck in New York City as a dirt-poor dancer with no money to buy a flight back to San Francisco. The day of his death and the funeral that I missed bum me out to this day.

Ah, the United States Navy. My father and the uncles on my mother's side were all Navy men. The best way to get into the States, and into a new world of chances, opportunities, and dreams, was joining the US Navy. United States Navy, thank you for not making Dada a dishwasher in a ship's galley. Thank you for giving him a chance.

3. The Beginnings of Woolly Mammoth Boy

...and so I was reborn again and again. There had to be a purpose and a reason. Ah, what a foolish thought that is! For what was... was. What will be...will be. And so, I was created once more to be born and destined to experience life once again, for good or for worse.

It really did not matter where, when, or who I was to be. What mattered was that whatever life I was offered, I would live that life with meaning. Nothing was guaranteed and all was up to me.

–Woolly Mammoth Boy Remembers

THE LONE, SINGLE CELL DRIFTED and floated in the great chaos of stars and clouds of cosmic dust. Slowly the cell began to rotate, first turning clockwise and then counter-clockwise, generating friction and heat. With each new rotation, slowly picking up speed, the lone cell began building enough energy to divide and multiply. From a single cell a many-celled organism continued to grow. Odd shapes appeared and disappeared. What seemed to appear at first as a wing started to solidify—wait, no—it changed again into what looked like a foot, or was it a reptilian eye, or a dolphin's fin? As the mass of cells continued to evolve larger and larger, no true shape ever manifested. This ever-changing organic life form floated aimlessly in the depths of the great Universe for many eons in a single, timeless moment. There it floated, protected by the Breath and Light of a Spirit with no name.

Then a time arrived when the consciousness of this lone organic being began to focus on one image, one idea: a large organic life form covered in a mass of dark brown, matted hair—coarse and bristly. From its torso of flesh and muscle sprouted four large stumplike appendages. Legs? An immense cranium slowly formed, large enough to support two long, curved tusks of strong white ivory—almost a third of its total body mass. Between these tusks a long, flexible tube of hollowed flesh sprang forth, and floated gently in space. Then, in a split second—in the time it takes a beam of light to travel through empty space—the shape changed again, into a small humanoid organism. This new transformation spoke a series of sounds: "Woolly Mammoth Boy." Then, this shape too disappeared only to reappear as a single cell. The process of evolution started all over...from scratch, from the beginning. Only this time, a sound resonated in the great void—a sound so deep in tone it shook the nearby stars: "Woolly Mammoth Boy."

After a timeless period, Thought appeared and directed itself toward the mass of organic material that had been floating in the great Universe of stars and black holes for a couple of long Times.

"So, you have a choice," Thought communicated without words to the organic mass, which was now a mishmash of bones, muscle, and flesh. "Who do you wish to grace with your presence?

"?&ierufhsakjgas*yrjkfhsduew#$$@cbsd," the organic mass replied.

"I did not quite catch that. Can you say that a little bit slower please?"

Taking a long pause, the organic mass spoke, "I choose two humanoids on the third rock from the sun of a solar system down the road a piece." The organic mass replied more slowly so it could be understood.

"Well, well, little one. Do these two humanoids have any distinguishable features?" Thought asked, without getting too nosy.

"Yes, these two humanoids are called Filipinos. They can be dark or light in skin tone, and short and stout in body structure."

"Filipino…is that spelled with a *P* or an *F*?" Thought inquired.

"With an *F*. You use a *P* for the country of origin—the Philippines."

"Ah, very tricky…could get confusing. Yet, I like this choice already," Thought smirked. "So be it! Good fortunes to you and break a leg, little one. Do these humanoids have a title, a name?"

"Yes, they do in fact have a clan name," the organic mass quivered in response. "Their clan name is 'Rubio.'"

"Do they have blond hair? The name means 'blond' in the Spanish language, I believe," Thought questioned.

"Naw, they have jet-black hair!"

Thought and the organic mass laughed a big, bellyache laugh.

Catching its breath, Thought said, "Well, isn't that just a kick-in-the-face joke! But seriously, little one, be careful; this could be a real roller coaster ride for you."

"Thanks. Can I proceed now to my destination?" the organic mass asked impatiently.

"Yes, please be on your way. Ciao! And remember…don't let the bedbugs bite!"

In a flash of light and darkness the organic mass zapped itself from one point in the vast Universe to another—toward the third rock from the sun of a solar system many, many light years away. As it transported itself to that third rock from the sun, the organic mass learned this rock had a name: Earth. Thinking to itself, the organic mass chuckled out loud, "What kind of mess did I get myself into this time?" But by that time it was too late to hesitate and change course. The jostling, quivering, organic mass was entering Earth's atmosphere. The time of its conception was at hand. Its life on planet Earth was about to begin—as a member of the clan "Rubio" in the twentieth century of the planet's modern history.

The mass thought to itself, "I remembered very little of what had gone before me, what other lives had been spent and how they lived out. I knew this was not the first time I had been on this rock. I knew nothing except that I had chosen a very particular species, and a peculiar set of parents. I entered the consciousness of my parents and I was conceived. The timing of my appearance may have not been right for them, but it was right for me."

Now was the time to be born and live.

4. An Immigrant's Son Born to Two Colliding Shooting Stars from the Deepest Heavens

There is always a reason for all that occurs in one's life. That any experience is left to fate is absurd. Your decision on available choices will point your ship from one course to another. To believe you are just floating aimlessly and at the whim of a powerful god or goddess who may be picking their teeth when deciding to strike you down with a light-bolt is a powerless point of view. And yet, you never hear the bullet that kills you.

–Woolly Mammoth Boy Remembers

I AM THE SON OF IMMIGRANTS who came from the Philippine Islands—one of the United States's former colonies. The Philippines are also known as "a friend and trusted ally of United States of America." I once told a friend about my Filipino heritage, and he confessed he did not know where the heck the Philippines were located on a world map, let alone that "Filipino" is spelled with an *F* and not a *P*. *Yikes!* My father was an immigrant right off the boat via a US Navy ship entering San Francisco at Hunter's Point Naval Shipyard. My mother and her family came over to San Francisco after the war, with Dada in the lead. Both my parents were new immigrants amongst a flood of immigrants coming to America right after World War II. I am a first-generation Filipino American, born in the USA.

How my parents met was a great mystery to me for many years. I only knew about the volatile relationship they had once they were married. This mystery remained until my mom told my daughter, Josephina Marie, the tale of how she met our dad so many years earlier. You may want to sit down, my friends, and hear this incredible tale of two shooting stars from a different time and place. A story of two people who were not supposed to meet, but did, and then collided with sparks and flames of great magnitude. I was told their meeting almost destroyed parts of San Francisco.

These two celestial beings came from very different parts of the earth, and this is very important to keep in mind. My father, Fernando Demagaba Rubio, was in his mid-twenties, a US Navy man and a new arrival to San Francisco from the Philippines when he met his future wife, Estella Lorreta Ponciano. She was just nineteen years old. Dad was born into a poor family whose status was very low on the social totem pole of the Philippines in the 1930s. This social environment still exists today. Presently, the Philippine Islands is the poorest nation in Asia.

My dad's daddy, my paternal granddaddy Rubio, was a real rolling stone who abandoned his family when my dad was a very young boy. Shoot! The poor fool was as good as dead to my dad because he gave him nothing except a bad legacy to live down. I once saw a faded picture of GrandDaddy Rubio. He was pictured in an all-white suit with a black tie, holding a white fedora in his very dark, brown hands. He looked very dapper and extremely handsome for the times. He had an irresistible, killer smile with a look in his eyes of worldly inspiration and desire. He wasn't the family type. GrandDaddy Rubio was a rolling stone; wherever he laid his fedora was his abode.

My dad told my siblings and me stories of growing up in hard times in Japanese-occupied Manila after the Philippine invasion on December 8, 1941. He told us tales of working the black market selling cigarettes—this is also when he started smoking those damn unfiltered Lucky Strikes as a nine-year-old. In those grim years of enemy occupation, he would sell anything worth selling to anyone who would buy anything. My dad could speak Japanese, and he told us tales of the shoeshining business he started. He made a great shoeshine box out of scraps and other materials found on the streets. He put that shoeshine box together with immense pride. Dad never finished fourth grade, and he was proud to say it.

My dad's home, or hovel, in the Philippines was a ratty hole held together by my paternal grandmother known only to us as "Lola"—*not* the Lola from the famed Kinks song, though. Lola was a she-devil on two short legs. I remembered Lola as a small, compact, flat-faced, and badass woman not to be messed with…ever! When I was introduced to her as a very young boy in the early '60s, she truly scared the shit out of me. She had beady black eyes and a perpetual mean face. I did not want to be left in the same room with her, which in her small silver trailer home in Vallejo, California was almost certainly to happen. This was an elbow-bumping place filled with statues of the Virgin Mary and weird smells. I don't think she liked kids. My mom told us stories of the hate that Lola had for her. Lola was a pretty scary lady.

One of only two known legitimate sons of my rolling stone GrandDaddy Rubio, my dad worked very hard to bring money in from the mean streets of Manila to help feed and clothe his younger siblings. There were stories of the sleazy extra money Lola would make as well. These stories, true or not, meant nothing to me. Wartime Manila was a tough town, and really, who gave a shit where the money came from? There were mouths that needed feeding and a roof to maintain. So no stone throwing from me.

My dad and his older brother, my uncle Narce, both joined the US Navy after the war so they could come to America, make the mean green, and bring the rest of the Rubio clan to the land of plenty. My mother came from the other side of the Filipino fence. Dada, her father, being a US Navy officer for some time already, was able to provide a lifestyle that kept his nine children and beautiful wife, "Mama," in a stable, lofty place within the rigidly constructed social ladder that was the post-Spanish Philippines of the twentieth century. They had "darkie" servants who were happy to make the equivalent of US pennies a month. All the pictures I have seen of the maternal side of my family showed elegance, lace, and the kind of gentleness that spoke of feather-light mosquito nets for the night, numerous servants for each child, running water, plumbing, access to higher education, and, of course, the bumping of elbows with other folks in that upper world so unattainable for many Filipinos like my dad. This, then, was the backdrop of these two colliding celestial beings, and here is the tale of their romantic meeting.

After the war the Poncianos moved to Daly City, which was the "Little Manila" of San Francisco back in the '50s. Mom was beautiful—*I mean drop-dead beautiful*—as were her four sisters. Mom had those richly exotic eyes from distant Southeast Asia that white people could only dream of. One night, Mom and one of her sisters went out on the town with no proper escort, which at the time was a very real protocol that had to be adhered to. Filipinos had been in America for a while tilling fields in the rich farmlands of central California—and being hunted and shot down by the white man for sport up until the '50s—yet after the war they came in droves. With these new Filipino immigrants came the old world ways of their homeland—hardcore Spanish Catholicism with a strong dose of Asian values that had been in place for centuries.

I forget which of my mom's sisters said to her that there would be a young man for her to meet on a double date, but in any case, my mom went along for the ride and met the friend of her sister's beau—my dad. He was a Navy man, like her dad, and that was a good thing for Mom. They hung out and had an evening—soda pops and seeing the sights of 1950s San Francisco—but the midnight hour struck, and off in a rush for home my mom and her sister went with the two Filipino men in tow. They were late!

Shit hit the fan big-time when Mama found her daughter, my mom, coming home late after curfew with a strange—and not properly introduced—Filipino man. Mama declared my mom a whore, a lowly woman of the streets, and the only way to remedy this dishonorable, despicable encounter was for this young dark Filipino man, my dad, to marry this sluttish daughter of hers—and pronto! *Whoa pony!* My dad never spoke of this, and I can only imagine his whole world shattering. He was in love with another woman, and the family of this one-time-date came from the lofty heights of the Philippine social world that was so foreign to him, as was the English language he was trying to master. Poor Dad!

Mom's dream of marrying a senator's son back in the Philippines blew up like a live grenade in her face. "Who is this guy? Fernando who? Where in the heck does he come from and what kind of living can he afford? I do not even know how to heat up a pot of water by myself! He will want children… My GOD!" she must have thought to herself. Ah, love…dear friends…sweet, sweet love.

The collision of these two celestial beings was like the smashing of two jets in a horrible mid-air collision. Fernando and Estella were to be married. The Ponciano clan's honor was saved—all was well, and no rung on the social ladder was broken. But my parents did not really like each other. They hardly knew each other. Two different people who never should have met were to be married. Truly, it was Murphy's Law in action, where anything that can possibly go wrong, does. Great beginnings! I am the second son and third surviving child of the four children born to Fernando D. Rubio and Estella L. Ponciano—a marriage forged in a deep, dark cosmos with enough fire and might to tear a whole planet to shreds! This is where Woolly Mammoth Boy enters, stage right!

5. Woolly Mammoth Boy Discovers Tears

Evolving through adaptation and then changing—this is the cycle of survival for any species. The constant strengthening of assets, and the detaching of known liabilities, is how a species is successful. For instance, that modern Homo sapiens developed the thumb, understood its usage, and was then able to obtain certain skills that separated them from the other living species, is a prime example. The catalyst for change begins with stress.

–The Queries of Woolly Mammoth Boy

THIS IS THE STORY OF how Woolly Mammoth Boy discovered tears and it happened in this way.

Forty to fifty thousand years ago, in what is now southern Germany, great herds of woolly mammoths roamed the area as the great ice sheets receded, shaping the Bavarian Alps. There were other heavily matted mammals roaming around too, like the woolly rhinoceros and the large and ferocious cave bears of the high peaks. There were savage predators that hunted the many different prototypes of the modern animals that exist today. The early ice age ancestors of modern-day horses, antelopes, and smaller mammals were sought after by the early homo sapiens, wolves, and the deadly mountain lion that sported a mane like today's African lion.

One warm day, Woolly Mammoth Boy was grazing along with others of his herd when he spied in the distance some two-legged creatures moving silently toward them. "Now what do they want?" Woolly Mammoth Boy thought, "I am many times their height and mass. I can sweep them away with the strength of my trunk and tusks, and pound them into dust with my powerful legs." Yet as the two-legged ones drew nearer and nearer they began making high-pitched noises, creating a commotion, and disturbing the other smaller mammals nearby, scattering them all. At first, the mammoths just watched as the two-legged ones started running toward them, and then, unexplainably, the whole herd began to run away. "Wait a gosh darn moment here!" thought Woolly Mammoth Boy, "Let's just turn around and stampede these creatures to dust." But he soon found himself running away from these small, puny creatures like his mammoth brethren. As he fled he started to cry, "What? What the hell is crying?"

Woolly Mammoth Boy felt the drops of water, his own water, falling down his hairy, matted cheeks. As he ran in frustration his tears, his *water, were cascading down his face faster and in greater volume. He was so angry and so extremely frustrated by running away; he was not able to confront his adversaries and smash them into bits with his rage. He just cried and cried, and kept running and running, with the rest of the herd.*

Well, fifty thousand years ago, as Woolly Mammoth Boy ran crying from the human hunters, he tasted the salt of his tears and knew the fear, doubt, frustration, and anger he could not express. In his urgency to flee he fell into a large natural depression in the ground that had been made deeper by the hunters chasing him, and had been covered by tree branches, which he did not notice. When he hit the bottom of the pit he felt one of his big legs crumble and fold beneath him. His leg was broken. He could not get up; he could not get out of the trap. Soon the hunters surrounded the lip of the depression above him, yelling down at Woolly Mammoth Boy victoriously; they started to hurtle sharp sticks and throw large stones upon him.

It was not long before Woolly Mammoth Boy felt his life energy drain from his huge body and lost consciousness. As he died he smiled with his large woolly mammoth lips and cried and cried and cried, happily...for he had accepted his demise.

6. Tying Shoes and Other Early Lessons of Survival

Once, on the great, open, and fertile plains that spread from the base of the towering blue-green glacial cliff walls, I was grazing with others of my kind. Being a woolly mammoth I feared little, for we were the largest creatures walking. I watched casually as a herd of horned antelopes grazed nearby. On the fringes of their herd I spied two great tigers with their curved saber teeth hunting silently. I watched as one of the smallest of the antelopes strayed from the main herd in its search for fresh grass. In a moment of quick movement and deadly speed, the predators singled out the young one from its herd and pounced. In the time it took me to grind two mouthfuls of grass, one of the killers had its prey gasping for air from its crushed throat, and it was soon dead. The tigers then fought for the prize. I learned something that day—do not stray in absent mindlessness. Now I had to remember what I learned, for my survival might depend on it.

–The Memories of Woolly Mammoth Boy

I WAS BORN IN THE CALIFORNIA city of San Francisco, on March 10, 1957, under the sign of Pisces in the Chinese Year of the Rooster. Pisces is symbolized by two fish swimming in opposite directions, one above the other. The City by the Bay is known for the Golden Gate Bridge, cable cars, and foggy summer days. It's a place where people leave their hearts. I am a first-generation Filipino American who cannot speak the language of my people in the Philippines. I was not taught *Tagalog*, so that my English would be untainted by any inflections that would give people reason to doubt I was an American. My early English was also accented by the streets of San Francisco. I spoke the English slang of a ghetto boy. *You can take the boy out of the city but you can't the city out of the boy!*

The early stage of my self-confidence was built on the following attributes: I was born a sickly, spacey-in-the-head child with bad lungs. I had large, flat feet attached to strong legs that supported a small, thin torso, topped with a large head that my brother called a "dinosaur head." (Little did he realize that it was not a dinosaur head, but my underdeveloped woolly mammoth head!) Being asthmatic, I wheezed at nighttime pretty badly. In the early '60s, inhalers had not yet been developed, so I just had to grin and bear it. My siblings would tell me I sounded like a purring lion. To me the wheezing was really loud in my head, but I could not turn it down like I could our new black-and-white TV set. I felt I was drowning with liquid in my lungs, and I could not sleep for fear I would not awaken. I developed the classic "shoulders in the ears" body posture from trying to strenuously breathe every breath I took with my upper body and shoulders, instead of using my belly to breathe. My squared-off shoulders later helped me carry the weight of the world, like the Titan Atlas did.

Being constantly sick was a drag. There are images in my deep memory of me looking up at bright lights, naked and crying; my parents are hovering over me, and dabbing me with rubbing alcohol. I am hot, very uncomfortable, and I just want to be in my bed sleeping like my brother. Why am I awake in the dead of night? I just want to sleep. Mom would tell me stories when I was much older about how I almost died numerous times as a toddler from pneumonia and high fevers. Whooping cough, asthmatic pneumonia, more deadly bouts of high fevers, and beatings made me a regular at San Francisco General Hospital in my early years.

Damn, I just wanted to breathe like my siblings, and be able to play like they did without losing my breath. Worse, I stuttered terribly when I tried to talk. I hated my breathing condition as much as I hated my stuttering. That's right, I stuttered like a deranged fool when I was excited, and I was excited a lot. I was a loud, pathetic mess. And since I spoke in the ghetto street slang of my San Francisco neighborhood in Bernal Heights, which was a mixture of mostly cussing and pidgin English, my speech was not much to listen to, even if I did have something to say. Mom would wash my mouth out with soap, but that did not faze me and my filthy cursing. Even Comet, an abrasive cleaner used on pots and kitchen tiles, didn't work. I was a nervous, jumpy, and scrawny kid who would bite his nails to the bone until they bled, and this habit would last for many years. Mom would put anti-nail biting solution on my fingertips, and though the solution put on my fingernails was laced with hot pepper, it was to no avail. I was a determined nail biter. My eating habits were also selective and spotty. I suffered from bad cases of constipation and diarrhea. Putting food into me and digesting that food was a challenge.

I slept badly and had a recurring nightmare. It started with a dark backdrop, void of any light, life, or sound, except for the image of a very large, obscene piece of butchered, bloody meat that hung from a deadly hook suspended from nothingness. From this bloody mass stretched a thin, an oh-so-very thin thread of sinew connected to another piece of large, hanging, butchered meat. It swayed so gently. God! When will the sinew snap under such weight? When will it snap, and when will the butchered meat fall into nothingness? When, damn it? When?!? This nightmare lasted until I was around twelve years old.

Growing up in my scrawny, messed-up body was frustrating for me. To top it all off, I was very uncoordinated with simple movements like walking, catching, and throwing or holding any objects; pouring my own glass of milk was a disaster ripe for yelling and a physical reprimand from Dad. I remember throwing rocks with my brother and the neighbor kids. We would see who could throw the farthest downhill on our very steep San Francisco streets. True to my nature, I was the only one to have my rock swerve off erratically to the right and break a neighbor's window. *Yikes! Flee! Lie! Pee in my pants!* I was always picked last of all the kids in the neighborhood for any game, if I was picked at all. Being very shy I would grab any opportunity to have a friend or share companionship when offered, even if it meant I was going to be used for another person's entertainment, jokes, laughter, or ridicule. I was so thin-skinned, and sensitive to insults and being laughed at, that I cried easily. I was a bully's dream come true, especially for my older brother, who tormented me relentlessly.

At this young age I was very hyper and could not stand still. My hyperactive energy was so out of hand that I could always be observed jumping around, running in circles, and behaving inappropriately. I was silly, acting out some made-up story in my head, and playing all the characters in the scene with the appropriate sound effects loudly, doing weird embarrassing dances all by myself. I was so very impulsive that it put me into terrible jams with authority, and that led to reprimands and disciplinary beatings. I became a habitual liar to survive. I lied so much I could not tell what was the truth. I did not want to lie, but I just could not help myself.

I was also known to exhibit an incredibly ferocious temper. I had an equally ferocious, filthy, and swearing mouth that would curdle the holy water at our local Catholic church, St. Kevin's. My anger would flare up easily. I had a very low tolerance for varying kinds of stimulations—loud sounds, overwhelming smells like a woman's perfume or cheap men's cologne (though I loved the smell of gas being pumped into my dad's '57 Chevy), unexplained changes to previously decided plans, or the stress I felt during transitions from one event to another event—any of these was enough for me to blow a couple fuses in my head. I would swing from happy to sad in a moment's notice.

My most extreme frustrations led to emotional meltdowns, and would often come from experiencing failure, or not achieving instant success at doing the most mundane of tasks. The same thing happened when I played games, like checkers, and lost. I hated losing, and I lost a lot. I felt most safe when I played alone in the cool dirt underneath the home addition my dad had built with his buddy from his old Navy days. Amidst the cold, grey, cement foundation I felt secure. In the darkness of being underneath the house I was in my own world. I also spent many hours playing alone in small cozy areas—underneath the sheets of my bed, for example—believing no one could see me and I was safe from all that was so threatening to me, especially my dad.

Years later as an adult, I would be diagnosed with Asperger syndrome, which was compounded by my post-traumatic stress disorder (PTSD) from being beaten, bullied, yelled at, and generally shit on. The PTSD was made worse by a traumatic brain injury (TBI) from the head bashings and beatings from my dad. It was said to me later as an adult that certain behaviors were hardwired in my brain at a very early age, and, therefore, I lacked "this or that" to be able to cope with stress. *Whatever*. The information I received as an adult helped explain why I acted as I did as a child (and as a adult), but no one knew about Asperger syndrome back in 1960s America. To the adults in my young life, I was just a hyper, nervous child who was also rigidly headstrong in his thinking, would lie profusely on a dime, was very spacey, and had no bodily coordination. The remedy for kids like me back in the '60s was corporal punishment in my elementary school, and for me at home it was also the belittling screaming and beatings from my dad. Now, if there was information back then about what is known today about autism, I believe many of us on the autism spectrum would have had the opportunity to receive the appropriate services that would have provided vital information to learn the basic social and living skills needed for a better quality of life.

My dad, being a young immigrant from the Philippines, was dealing with a lot. Between raising a family he was really not ready for, and trying to "keep up with the Joneses," Dad was just stressing all the time, it seemed to me. He was a chain smoker who was either silent and brooding, or screaming and angry. *Damn, I guess the apple does not fall far from the tree.* Dad was trying to deal with the English language, which was so vital to opening the doors of opportunity that were necessary to support his new family. He could speak eloquently at times, but he also made up words he did not know. I would do the same later in life. Dad had to deal with the patronizing racism of the late '50s and early '60s that was so acute in Californian society for a person of color, especially one with brown skin and black hair. You were either a "wetback" or a "chink" before you could even open your mouth.

During this time he relied on his limited parenting skills, which were nonexistent—except for an uncontrollable temper of swearing, yelling, and giving out severe beatings—to raise his growing young family.

My dad was capable of being loving and funny, but he only seemed to express these feelings for his own benefit. His was a tough mix of influences—a strict and devout Spanish Catholicism, the moral values of an Asian man, a fourth-grade education, and the trials of being a father in a new land. There's nothing in this mortal world quite like such an upbringing.

My older brother, Fred Jr., was my parents' first child. By the time I was born he was already suffering from epilepsy, a result of my father's beatings. My younger sister, Valerie Joyce, would be born two years later, finishing off the Rubio clan's offspring. I also had an older sister, Sabrina, who died of a mysterious cause as a baby not yet a year old. The "skeleton in the closet" is that Dad, against my mom's pleas, went into Sabrina's room to quiet down my older sister, who was probably colicky and having a crying fit. By the time he left the room Sabrina had quieted, and passed away later that night. I was later told, when we would visit Sabrina's grave on her birthday, that she had died of pneumonia. This helps explain why Dad made a weird trip to Alaska soon after her death, and contracted tuberculosis while in that frozen tundra. He later said he had paid for his sins while up there. I did not know what the hell he was talking about until much later.

I often wondered as a depressed teenager, and as an adult, why in the hell my mom and dad decided to have another child—me—after the passing of my older sister. Why my mom stayed with Dad I could explain: she was trapped in that messed-up Catholic ideology of the '50s which did not, and still does not, allow the use of birth control or divorcing your abusive spouse without being condemned to hell. So, I was born, but it did not seem to me that I was really wanted in their lives. Dad was always pissed off at me, or vacant in deep thoughts, and Mom was always preoccupied or fluttering about. I knew her love was there though it felt like a tired, sad love: the same feeling you get when looking at a wilting red rose. I mean, I realized I was not the pride of my father for I was not the firstborn son—I wasn't even really the second child. I was the very peculiar third child in the family; I had an oversized woolly mammoth head and stuttering speech. I was clumsy, sickly, spacey, not too bright, and very hyperactive.

I was the lightning rod for my dad's extremely harsh disciplinary beat-downs. One of the many accolades my dad constantly bestowed on me through the years was, "You are not a Rubio! You are sickly like your mother! You are Ponciano! You are not my son." I guess Dad kicked me around because he figured he messed up his first son's noodles too much for any further damage. My dad's ass-kicking sessions were fueled by his own strict models of living life, which included a very low tolerance of anyone in his family who was too slow or clumsy, either in thought or action. Efficiency and promptness were key; do not waste Dad's time.

My dad hated weak people, slow people, and stupid people—and he felt I was all of these things—and because of his anger, I started to lie. I was prone to go into a "spacey" frame of mind at the drop of a dime, and then I would shut down, stop speaking, and get everything all mixed up. I would leave my body and float high above that mumbo-jumbo hell called home. For example, there were many occasions at the dinner table when my dad would swing a banana in front of my face like a pendulum. To the delight and laughter of my family, I would stare blankly into the space in front of my face, not responding to their ridicule or the swinging banana. Little did they know I was floating above them all, and looking down at them with my woolly mammoth tusks gently touching their heads!

I remember at the age of five being made to stay up into the early morning hours on a school day for not being able to recite the alphabet past the letter *G*. In the brightly lit living room, while my siblings slept, my dad screamed, yelled, and hit me as my mom cried. I stuttered away, shaking, crying, and having a hell of a hard time getting past that damn letter *G*. Early homeschooling technique at its best!

As I said, my dad lived in a sick world—the corporal punishment favored by Spanish Catholicism mixed with a tinge of Inquisition-like malice, all combined with a sprinkle of Japanese torture techniques he picked up as a kid in the Japanese-occupied Philippines. It was very painful. One punishment I received for spilling milk on a newly cleaned kitchen floor made me question why was I even alive. Dad spilled a handful of white rice on the linoleum-tiled kitchen floor, and made me kneel on those rice kernels with my arms out on my sides, like Jesus on the cross. He would hit me if I lowered my arms. My baby sister watched this spectacle with the orange light of the setting sun filtering through the kitchen windows. I remember thinking this was the craziest shit in the world. All the beatings ended by going to bed, praying with a black-beaded rosary, crying and tired. *Good night Dad...Good night Moon, Good night cow jumping over the Moon...*

Needless to say, I started to learn survival skills, like leaving my body to hover over myself and watching all this mayhem occur from a safe distance. Another survival skill was extreme lying. My mother's teaching skills were less physical, but very effective. I remember the time I had to learn how to tie my shoes. I was four years old or so and living in Sacramento, California where it seemed that in the summer time the air and sidewalks boiled, and my Auntie Licha's sweet iced tea was nectar sent from heaven. Well, one summer day Mom gave me my black-and-white Converse tennis shoes, and walked me outside of our home in the cool, early morning and said to me, "Ron, I will not let you into the house until you learn how to tie your shoes yourself." Now, why my mom did not do the decent thing and show me at least once how to do this intricate task I do not know.

So there I was, sitting on that awfully hot sidewalk outside our house while my "hell on wheels" temper unleashed upon our neighbors' ears for hours. I struggled, fought, bit, and threw against the road those bastard little tennis shoes. Calls from our neighbors to my Mom to bring me inside fell on deaf ears. They were not to be relieved of my incredibly creative, foul, and swearing mouth. I screamed at full volume for hours. Finally, by the time Dad came home at 5:00 p.m., my shoe-tying lesson was learned. Years later, in high school, a friend's mother was waiting for me to tie my shoes so that I could hang out with her son when she observed my very peculiar shoe-tying technique. She said to me in the sweetest voice, "Oh, my dear one, how did you learn to tie your shoes like that?" Hearing my tale, she ended up almost crying right then and there. She came to be my strongest ally when I needed a place to stay and escape my dad's home of hell.

I would learn other survival skills as I got older—like running fast from the white kids who wanted to torment me, or acting really stupid and naïve so people would take the time to teach me new things. I made them feel sorry for "the stupid poor kid." But the best survival skill I learned was to travel to places in my creative mind, where I could see myself as a bird flying away from the madness called living and growing up. I was going to survive.

7. Woolly Mammoth Boy with Hungry Hunters and the Ice Age

Time layered upon time. Lives and memories deeply embedded into our soft tissue. What can one actually recall from one's former lives?

—Woolly Mammoth Boy Remembers

Before I, Woolly Mammoth Boy, was to meet my chosen humanoid parents in the twentieth century of Earth, I was in a land now called southern Germany, in the time of the planet's most recent Ice Age—45,000 years ago. I saw others like me foraging in a vast plain, with mountains in the distance still being carved by the receding ice mass. Ferocious mountain lions and huge bears haunted the high peaks and their cold, deep caves. The plains themselves supported life forms all destined to go extinct in the future, except for one. This frail life form was very clever. It stood upright on two legs, and had learned to make sharp hunting tools out of flint gathered from the hills. It moved in small bands of its own kind, and clothed itself in animal hide—furs it had skinned from butchered woolly mammoths it had hunted, killed, and eaten. In fact, these creatures, now called *homo sapiens*, hunted, killed, and ate anything in sight, and then moved on. Pesky little things!

I saw animals with similar hides and fur, but my kind was the tallest and largest. My kind had a pair of mighty tusks that persuaded even those large mountain lions to give us woolly mammoths a wide berth. In a herd we mammoths were invincible, but alone we were vulnerable. Isn't that the story of life, though? Being alone is cool, but being in a herd has its advantages, even if it can be stifling and confusing.

Those gifted with a high-functioning autism called "Asperger syndrome" would have to deal this behavioral dilemma thousands of year later as well: To be alone or to be with others? You see, being alone is great: you are accountable to no one but yourself, you can eat what you want, sleep in, and let your hair grow long. Yet, being alone is lonely and cold at night without the warmth of others; being alone you are left to fend for yourself, and you tend to forget there are others out there who can help you when you are stuck in a tar pit. To be with others has its curses and benefits as well. For instance, in a group sometimes you have to adhere to dogmatic and rigid beliefs and "laws" that make no sense, but they allow for safety and structure in a social community. At the same time, being with a group allows you to enjoy the common table and fare, learn the newest jokes, and keep up with the times. And, if you are so inclined, you can find a mate in the group you belong to. Decisions, decisions—to belong or not to belong. To be alone or not to be alone.

As a woolly mammoth, I chomped on the tall green grass that grew in abundance on the great open plain where other giant mammoths grazed. From the corners of my eyes I saw giant woolly rhinoceroses foraging nearby, also in their herds. The smaller herds of brown antelopes and the dog-sized creatures that were the ancestors of the modern-day horse moved in their skittish, scared ways, always wary of predators lurking on the outskirts of the plains.

Suddenly, I saw a flurry of movement in the nearby herd of antelopes. There was a smaller bunch of those skinny two-legged creatures throwing sticks at them. I saw some of the antelopes fall and not get up as the others of their herd fled. How did those little two-legged creatures get close enough to take down the antelopes? And why were they clothed in antelope furs? Why did they have horns growing out of their heads like the antelopes they were hunting? "Damn!" I thought, "Woolly Mammoth Boy, you better keep an eye out for those little bastards." Now what was I doing? Oh yes, I was eating!

The great ball of heat and light burned directly overhead and I saw the other mammoths start to move on. So with a few last mouthfuls of prairie grass, I moved on with my herd, chomping and trying to figure what I was thinking about those two-legged creatures nearby a moment ago.

"It doesn't matter...the herd is moving on."

8. Dragons on the Wall

"Little One, are you okay?" asked Thought to the little boy I was now living as.

I was in deep torment. "No, I am not okay. I am sad. I do not understand the pain I am having to suffer."

Thought responded to my anguish. "Little One, I will give a gift to help you. It is the gift of vision."

I heard the voice in my head, and smiled. "Be careful, others will not understand...LOOK OUT!"

—Woolly Mammoth Boy Remembers

By the time I was five I was very messed up. The year before, at age four, Dad came home from Livermore Sanitarium recovering from TB. As the story goes, we were all laying down to sleep when I got up to go to the bathroom. Dad got pissed off, grabbed my legs, and whirled me around until the front of my head slammed into the headboard. I was sent back to my bed crying. Mom said I cried and cried all night as the front of my skull swelled up dangerously; my eyes were swollen shut, and grew black and blue. The next morning Dad left us to go where he had found work, which at that point was away from us in other towns. My mom, frantic and ten months pregnant with my sister, called my grandfather and they rushed me to the hospital. The doctors did not think I was going to make it because of the swelling and internal bleeding. I was given my last rites. They told my mother I probably suffered major frontal lobe damage, which is the part of the brain that controls thinking processes like the ability to reason. Sounds like TBI—traumatic brain injury—to me. Throughout my growing years my dad, even after my parents got divorced, would continue to hit me on the head.

Special foot rollers and special shoes were bought for my flat feet (I noticed that elephants do not have arches, either). Special things for a special kid. Special people for special people. My younger sister of two years, Valerie Joyce, was my best playmate, and I was on her level in so many ways. I was very socially awkward because of my speech, and my clumsiness was evident even in playing the simplest of games. My temper was legendary and violent. I would go from laughing, to frustration, to complete foul-mouth swearing and screaming in sixty seconds. I was a madman. I would be found running around the house or dancing at a delirious speed by myself, and I would not stop moving even if my life depended on it. It was as if I was on borrowed time and I wanted to live each second to the max. You could find me crawling under things and cracking my head open on sharp corners. I was just a bewilderment to my mom, who did not quite know what to do with me except to let me play by myself. For hours I would make all the sound effects from the World War II battles I played out in my drawings, or with the plastic toy figures I had amassed. I was an obsessive collector.

My mom said to me years later that all my aunts and uncles noted how considerate and kind I was to my younger sister and cousins. It surprised them a bit because it was one of the few times I actually stopped and did something for someone else. This makes more sense if it is considered that most people with Asperger syndrome are usually too self-absorbed to be aware of those around us. In other times, I was off in the visions in my mind.

Freddy Jr., Valerie, and I weathered my dad's raging and my mom's "little helpers"—the pills she was now fond of taking. Mom was a bundle of nerves and had attempted suicide on several occasions by the time I was seven. Dad was not home much, since he could only obtain work away from San Francisco. He would be away for days on end, it seemed. Mom was by herself a lot of the time unless her sisters came over or Dada dropped by to see how his daughter was doing.

Something that really shaped my character was Fred Jr.'s epilepsy. It scared the living crap out of me, and yet I could not back away and hide from his seizures; he was my older brother who bullied me when was he well but was so helpless during his seizures. I really loved him despite every mean thing he would do to me. He was my older brother, and since I had to sleep in the same room as him it was my job to wake up during his nightly epileptic fit—a condition he was gifted with from the jarred-up brain he received through the beatings he had taken years before.

Since Fred Jr. was two-and-a-half years older than me, I thought it was out of place for me to have such responsibility over him. His bullying always reminded me that he was older than I was. He would put me in my place for being the dorky, odd-shaped-head younger brother who could not handle anything without breaking it, and yet those ghoulish sounds that emitted from his seizures startled me into action from the little sleep I got, no matter what I felt about his animosity toward me. In the darkness of the early morning I would freeze in fear upon hearing the scary sounds of moans and groans that came gurgling forth from the other side of our shared bedroom. Then I would fly to his bedside in urgency; the only thought in my frantic mind was getting to him before he bit his tongue off.

Springing out of my bed to turn on the lights, I would witness my brother in his epileptic agony. His eyes rolled up in his head and he was thrashing wildly as I screamed for my mom's help. Mom quickly called the fire department—all seven numbers one at a time on our rotary phone. The 911 emergency setup was still years in the future. I was fighting my older brother in his seizure. After what seemed like an eternity to me, Mom would make it to my side to help as I struggled to place a cloth in his rapidly opening and closing mouth.

Soon the fire department guys would arrive, and the whole house would be bright with glaring light, busy with the bustling of big men in firefighter uniforms, the sounds of walkie-talkie communication crackling in the morning air, and the comforting words they offered Mom. All I could feel was the incredibly suffocating space of the bedroom filled with big bodies, and the loud voices making a wall of sound. Propping my brother up in his bed, a firefighter would slap him until he came to, back into the world of the living, and away from the world of the zombies. Slap! Slap! I hated watching them do that to my brother, hitting him on the face as he was helpless in their arms, but that was all they could do to bring him out.

Fred Jr. would finally come back from his epileptic hell, exhausted and totally out of it. He would look at all of us standing, looking at him, with a look on his face not knowing what happened. Then he would close his eyes and fall into a deep sleep and be out, just like that. The firefighters would make sure my brother was stable, make contact with the firehouse, and then leave. The house would settle down as my mom stared at my brother, turned off our bedroom lights, and I would crawl back into my cold bed, wide awake with my heart pounding, knowing I would be getting up for elementary school in a few bleak hours.

I hated what was happening to Fred Jr. I hated that I had to be sleeping in the same room with him because his fits scared me so. But, like I said, I loved my brother and wanted to be there for him because he seemed so helpless in those moments; still, doing this for my brother did not stop him from bullying me or from making fun of me when he was himself. Damn! I thought that was the way of all older brothers in the world.

When Dad was around for the holidays, those special religious days like Christmas and Easter, we had to be on our toes. I knew he loved us but the way he taught us and disciplined us was pretty damn cruel and hurtful. Years later, looking at old '60s reel-to-reel films or old photos, it was plain to see the pain we suffered during those "joyous holidays." Those damn bright lights in our faces and our eyes squinting, with our best Christmas clothes on and presents in our hands in a very choreographed photo, it was not hard to see the recent tears and crying faces that we tried hard to mask. My little sister was too happy about her presents to register the chaos, but my brother's face and my face would show the evidence of the violence.

Going to my Dada's house for the holidays was marked with Dad's screams to hurry up; he would hit us as a reminder of our lagging speed to get into the car. I remember the sniffling and sadness that came along with Dad telling us to stop crying and get our shit together before we arrived at our relative's house. If we didn't there was always more where that shit came from, and it could happen right then and there in a moving car. Entering my grandparents' home, where all my mom's sisters and brothers were with their kids, we shifted our emotions and put on our happy masks. Yet, all my cousins knew what had happened, and I knew my mom's siblings knew as well. Us kids looked forward to the presents, but we all hated those holidays when Dad was around. The moments were filled with dread.

Driving around with Dad was a scary and anxiety-filled time regardless of where we had to go. His rage filled our travels with stress and tension, and may have instilled a pattern in me that I repeated as a father traveling with my own kids. Transition and timing, and having to wait on everyone who was moving slower than a slug, drove me crazy. I just wanted to travel more my speed—the speed of light. Damn! What a bitch it was having to wait on the speed and timing of others! Why couldn't people just go at my speed, the speed of life, the same speed that my dad had beaten into my bones and into my muscle memory?

When I was away from all this madness and finally back home, I would lie on my bed and look at the walls of my room. The textures and shadows brought out by the bulb over my bed would reveal a world of dragons and animals. The embossed paint streaks created images that were so clear to me, and yet my siblings could not see them at all. They could not see the faces, so grim and silent—the dragon and lion heads, and the great battles between the knights. When I invited my brother into the world I was seeing, he would, after a few impatient seconds of trying to see what I saw, say I was stupid and would walk away with a grunt and a slap to the back of my head. My younger sister tried to see them. Valerie Joyce would stay with me and tell me to point out to her what I saw. Little by little she saw what I saw, but it would take time to bring Valerie Joyce into my world.

To this day I can see images and shapes in the bark of trees, the paint on the ceilings, the clouds in the sky, the crags on the mountain, or when the summer wind goes through the tall grass creating vanishing and reappearing faces. This is my sweet world where I can invite you in or keep you out. I only have to stomp my big, flat woolly mammoth foot and say, "NO! You are not invited." I did not let too many people into my world. It was too hard to explain what was so easy for me to understand. They would just laugh at me anyway.

    I would also go to other places that held my secrets. I would find the cool, dark, shadowy places under the addition my dad had built, and go where the minute world existed—a world where the tiny fairy people lived. For hours I would stare deeply and intently, not moving, just watching the tiny insects scuttle to and fro in their world of semidarkness. The cool air passing under the addition had a strong scent of dirt and anise. The cool, grainy dirt felt good on my face. My family did not know where I was, and no one cared to look where I might be anyway. This tiny world was quiet and I imagined that they, the little insect and tiny fairy folks, were all safe, happy, and wanted me to join them. As I grew older I would still initiate this deep, introspective observation of the physical world around me. Wherever I traveled or found myself there were always places of magic and enchantment that I could find on my own. It could be in dank alleyways in the great cities of cement, or in the deep redwood forests. This was my gift, it was dear to me, and I would share what I discovered with others, but it disappointed me that they did not see the magic and energy I saw so clearly. They just saw cement.

…
Part 2: Little Big Man

9. Woolly Mammoth Boy Is Reborn

Ah, to be reborn! The bliss of knowing that you remember that you have forgotten it all. All that was…was. And all that will be…will be.

—Woolly Mammoth Boy Remembers

THE SINGLE CELL THAT FLOATED in the Great Void had been adrift in the timeless nothingness, bored. Soon the single cell began turning, creating heat and friction, starting the process of multiplying to become the multicelled complex that would transform into a living organism again…but what?

Thought was asking the same question.
"Little one, what are you becoming?"
"What was I before?"
"A woolly mammoth?"
"How about it…a woolly mammoth again? Your thoughts?"
"I am not sure this is a good idea. You did not do so good last time, and you didn't make it to the Filipino family you were supposed to hook up with, either."
"I did not?"
"Naw…you were killed, eaten, and your hide was worn by others."
"Damn!"
"Yes, it did not turn out the way you hoped it to be. But you did leave part of your spirit body in the scrawny Filipino kid through osmosis wave thought pattern imaging."
"Really?"
"Yes, the kid has a large head with a shock of black hair on top of it. And he also has a pair of big flat feet that are not in proportion to his legs…an odd-looking lad. That is as close as you got to making it to him."
"Damn!"
"Yes. He is in a jam right now and he could use some help. He is a bit spacey, he sees 'things,' and his biological father really does not like him."
"Cool!"
"Yes, yes, so you think, little one…anyway get to him and inspire him…he really could use some help."
"I'm on it!"
"So finish up and be on your way…you have not finished your work… your karma is not fulfilled."

And so the multicelled organism, the former Woolly Mammoth Boy, now started to multiply more quickly, changing from shape to shape, a formless mass to another formless mass. The now-living organism could not wait to create a creature that would be helpful to his earthly shape that was evolving without him. It just could not make up its mind on what the end product would be. The organism was already moving through the Void towards a selected solar system so far away.

Even as it seared into being from the intense white heat of entering the atmosphere of the planet Earth it was still making up its mind about what it wanted to be.

"To be or not to be...hehehe!"

10. "President Kennedy has been shot in Dallas!"

History repeats and repeats itself. Lessons to learn, great opportunities to grow! And like a slap in the face we are awakened...then, we shake it off and go about what we were doing like nothing happened at all.

—The Queries of Woolly Mammoth Boy

I GREW UP IN A FEW places in California before Mom and Dad settled into a two-story, two-bedroom home on 351 Prentiss Street in Bernal Heights, which is just south of San Francisco's Mission district. From my bedroom I could see the city of Oakland across the bay. The fog would roll in at night and the foghorns would moan their mournful songs in the darkness. There were a few lucky times when I saw the conning tower of a US Navy submarine leaving its dry dock at nearby Hunter's Point Naval Shipyard.

My first friends were two black kids, Wayne O'Gilby and Otis Dotson. I lived in an area where white people represented a very small minority. The neighborhood was filled with people who were Black, Filipino, Chinese, Japanese, Chicano, Mexican, Italian, and a very light sprinkling of poor white Irish. This was a very different Bernal Heights than what the generation of yokels experienced who moved in later, during the late 1980s through today. With their groovy coffee shops, weird clothing stores, yuppie-ing white families with their dogs, and politically correct mixed-gender couples, these "gentrifiers" drove up the cost of living so that many people of color could not afford to stay in the neighborhood. Agh!!! No, the Bernal Heights where I grew up in the early '60s was a small, tight community. We had our own movie house where 10 cents bought you a double feature; St. Kevin's—the Catholic Church where I was baptized and served as an altar boy; a very nice public library; and several family-run stores where I bought my Revell plastic models of World War II airplanes, ships, battle tanks, and glue—not to sniff, but to actually glue the plastic parts together. We had our little Bank of America; these very true San Francisco families of all colors were living simple inner-city lives.

I went to Paul Revere Elementary School just down the hill from where I lived. Years later, in 1976, my elementary school would be painted in red, white, and blue colors to look like a giant American flag for the bicentennial. I once saw my "flag" elementary school from the sky on a United Airlines flight out of SFO that was taking me back to New York City where I was then living.

My home back then was filled with violence, sadness, and only sometimes had a "family feeling." At least that's how it appeared to me, especially when I was not in my fantasy world where I was safe and did not have to inhabit my human form. By 1963 I was out of the woods with my major illnesses, except for my bouts with whooping cough, measles, and chronic asthma. I did not have to wear those silly-ass shoes anymore; they did nothing for my flat feet except make me cry from being so uncomfortable and different from my siblings. My training as a professional dancer in New York City sixteen years later would help me reclaim those coveted arches in my feet, but in 1963 I was still a flat-footed six-year-old boy. I was stuttering less, but I was still scared and had not grown much. I still had my large "woolly mammoth head"—not a "dinosaur head" as my older brother would continue to say to me—and I was still maddeningly constipated and scared shitless of overflowing plugged toilets.

I could not make any sense of my schoolwork, nor did I have the attention to care about it anyway. I was very hyper and silly; I was the class clown in a cute way. I would only settle down when I started to teach myself how to draw action figures from Marvel Comic books in the style of the late Jack Kirby, who is still my hero. I could draw for hours. My mom told me I would read the *San Francisco Chronicle* by myself—another thing that caught my wild, uncontrollable attention. I could not read out loud, and when I did not know how to read a word I would just make it up.

At the time I was really into NASA's Mercury and Gemini space programs, the US space competition with those damn communist Reds, and the developing war in Vietnam. I would cut out every article on the space race and draw with great detail the Mercury or Gemini command capsule. I collected anything space. I bought and glued the newest Revell plastic model of every space vehicle I could get. In fact, the only time I was ever interested in a school report was when I chose to do a report on the planets of our solar system. I got to draw every planet. I wrote the report in such a small print that I could not read it at all when I looked at it as an adult. It was only then, many years later, that I realized the A+ grade my teacher gave me for the report was because of the effort I put into it. It was the only report I ever did for her.

In the early days of space exploration, I remember being aware of the plight of the space monkeys those damn Russkies were using as guinea pigs. I felt so sad about those primates who were going up into space to orbit a couple times and then come crashing back into Earth. No survivors. My sense of injustice and unfairness for others was starting to grow, and it began with the plight of those space monkeys. Later, this sense of unfairness would reach a more personal level.

About this time Dad and Mom were fighting like crazy. I remember the beatings getting more and more violent and frequent without any clear reason or provocation.

One time, Dad beat me good on a Sunday before going to church for not putting my clothes drawer in order. But damn it...I *had* put it in order! I wasn't stupid enough to provoke a beating from Dad by not getting my drawer together. It seemed that Fred had thrown something into my drawer unfolded *after* I had organized it and had moved on to another assigned chore. During inspection by Dad, the unfolded item in my drawer was found and my older brother, not wanting to get an ass kicking, did not say it was him who put it there. My dad was furious and laid a heavy one on me. I tried to tell him I did not do it, but he thought I was lying, and my stuttering only made it worse. So he beat me, told me to get ready for Mass, put pomade in my hair to slick it down, combed it back, and sent me off to church with a promise to continue the beating when I got back. I tell you, I was starting to have serious doubts about religion, church, violence, and how they were all tied together. Dad was a very religious man, but it did not seem right to be going off to church knowing I was going to get more of a beating when I came home. I just left a man who prayed every night for forgiveness. It made no sense in my six-year-old woolly mammoth mind!

Things came to a head with Dad and Mom when, in a fit of the crazies, Dad picked up a wire hanger and laid it to my bare buttocks and the back of my legs. Mom took me to San Francisco General Hospital in tears with a couple of her sisters. Dada was there and was pretty pissed off. Dad fled and wasn't seen around the house for weeks. I was really hurting and could not understand why in the hell I got the wire hanger beating. Nothing made sense to me. Mom did not press charges; back in the '60s the cops would not go after an abusive parent unless charges were filed. They had to disgustedly look the other way. My parents separated. Dad took off.

Mom was alone with three kids now. Her oldest son suffered from epileptic seizures, her second-born son was so traumatized he could not poop, think straight, or act "normal," and the youngest child was a little girl only three years old. I remember watching TV one day by myself in a silent home when Dad walked in. I was happy to see him since he hadn't been around in a while. My older brother and younger sister came in the living room. We were all happy to see him. He wanted to talk to us. He started to tell us how sorry he was for the mess the family was in, and that Mom and him were getting a divorce so things could be better at home. My older brother was bummed; I did not understand what he was saying because I was paying attention to the TV, and my sister was playing nearby.

Just then a news flash came on, cutting into what I was watching: "The President of the United States has just been shot in Dallas! President Kennedy has been shot and killed in Dallas, Texas, this afternoon!" Dad stopped talking about divorce, my brother turned up the TV, and I just looked into our little black-and-white screen as scenes of the Presidential motorcade were shown, along with the bedlam of people crying and all the hell that was breaking loose in Dallas. Dad looked at us and did not say anything. Mom came into the living room and said nothing. That's all I can remember. Mom and Dad were going to be divorced and President Kennedy had been shot and killed in Dallas, Texas. It was November 22, 1963, and the world of Woolly Mammoth Boy was to going to change big time.

11. Woolly Mammoth Seagull Boy

Life's quirky moments are fleeting, so enjoy them. It hurts too much to try to avoid them anyway.

–Woolly Mammoth Boy Speaks

I FLEW HIGHER AND HIGHER WITH each sweep of my great, white-feathered wings—what a difference from my previous life as a woolly mammoth. The foggy air was wet with moisture, but it made no difference to me. It bothered me not, for my downy seagull feathers kept me warm and waterproof. The sun was shining brightly above the foggy canopy that covered the vast city below me.

Yesterday, I spied the little child who was part of me. The kid's head was larger than his body. He was walking up a street when I spied him from above. I was immediately drawn to him, not knowing anything about this scrawny little kid except that I knew him but he did not know me, and that we were destined by the Powers that Be and the future that connected us to meet.

As I flew over him for a better look I gave a nice loud call to catch his attention. At that moment I inadvertently let go the contents of my bowels, barely missing his jet-black hair, which made him a pretty good target against the grey sidewalk. My droppings barely missed him as he dodged clear. The little kid looked up at me and waved in greeting, and yelled something I could not catch. How nice of him, so I gave another greeting, and came to rest nearby on some thick black cables. I felt an aura of energy from the little kid that spoke of sadness and fear. As I watched the little boy walk below me, I started to preen myself to get ready to head out for some food.

I jumped off and headed for my favorite place near the big orange bridge where the fishing was good and the others of my flock would be hanging out. "Grab me a fish and sing me a song, or I'll scavenge some junk floating on the water or on the streets where the people congregate"—it is a good day just being me. I knew I would see the boy again. I would be observing and watching over this boy as he grows to be a fully developed human. If not in this avian form, it will be in another life form altogether.

12. Trouble at Paul Revere

You can bump into a wall once, maybe twice...then you better wake up! Because the third time may not be all that pretty.

—Woolly Mammoth Boy Speaks

"Mrs. Rubio, what are we to do about your son, Ron?" Mr. Soso sat back in his wooden chair looking at me as he waited for my mom to answer. Mr. Soso was the principal of Paul Revere Elementary School, where I was now in second grade as a seven-year-old street kid. "He plays too much in class. He disrupts the class with his clowning and joking around in very inappropriate times. He does not do his schoolwork at all; he just draws and plays. This is the third time this week and it is only *Wednesday*."

Mom was tired of my behavior. She was stressed out as a single parent of three kids, and I was a very high-maintenance child for her to deal with. Mom was young and depressed. Dad was no longer living at home, and financially things were very tight. Before splitting up with Mom, Dad had built a small one-bedroom addition to our home on Prentiss St. with his old buddy Palmer (from his Navy days). In fact, in an attempt to try and make ends meet my Mom had one of her older sisters move in with us, along with my auntie's musician husband and their two kids, my younger cousins. As my dad and Palmer were building the addition, I remember seeing them smoke their Lucky Strike cigarettes as they planned, discussed, and worked on the place. I observed how very cool it looked when they lit their smokes with a one-handed flick from their saved Navy lighters. They would hold their cigs in a military fashion—from a cupped, hand-held position—protecting their cigarettes from an unfelt breeze.

The addition was built on a cement foundation with the general principles of carpentry, plumbing, and electrical in mind. This would be the first of many carpentry endeavors my dad would undertake in his lifetime. He was self-taught and highly motivated. Corners were a little off here, angles a little off there, but it stood and was habitable. The extra money from renting to her older sister helped Mom, but she continued to be really stressed out. Life was just plain hard for Mom in 1964 in San Francisco, and now she had to take almost-weekly meetings with the school principal about my behaviors.

"Mr. Soso, I am not happy to be in here again." With that, Mom shot me the look only mothers know to make that told me many crucial things in one complete package: Primarily, the look said, "This is extremely embarrassing for me to be here...AGAIN!" Secondly it said, "Ron, my son, you are a pain in the ass," and finally, "Boy, wait until we get home!" It's simply amazing how one look can freeze somebody's heart! "Damn!" I was thinking to myself. I was trying so hard not to pee in my pants!

"Mr. Soso, please...I give you permission to do what needs to be done at this school to keep my son in his place. I am sorry for the inconvenience he has caused you and his teachers." Mom paused, looked at me again, and said, "If that is all, Mr. Soso, I will be leaving now. Thank you, Mr. Soso." Mom got up from her chair and Mr. Soso out of his. He motioned me to stay seated as he shook my Mom's extended hand in his—engulfing her petite little hand in his huge bear paw, and then escorted her to the door. Mom did not turn around to look at me as she left. "I must have disgraced her and pissed her off really good," I was thinking to myself.

Upon seeing my mom out the door Mr. Soso turned on his heels and faced me. He looked down his bulbous nose and stared right at me with his two large bear paws fisted on his hips. "Shit! I am dead," I thought.

"Well, Mr. Rubio, what am I to do with you?" Mr. Soso asked, not expecting an answer. Mr. Soso, towering over me, scared the gas out of me, and so relying on my disciplinary experiences with Dad, I said to myself, "Shut up and be still." I knew I would just stutter aimlessly anyway even if I tried to speak. I followed him with just my brown eyes, my head still, as he made his way around his massive wooden desk to his wooden chair. He sat with a thud and a squeak, and looked at me again as he rolled his chair closer to his desk and paused.

"I do not like to see you in my office, Mr. Rubio." I hated the way he said "Mr. Rubio." I knew something bad was going to happen. He opened his top right drawer and took out a large, wide, wooden twelve-inch measuring ruler. "I do not like your disruptive behavior in class, your fooling around, and not doing your school work." The ruler played in his big left bear paw. My eyes were fixed on the ruler.

"Get up off your chair, come around my desk, and stand before me." Mr. Soso ordered me with a deadly calmness in his voice that got me shaking in my knees. Now, when my dad was going to hit me his whole body shook; he yelled and swore at me, cursing my stupidity, but Mr. Soso was calm and rock steady. Damn! I wanted to disappear. I made it around his large wooden desk and stood in front of him. Even seated he was still taller than me. He then took my left hand into his big right bear paw, and held it with my palm facing upward. I was looking at the wooden ruler the whole time.

"Mr. Rubio, I do not want to see you in here anymore." We locked eyes and the air in his office became very still. Then he struck the open palm of my hand with the ruler. *Whack!* The sound was so loud in my head. I was stunned by the stinging in my hand, and I lost my breath. Then again. *Whack!* I tried to pull my stinging, throbbing hand away while still looking into his eyes. Then a third time..."Oh, lucky three"...*Whack!* And with that last strike the pain exploded out of me and I screamed and cried as loud as I could. "Damn! Motherf*cker!!!" I screamed. He hit my hand again for swearing...*Whack!*

"Go sit outside my office until you can pull yourself together, and then go back to your classroom!" I could not move, frozen by a sobbing seizure. "Get out of my office! Now!"

I stumbled out of Mr. Soso's office and crumbled into the waiting chair. His secretary did not look at me, and the student office helpers looked in the other direction. I had felt pain before—a wire hanger to my bare butt was pretty up there in the pain scale—and yet the striking of my open palm with a stiff, thick, wooden ruler, wielded in the hands of a balding grizzly bear, was another form of discipline that was surely made in a dark place in the universe! I made it back to my classroom somehow, sniffling, my body jerking with dry heaving sobs, totally embarrassed, humiliated, and very angry. No one talked to me, and my teacher let me silently sob away until I fell asleep at my desk, my head cradled in my folded arms. The next thing I knew the school bell rang. I awoke and it was time to go home.

In telling this tale I am reminded of another story. As a mentor to young people I had a client in 2009 who, besides being Aspie, was also diagnosed with obsessive-compulsive disorder (OCD). Damn those labels! When flooded with emotions and trauma he wanted to cry, no matter where he was. He said crying made him feel so much better, and it was a way to release the pain. He would cry in school and in public places as a young boy, and as a man. He once cried at a family gathering, embarrassing himself and his family.

When I started to mentor him he was 23. By this time he was better at not crying in public; he found it helpful to return home, where he lived with his parents, go into his room, and in the loneliness of his haven he would have a serious crying session. He cried and cried. He once felt comfortable and safe enough to cry in front of me during a session. I observed how he sobbed and cried like a little boy. I worked with him to find alternative ways to express his fears, anger, and frustrations when he felt bombarded with stimulation from the public world and the inevitable desire to cry which would come upon him. I suggested strategies which offered him the opportunity to cry safely, so he could discharge the energy he was feeling instead of bottling it up and exploding at home, or in an inappropriate area.

I have nothing against crying. I myself was an avid crier through elementary school up to high school. I once belted out a hurricane of tears in a junior high school band room. My music teacher was freaked out by someone crying at my age, and yet he showed compassion, stayed with me, and helped me through the embarrassing moment.

As the tears ran down my face, where my woolly mammoth tusks once were, it felt great.

Now, as a grown man, I still have the strong desire to cry like a baby at times. It is said that grief is the opposite side of the coin of unexpressed anger. This is surely true! Sometimes I want to scream, yell, and destroy something close at hand, and then I want to cry so hard until I am tired enough to drop into a deep, deep sleep. It was like this after beatings from my dad, but as I got older I would rage instead of cry. I told this mentee that I wanted to cry like him without giving a hoot about what the world would think of me. I told him this once in a session together. He was amazed. Yet I told him I had to learn when it is an appropriate time to cry and when it is not an appropriate time to cry. It was important for me to learn how to discharge the energy of rage, to breathe into myself in order to come back to sanity, and to face and solve whatever was driving me to cry. It is easier said than done. Crying is good.

I don't remember too much of anything of the two-and-a-half-block walk back to my house except a big fat white seagull flying overhead squawking and nearly pooing on my head. "Screw you!" I thought to myself as I dodged the falling bird ca-ca and flipped the gull off. The seagull squawked louder and flew off to settle on a nearby rooftop.

I made my way home dreading what my mom had in store for me. Mom was not cruel in her disciplining ways as Dad was, but she had her own brand of convincing consequences.

13. Why Humans Love and Hate, According to Thought

Hear, my darlings, of Love and Hate, and the mysteries of relationships...

—Woolly Mammoth Boy Speaks

"WHY DO HUMANS HAVE TO deal with the emotions of love and hate?" Woolly Mammoth Seagull Boy asked aloud one evening as he perched high on a rock above the roaring Pacific Ocean just past the Golden Gate Bridge. Though Thought was engaged with billions upon billions of other conversations throughout the Great Cosmos at the same time—with a myriad of creatures both humanoid and beyond—Thought answered immediately.

"Well, the reason humans were given emotions of love and hate, my little one, is because, like no other creatures on their planet *Gaia*, humans were given an emotional struggle or curse, so that they may work out their large self-centered egos and desires to find the true human emotion that surpasses the emotion of love—that which balances the emotion of hate—and find the harmony that exists in the Great Cosmos. It allows the humans to fulfill their emotional karmic debt so they can be as you are, Woolly Mammoth Seagull Boy, and like all the other beings and nonbeings of the Great Cosmos—free to choose to be reborn and come back as many times as they wish in any form, or until they have completed their *karma*, before moving on to any place in the Great Cosmos." So answered Thought with a gleam.

"Will the humans ever discover this true emotion?" Woolly Mammoth Seagull Boy asked as he plucked at a ripe sand tick from under his wing.

"Surely, little one. You did, and so have many other beings and nonbeings since the first fires existed, and since the first act of procreation consummated the union between two humans," assured Thought.

"What is the true emotion?" squawked Woolly Mammoth Seagull Boy. "I do not remember it from my past human lives."

"Well, well, my little one," glowed Thought, "If I reminded you of the true human emotion that surpasses love and hate, you could accidentally tell that little boy you have chosen to ward, guiding him to the answer, and thereby condemn him without his consent to have to come back as a human all over again. He must find the answer on his own like all other humans. So I am sorry I cannot reveal this to you."

"I would not want that for the little boy, to condemn him in any fashion. His life is pretty messed up as it is," said Woolly Mammoth Seagull Boy as he gazed unblinking into the western horizon where the sun was sinking into the ocean and the ominous dark fog bank lay lingering off shore, just before it rushed landward as the heat of the sun vanished, to cool the San Francisco evening air.

"The answer, little one, lies in the depths of a true human understanding of each other, a true act of communication, a true act of self-sacrifice; an understanding that is beyond all the glitter of good deeds well done, or the sparkle of good intentions promised, or the romantic emotions that blind one from the true connection between humans." Thought paused and gave a deep rumbling sigh.

Woolly Mammoth Seagull Boy took a deep breath and squawked out loud to himself, saying, "I will be more observant of humans and see what I can learn about them as it concerns this love-hate question. I know the answer, or I would not be here right now as a seagull, who once was a woolly mammoth, who once was a human...I just can't remember."

Thought said no more, nor did Woolly Mammoth Seagull Boy. There was silence. The sky grew darker out beyond the landfall where the seldom seen deep-sea creatures came up from the depths to hunt in the shallow upper waters. The night sky above San Francisco grew lighter with the turning on of the streetlights and buildings lights. The silence was punctuated by the crashing of dark waters upon the craggy rocks below Woolly Mammoth Seagull Boy. He had almost forgotten what he had been talking about with Thought when he came out of his seagull brain and said out loud, "I want to help the little boy very badly...in a sense the little boy is me in another time and space. I am part of that little boy."

Thought replied, "Yes, I know you want to help the lad, but be wary, little one. I will not warn you or try to stop you should you try to help him. What will be will be. Remember, little one, for every action there is a reaction. No deed is left unanswered in the Great Cosmos, where all voids are meant to be filled and nothing is left undone."

The wind started to pick up as other seagulls were making their way inland to the city where they would find shelter or a good night feeding on trash. The night wind made the dry, tall grass, which clung to the cliff rocks, rattle and hiss. It sounded like a thousand snakes.

As Woolly Mammoth Seagull Boy opened his wings and took a little hop to start gliding into flight, he thought he heard something in the wind. The rattling and hissing sounds confused him; he heard something in the air, but he was not sure. He shook his head and squawked, trying to clear his ears.

"Damn! What was that sound?" he asked out loud. He heard it again but very, very faintly this time like a mermaid's haunting siren song.

Compassion.
Compassion.
Compassion.

14. The Altar Boy and His Fall from Grace

Rituals and ceremonies of any organized religion have great purpose in our lives. These rituals create order and boundaries for our minds and spirits to follow...if we choose to follow these strictures. Personally, I did not see the value in them. Life was complicated enough without putting energy into the fears and restrictions of others.

–The Observations of Woolly Mammoth Boy

I WAS BAPTIZED AT ST. KEVIN'S, a Catholic church serving the souls of the neighborhood of Bernal Heights, San Francisco. The smell of St. Kevin's was one of oiled wood with a nice patina, dusty prayer book covers, and leftover perfume and cologne fragrances from the many parishioners that came in from 6:00 a.m. until sundown. The stained glass windows were hauntingly beautiful, and depicted the sad Stations of the Cross as the sunlight filtered through the dark blues, reds, yellows, and greens of the windows. I loved stories and each stained glass window had a story to tell. The church bell was a real bell that called the Bernal Heights people to its simple hall.

As my mom, siblings, and I settled into being at home without Dad, we developed some very peculiar ways. At night Mom would gather us into one of the two bedrooms and give us a pee pot for our nightly bathroom needs so we would not open the locked bedroom door and leave the safety of each other until the coming of dawn. It was like we were barricading ourselves against the night creatures of spookiness, danger, and fright. I think it's a Filipino thing—the superstition of the bogeyman, and things that go bump in the night—as well as the real threat in the Philippines of robbers and poor folk breaking into homes for things they do not have. Later in my life, my third wife had a Filipina maid who would lock herself in the child's room with my wife's youngest daughter, and leave every light turned on for the whole night. Needless to say, I voted to boot the maid when I entered the family—no need for that paranoid stuff in my home!

I never really knew my mom as a religious person, let alone as a practicing Catholic, during the years of my early childhood. I believe she went to most of the Catholic high holy days, though. For her, praying for a safe night's passage, protected against evil, did not quite fit into the nighttime protocol.

My dad, on the other hand, made us go through the rosary every night with him plus some more prayers for good measure. In the Philippines, the mysteries of the supernatural walked side by side with the waking world of the living, but maybe that's just a Catholic thing too. I mean, you have a lot of sinners—wandering souls stuck on Earth from their wrongdoings—or people who have been murdered, those that have died before their time. It felt like these people could not ascend to the pearly gates of Heaven, and had been damned to wander the Earth amongst the living. I know many Latin Americans, Spanish, and Irish Catholics who hang on to similar superstitions.

So, that's how I grew up. Nighttime was a scary time to be alone. It was not a safe time, and you'd better watch your back—don't look down that dark staircase because something in the deep shadows may be looking for you, ascending the stairs. Whatever you do: DO NOT UNLOCK THE BEDROOM UNTIL DAWN! To be honest, I do not disregard the belief in spirits amongst us, but I believe you draw those spirits and bad juju energies toward you: like begets like, and fear begets more fear.

So when the opportunity offered itself to become an altar boy at St. Kevin's it seemed like a cool thing to do. My older brother did not want any part of it. The small group of boys who had accepted me into their social circle had all decided to become altar boys too, so we all thought to join up together. I was already enrolled in after-school catechism classes, so what the hell. I joined up for a tour of duty as a cadet in the Army of Light. I was eight years old, and would serve two one-year tours of duty.

I went through altar boy "boot camp," and learned the proper etiquette to follow pre-, during, and post-mass. I was taught the service format for each of the high holy days, and how to hold the incense—that swinging metal thing with the chains—without burning yourself, getting smoke in your eyes and throat, or loudly hacking in front of the congregation. I learned how to *not* fall asleep when on "stage" and sitting on those damned hard wooden benches. The head priest, Father O'Connor, would drone away in a heavy Irish brogue that I could barely understand. I had to fight very hard to refrain from laughing and to resist waving to my friends and family seated in the congregation. I learned to say the right Latin response at the right time without just mouthing it, and, most importantly, how to look like I understood what the heck I was doing up there in front of the congregation. Then, and only then, were you assigned a mass to serve with a priest.

My first assignment was the early morning mass—a Monday through Friday "show time" before school at 8:30 a.m. Among my fellow altar boys, we called serving a mass "doing a show." It was as if we were performing on stage like our favorite Motown bands—The Temptations, Marvin Gaye, Gladys Knight and the Pips, Smokey Robinson, and that white, British band:

The Beatles. The morning mass was the hardest because I had to be at church by 6:30 a.m. and prepare the "stage" with all the right stuff for a 7:00 a.m. curtain call. I would roll out the white, thin cloth that covered the main table, and set up the water- and wine-pouring bottles—knowing that Father O'Connor did not like any water in his wine mixture. I then had to set up the big candles and light them, turn on the main stage lights, and pick out the proper vestment worn by the priest for the service during the week (there was a special vestment for each Sunday of the year, and for the high holy days). The Bible the priest would read from also had to be set up, and finally, I had to get myself dressed and ready to rock 'n' roll.

I loved doing service—from the prep work to blowing out the candles at the end. I mean I loved every part of it. Everything had a purpose, a place in the show, a social timing that did not change, an answer or reason for anything you said or did. I loved the structure of doing mass. It was such a relief to my spirit and mind, since most of the time I was bombarded by the very unstructured, unpredictable, and sometimes-violent world I was trying to understand and be part of just to survive.

During the weekday mornings it was just Father O'Connor and me, and during Sunday mass there were two other altar boys on board serving the priest. I would get to church early after waking around 5:45 a.m. I would wake up on my own; check in on my older brother, younger sister, and Mom who were still sleeping; make a little breakfast; wash up; and get out the door for the seven-minute walk in the early dawn light to St. Kevin's. I corralled my intense energies to my duty.

After entering the church, I would go straight to the altar-boy room and get my service undergarment, a jet-black ankle-to-throat gown upon which were thirty shiny buttons to button up onto my scrawny frame. I loved that the best—buttoning all those buttons up to my throat, and putting on my "uniform shield." To this day I love wearing turtlenecks and having my throat covered. Feeling the cloth around my neck and all buttoned up made me feel where my body was in relation to the world around me. It also made feel safe, like having a thick, heavy blanket on me at night when I went to sleep. I liked the feeling of containment around my body. *Please hold me tightly... someone... anyone.*

After doing all the prep chores for morning mass, I would go into the priest's changing room and open that long, tall, deep closet filled with beautiful vestments, one for each Sunday of the year and the special ones for the high holy days. The vestments all had different symbolic, magical design patterns, and came in different shades of colors: deep purples, rich reds, blues, golds, oranges, and pearl whites that looked so creamy and light like an angel's wings. I would just stand there for a short, sweet moment and look at them all, and then I would start at one end of the closet and go down to the other end, passing through all the vestments, touching them all, running my fingers down them to feel their soft holiness. It was the best part of prep time for me. It was my alone time and a very quiet time of the day: the early morning. Aspies do well when there are defined parameters to follow. Recognizing structure and the benefits of having structure, or developing structure to help organize how one sees and functions in the world is paramount. Not only for the Aspie individual, but the neuro-typical ("normal") person as well.

The morning mass would bring the dregs of the neighborhood from out of the cold, foggy streets. The small morning congregation was made up of drunks, derelicts, women of the night, and those going off to work early. As the moment came for the parishioners to receive the "Body of Christ"—a little paper-thin rice wafer—I would hold a gold-plated dish underneath the chin of the parishioner as Father O'Connor placed the wafer onto the tongue of the receiver. I would hold my breath as I looked down the gullet of these early morning souls receiving the sacrament of Holy Communion. I would wonder: What were their sins? Where did they sleep at night? Which bench had I seen them on, in which alleyway had they been lurking? Some had no teeth, or they had brown-yellow ones. The sight of their dental hygiene, or lack thereof, reminded me to keep up with the brushing of my own teeth. Despite appearances, in the end they were all saved and received forgiveness for their sins once again. What a great deal! Then they could go back out in the world and do it all over again!

All went well during the years I served at St. Kevin's, but, in the end, I started to grow disenchanted with the church and religion. I had been drilled in the Ten Commandments, had read and studied the Bible with the Catholic Sisters in catechism class, and I had recited the Latin prayers. I went to church every Sunday with my hair slicked down with pomade hair grease. I read stories of Jesus getting mighty angry and throwing the selfish sellers and their gold coins from the church turned into a marketplace. I was lectured on how to be good to my fellow man, and all that stuff. But as I got older, I saw how the men would look at each other's wives secretly; how they talked about "nigger" this and "chink" that; how the cigarette smoke filled the church basement during bingo nights, the money being jingled in fat hands; and how my God-fearing dad would beat me, even after he was out of the house, because Mom would let him visit to keep "his children" in place.

I was losing my faith in the Catholic Church. If there was a God, why in the hell was this man still beating on me!?! I am blessed I was not molested like altar boys in other parishes—keeping their deadly silence within their churches' white walls. No, this church-religion thing was not working for me. My rigid thinking of right and wrong, of fairness, my literal thinking of everything taught to me in church, led me to want to leave it behind.

The shit hit the fan when one of my fellow altar boys had a great idea. Well, at the time it seemed incredibly brilliant, at least. There were a lot of shiny quarters inserted into the candle tables. Twenty-five cents went a long way back in the 1960s. All seven of us altar boys saw—and ourselves had placed—a quarter to light a prayer candle. The idea was to heist some of those quarters from the candle tables and split the takings. All seven of us had a role in the scheme. Some of the braver, cooler ones had butter knives from home to slip into the slot to extract the quarters; others were to tip the candle tables so the quarters would slide down the butter knives, while still others were lookouts. I was a lookout. Being the most timid, shy, and awkward kid of the "wild bunch," the ringleaders gave me the simplest of tasks.

The scheme went off without a hitch—we all knew the timing of the church activities, for we were the observing eyes of St. Kevin's. The first time we pulled a heist we grabbed enough quarters to really score a solid load of candy per person. Back in the '60s, a penny could buy you one Bazooka Joe bubble gum, or one stick of red licorice, or a Tootsie Roll. I spent my split of the take on a sugary roll-bready-thing, and a Marvel or DC comic book. This thieving went on for months until the conscience in my "wanting-to-do-the-right-thing" spacey head led me to confess to my mom and give up the gang of thieves. I did not want to keep living a lie by stealing from the church, and my mom was furious when I told her about our scheme.

At the meeting with Father O'Connor, Mom, realizing I wanted to come clean, told Father O'Connor that the trade for her son giving up the rest of the gang was to give me the status of an anonymous call-in about the stealing. It was not like I was being hidden in the Witness Protection Program, but Mom had made the deal with Father O'Connor to protect me from the wrath of my gang and from being labeled a "dirty rat fink" by my schoolmates. No one ever knew it was me who had sold out the gang, and I was relieved to get that deceiving monkey off my back and come clean. I would not do that again. Stealing was not my thing.

The gang was busted up and hung out to dry. It was sensational news for the church and the congregation. All seven of us were banished from the altar boy corps. I never went back to St. Kevin's because the incident pushed me further toward my decision to stop being a practicing Catholic. I fell from the grace and ranks of the Army of Light and from the house of my little neighborhood church of gamblers, hypocrites, bigots, liars, and wife-chasers. I was not the least bit sad about it all, except that I would miss my special, quiet morning time in the priest's room with a closet filled by many-colored, soft, and holy vestments.

All seven of us were gathered in the administrative office of St. Kevin's refectory in the presence of Father O'Connor and told we were banished. As I walked away from the church for the last time, I felt like that TV Western called *Branded* with Chuck Connors. The show opens with a scene in which a Union cavalry officer (Connors) is wrongly accused of a crime and is disgraced. All his insignias of rank were torn from his uniform, and the final insult was his saber being drawn from its scabbard, broken in half, and thrown to the dusty ground.

I left the church, crestfallen and embarrassed, when suddenly my attention was attracted heavenward by the sound of a seagull's screeching call. High above flew a lone seagull who seemed to be shadowing my steps, and soaring free from the world of humans. I envied its joy of flying through the vast, blue San Francisco skies. I hurried home so Mom would not get mad at me for being late. The early evening fog was coming in and this lousy day was gratefully coming to a close.

During these "fatherless" years I was teaching myself many survival skills. I taught myself how to cook and make simple foods for myself and my sister. My older brother did his own eating thing when Mom was not around. I ended up burning myself and my food frequently, but I got a few dishes down. I started drinking coffee rather early because I made Mom coffee in the mornings. Mom liked her coffee hot, a little creamy, and really sweet. I also taught myself how to ride a bike. Those pansy-ass scenes on TV shows—with the nice parent helping their kid with those first precious moments balancing their little world as the kid takes the first bike ride—were from a fairytale movie for me. I envied my friends who were riding their cool Stingray bikes around the neighborhood.

So, one grey San Franciscan day, I asked a kid who was kind-of my friend but not really, if I could borrow his bike for a couple of hours. He said sure. I went to the widest street in our neighborhood. Minding the cars, I got on that bike and punished myself for a couple of hours by pushing off, trying to balance, pedaling, and then crashing horribly. This sadistic, painful bike lesson lasted for two frigid hours. I swore, cursed, cried, and yelled until I could pedal that damn bike one complete San Francisco street block without crashing. I learned to ride that bike—the world be damned! I did not need anyone's help, but I was also sad that I had no one to help me.

Thirty years later, I would be helping Aspie teenagers learn how to ride a bike because their parents couldn't, or wouldn't, teach their son or daughter out of fear for their kid or their own lack of faith in their kid's ability to even try to learn. Balancing, coordinating legs for movement, remembering how to brake, looking out for things to crash into, and just the plain old bruises and cuts of learning to ride a bike is just too frightening for most people. For uncoordinated individuals with a clearly fearful outlook toward the physical world, most Aspies shy away from learning how to ride a bike at an early age. And if the unwilling bike learner complains loudly and often, and resists help strongly, and just makes it a hellish annoying experience for the parent/trainer, well then, the project of learning to ride a bike might be dropped forever. You would be surprised how many Aspie kids and adults never learned how to ride a bike from their parents...sad.

My world was weird and alone and that was fine. I would learn to live in this crazy world my way, and that was that. As for the concepts of God, Heaven, and Hell, well, I would have to find my way through this. I figured as long as I was good to others I would be okay. It felt strange to me that while in church, we always had to look upward to "see" God. I had thought, from my catechism classes, that God was all around us all the time. In fact, I thought God was supposed to be in us all, and that we were made in God's image. If this concept were true, I thought, then how in the hell can we be born with original sin as babies? This religious stuff made no sense to me. So, I would let it ride for a while. I figured if I was going to Hell, or going to the grey netherworld of Purgatory, well, that would have to be the way the ball bounced. I was only nine years old, and if God was going to be that mean I really could not do anything about it. I could not stop Dad beating on me when he wanted or stop the world from laughing at me, either. I would survive this world on my terms. Really, what choice did I have?

15. Learning Gentleman's Manners and Fire on Witch's Mountain

I learned from watching the older mammoths. I watched amazed how the elders knew to create an outward facing circle when approached by the saber-toothed predators. The images taught me the silent language of their bodies. Then, I only had to remember what I had learned, for I knew it would come in handy one day.

–Woolly Mammoth Boy Remembers

The year after Dad was out of the house, life at home was different. I missed him. I mean, he still was my dad no matter how much pain he inflicted upon me or how much fear he instilled in me. Other kids had their dads and I did not have mine. The house was packed with action because my cousins lived downstairs, and Mom had her sister and brother-in-law around. When they moved out Mom was strapped for cash, so she decided to get a night job with Kodak films working the graveyard shift in the film processing plant in San Francisco.

She prepared us for our dinners with a new fast dinner product called Swanson's TV Dinners. Plop those bad boys in the oven and you have a special meal in thirty-five minutes. Amazing treats. Before Mom left for work she gave instructions to make sure everyone washed up before going to bed, and she got us ready for school the next day by laying out our clothing and helping us with our homework. Fred was not available in the evenings after Mom left around 6:00 p.m.—he would do his own thing or go visit friends. Fred just wasn't around for us siblings, and Mom looked to me to help out now that Dad was out of the house.

First I would put Valerie Joyce down for bed by playing with her in my very silly and creative way. I would dance around in my mother's shoes or perform some storyacting games I made up. We played for hours, and then I would clean up and do my homework. Fred did his thing and put himself down. I would check in on him off and on throughout my night watch; it would be two more years until his epileptic seizures got under control and would lay dormant inside of him. I made it my duty to stay up for Mom until she got home around two or three in the morning.

Being a nine-year-old boy, I thought nothing of all the responsibilities that were laid upon my young woolly mammoth head. I thought it was a natural part of doing a "warrior kind of thing"—I was on guard and watching the gates so no intruder would get in. I thought my Dada would be proud of me. I was like the Marine sentry at the gates to Hunter's Point Naval Base. Years later, I would realize that these "night watches" were a hell of a load to carry for a young boy. No one in the house was older than ten-and-a-half, and I was only eight tugging on nine, but, Mom had to pull in the extra dough and I was up to the task of helping her.

Most nights I would stay awake until she got in. Other times I would be asleep on the couch, and I would awake to hear the front door unlock and open. I had acquired the hypervigilance of someone waiting for danger to appear, or waiting to be smacked or yelled at. Mom would greet me and then turn on the TV, set up the ironing board, and start ironing to work out her graveyard shift energy. Mom kept me up to watch movies with her while she ironed. We would watch TV movie classics like *Wuthering Heights*, *From Here to Eternity*, *On the Waterfront*, and many more. Mom would say, "Ronnie, this movie will really make you cry," and it would. I did not understand what was happening, but I got the feeling that this time watching movies with Mom at three in the morning was an important time. I was learning how to express loss and agony.

It was from watching these movies that I started to be mentored in the social nuances of the 1940s through the 1960s. These were gentlemen's manners from such actors as Jimmy Stewart, Cary Grant, Gary Cooper, Clark Gable, Spencer Tracy, and others. I guess this could be called "male mentoring by the silver screen." I figured what I saw the men in these movies doing—opening doors, holding themselves with gentlemanly grace and surehandedness, speaking politely, being helpful and brave, thinking of others, and being funny at the right time—were behaviors to emulate no matter how "pasted on" they seemed. These early "movie lessons" would help me tremendously as I grew older.

My "pasted on" gentleman's manners would help mask and cover my more turbulent, erratic behaviors. Later, becoming a dancer in my early twenties would help me to "anchor" or fix these gentleman behaviors in my mind and body, but that was years to come and too hard for an eight-year-old to understand. So I soaked up these movies and stayed up with Mom as she ironed our clothing to tire herself to sleep. I would cry and laugh with her while watching these movies until I fell asleep on the couch, then Mom would carry me to bed, only to awaken a few hours later to go to school. In those years I did not sleep much.

It was on one of these night watches that the witch's house on Bernal Heights burned downed. Mom had already left for work and all was fine until we heard a lot of sirens. From the street we heard excited voices. We peered out our windows to see what the excitement was about. To my amazement

I saw the old witch's house on fire up on the Heights. There was an old lady who owned and lived in the only house on Bernal Heights proper—up on the Heights themselves. Seldom seen, she was shrouded in mystery and gossip. No one really knew when she arrived at the house or even knew her name. To us neighborhood kids she was a witch. We knew she was unkempt in her appearance when spotted, and she had a mass of white, long hair that stood out from the dark clothing she wore.

Bernal Heights were made up of two connected sizeable knobs of protruding earth—one taller than the other—and straddled the south end of the Mission District. It gave a splendid view of the whole city of San Francisco, the East Bay and the lands beyond where the sun rose in the morning, the lands south of San Francisco proper where Hunter's Point Naval Base was situated, and all the way over to the distant hills in the west, which faced the Pacific Ocean where the fog came from. I would climb Bernal Heights and imagine it as my Wuthering Heights, and I was Heathcliff. Bernal Heights was nestled in a valleylike landscape—the Heights were on the north end, a large bowl filled with little homes; Cortland Avenue, our main street, cut east to west in the middle, and a lower ridge rose a mile and a half on the south end of the bowl. Our house sat on the southern side facing Bernal Heights to the north. Our neighbors were all standing in the middle of the street looking north across the bowl and up towards the Heights. I imagine the whole district was out on the streets watching the house go up in flames. The firefighters allowed the house to burn.

I was chilled watching the spectacle for it was not less than a month since the gang had decided to peer into the witch's house and see if we could see her doing something sinister. It was near dusk and the nine of us walked up toward the Heights, and planned out loud. Since I was the smallest and the most naïve, I was volunteered to sneak up close to the house and do a "look-see," and then get the hell out of there. My gangmates were going to cheer me on from a safe distance. I crawled on my belly like a snake until I was up close to the witch's house. I remember clearly smelling the anise-licorice plants and the smell of earth and grass as they brushed against my face. As I neared the witch's house, I looked back to see my mates who were all looking at me with fear and excitement on their faces. I edged myself to the side of the house to where the closest window was and slowly, like a shadow, I stood up.

I remember thinking, "I hope I don't start wheezing, then witch will hear me and grab my sorry soul!" Now standing, I saw the faint glow of a light or candle within the small cabinlike house. I checked in with my gang mates and they were all urging me to peer in for a better "look-see." I held my breath and peered into the witch's house. My view was partly obscured by faded, old, white drapes. I started to scan the room when I saw the shadow of someone's figure walking across the room. I ducked and almost peed my pants. Seeing my reaction the gang became one with the grass as I heard their hissing whispers to shut themselves up. I heard nothing from within the house so I thought it safe to stand up for another peek. Again, I rose from the ground like a misty shadow, raised myself to the window so only my eyes were above the windowsill, and then I froze. There, waiting for me in the darkness and silence on the other side of the glass window, was the witch! She looked at me as our eyes met. Her white hair was ratty and in disarray.

I could not tell if she was white, black, or brown in skin. Her clothing was dark and old looking. She seemed puzzled and then annoyed by me standing looking at her. When I saw the annoyance on her face I must have yelped as I turned and ran. I peed in my pants. My friends were already gone for they saw her move to the window but gave me no warning as they fled. We all ran down the Heights in a flash like the wind. I ran and ran until I got to our rendezvous point behind the library. They were laughing as I pulled in with the front of my pants noticeably wet with urine. I grew dangerously angry with them. I hated to be laughed at. I must have swung at the first kid near me, felling him with a clear punch before the rest of the gang got to me and held me down. I yelled at all of them for leaving me, and kicked and screamed until they let me up and I ran home. Mom was getting ready for work and I rushed by her to hide my pee-stained pants. She said goodnight to me through a closed bathroom door. She was used to me peeing and having accidents in my pants as a boy. I waited until the coast was clear and then I emerged, relieved. I was safe at home and had not been turned into some inhuman creature by the witch.

I watched the witch's house burn that night, the flames shooting out the windows, it looked like angry eyes. Word went around at school the next day that no body was found and that the house was burned completely to the ground. We all went to the witch's house after school and picked through the still smoking hot embers. Nothing was salvageable.

Years later I took my daughters up to Bernal Heights to look at the city view. We meandered toward the old stone foundation of the witch's house that was barely still visible. Bernal Heights had changed in the thirty-eight years I had been away. Even with the new coffeehouses and the silly stores of the "yuppified" area that now covered what had been my childhood stomping grounds, I could not keep the chill out of my bones as I stared at the dim dirt outline of where the witch's house once stood.

As I told the story to my girls we started poking around. I was able to clear some ground and weeds when I bumped into the remnants of a set of stone stairs leading down to what was once a cellar. I walked down the stone stairs with my girls looking at me in the bright sunlight. I brushed some bushes away at the bottom of the stairs and saw an old door half buried in dirt and weeds. I looked back at my daughters to see their excitement and fear of my discovery. I was going to try and pry the door open when my girls started to beg me to leave the door alone and get out of there. Though the sun burned brightly above my head I felt my daughters fear and something else—my own childhood fear rising. Did the witch escape through the cellar door that fiery night? Where did the door lead to? Did her bones lie on the other side of the door? I felt something pull on my heart, and I got out of there quickly to rejoin my relieved daughters. I thought it best to leave old things lay in their dark slumber. My daughters and I laughed as we left Bernal Heights on that beautiful bright spring day.

Woolly Mammoth Boy watched the boiling red sun set beyond mountains that edged the deep valley where he stood. He heard the wind rustle through the trees that surrounded him.

"Yes, I hear you," he said into the cool dusk air.

"Penny for your thoughts...or maybe an Indian nickel?" Thought whispered as a cricket.

"I was pondering on how the manling is learning without a man-bull around," Woolly Mammoth Boy answered. "There are no man-bulls present in his young life. There are no effective teachers for the manling to learn from."

"Yes, the lad is teaching himself many things quite creatively. I can only surmise he understands he must survive to adulthood and he has no one to teach him at this time." Thought was in Woolly Mammoth Boy's ear as an irritating, buzzing gnat.

Shaking his heavily matted, tusked head vigorously, Woolly Mammoth Boy sighed, "Do you mind getting out of my ear? Yes, the young manling has had so much laden upon him, and yet he perseveres. He does well seeking the answers on his own."

Saying this, Woolly Mammoth Boy saw the young bull mammoths setting up for the night's security. He watched them and slowly left to join them. He had learned from his older brothers the responsibilities that a male mammoth had to the herd.

"Fear not for the manling...he will learn from what resonates with him," Thought screeched as a nighthawk leaving its perch for hunting in the early black night sky. "He perseveres."

16. Abandonment Issues and Mom Dates Hank Williams

To be alone in the Great Universe is not really being alone. There is fulfillment in emptiness...so it is said in the Universe. In emptiness there is wholeness. "Yeah, right," I said to myself as I looked across the Great Plains where I grazed. I could not imagine being without my fellow mammoths. I looked at the orphaned little one feeding at my feet, whose mother was killed by a saber tooth. I wondered if he felt the same.

–The Queries of Woolly Mammoth Boy

MOM WORKED HARD TO KEEP the ends met at home. She was a single parent who had to find a solution to her oldest son's epilepsy; work with my peculiar, awkward, and hyper behaviors; and be available for her youngest daughter. Mom still grieved for her dead daughter, Sabrina, who would have been my older sister, from so many years ago. Mom worked the graveyard shift at night and was a very nervous woman. Back in the '60s there were a lot of "mother's little helpers" that you could get over the counter or through prescriptions. Mom had a variety of personal options to keep her head in one place. Needless to say, a person can get out of control when dealing with stress, challenges, and taking drugs.

By the time I was nine years old, Mom had tried to take herself out of the picture—out of our lives—four times by overdosing on pills. I remember the frantic calls to the hospital, and the rushing of relatives over to our house as Mom had her stomach pumped and had her emotional mind stabilized. The first two times I could remember the intense energy in the home as they packed Mom up to go the hospital, and the severe scolding of us children for being...children. We screamed, fought, and played with the exuberance of youngsters. Fred was a bully to me and we fought. I was hyper and clumsily mobile, which led me to often crack my head open while playing by myself. I would have to go to the hospital for stitches—and then there was my little sister who was just being a daughter wanting her mother. With Dad not around the fear factor of his beatings disappeared, and we were to able take advantage of the situation and just be children. Mom was also recovering from her abusive husband.

I watched and learned. How did my parents deal with stress? Dad raged, yelled, cursed, and went bloodthirsty berserk; Mom took drugs or, when it got too much to bear, she would try to kill herself. I was so angry with my mom after her third attempt on her life. I remember my Dada coming to our house for the third time in two years to see his daughter being taken to the hospital. He looked at us, his grandchildren, as we huddled around Mom's bed before the ambulance came, and he scolded us, "Look what you did to your mom, look what you have done!" I was furious! I was so angry with Dada for saying that, and so angry with my mom for trying leave us kids. To leave me! How could she? Did I not work hard to please her and take care of the house for her, take care of my brother and sister for her, stay up for her after she came home from her graveyard shift? And all she wanted to do was check out and leave me! I thought this was a real pisser. Who in the hell was I to trust to be around for me? I was scared to be alone. If I like someone and share my life with this person, will he or she be my friend the next day? And if I they say they love me, why do they want to go away and leave me? *Who in the hell was I supposed to trust?!?*

Now, I cursed like a true sailor, and had my dad's temper and anger. My mom's suicide attempts built up such abandonment issues in my spirit that I started to really lose it. My grades went to hell, I became even more unmanageable, and I raged and fought. I became depressed and more apt to play alone than ever before. I lost whatever confidence I had and became more of a loner, even in the small gang I hung out with—I was becoming too weird and distant for them to understand. I trusted no one except my younger sister, Valerie Joyce. I saw the world as a very precarious piece of rock to live on. When would it all disappear? Would I awake one morning and Mom would not be there anymore?

The church was out of my life and I had no God, no religion. I feared little and all. I was molding into the human I would be for the next thirty years. I wanted to find love—like in the movies I watched with Mom. In the movies things always started out okay, then got shitty, and then there would be a happy ending—but only after everyone took a major hit and realized the folly of their ways. I was hoping for that kind of scenario to develop for me, but that was for another movie; it was nowhere to be found for me. To make things worse, Dad was back in the picture with biweekly visits to discipline us, and so the beatings started back up. The tension was unbearable and yet all children are resilient; so my siblings and I endured, laughed, played, and still remained children. I was just a decayed mess inside. In my universe, I could be safe in my very own fragmented world of fantasy and play. I truly whistled while I worked.

By the time I was nine years old, Mom started to date, and this was a good thing because with Mom dating, it brought an emotional stability to her and to us kids. This was nice to have after so many years without it in the house. Mom was still young and very beautiful. She would go out with her sisters on the weekends and dance her butt off. Mom loved to dance. There were a few men Mom brought home for us to meet and judge.

One of the first men to enter our home was some white hillbilly kind of guy who loved country music. Where Mom picked this guy up was a mystery. He would come over and put an album on the phonograph—Hank Williams, Johnny Horton, or some other knee-slapping country music. Now, growing up in San Francisco, Motown music was the only thing for me. I was dancing in my falsetto voice to Marvin Gaye, Stevie Wonder, The Temptations, Aretha Franklin, and on and on. Country music was just too outright weird and white for me. The only white band I was listening to was The Beatles. Mom asked us what we thought of her country-boy boyfriend, and I let her know when it was my turn to speak: "Mom, he is a nice guy, but he is weird and his music is weird and I don't think so." We did not see him much after that. Other men came and went: a doctor and an Italian dude. One weekend night Mom went out with her sisters and had a great time. She met this guy who seemed good enough to bring him home and meet the children. This new guy was a young white guy with a funny name. His name was Horst and he would change our lives.

The lone injured deer hobbled aimlessly. Left to fend for itself by its herd, the distraught, abandoned mammal cried its plight into the dry, still air.

Woolly Mammoth Boy stood grazing nearby. He turned his head to see in the distance a pack of hyenas trotting toward the injured deer...they had picked up the fear scent in the air that the injured deer emitted so easily.

"Why was it abandoned by its fellows?" Woolly Mammoth Boy asked a black buzzard tearing dead flesh off a decaying carcass.

"The injured one was no longer able to keep up and was a liability to the herd," answered Thought between bites of sinew.

"Why did the manling's mother abandon him?" Woolly Mammoth Boy said, watching the injured deer trying to flee its impending doom on a broken leg as it caught the scent of the hyena pack.

"Humans can be weak in their fragile minds. The manling's mother saw this as the only option to her despair," Thought answered as a slithering snake at Woolly Mammoth Boy's foot.

"The manling is grieved by her actions...it has wounded him. Will he...?"

Before he could finish his query, the sounds of anguished death tore into the air; the hyenas had caught up with and jumped the injured deer, and they began to eat it alive.

Transfixed by the gruesome scene, Woolly Mammoth Boy heard a whisper in his mind.

"Yes, he will survive this, and yes, the manling has been wounded deeply."

17. Across the Bridge and Back

When in doubt...go! Leave and just go! This sounded like good advice to me. Yet in the Great Universe I was told that you carry yourself wherever you go. Well, isn't that like being between a rock and a hard place? I also heard this in the Great Void: that it is you who changes and not them. Go figure.

–Woolly Mammoth Boy Speaks

THE YEAR 1966 STARTED WITH a bang. The war in a far off place called Vietnam was escalating from its beginnings in the late 1950s. The space race with the "Russkies" was picking up too, and the civil rights war was being waged on the streets of America. I was nine years old. At this time of my life, I was to experience death for the first time. It was the day I heard the news my cousin Don had died. Cousin Don was the oldest male Rubio child in both Rubio families—my father's and his older brother's, my Uncle Narsie. Don was another strong, young, first-generation Filipino American who, because of his mother—my aunt who was a southern white woman—had the good looks of mixed blood. Don was very popular in school and had many friends.

A few years before their divorce, Dad moved us out of San Francisco for a year to live near his work at Mather Air Force Base, and near his older brother who lived in Sacramento. I remember those hot days—the sugary iced tea Auntie would make, and learning how to tie my shoes. I remember Don as a playful older cousin who was protective and generous with pranks and laughter. Then the Vietnam War heated up, and Don enlisted in the Army and was shipped out. His letters coming home from the war front, though militarily censored, spoke of his camaraderie with his fellow Army buddies; of him being point man while on patrol; the hot humid jungles; and an enemy, "Charlie," who was fearless, dangerous, and smart; and of course, the inevitable message "I will be home soon."

Don had made the rank of Sergeant and he was very proud of his accomplishment. He looked after his buddies and was respected. I remember the day we received the news that he was coming home. His tour was done and he had survived one year of war that already had taken thousands of young lives, both American, allied, and Vietnamese. We had already moved back to the San Francisco Bay area from Sacramento because Mom was homesick for her relatives, so our family was going to travel up to Sacramento to welcome Don home. We were all excited to see him. It was to be a glorious homecoming. All his friends were to give him a warrior's welcome.

On the night of his arrival, not more than a couple of hours after being home, Don and his best friend went out on his friend's motorcycle to pick up another case of beer for his homecoming party. Don rode behind his friend as he took him on his victory ride. On his way back from the liquor store a car illegally turned in front of them and collided with them. The impact of their motorcycle with the front of the car turned the car's fender into a twisted, upturned, and jagged blade—a steel knife that first sliced his friend in two, and then cut through Don's body as he passed the impact area, before hurtling him up 15 feet in the air where he smashed into the street light that showed green: his right-of-way.

Don and his friend died instantly.

The Vietnam War was over for Don, and he had survived it only to come back to die on a American street buying beer for his own homecoming party. A royally f*cked-up situation. The world, as my family and I knew it, stopped. Everything turned to grey and sadness, longing and despair. I kind of understood the loss of my cousin Don, but the sorrowful cries and the darkness that accompanied my aunt and uncle's loss of their son, I could not fathom or comprehend.

The funeral was surreal for me as a boy. I saw Don dressed in his Army uniform with his army nametag proudly on his chest: Sgt. Don Rubio. The mortician did a great job putting Don and his best friend together. His porcelain-soft face looked like a mask to me. He had a small smile on his lips. His chest puffed out under his uniform, and hid where he had been cut in two. His head looked put together correctly from the damage he had suffered smashing into the street light. I thought he was going to wake up and say to me, "Hey, Ronnie boy!" No dice. He was dead. He looked like the very big GI Joe doll I used to played with. His skin didn't look right to me. Friends placed items of love in the casket.

As I stood at his open coffin to see Don for the last time, I floated out of my body and was damned to a spacey purgatory. My brother pushed me along so others behind me could view Don's body. I did not cry. I could not cry. I did not know how to cry for someone or for something that had died. I did not even cry when my pet turtle died and had been flushed down the toilet by Mom before I got home from school. All around me the packed chapel was filled the sounds of breaking hearts and moans of darkness and grief. Don's death killed his father, my uncle, who died of a broken heart. Uncle Narsie grew white hair and would die before his time.

I never rode a motorcycle and never wanted to. I imagined my cousin Don smiling, his face calmed by the warm Sacramento night air, eager to down a cold one, and rejoicing with his best friend riding free into the night. Cousin Don rides a Harley in heaven with his best friend, forever.

Forever.

Forever.

Forever...

The biggest news in the latter part of 1966 for my family was that Mom began dating a guy named Horse. Actually, his real name was Horst, but we kids could not pronounce it correctly, so we called him Horse for the longest time. When we realized his name was not "Horse" but "Horst," we felt like fools. He was a young Austrian with blue eyes that looked like cold stones to me. His face was chiseled in a handsome way, like the actor Cary Grant, with lines down the sides of his face, and a large nose that looked very different than the flat, wide Filipino noses we had on our faces. He spoke his English with a weird accent. His hands always smelled sweet; in fact, he smelled like sugar. Later, we found out he was a baker. He drove a white Chevy Corvair, an odd little car whose engine was placed in the rear of the car where the trunk normally was. Weird!

That Mom was dating this young guy felt right. Horst was very polite, and I could see that he was nice to Mom and real to us kids. Fred was okay with him, and Valerie Joyce loved being picked up by this strong man. Horst was very different than Dad. Dad was dark brown and Horst was white. Dad was small in stature and Horst was taller and broader. I had mixed feelings about Horst; I did not want anyone replacing my dad, but Horst made Mom happy. The dating went well for months.

Over dinner one night Horst asked a question to my brother and me, "Would one of you like to come to my place in Oakland and stay the night?" My brother Fred looked at Horst like Horst had two heads. Horst lived in the East Bay, far from San Francisco (so it seemed to us), across the water and over the Bay Bridge in a land we had never been to, except to drive through to visit some Rubio family members up in Vallejo. Horst lived in a strange land. I looked at Horst and said, "I would like to." He looked at me and smiled and said, "Okay, Ron, one day next week you will stay overnight with me." Mom looked at me with a very weird look in her eyes. Her peculiar, quirky, little boy wanted to sleep over with a stranger in a strange land. My siblings looked at me and there was silence at the table. I was grinning from ear to ear.

Now, what Mom did not know was that I was a regular traveler of the MUNI bus system in San Francisco. When Fred allowed me to hang with his friends, one of the things we would do is follow a particular bus route in relay fashion—one kid would run after the bus, and when he got tired the next kid would take over until we found the end of the bus line. Why we did not pay the 25-cent bus fare was not to be questioned by anyone. Fred, who was the leader of this pack of older boys, wanted us to do it this way. In this fashion we learned different routes around San Francisco. One day, I got the brilliant idea to actually get some loose change out of Mom's purse and pay for the MUNI bus, ask for a transfer, which was good for the round trip, and, by myself, explore the city.

I went to the San Francisco Zoo alone. I went downtown to see the skyscrapers shoot toward the heavens high above my large woolly mammoth head. I traveled alone down to Fisherman's Wharf for sweet chocolate bars from Ghirardelli Square. Mom and my siblings never knew of my solo traveling around San Francisco. I loved it so much. I was alone in my adventures with no one telling me how stupid I was, not wanting me to be around them, or letting me know how pathetic, clumsy, and embarrassing I was to be around. No, this was my adventure. My life. So going to Horst's house in the foreign land of Oakland was going to be my adventure supreme!

The following week came and after dinner one night at our house Horst said to my mom, "I'll be going home now and I will take Ron with me." Once again Mom gave me that look like she did not know who I was—how can Ron be this way? Fred gave that look of "Good luck, fool," and my little sister cried. I was her best friend and she wanted to marry me someday. I told her that was impossible because we were brother and sister. Leaving her was not a good thing, but I told her I would be back the next morning. I would tell her about the whole adventure, and we would play and play. I left the house with the clothes on my back, and then I was in Horst's weird car with the engine in the back, heading toward the Bay Bridge through the city of San Francisco.

We crossed the Bay Bridge and as I looked back toward the west and San Francisco I realized, how in the hell was I to return? The city lights were different in Oakland. We hardly spoke as he drove, and I never heard any discussion at the dinner table that night between Horst and Mom about how I was to get back home. I was too excited about the adventure to worry; I figured Horst was going to drive me home.

Horst pulled up to this big white building with many windows. It looked like a miniature skyscraper I had seen in downtown San Francisco. Horst told me this was an apartment and he lived there. We entered this strange building with many strange smells. Walking up some flights of stairs, I started to realize I was truly in a very strange place with a very strange man who hardly spoke to me. We entered a dark one-bedroom apartment. He showed me some art books because he knew I liked to draw. I was starting to like this guy. Horst told me he had to wake up early for work, and I would have wait for a bus that would take me across the Bay Bridge back to San Francisco, and that it would drop me off at the bus transit station at 1st and Mission Street. We got ready for sleep, got into his big bed, and he turned off the light. Horst was out cold before I knew it. I was of course wide-awake, listening to him breathe as he slept. I never heard another man breathe before except my dad when we used to take naps together when I was a kid.

The room was very quiet, still, and pitch dark. I had never been in a darker room before. I did not have Fred and his epileptic seizures to think about. This was a very new experience for me, and I felt really out of place. I fell asleep for what seemed like minutes, only to be abruptly awakened by a very loud alarm clock, which of course I did not know was next to my head. Soon Horst was up and telling me to get dressed. Damn! It was still dark because it was only 4:00 a.m. in the friggin' morning! Horst gave me some money, I put it in my pocket, and then Horst told me I had to wait for this bus at this corner, wait until it comes, and then board it and get back to San Francisco. "Sure," I was thinking to myself, this will be real easy.

We left his apartment and were out in the cold morning air; the sky was sunless. It was the dark before the dawn. I was thinking to myself: was I awake, or was this all a dream? Horst drove to a street corner and told me to get out of the car. He repeated all the traveling instructions once again and then he said "Goodbye," waved, and pulled from the curb and was gone. Damn! Which bus was I to board? What was the number of the bus again? I was starting to realize I was cold and on a deserted street corner in a strange place. I stopped myself from crying. "Get a grip, Ron! I am nine years old and I can do this." Looking back at this situation as an adult, I was very lucky some goddamn pervert did not drive up and snatch my sorry ass off that street corner.

So I waited on that corner as the first buses started their day. People gave me strange looks. One asked if I was a runaway, and I said, "No." Bus after bus stopped and continued by. It did not occur to me to ask anyone for help. The morning grew brighter and brighter. Finally, a bus driver opened his door and asked me where I was going. After telling him, he said, "The Number 57 bus is what you need, kid." Damn! I had let over four "Number 57" buses go by in the many hours I stood at that street corner. The next 57 bus that came I finally boarded and was on my way home.

I watched in total amazement as the enormity of the world passed around me. All the strange traffic of trucks, cars, and buses all heading toward San Francisco; I tried not to stare, but the people on the bus looked like they were dressed up for some sort of dance party, or so I thought. Seeing the familiar San Francisco skyline appear was simply glorious! The 57 bus reached its destination and disgorged its payload. I was a small kid thrown into the madness of morning rush hour; it was 8:00 a.m. and I was starving. I looked at my money supply and saw that I had enough for bus fare if I begged for a nickel, or I could by food (candy), and walk the thirty-odd blocks back to Bernal Heights. My stomach won over. With the 20 cents I had, I bought five red licorice sticks (mmm...soft and sweet!), five Bazooka Joe bubble gums (chewy—not hard and brittle), one Payday bar for a nickel, and one hard candy necklace for the remaining nickel. I loaded my supplies in my pocket and started my long walk home, right up Mission Street that I knew so well, then right up the north side of Bernal Heights, across Cortland Avenue, up Prentiss Street, and to my front door. I reached home around 10:30 a.m. I was pooped out. My family was just starting their day as I walked up the stairs into the kitchen. They kinda greeted me, Valerie Joyce more than Fred or my mom. It was as if I did an ordinary everyday thing, and it was not a big deal. I was a bit disappointed in their attitude, but no matter—did I have a story to tell little Valerie Joyce!

    I drew my little sister in to me and went downstairs and outside to our backyard, gave her the last of my candy supply, and danced around as I half-sung and half-told her of my journey that took me across the bridge into a strange land and back. She smiled and chewed on the candy as she sat delightfully watching the show. I had gone and come back. I did it on my own. I had improvised and created something out of nothing. I was proud of myself as I went downstairs to the basement to play inside the dryer like I was an astronaut I had seen on TV.

"Well done and thrice blessed, my boy!" Woolly Mammoth Boy heard from a blue bird chirping at him while perched on one of his long, curved white tusks.

    "For what?" smirked Woolly Mammoth Boy as he released his bowels in the early morning light.

    "For looking after the boy as he tested his 'wings,' so to speak," answered the blue bird as it picked bugs off the tusk where it rested. "The lad could have been snatched off that lone street corner by one with bad intentions so easily."

    "Well, yes...of course, I was looking after the manling, for he is brave for one so...so..."

    "So naïve," Thought finished.

"Naïve? Yes, I guess," Woolly Mammoth Boy said to a large shiny black dung bug scurrying over his steaming stool. "He is so trusting, in a way that speaks of an awareness that he must have acquired from a place other than his birth planet."

"First, thank you for the hot meal," said the dung bug Thought. "Secondly, are you hinting of where he came before he chose this 'Earth'?"

"Well, yes. There is something about this manling," Woolly Mammoth Boy said into the brisk early morning as he watched the rising sun. "He has latent intelligence from another place, another universe."

"That he has. And he will learn how to access this knowledge as he grows," Thought gestured as a fleeting cloud before the brilliant sunrise.

18. Laundry, Doughnuts, and Racism

I once watched a pack of Hyenas tear apart and kill one of their own kind. The victim was new to the pack, and it had entered and tried to become one with the others. I was surprised by the savagery it met. I knew the filthy beasts as fierce scavengers and hunters. I had just never seen them attack one of their own. They did not even eat it. Was it because this stranger looked or smelled differently than the others? I was glad I was amongst my own kind. Yet that Hyena was amongst its own kind. My, oh my! What a strange Universe!

–The Queries of Woolly Mammoth Boy

MOM AND HORST (NOT "HORSE" anymore—we finally learned how to say his name correctly) were married in the summer of 1967. Horst was younger than my mother by six or seven years. He was amazing to have fallen in love with a divorced woman with three kids, but Mom was a beautiful island woman and that was that. Her magic juju love net was cast and Horst was caught—lucky for him and us! After the marriage ceremony and the honeymoon, Horst asked us boys if we wanted to take on his last name, "Hittenberger." Horst's full name was Horst Herman Victor Hittenberger. My brother said "No way!" Mom told Fred not to be rude. I pondered my choices: Ron Rubio or Ron Hittenberger? "Ah, Horst, I'll stick with Rubio," I answered, as Mom gave me "the look." And that was that; we kept our birth names, our Filipino names.

One of the first things Horst did was move us out of San Francisco across the Bay to Piedmont. It was here I immediately understood the phrase, "learning both sides of the fence." I grew up in San Francisco in a neighborhood where there were not many white people. I mean *white* people. Most of the white people in Bernal Heights were dark-haired and poor. The white people in Piedmont were light haired and rich. Piedmont was a city within a city. It was corralled by the surrounding city of Oakland, but Piedmont was cushioned and isolated from the "darkies" of the surrounding neighborhoods. Piedmont was 90% white, upper-class; I came from 90% mixed-color and lower-class—a very different social and economic environment.

The race riots of the early 1960s that had spread north from the south and LA, hit the San Francisco Bay Area in small pockets. My black friends told us to stay indoors during these turbulent times. One time I got caught outside the safety of my home. School had been let out early because of the rioting, and I thought I could use the time to visit a friend. On the way to my friend's house three older black kids, Fred's age, stopped me, pushed me, and slapped me around a bit. They recognized me as being Fred's dorky little brother, "little Rubio," and did not lay it into me too badly. It made no sense to me. These black kids knew my brother and me, and they still raged on me. I guess being brown skinned did not save my ass. Black is Black and White is White. Where did the brown person fall in this racism? How about the yellow person and the red person? This was all very confusing to my woolly mammoth head. People hating each other because of the color of their skin... weird!

When Mom and Horst told us that we were moving, we all had a shit-fit! Fred had a lot of friends and was in junior high school. This is a very important time in a young person's life; it is not to be messed with if possible, and Mom and Horst were definitely messing with Fred's life. As for myself, I was just starting to get into the social groove after so many years of being out on the fringes. In fact, a girl liked me! I was in fifth grade and really rockin' my life in school. I was melting down less and was a solid C+ student. The news of moving was not cool with me either. Valerie Joyce was okay with it, but she did not like the change. Piedmont, Horst said, had better schools, and a better neighborhood. He could have just said there were not as many black people there. Damn!

As the move to Piedmont became more of a reality, the "goodbyes" started. Fred was not displaying any sentimental BS about moving, whereas I was a bit distraught. I was worried; I was no longer stuttering as much, but I was not really speaking English that a white person could understand. I spoke an inner-city English slang where every other word spoken is a curse word, or "filler word" mixed in with street codes. So, out of a ten-word sentence, three words were actually of substance and relevance. It had also taken me years to be accepted by my friends, and they were of color: chicanos, Filipinos, Asians, and blacks. How was I going to make it in Piedmont? I promised my friends I would visit and stay in touch. That would not happen as planned. The sweet girl who liked me, and I her, we would say our farewells with a sad, shy smile. The Rubio–Hittenberger family packed up and moved out of the ghetto into my social hell in the middle of the school year. Damn!

I was introduced into my new fifth grade class where I was the only kid of color, except for one Chinese kid who was brainy and spoke like he came from this other side of the fence like the rest of the white kids. There were no Latino kids or black kids; there were no "cool" kids at all. My clothing reflected my street upbringing—dark in color, mismatched, and used. My brother and I fought daily with the white boys. Fred took this move hard and really had to chisel his place in junior high school where kids were just plain-ass mean to outsiders. I was hard to understand at school because my English was so bad and I started to stutter again a little bit for I was very anxious and nervous. Once, I had to fight white boys because I looked at a white girl. I had never seen a girl with blond hair in real life, only in movies. I fought white boys because I walked "ghetto"—which is to say with a lot of attitude, partially dragging one leg in my stride. I fought white kids because I was slow in my schoolwork; to them my stupidity was justified by my color. I fought white kids because I was the wrong color. I fought white kids because they looked at me the wrong way. I was humiliated and embarrassed most days. I spoke little and played even less with the other kids. Actually, no kids wanted to play with me.

Valerie Joyce came home one day crying and I was fuming when I saw her in distress.

"What happened, Valerie Joyce?" I asked.

"Kids were making fun of me, Ron!" she sobbed as she told her tale. "They wanted to know why I wore the same clothes every day! I was so embarrassed, Ron."

"Don't you worry, Valerie! Who were these kids?" I shook and trembled with rage. Rage at the injustice. Rage that anyone messed with my little sister. There was going to be some reckoning. I may not speak the English these white kids could understand, but I did speak a "beat down" they would understand.

"The Kyle brothers," Valerie Joyce answered, between sobs.

I heard that name and my world turned red. There were two Kyles: one was in my grade, the other in my brother's. I left Valerie Joyce after drying her tears and promising blood. *You can take the boy out of the city, but you can't take the city out of the boy.* The Kyle brothers messed with the wrong kid that day. They were dead meat.

I ran from our home and hunted for the bastards. I found the Kyle brothers playing in the schoolyard behind the football field near my school. Those two dead meats were playing tetherball. They saw me coming and started to laugh. They said something to each other and separated. I approached the two, keeping both in my sights.

"So which one of you motherf*ckers made fun of my sister?" I was the only one in my family that swore. I had started at an early age—lessons from my dad—and I did it well. I had also learned how to flip people off when I was in fourth grade by sliding a pencil under the first and fourth finger—at the first knuckle and over my third finger—then withdrawing the pencil. (Teaching this to my brother and sister was a huge mistake: for when Mom found out how this "flipping off" had entered her home, she immediately taught me the meaning of a "wall-to-wall carpeting" beating. She would drag you by the hair and beat you from one end of the room to the other, wall-to-wall carpeting.) All of this meant I knew how to be "city"—as the Kyles were going to find out.

"So which one of you f*ckheads made fun of my sister?!" I repeated.

"I did, Jap boy," answered the younger Kyle brother, the one in my grade.

"Listen, asshole, I am not a Jap."

"You look like one."

I felt the tears start to well in my brain and the anger rage build in my asthmatic lungs. Before he could say another word, I was a flurry of fists and kicks, pulling his hair and biting on his face. This was "city" fighting, and you messed with my sister.

The younger Kyle did not know what hit him. I was crying, screaming, and uncontrollable. I was the berserker from your nightmares come alive. The older Kyle brother wanted no part of me. He figured if he messed with me he would have to deal with my brother, Fred. He stayed out of the fight. Kids pulled me off the bloodied and messed-up Kyle. I was sobbing and gasping for air and I wanted to finish this kid off. The Kyle brothers retreated a safe distance, and I eyed them like a wild thing, ready to apply the *coup de grâce* on their sorry asses. We parted and I went home crying, satisfied and tired, only wanting to sleep. *Don't mess with my sister and don't mess with a Rubio!*

Mom asked me what happened. When I told her she just said wash up and get ready for homework. That was it. I guess I did what was expected of me as Valerie's older brother. Defend and protect. Needless to say, we did not get much hassle after that. The fighting slowed down when the school bullies and other assholes figured that if you do not want to be disfigured by Ron, don't mess with him or his sister. Now, I was not a fighter. I'm just a guy that goes into "berserker mode" at the flip of a coin. I am my father's son, and the apple did not fall far from the tree.

We settled into school life as best as we could as kids. Racism was tough and ugly. I hated to be defined by my skin color and not for who I am. I already dealt with growing up in a family that saw me as weird and dorky. I always felt out of place with them, and now I lived in a place where I had to be concerned with my color as well. Damn! This was too much. Yet, I knew I had to live on. So I lost myself in drawing a lot, and excelled in art and military history. I started playing music in San Francisco: Horst bought me my first trumpet in Piedmont, and I took to playing that horn like a dog takes to chasing cats. I played my heart out in the backyard. Our neighbors never complained because I played quite well and I could hit those high Cs with clarity and strength. It was as if the trumpet was my true voice, unfettered by shame, stuttering, and sadness. I played the blues and I played them well.

Valerie Joyce was still my best friend. She was two years younger than me. We would play for hours just like we did in San Francisco—her Barbie dolls "hitting up" on my GI Joe action figures. Being younger than me, Valerie understood my childlike behavior and creative imagination. Once we found a whole book of unused banker's checks. We must have played banker and customer for days. We signed our made-up names just the way we saw Mom and Horst do. With an overly gestured flurry of the pen our signatures would appear, and we would sign names like "Frank Frankly with Frank," for financial amounts that were astronomical. I was so happy playing with Valerie Joyce. I laughed and was free with my creativity, but my behavior was very different at school. I did not play with kids my age and did not make any effort to try to understand their game-playing; their rules made no sense to me. Nope, Valerie Joyce was my best playmate.

Horst was an enterprising young man who saved his money, which he made as a top-notch baker and cake decorator at a well-known bakery in Berkeley. He also invested his money in property and a laundromat—an enterprise he brought my brother and me in on. For allowance money we had to open and clean the laundromat every day around 6:00 a.m. before school, and clean the apartment he owned twice a week after school. Both places were a long bicycle ride from our house in Piedmont. Fred and I traded weeks opening the laundromat. Whoever opened the laundromat in the morning was also tasked with bringing home a dozen freshly baked donuts from the donut store next door. I did not mind opening up shop early in the morning because I was used to waking up early from my altar boy days, serving the early mass "show." I would zoom down the deserted early morning streets of Piedmont to the laundromat, open it, clean it, scrounge some extra coins left in the machines, buy a few extra donuts for myself, and still bring a box of hot donuts home and wake the family. It was one of the few things I enjoyed in those early days living in the new land of the white people and their harsh ways. Those donuts were the sweetness that hid the bitterness growing in my heart from the unfairness brought on by the color of my skin.

My younger brother Shawn Hittenberger, the son of Mom and Horst, was born in January of 1968. I did not like the "step-brother" title or even "half-brother"—Shawn was my brother and that was that. I loved him so much. I changed his diapers and played with him every day. He looked different than my brother and sister. He had a long nose and light, olive-colored skin with beautiful "island" eyes. He would pass as white. Nice mix.

My family was a real mixed-race family now and that was that. Life was really shifting, and I was trying hard to understand all the social changes. The civil rights movement was heating up under people like Martin Luther King Jr., and the violent, loud voice of the militant Black Panther party in the neighboring city of Oakland got me thinking. Where did a brown kid like me, who by this time had been called, "chink," "Jap," "slant-eyed," "wetback," and "gook," fit in this very pronounced "white–black" thing called the civil rights movement? Was I going to be a sellout? Someone accepted by white people, an Oreo Cookie—black on the outside and white on the inside—like I heard some "colored" people say. Would I risk being alienated by my own kind?

Like Sgt. Schultz from the TV show *Hogan's Heroes* would say, "I know nothing, I see nothing." Maybe that would be the safest route. I did not know, but I was soon to find out. Hell was around the corner for America and this was my time.

Woolly Mammoth Boy slammed his large curved tusks into a massive, blackened, ancient tree that had been blasted by lightning into a stump the size of a small hut. He would back away a few paces, then charge at the blackened stump trumpeting a battle cry; stopping before the ancient tree stump, he swung his massive head to smash large sections of the dead black wood to smithereens with his steel-hard tusks.

"Training are we?" croaked a large spotted lizard Thought watching the vigorous spectacle.

Breathing deep breaths and exhaling with the bellow of a thunderstorm, Woolly Mammoth Boy turned and stared at the lizard with a heated look as if to flatten it into the dust.

"Hold, boy! You have the berserker upon you!" spat the lizard.

"Well, then be off! And leave me be!" bellowed Woolly Mammoth Boy to lizard Thought. "My manling battles the same way! We are one and the same in warring!"

"Young one, why unleash such fury upon the earth?" sighed the ancient, blackened tree stump. "Is there no other way?"

"The manling defends his sibling—his own very existence—from predators that surround him! The manling has the berserker in him that enables him to survive!" bellowed Woolly Mammoth Boy to the large mangled stump before him. "I, too, am a warrior for my own herd-mates. I, too, must battle the saber-tooth, the pale two-legged ones, and the giant *clawed predators for my existence. Be off!"*

"From the act of inflicting pain comes pain..." Thought said through a blast of dust and wood chips, for Woolly Mammoth Boy had once again resumed attacking the dead stump with the fury of an exploding volcano.

19. Fast Feet Bilbo Baggins, and a Rite of Passage

"Little One, you will continue to grow. I know you are having a hard time," Thought gestured to me. My woolly mammoth head spun with sadness and pain.

"I am not sure I want to continue," I answered to the mist in my mind/soul.

"Oh, but you must, Little One. You will find a way." Thought smiled and smirked.

"Who will teach me? Who will show me the way? Who?" I pleaded.

Thought was quiet for a while and then answered, "Little One, my little dear Woolly Mammoth Boy, you, of course." With that, Thought laughed a bellyache laugh.

–Woolly Mammoth Boy Remembers

BY 1969 A SMOLDERING FIRE was burning in the American consciousness. National anguish followed the assassinations of Martin Luther King Jr. in April 1968, and Democratic presidential hopeful Robert Kennedy in July of that same year. Also, at the '68 Democratic National Convention in Chicago, violent police brutality against protesters was a sad, televised affair of a power base gone out of control. The anti-war movement was picking up and so was the race war. The anti-war demonstrations on the campuses of UC Berkeley, Ohio State, and other major colleges beckoned in the age of student power, and showed the potential strength of grassroots movements. In the city of Oakland, California, the Black Panther party was arming itself and bringing war to the established white power. White cops endeared themselves to the Black Man in the form of brutal, racist police action in the streets. Recent and deadly race riots in Watts, Detroit, and other major cities were very real and could not be hidden or denied. For my family, 1968 started with the birth of my baby brother Shawn in January. Also that January of '68, a surprise coordinated attack called the "Tet Offensive" by communist North Vietnam and the Viet Cong was sprung against all major points over democratic South Vietnam. The Tet Offensive came right after American military high command called the war against communists "under control." Though the Viet Cong and their North Vietnamese allies were defeated, it was a rude wake-up call to the American public that this "Vietnam conflict" could go on for a long time, and it went on for another seven years. Newsstand magazines showed the faces of American war dead weekly and constantly. I was twelve years old in 1969.

My life in Piedmont had mellowed to an easy truce between a low level of tolerance amongst my predominantly white classmates and brown boy me. My siblings and I were starting to dress and act like our white peers. I was still not really accepted into their social circles, nor did I want to be accepted into them. I felt safe on my own, and in my relationship with my younger sister, Valerie Joyce. My older brother, Fred Jr., took an incredible turn in his life and became a true example of "identifying with your oppressor." One day, Fred Jr. came home very sad and extremely angry from Piedmont High School. He was fourteen-and-a-half years old. He was so angry at being a brown-skinned person. "I hate being brown. I am not a Filipino. I hate being poor and I will not be poor again," he said.

In an angry diatribe Fred Jr. ridiculed us, his own blood family, and disowned us. From that day forward he began a daily ritual of pressing his nose together with his hands to re-create a "white" nose from the flat nose he was born with. Fred Jr. kinda did the Michael Jackson nose thing to himself. Fred Jr. plucked his thick Spanish-Asian eyebrows to be more "white" and to look less ethnic. He made a mess of it and looked like he ran through his eyebrows with a dull lawn mower. He would not recognize us in public, and instead he would walk behind us wherever we went. He once invited a girl from school over to our home (the only black girl in Piedmont High, no less!), but before she arrived he told us that we were to take on different personas, and that these would elevate us from the lower caste we were stuck in. According to Fred Jr.'s story, Horst was an architect, Mom was a nurse, and Valerie Joyce and I were very smart and talented in music. We all told Fred Jr. to shove it. He was not pleased.

That year Fred Jr. worked a summer job and made $1,500. That was a lot of money for 1969. He changed how he walked, talked, and dressed himself. Years later, I realized that this was his way of surviving the incredible task of assimilating and adapting to an hostile environment. Though he was basically an "Oreo cookie," I would credit my older brother with being the icebreaker, the one who forged a path for others to follow. Fred Jr.'s behavior, though extreme to me, was on the right track with my parents—at least, that's how it seemed.

Personally, I rebelled against money, greed, and mean, racist, fake people. I identified with the hippies. I was a member of the counter-revolution. I hated what money and elitism had done to my blood brother and the people around me. My brother grew to really hate me, but I could only feel sad for losing him, and watch him lose himself. Fred's school peers embraced his newfound self. He started to be invited to parties and became a larger presence in his high school class. He was no longer my brother. Very, very sad.

During this time Fred Jr. really got into Nazi Germany history, and always took the Germans' side when Dad would take us to one of the many World War II movies out in the theaters during his weekend visits. Weird! I watched my brother turn into someone else, someone I did not know and would not know for the next thirty-odd years. He became a cutthroat in money dealings with the family, and was just plain mean-spirited when it came to the plight of the poor and disadvantaged. This was a sad time for me.

Money issues also reared their ugly head in our family. Being a child of a divorcee was a drag—either Mom got child support if we were with her, or Dad did not have to pay it if we were with him. I felt like my sister and I—forget about Fred Jr.—were only worth having around for the money one parent would receive or not receive. Dad was living nearby and had remarried as well, also to a white person. Strange. It soon felt like we kids were all about money. This situation made me very sad and depressed. I hated money, greed, and mean people. Someday I knew that life would be different for me...but not now.

We would visit Dad on weekends and stay with him in the summer. This began my training in construction from a self-taught carpenter—my dad. Because he had a temper and a strong intolerance for slow, stupid, sickly people, being with my dad did not go well for me. I was just his stupid, slow, spacey second son. His first born, Fernando Jr., hated working with his hands and was turning into a typical lazy teenager. Fred remarked once that the only thing he would pick up was a pen to sign checks, and he would fulfill that self-made prophecy later in his life. In those early years he argued and refused to work, but I did not mind because I liked working with my hands.

My obsession with putting objects in order came in handy working a trade like carpentry. Dad put me to work but showed little patience when teaching me new skills. His weird Filipino use of language did not help either. For example, the word "goop" could refer to wood glue, roofing tar, window caulking, or anything else that came out of a tube. Dad would get pissy real fast if I could not figure out what he wanted, so I had to put the pieces together quickly: What was the job we were doing? And what, therefore, was the correct "goop" he wanted for the job? Yikes! My mind was working more out of fear than trying to learn. Dad salvaged everything and saved everything bent, broken, and maybe fixable. I straightened out bent 16-penny framing nails to be reused. His wartime experience growing up as a young boy in the Japanese-occupied Philippines taught Dad to save anything and reuse everything—*"No wasting, damn you!"* He was always building something. By twelve years old, I had built storage sheds, an in-ground pool, and numerous other carpentry projects he had going.

The last year of elementary school found me floating in a realm of fantasy and make-believe to escape all this madness of life at home. I would ride my blue Stingray bike with my banana bike seat everywhere. I loved being alone or playing with my sister. I was not playing with too many kids my own age, but I did get along with kids younger than me. I had one friend who was also a loner. We met in the school band, and he was picked on too, but he was white. We made a pact that when we grew up we would search for the "Bigfoot Monster" that haunted the Northwestern states. That never happened.

In sixth grade, my elementary school principal saw I had read *The Phantom Tollbooth*. He pulled me over and he said to me, "Ron, have you ever read *The Hobbit* by J. R. R. Tolkien?"

"No," I replied.

So I took the book out from the library and fell in love with the first paragraph. I was hooked. I read that book over and over again. My principal said to me after he saw I had read *The Hobbit* five times, "You know Ron, Tolkien also wrote a trilogy called *The Lord of the Rings* to which *The Hobbit* is a prequel."

What?! Damn! I asked immediately for *The Lord of the Rings* for Christmas. It would be the first of my thirty-plus readings of the famous trilogy. I moved my reality into a world of heroism, adventure, the small and weak against the large and strong, fighting the good fight, making do with what you had, and traveling alone upon deserted paths with a wooden staff and lots of non-perishable Elven waybread packed. Hobbits were the perfect characters for me. They had big feet like me, and did not want to be brave but were the bravest of all without even knowing it.

A year and a half after leaving the streets of San Francisco, I was starting to define who I was in my new school. One day all the kids were lining up to do foot races at the morning recess. I stayed off to the side near the fence and watched. One kid named Bob Morgan challenged every kid to race and beat the tar out of any challenger in a 50-yard dash across the play yard. He had blond hair and was about my size and very fast. I stood up from my corner where I was sitting and walked over to Bob and accepted his challenge. Now, all the kids knew me as the crazy, skinny brown kid not to be messed with when I was angry, and that I was a loner. Bob looked me up and down and said, "Okay."

We lined up and all the kids were watching. Bob was the fastest kid in our school, and, both being sixth graders, we were the oldest in the school. We lined up and some kid called out, "Ready...On your mark...Set...GO!" Bob and I were neck and neck all the way to the finish line. This was a first. The schoolyard kids were amazed that I had stood up against Bob and tied him. The recess bell rang and Bob said something stupid like, "I was tired and I could have beaten you." I looked at him and was about to pop him in the face, but I stopped because I realized I really had him; I had gotten under his skin. Bob was experiencing self-doubt.

"Well, Bob, why don't we race at lunch time when you are rested—no excuses." He shot me a look and I to him. The other kids were salivating at the prospect of a race in which Bob Morgan could actually lose. During class time I saw other kids go to Bob to cheer him on and tell him how he was going to kick my ass. No one talked to me. At lunch the same scene was set up: Bob Morgan and I lined up on the starting line and the same kid called out "Ready...On your mark...Set...GO!" Bob and I flew with our feet barely touching the cement schoolyard, and once again we tied. The kids around us actually gasped. Bob Morgan had met his match. This brown boy tied him twice. The kids called for a third and deciding race. I was ready for eight more races; all this racing was peanuts to me. Running up and down San Francisco streets after MUNI buses had made my legs strong. The third race was another tie.

Bob turned to me, smiled, extended his hand, and said, "Good race!" I agreed. We became friends. And that was that. I had defined myself at school as the kid who tied Bob Morgan three times, the fastest kid in school, and I was also crazy when I was fighting mad. Not bad for a day's work. Life was changing for me.

During the last months of elementary school before heading off to junior high, I was chosen from my class to go to a conference to hear the anthropologist Dr. Richard Leakey speak about his work in Kenya, Africa, and his recent ancient ape-like humanoid discovery he named "Lucy." My teachers knew I loved human history—mainly military history—and that I was well-read. The conference was a tremendous opportunity for me to hear how we had evolved as a species. At one point in an open discussion where Dr. Leakey was taking questions a huge black woman stood up and practically screamed, "Are you insinuating that black people came from the apes?" The crowed held its communal breath. Up to this point all the questions to Dr. Leakey were scientific in nature and this woman was very heatedly calling up the "race card." This was during the time of the civil rights movement, the race war was being waged on the streets of the United States, and insulting one's skin color or how one looked was a way of getting yourself killed.

This black lady was picking a fight. Hell, even I could see that. Maybe Dr. Leakey, being an Englishman, was not aware of all this race stuff, being out of touch in the Kenyan dry lands digging in dirt and all that. Dr. Leakey kept his eyes on her; his reply was simple, clear, and almost fatherly. "My dear lady, I am saying that we ALL came from the apes!" The audience let out an audible sigh, laughing the nervous tension away. The brute of a black woman sat down hard with a huff. She was out to pick a fight and failed. I raised my hand tentatively, and Dr. Leakey looked in my direction and called on me. With a quivering voice I stood up and asked my anthropological question, and the whole energy changed in the room as he looked at me, smiled, and answered. Now, his response to the black lady struck me like a bolt of lighting. Dr. Leakey was saying that, basically, we all came from the same human evolutionary tree. This meant that all those mean, uppity white people also came from the apes, and that we were ALL equal. I was going to keep this fact up-front-and-center in my thoughts.

It wasn't just the social climate of America that was changing; my home life was transforming too. Horst had been living with us for over a year now, and he brought a whole new tone to our family. He introduced us to hiking, beaches, and Muir Woods and the giant redwood trees, in addition to the cheese fondues, salami, and buttery croissants he brought home from his work at the bakery. Horst was impulsive when it came to the outdoors. One Sunday, sitting around the breakfast table, he asked my brother and me if we wanted to go hiking. I said, "Sure." What I didn't know was that Horst wanted us to climb Mt. Whitney with him, the tallest mountain in the continental US of friggin' A, standing at 14,966 feet above sea level.

The next thing my brother and I knew we were out the door with Horst, after saying a quick "Bye" to Mom, Valerie, and my baby brother. We got packed with the very little camping gear we owned. Boots and other essential hiking gear for an arduous trip just did not exist in our home. We were going to make the ascent up Mt. Whitney wearing thin black socks and Converse tennis shoes! We jammed into the blue family AMC Rambler station wagon, and drove for what seemed like a four-thousand-year car ride from the San Francisco Bay Area to the dry, inland, desertlike terrain skirting Death Valley, California. Horst flew the Rambler down long straights of hot, dry asphalt. Finally, we arrived at base camp by midnight of the same day.

We broke camp in the predawn light, awakening stiff and sore in the station wagon where we all slept. We did not have a tent. From there we hit the trail with the little food and water we had packed into a very large, metal-framed backpack. Like I said, Horst was a bit impulsive when it came to the outdoors. His plan was to attack the monster 14,966-foot mountain in one day and be back at base camp by nightfall. My brother and I, being two ignorant kids from the streets of San Francisco, had no idea of the physical mayhem we were getting into. Needless to say, with Horst setting the pace, we made summit by early afternoon. Or at least my brother and he did—I fainted a mile from the summit. The air was thin, we had no food or water in our bellies, and it was my turn to carry the backpack up that final mile toward the peak. It was a stumbling, wavering climb for me until I just collapsed on a boulder off the trail. Horst and my brother continued to the summit and promised they would sign my name in the visitor logbook at the top. Horst told me to head back down, and that I was to meet them at base camp later. I started the long trail back down the mountain alone and delirious. Horst treated us to steak in the town of Lone Pine at the base of Mt. Whitney that night. We ate like victorious warriors.

I was proud of what I had accomplished, but pissed off I did not finish after all that work. We were home by afternoon the next day. We had scaled the highest mountain in the continental United States in a single day. Most sane people would have planned for a 2- to 4-day ascent, stopping and making camp at the beautiful lakes on the way up the mountain, but Horst had us back home after a total of just three days after leaving the Bay. Crazy shit!

Horst also had a wooden 27-foot-long sailboat that we sailed through the San Francisco Bay to Angel Island, and on which we made special trips beyond the Golden Gate Bridge, only for a short distance, on good days. The smell of salty air, racing wind, and being topside was very exciting. Below deck, Mom and Fred Jr. were green-faced and seasick, refusing to come topside. Since I was the only kid in the house with an interest in music—and since Horst had played trumpet as a kid in Salzburg, Austria—he supported my horn-playing by buying me my own trumpet. Horst painted oils and he saw that I loved to draw and had a pretty good artistic eye.

(Thank God the personal computer and computer gaming did not come out until years later! Had the Apple computer been available to an obsessive-compulsive wild Hobbit like me, it would have destroyed any ambition to do anything creative or healthy for myself. Years later, as a mentor to young men on the autism spectrum (AS) in the early '90s, the single most devastating component I had to deal with was the abusive and extremely addictive habit of intense computer gaming and use that would literally consume 4-8 hours a day for my AS clients. I was saved from this brain- and spirit-killer by being 20 years older!)

Seeing that art was in my veins, Horst turned me on to his library of *Time-Life Books* on the great masters of classical art. From Goya to Michelangelo, El Greco to Leonardo da Vinci, I soaked it all up and could easily copy any drawing from these books. Yet the most important thing Horst ever gave me was myself—he awoke me to the bigger world and offered it to me. Up to this point nobody really paid much attention to me except my younger sister. My own dad did not like me. He would say to me, "Ron, you are like your mother, sickly and stupid. You are not a Rubio. You are a Ponciano." Thanks, Dad. My brother despised me. My mother was now occupied with her new son and was often unavailable, and Valerie Joyce, well, Valerie Joyce understood me and was my only ally.

I was fearless about traveling on my own and had been for a long time. I had proved it to the family at nine years old when I crossed the Bay Bridge, stayed at Horst's apartment, and came back on my own. One night at the dinner table after a weekend at the beaches of Point Reyes, a national park located about sixty-or-so miles north of San Francisco in Marin County, I said out loud, "I would like to go camping by myself." Everyone stopped eating and looked at me. Uh-oh, there goes Ron again. Fred Jr. told me to shut up, Valerie Joyce looked scared, and Mom gave me the same look she did when I was nine and wanted to travel alone and sleep at Horst's apartment.

Horst simply asked me between mouthfuls of dinner, "Where do you want to go camping and for how long?"

Mom looked at her new husband and said, "What are you talking about, Horst? Ron is not going camping by himself!"

Horst just looked at me and repeated his question, "Ron, where do you want to go camping and for how long?"

I was now looking only at Horst and said, "I want to go to Muir Woods and Point Reyes. I really liked it there. We have been there a few times already. I was thinking about camping for a week or ten days."

Mom looked at me with shock, and then to Horst and said, "No, no, no! Ronnie, you are not going anywhere by yourself. You are only twelve and that is it! Horst?"

At the calling of his name Horst just looked at me as I was looking at him and said, "Estella, let the boy go." The dining room was so quiet I could hear my wheezing lungs.

"Horst, NO! Ronnie is too young to be on his own, to be traveling around at twelve by himself, how will he feed himself, where will he sleep, who will look after him?"

Horst just looked at me and said, "Ron, answer your mother," and continued eating while watching me.

"Well, Mom, I will buy food supplies with my savings, I have a cloth sleeping bag (which weighed a little more than a third of my body weight!), and we have extra backpacks. I'll be ready to travel. I'll be safe, Mom...I promise, Mom." Mom was aghast and her mouth was wide open. Fred Jr. just looked at me with a blank stare as if to say that this would be a nice way of getting rid of me, and my poor sister, Valerie Joyce, she looked sad and almost started to cry.

"Horst!" Mom cried out.

Horst stopped eating and studied me and then calmly said to his new wife, "Estella, let the boy go. He wants to do this. Let the boy go."

Mom paused, studied me, and was quiet for a time. I saw concern, anger, and bewilderment in her eyes. Mom heard something in my stepfather's words, though: "When were you planning to go, Ron?" she finally asked. I was stunned by the flow of events. Mom was actually considering my request.

"Well, I thought soon, before it got too cold outside."

Mom looked at Horst again and said, "Clear up the dinner table and get to your homework...everybody!"

That night I could hear Mom and Horst talking loudly about me in their bedroom. Fred Jr. said to me in our room, "Ron, you really want to do this? This camping by yourself?"

I looked at him and replied, "Yes." And that was all the conversation my brother and I had about my solo camping trip.

My sister was very concerned, "Ron, this is crazy! Something might happen to you."

I reassured my dear sister, "Valerie Joyce, everything will be okay. Don't you worry, Valerie. I want to do this. And when I return I will have a tale to tell and we will play and play!" This did not please her one bit, for she was too old for that type of bullshit reassurance. I was her only friend, and had protected her and had taken care of her since she was young. Once, years ago, I stood up against my dad, protecting my sister when he wanted to spank her for some reason. "Oh, little big man, huh!" He beat me good, but he never touched Valerie with an open hand. "Don't leave me, Ron." I did not answer her.

The next day Horst said that Mom and he had agreed to let me go and I should start planning a departure date. "Damn! What have I done?!" I thought. I was actually scared. My impulsive self had gotten the better of me. No! I can do this. I will go on this camping trip alone and come back to tell a great tale to Valerie Joyce and my whole family. The plan was set and I chose a date that was two weeks away. I would miss school and that was that. I worked hard for extra cash and started to buy my supplies. Horst gave me a metal frame backpack that was almost as tall as I was. I went to Sears and bought a nice, sharp camping knife that came with a leather sheath—my "Sting," just like Bilbo Baggins had—a canteen to be filled wherever I could find water, and a new wind-up alarm clock that gave a distinct "tick, tick, tick" sound. From the drugstore I bought a new tube of toothpaste and a toothbrush. From the supermarket I bought four jars of beef jerky and repacked them in plastic bags, five bags of lemon drops, and numerous boxes of a new product called "Pop Tarts" with a strawberry flavor, sold as a thin, breadlike morning snack. I figured I had to bring nonperishables like they did in *The Lord of the Rings*.

When all was packed, including that very heavy cloth sleeping bag and some clothing, I was weighted down big time. I only weighed at most 95 pounds—wet and with cement shoes! My backpack weighed 65-plus pounds fully loaded. I had bought a map and went over my route with Horst, Valerie Joyce, and Fred Jr. looking on. Mom would not be part of the planning stage, she was too nervous. My plan was to travel across the Bay Bridge by bus back to San Francisco, catch a ferryboat from the Embarcadero to Sausalito on the other side of the Golden Gate Bridge in Marin County, and then it was all "thumbs and a smile" hitchhiking from that point on. I was to be away for a little under ten days, or as long as my food supply and the very little money I had left lasted. Back in the late '60s and early '70s it was still safe to hitchhike. There were weirdos out there still, and it would have to be my good fortune not to run into any of them...or else I would have to kill them all—that is what my brave self said, at least!

I would realize later on in my adult life that this was my Rite of Passage. Horst was actually letting me go and see this world as he probably did in Austria when he was a young boy. His father had been killed in World War II, and he explored the world and left Austria by bike to Switzerland to become a master baker by apprenticeship when he was fourteen years old. Horst was giving me this opportunity. I never consulted my dad. I do not remember him ever asking or being interested in this adventure of mine. So all was set, and I was going to be initiated by the vast, glorious, natural world I did not fear. It was people I feared, not Nature. I was to leave the next morning. I was given some extra cash by Mom, but she offered no words of advice. She was letting her twelve-year-old son go on this mad adventure.

Early the next morning I awoke. Horst had already gone to work but left no note on the morning table or words of encouragement—nothin' from him at all. I put on my black Converse tennis shoes with my black socks and blue jeans, a nice shirt and a hooded sweatshirt, and went downstairs from my bedroom to a quiet kitchen. I ate in silence looking around at the familiar settings as if for the last time. My siblings slept on, as my mom did as well. I walked out the kitchen door and whistled as I walked to the bus stop. The morning was brisk in temperature and quite cool, but looked as though it promised to warm up and be sunny. The damn backpack weighed a ton, but it was reassuring to know it was filled with supplies that would keep me fed for a while.

The walk to the bus stop was a tune-up to adjust the straps of my backpack and my clothing. I made the 7:00 a.m. bus to the San Francisco Terminal, and was in San Francisco by 8:00 a.m. I made the 9:00 a.m. ferry to Sausalito. The ferry ride was opposite the rush hour traffic heading into the city, so it was almost empty. I rode on the top deck and watched the morning energy take over the bay. The Golden Gate Bridge looked ghostly in the receding fog. Tons of seagulls flew here and there for their morning feed. The salty air felt great to me and the wind on the bay was exhilarating to my Woolly Mammoth Boy spirit. I was truly on an adventure of my own making and I was fearless. I did not know this was my Rite of Passage at the time. I had a sense that what I was doing was big, but only vaguely. To me it was an adventure; it was my vision that I had and I was making it come true—impulsive or not.

In some countries in the world, the rites of passage are a special time for the whole village. For young boys and girls this time of defining oneself in relationship to the tribe is one of great pain, fear, and awakening—a dying and being reborn. It is a time in which the ancestors rise up from the dust of their peoples' past to evoke their ancient power and voices into the present lives for the future of the tribe. It is a time of learning to serve the "greater" rather than the "lesser." In the cultures of indigenous people, untouched by modern religions and their trapping of gifts and glitter, the rites of passage play a very important role in holding together the fabric of the people.

This was my time.

As the ferry from San Francisco neared the docks in Sausalito, I started to lock and load myself into a life-and-death frame of mind. I was alone. My knife felt good in its sheath on my belt. I secured my backpack after getting a few sticks of beef jerky out from a side pocket, and prepared to disembark from the ferry. The people onboard the ferry looked at me with questions and smiles. Where in the hell was this kid going? Is he running away from home? Shall we call the cops on him? Even though I was twelve years old, I looked like I was nine because I was so small for my age, and the size of my backpack overwhelmed my slight frame.

I saluted an imaginary Marine posted at the top of the plank and made my way down to the wharf. I looked up at the wheelhouse and saw the skipper smiling at my act of protocol. He saluted me. The morning sun was burning off the fog and the day looked promising. The plan was to make my way to the top of Mt. Tamalpais, a tall mountain that governs the Marin hills, and then make my way down the other side to find a place to camp in Muir Woods Park that night. Horst had taken the family there and I really enjoyed the majestic, aromatic smell of the redwoods, and thought of them as the forest of the Ents, the forest guardians from the world of Tolkien.

I made my way to Highway 1 and put my finger out to catch the first ride. At "Tam Junction" the traffic was brisk with commuters heading in the opposite direction, toward the Golden Gate Bridge and into San Francisco, so there were fewer cars heading north into the Marin coastal hills. Cars drove past me without stopping and I was getting kind of bewildered. I knew nothing about hitchhiking and this was my very first time alone…really alone. An old truck pulled up and this man opened the passenger door and said, "Where you headed boy?"

I looked at him and slowly loosened my knife in its sheath. "I am headed to Muir Woods, from Mt. Tam, sir."

He looked at me with a smirk on his face. "Do your parents know what you are doing?"

"Yes, sir."

"You running away?"

"No, sir."

"Get in kid, and I am no 'sir' to anyone." I saw his name stenciled on his green, faded army jacket.

"Yes, sir."

I climbed into his truck after getting my incredibly heavy backpack off me, which I threw over the rail and into the truck bed. Damn! I almost couldn't get the damn backpack over the truck rail! I did not plan on being able to throw this 65-pound backpack over my head and over the side of a truck if I needed to. I guessed I would have to grow stronger on this journey.

So there I was, a twelve-year-old kid taking his first hitchhiking ride, with so many miles already between me and my home. I felt so damn good about myself. I felt like I was on a journey where I would face challenges like in *The Lord of the Rings*. I was on my own. I controlled my world and my timing. Nobody told me what to do and when to do it. Traveling alone seemed so easy to do because I was already used to having to deal with a hard life and solving problems if I was going to survive. This was peanuts! I was smiling to myself as I looked upon the new morning in a comfortable truck ride going up Mt. Tam. The man did not talk to me and we rode in silence.

Finally he spoke up, "I am headed to Muir Beach. I will let you off at a good junction point."

"Thank you, sir." I am glad he had said something because I was about to start humming to myself, forgetting I was in a stranger's truck. That would have been embarrassing!

All too soon my first ride was over and I was left off at a junction: one road heading down to the ocean and the beach, another to the top of Mt. Tam, and another going around the mountain toward the east side. I knew where I was. Yes, I had studied park maps of the area and Marin County before I had left home. I had remembered from *The Lord of the Rings* how the Hobbit Frodo reminded his cousins to study maps while staying in Rivendell before beginning their fellowship and their mission of the Ring. I studied maps as well, so as not to be left quizzical as to where I was in the land at any given time on my journey alone.

As I stood at the junction at around 11:00 in the morning, I watched as the sun burnt away the fog over San Francisco Bay. At first only the two towers of the Golden Gate Bridge were visible from my vantage point. Then, slowly, the Golden Gate Bridge with San Francisco in the distance became crystal clear, emerging from the soup of fog and mist. I enjoyed this spectacle tremendously. I broke out some lemon drops and waited for my next ride.

Thumbing a ride was easy, but waiting to be accepted by a new driver was a drag. Acceptance was an issue that would be vividly illustrated numerous times throughout my life, but putting myself in a position that required being accepted by others was an unstoppable attraction to me—like a moth's fatal attraction to a flame, or the mongoose's joyous desire to do battle with the king cobra. Waiting to be accepted was painful; it meant feeling the burn of loneliness, and the poisonous bite of rejection and ridicule. The flip side of this longing to be accepted, validated, and loved, was my strengthened instinctual impulse to pull back and be left alone, safe under heavy blankets where it was dark and cozy, where no one could see me, or so I would think. Being social…bah humbug! Being accepted is a bunch of crap! But I could use a ride.

Fortunately, my next ride came sooner rather than later and took me to the top of Mt. Tam. The sun was strong as I walked around enjoying the sights from the summit. I felt and noticed people staring and talking in my direction. I wanted to become invisible. I wanted to be with the nature, life, and far away from people. Their energies were jarring my thoughts—"Leave me alone!"—I wanted to yell. Instead, I lugged my way off the summit and headed back through the trails that led from Mt. Tam to Muir Woods. There would be peace in the deep redwood groves of the park. I got a ride immediately, and after the usual barrage of questions and looks of "What a ballsy kid" I was let off at the front gates of Muir Woods, "Thank you, sir."

I knew the redwoods would soothe me. When Horst first took us to Muir Woods, I was struck by the potent Earthpower displayed all around me. Having survived my boyhood traumas, I intuitively felt the presence of the healing Earthpower that exuded from the immensely tall redwood trees rooted all around me. My senses were flooded. I stood and took deep breaths of the magical redwood forest air, and stimulated out through the deep, rich fragrances emanating from the moist redwood bark. The salty ocean air permeated the woods. My ears could discern the heavy silencing of the sounds made in the forest; it was as if the trees absorbed all vibrations and sent them back out through the ground. As I stood there, alone, without my family, I had a sincere sense of belonging—a belonging to nature and a reconnection to the life energy here on earth that was all around me.

The sun was not yet strong enough to evaporate the moisture that hung heavy in the deep, forested canyons of Muir Woods, so I started to move to an area away from all the tourists and external sounds that came from people and their things. The deeper I hiked into the redwoods, the deeper I fell into a trance connection of quietness and stillness that settled my chaotic mind energy. My body responded to the rigors of hiking up the redwood trails with a determination bordering on a self-imposed military mindset. I was focused only on accomplishing my current mission at hand: climb this motherfu*ker of a trail with all this packed weight and try not to whine too much. And, oh yes, one more thing: please make it look easy!

I loved it!

By late afternoon, I decided to hole up off-trail near a baby stream. The day wore on as I sat next to this stream; a break in the canopy above let in a brilliant hot ray of sunlight. Nice. I did not bring any books, diaries, or blank journals. I just brought my insanely creative, active mind along for a ten-day solo camping trip to keep myself occupied. I told stories to myself, drew in the wet banks or in the clouds in the sky, and sang of ancient people and kingdoms made up from my library of fantasy motifs in the storage files in my head.

Soon I knew the sun would go down and that meant I had to activate the evasive planning options I had thought out earlier. In my head I had already prepared for my first night alone in the woods by myself: Do not be awake when the sun goes down, and awaken when the sun rises the following morning. The plan was simple: no fuss no muss. I figured I would be asleep, safe in my sleeping bag as the night creatures of the woods roamed and hunted in the dead hours of night, and then awake to the protective gaze of morning sunlight.

I took out the Weston clock and wound that baby to the max. I needed the timing to be perfect. *NO FEAR.* I made a camp for the night and spread my bag right across the ground. I had no plastic tarp to keep me dry; I hadn't thought that far. I laid out my trusty blade next to me, ready to rock 'n' roll. Flashlight: check. I opened my new king-size tube of toothpaste and washed up. I got into my bag fully clothed and with socks on. Perfect so far. The time was 5:00 p.m. and the shadows were deep in the north-facing redwood canyon I was in. I was in the bag, zipped-up, clean, and already drowsy. Perfect! I fell asleep looking forward to the dawn and the safety from the night spooks. Perfect!

I awoke to a throaty owl call. I did not know where I was. Night sweats soaked me and the inside of my sleeping bag was very damp and clammy. I could not see a thing.

Then, slowly, a star-sprinkled night sky shone clearly through the openings in the black forest canopy. According to the glow-in-the-dark arms of my clock it was 2:30 a.m. I was terrified and spooked out. Night was jet black and I could not see my hand in front of my face! *Damn! Save me! What the hell happened? Why am I awake right now? I am five hours too early! Now I am awake to the black night of fear!*

The night creatures were roaming.

The night wind was moaning.

What was that sound?

Is something rustling nearby?

I slowly reached for my flashlight.

I drew my blade quietly, but my damn knife didn't glow blue like the real "Sting" did whenever there were evil Orcs lurking around. Damn, my luck! It will be a bloody battle to the finish, and I hope my family will be able recover my body—if they can even find it in this obscure part of the park! Maybe they will be able to see how I struggled against the night monsters, and that I had died valiantly.

I turned on the flashlight shining it on the nearest sounds only to be rewarded by the numerous pairs of eyes belonging to a family of raccoons hanging out in the nearby stream. I had never seen a live raccoon, let alone a troop of them, and this really freaked me out. "I will kill quite a few of them before they get me," I thought. I prepared myself should the raccoons meander in my direction. Of course they did not, and instead they all ran into the blackness of the bush. I turned off the flashlight, lay in my bag and listened, keeping my eyes opened; I could not see a damn thing except the stars that appeared out of the blackness in front of my face.

I settled down my fears; I slowed my racing heart and started to listen to the sounds around me and registered the night smells that enveloped me. I was lying nestled in my bag on a thick bed of ferns, redwood flakes, and needles. The sound of water was distinct, clear, and playful. The smell of the redwoods filled my senses so that I was comfortably breathing. Little sounds, terrible sounds, hisses, growls, tweaks, and screeches, the night blackness was very much alive. I breathed into the stillness like I was hiding from a beating.

I feel safe.
I feel accepted.
I feel part of.
I feel received.

Betrayal lingered not in these woods.

The fear of the deep woods—of the unknown—disappeared from me, and the events of that night watch would set a precedent on how I would face the world around me from then on. Here I learned another survival tool: Be quiet and observe. Become one with the surroundings: Fox Spirit. The morning brought a fog-enshrouded landscape, heavy with dew and wetness. I felt the morning weight of the forest power slowly awakening. I jumped out of my sleeping bag singing one of my made-up songs. It was 6:45 in the morning, and the beginning of my second day. The journey amongst and through the Marin Headlands and then down toward Point Reyes along the grand Pacific Ocean took me three days. I was alone in fog, sun, lonely empty hills, and the great world.

I saw myself being able to be alone in this world—being able to make sense of it and survive. There were nights in the early part of the journey where I was terrified; I was scared for different reasons, and had to face the long dead hours of the night tucked deep into my sleeping bag, fearing I would feel hands, claws, or teeth upon me. The mornings after such nights birthed strength; such fear gave "learning courage" a new meaning to me. I evolved with each moment of each day and each night alone as a life lesson in "going with the flow."

I had learned about courage a little bit from gang fighting as a kid on the streets of San Francisco. In those situations you did not let a friend take a beatdown if you could help it even though you might take a beating yourself. Courage to face a disadvantage in odds of fists and kicks for a friend was not taken lightly by others in the gang. To show cowardice resulted in a blacklisting that followed you everywhere. You were not to be trusted

because you ran on a brother to save your own hide.
I had your back.
I would hurt for you.
I will show courage under a fire of kicks and fists!
Yet, this was a different kind of courage I was learning about. This was a courage borne from solitude and loneliness. The willingness to be alone.

My journey, my rite of passage, finally hit the "high tide mark" around the eighth day. The Pacific coastline along Point Reyes national park showed no pity upon one going through an initiation alone, or on a dream. The cold, bare sand dunes offered little shelter, sand filled my sleeping bag, and the constant moisture in the morning air dampened my bag and doubled its weight. Also, by this time my food supply consisted only of a few precious packages of Pop Tarts, one three-quarters-full bag of hard lemon drops, one package of twenty-five sticks of beef jerky, and water wherever I could find a working water faucet. Feeling tired, spent, and ready to come home, I turned around, faced south, and started walking, always heading in the direction of San Francisco in the far distance.

Up to this point in my journey all my rides had been great, and the experiences with each driver, male or female, were very rewarding. Most of my drivers felt they were witnessing the ending of a time when one could wander and journey to find oneself, to initiate oneself to the great world around us, and all the people, earth, water, and mountains that exist. I was safe and in control the whole time. I had survived my initiation: I was no longer a boy, even though I had felt a growth beyond my years for a long time already. Many responsibilities had been forced upon my little Woolly Mammoth Boy shoulders by my mom since the divorce back in 1963. I was warrior born. My Dada would be proud.

During the last two nights on the Pacific coast I used my resourcefulness and survival skills to find some empty research cabins that were vacated for the season, and that had been built right on top of the bluffs facing the pounding blue-green waves. Those dark nights alone I laid terrified in a wooden bunk, as the flimsy, empty, dark, and wooden structure at the brink of the great ocean moaned and groaned while the night blew in harsh winds, and the howling restless banshees rocked the brittle wood-framed structure. I feared I would be washed into the dark waters never to be found. Sleeping outside was too terrifying in the Pacific storm's vengeful wrath, so finding an alternative place outside would be futile, I surmised. So it was inside, though dry and warm, that I cowered and laid in fearful wakefulness.

On the tenth and final day of my journey, I had somehow made my way to the last onramp out of Tam Junction before the Golden Gate Bridge. It had taken a series of rides to get me there. It must have been rush hour because there was a hell of a lot of traffic, and the sky was turning into a dusky rich blue with orange hues that foretold very cool evening temperatures.

I was tired, bone cold, and weighted down by a damp, dirty, and sandy sleeping bag; I was down to a few lemon drops, and only had a quarter of my rusty-tasting canteen water left. I held out my thumb and smiled into the oncoming car lights that blinded me. I had been waiting for about 20 minutes when I heard the screech of a passing car stop behind me. I turned around, picked up my backpack, and ran toward the ride. A beautiful young woman with light blond hair waited for me in the open cockpit of a white MGB roadster—a two-seater car. I stopped and gawked as I looked down into the cockpit of the car at this beautiful, angelic, living painting of a woman. She looked up from her seat and said, "Where are you going, babe?"

I snapped into cognition and said, "I am headed to the bus terminal on First and Mission in the city." I thought I was talking to Love embodied. My twelve-year-old mind and body were racing.

"A little young to be traveling alone, aren't you? Well, get in, babe. Let's go." I knocked my tired bones into action, threw my backpack into the back area of the MGB, and jumped in to sit next to this beautiful angel. *Take me anywhere!*

My last ride that took me across the Golden Gate Bridge was in a sports car driven by a young beautiful woman who would look over at me and smile as she weaved quickly through the early evening traffic heading toward San Francisco. Damn! No one is going to believe me! Halfway through the ride over the bridge she started to ask me questions and I was more than happy to talk. I hadn't really spoken to anyone for any length for ten days. I prayed I would not stutter, and I did not.

"You hungry, babe?" I was stunned by the implications of eating anything other than lemon drops and beef jerky.

"Yes, I am very hungry," I said, trying not to sound too needy.

She looked at me for a moment and said, "Well, looks like I am going to have to take care of you, won't I babe?" I melted into my seat. That was the nicest thing anyone had said to me for a long time. I felt the power of the MGB vibrating through the seat I was sitting in. The car hummed and this angel woman was going to take care of me.

"Thank you so much," I sighed and did not take my eyes off her again until she stopped in front of a new restaurant called "McDonald's."

"C'mon babe. You are going to eat."

I entered the brightly lit restaurant blinking like an owl. She ordered for me: a cheeseburger, fries, and a coke. She sat across from me as I ate, and just watched me. I ate the food set before me ravenously as I looked into her eyes the whole time. She did not ask any questions; she just watched me eat. I finished the food without knowing it. "You still hungry, babe?"

I nodded, "Yes."

She got up and ordered a second round of the same items, and I chowed the second order down just as quickly. When I finished eating my cheeks and belly both felt very warm. It was the first cooked food I had eaten in ten days. I smiled at her and she returned it with a gleaming bright smile. "Okay, babe. Let's get you to the bus terminal so you can get home."

We started chatting as she drove me across San Francisco toward the bus terminal. She was so amazed at the story I told of my journey alone. "You are very brave." I felt so safe in her presence. She recognized me. She saw who I was and accepted me. I did not want her to leave me ever, though I knew she would have to. We pulled up in front of the bus terminal and she turned off the car. "Here, babe, here is some money to get you across the bay." She handed me some bills and I slowly pulled myself out of her car. Soon I had gathered myself on the sidewalk and stared down at her in her MGB. She started the car and it purred and rumbled into wakefulness. "Take care of yourself, babe. It was so nice to meet you."

I was lost for words and mumbled "Thank you" out of gratefulness. She pulled away from the curb and drove away into the evening traffic. I was alone once again, and I had to really kick myself into action. My belly was warm; my heart was soft and sad. I entered the bustling bus terminal and slowly made my way through all the grown-ups going nowhere and everywhere. I found my bus and boarded.

The forty-five minute bus ride went quickly. I walked the last two miles in the evening lit streets of Piedmont to my home. I was lost in thought. I felt like Bilbo Baggins coming home from the Lonely Mountain after an incredible journey filled with dwarves, war, treasure, and life-or-death risks. I stood in front of my home in Piedmont for a very long time. I had seen a lot and experienced a lot in ten days. I felt I was coming into someplace very foreign: my home. I felt different about myself. I walked up the dark side driveway to enter the house from the backyard and dining room. I stood in the darkness beyond the dining room light and watched as my family were sitting down and having dinner. I had not contacted my family the whole time I was gone. Yet here they all sat, eating and living their "normal" life. Baby brother was raising hell in his high chair. My sister and older brother were eating food; their muffled voices carried through the sliding dining room doors—they sounded like animal sounds.

I walked up to the dining room door and opened it. The flood of warm air enveloped me. Everyone turned toward me. My sister screamed in delight. Horst had a big smile on his face.

"Hi, everyone. I am home." I entered my old life with a sigh and a smile.

In a far distant glacier pass, a large herd of woolly mammoths foraged peacefully.

Woolly Mammoth Boy swayed from one foot to another while munching on some fresh grass as his long, flexible trunk ripped large clumps of sweet grass from the moist glaciered soil.

He had observed how his earthly reincarnation displayed tenacity and creativity in creating a Rite of Passage on his own, and how he had survived it.

"Not bad for a little squirt! Thank the Great Spirit he had that man in his life to support him," he said.

"I believe the man's name is Horse," chimed in Thought.

"Nope. It is Horst and not Horse," Woolly Mammoth Boy corrected.

"Yes, you are right. Horst it is," sang Thought. "That young manling sure has had to really work hard on creating a voice he can call his own."

"Yep," Woolly Mammoth Boy said with a mouthful of sweet grass. "His male sibling did a pretty good job finding his own way. His way was a little tough on the others, but he did what was right for himself. What may appear as one thing to one person may appear as a completely different thing to another person. Not bad."

"This charge of yours...Ron, I believe he is addressed as...seems blessed with unseen fortunes. Your doing?" whispered Thought deeply into Woolly Mammoth Boy's mind.

"I am making sure that the young manling is connected somehow to all that is available to him," Woolly Mammoth Boy replied to the light wind that blew.

"Oh, like the cutie with the sports car?" chuckled Thought.

"Yep," Woolly Mammoth Boy answered as he tugged on a nice tuft of sweet grass. "That boy is connected to the abundance of the Universe. He will understand how to access this prosperity more easily as he grows."

The herd started to move on down into the deep valley. Woolly Mammoth Boy took one more mouthful and started to follow the matriarch as she led the herd into the valley that was swallowed by the dark shadows of high mountains surrounding them. He saw the young boy's smiling face in his mind.

"He really does have a woolly mammoth head under his human skull," he thought. With a grunt, he hurried to catch up with the herd.

Part 3: Far Away Places

20. Over the Hills and Far Away

The migration took the herd into the deep valleys where the grass was greener and the water plenty. We lost the weaker ones and the old ones as we crossed the high country. The predators that followed us took them instead of the healthy—the ones who had the strength to make the journey. The bones of the fallen remained in the frozen heights. That is the way it is in life, you lose something to gain something. You feed the predators to save the herd.

–Woolly Mammoth Boy Remembers

PIEDMONT MIDDLE SCHOOL HAD BEEN a social minefield for fitting in and being accepted. I was feeling more alone and out of place. The only blessing at the time was my Math teacher and my English teacher. These teachers allowed me to hang with them on their morning breaks on different days while all the other kids were outside playing. I was drawn to them because they extended energy out to me; they gave of themselves, and, most importantly, they saw me and heard me. It must have been odd for them to entertain me just by listening to me speak of things so foreign to my classmates: racism, aloneness, wanting of validation. I often think of how Mr. Math Teacher and Mrs. English Teacher had so easily read how lonely I was. I was only one of two people of color in the whole class.

My depression and the energy-draining thoughts of failure continued eroding my self-confidence when dealing with my peers and family. Though happy and playful at home with my sister and baby brother Shawn, I was normally quiet, introverted, and thoughtful about the world around me. If caught by the full moon cycle crazies, I would be the annoying joker, singer, and the one looking for attention in a display of erratic and loud behaviors.

I had no true friends yet, only "acquaintances." These kids were from my symphonic band and art classes. Acquaintances, as I understood them, were like "friends," and so you could be friendly to them—but not too friendly—because you were not really "friends" with them, they were acquaintances. I understood I could not trust or share my heart with them. Huh? Social life was confusing! Like I said, middle school was a social minefield.

By 1971, I was a freshman at Piedmont High School. I was known as Fred's little brother and though he hated me and would have nothing to do with me, his friends and the school at large presumed that blood was thicker than water, and so no one messed with me. I had used my running skills to try out for a position on the JV football team in the fall of '71. I was a punt and kick-off return man, a safety on defense, and a wide receiver on offense. I was small but fast, and when I hit you, you knew. I threw all 110 pounds of my pent-up wild animal fury right at you. I wore the number 55. It was the only number left. Not exactly the number for my position, and I got the last pick in all my football gear: an oversized helmet and shoulder pads better suited for the position of a linebacker, but what the hell—I was playing football and I could be part of a group, even though I was a ghost in the locker room. No one really offered me friendship. I just did my job on the team when called upon and played the game hard. I was a perfect company man. I did my job the best I could using the training given to me for my position, while throwing in all my natural talents. Everything was cool. No complaints.

I got something out of playing football. The physical training grounded me. I still had a temper; I would rage and melt down when my rigid thinking and anxiety around transitions arose, but the physical training of football opened me in another way. I had to deal with things as a team. The rigorous physical exercises taught me what I could and could not do, and seeing what other kids were doing successfully in their positions on the team was inspiring to me. I started to get a sense of my physical boundaries. I was starting to understand where my body ended and where the space around me started. Through football I slowly created a physical presence about myself that people around me could no longer deny: I existed. That fall of my freshman year I was invited for the first time to a fellow football teammate's beachside home in fashionable Aptos near the Santa Cruz beach: I was slowly being accepted by my peers on my own terms.

I liked to brag I was a solid C+ student with terrible handwriting, undiagnosed learning disabilities, and prone to attention deficit wanderings in the classroom. I remember having to grade myself in all my subjects, and my parents had to sign off on the self-evaluation. I had given myself mostly As. Horst and Mom laughed when they saw my self-evaluation, and asked me how I could give myself the grade "A" when all my grades showed either C- or C+. My answer was simple: Nobody knew how much I was trying. I believed I deserved an A for trying in every class I was taking, and I was trying really hard. I did not understand that this was not the way the world turned. You were graded not only on how hard you tried but also on what you actually produced. Damn!

I was immature in my interests and hobbies. I was keenly obsessed with drawing superheroes and fantasy characters from my Marvel comic books with a fervor; I still played with toy figurines and continued playing improvisational theater games with my sister or by myself for hours—

definitely not what my peers were engaged with in their lives. I was engrossed with reading the news of the Vietnam War, NASA space projects, and the civil rights movement. I was excelling at my trumpet, and enjoyed riding my Stingray bike for long distances and periods of time. In addition to playing in the symphonic band I joined the marching band as well. I was obsessed with J. R. R. Tolkien's world described in *The Lord of the Rings*. I was a "freak-out machine" when it came to facts, dates, or anything related to the Tolkien trilogy. If you wanted to know a particular fact about a certain battle between the Elves and Orcs, or if you wanted to write your name in ancient Elvish script, I could help you, but these were not the interests of most of my peers, especially at the age of fourteen-going-on-fifteen years old. Most of my acquaintances were into girls, and so I was being left out.

I had started to listen to music on the newly founded FM underground station KSAN out of San Francisco. Being a trumpet player, I enjoyed listening to a wide spectrum of music: classical, pop, Broadway musicals, street music (meaning R&B), and the White Man's rock 'n' roll—not the '50s stuff, but the rock 'n' roll of the '60s and '70s. Rock from the '50s conjured ugly memories of sadness from my childhood. The rock 'n' roll I was into spoke of revolution, drugs, free spirits, and self-awareness.

I was really getting into a poet-musician named Jimi Hendrix. I stayed with my dad and his new wife in their home in Contra Costa County during the summers—forty-five minutes east of San Francisco in a brown, dry land. One summer I heard a Jimi Hendrix tune on the FM radio—"All Along the Watchtower," written by Bob Dylan. Hendrix's soulful voice and not-of-this-planet guitar playing resonated with something deep in my heart. I was hooked. Jimi Hendrix became my mentor in the training of expressing spiritual and emotional visions without the restraints of the status quo. It helped initiate a deep study of my own insides—why I loved, cried, laughed, and survived. It helped me to continue living in a world that made very little sense to me.

I was inspired to begin writing simple poems, holding them dear to me and treasuring my written expressions like the sacred writings of a forgotten people. I was expressing myself to myself. No one was listening to me anyway—neither my family nor my classmates. I would imagine someone finding my writings long after I died, in a dusty old room somewhere, saying in a melancholy voice filled with a certain kind of awe, "This poet said a lot with his writing and he was so sad."

All the hard work I did with Dad that summer of 1971 put my out-of-body consciousness back into my body instead of letting it float away somewhere in Trauma Land. Muscle appeared on my scrawny body, and a hunger to eat and gain weight grew. I was learning executive skills that taught me to do one thing first before you did another thing—a very critical skill that could be applied to all aspects of life. Sometimes Dad would hire a few neighborhood kids, and I was starting to understand what it meant to be on a crew and think like a team. My swearing and cursing was perfect for the job as a carpenter. Being at my dad's home during the summer meant being on the border between the suburbs and the country. I was black from the sun working with only shorts and a carpentry belt in the dry, 100+ degree summer days. The new aromas of certain bushes and trees, and the silence of the plain, brown, dry landscape so familiar to the inner lands far from the California coast, were all appealing to me. The land resonated with the solitary and emotional me.

But despite all these things I was doing with my dad—things he liked to do—he was still very impatient with me most of the time, and so the bullying, physical intimidation, and screaming continued in his home with his new wife. I just could not please the bastard. He was just a rigid thinker and stuck in his ways; he wanted blind obedience and no questioning of his logic. Though I was learning, I was still slow and stupid in his eyes. I was also at an age when I was establishing my own voice and identity, and he was not into the "free spirit" in me.

My two years of junior high school had opened me up to new faces, but I was held at bay romantically. In eighth grade I was voted "Best Personality"—an award that basically said I was a nice guy, but not attractive enough for romance. The classic line, I think, went something like this: "I like you as a friend, Ron. You are such a nice guy. I can really talk to you about things I cannot talk to my best friends about." Puke and double-puke!

I had liked a blonde-haired girl in elementary school and fantasized she would notice me, but she did not know I even existed. This was a sad and confusing affair for me. Then something happened I had not expected. I fell in love with a girl that actually found me appealing. She was in my art and music classes. Perfect. But, now that I caught the fish, what do I with the damn thing?!? I asked her out to a school dance—and she said yes. She liked me! I was funny and cute, and very, very shy. I thought of the girl in 5th grade in San Francisco before I moved to Piedmont and how we were attracted to each other. We had spoken once or twice, but only through her friends. Here in Piedmont, I was older and now doing more of the inviting and reaching out, though awkwardly. I was learning and trying out my social wings.

I held love in a chivalrous light. I placed women on a white pedestal high above my mortal heart, to be adored, protected, and fought for. It was a very *Wuthering Heights* perspective on love. Heathcliff, the lead male character in the story, held an undying love for Catherine—a love that transcended mortal death—and this was to become my model for love between a man and a woman. It goes without saying that my view of love was not modeled after the love displayed between my mom and dad. No, their love was a love from a dark hell. The meaning of love that I held sacred in my heart was from another time and place, and that was a time long gone—probably 150 years earlier, as it was expressed in the Deep South by a Southern gentleman's love. It could also be found in the love of knights and maidens courting without physical touch, or in the display of warrior deeds and poetic words sung to win a woman's heart. But my model for love did not go over well in the mid-'70s. I was obsessed by a dire infatuation with the female of my focus, and all my heart was deeply embedded in poetic prose that I thought could be expressed by my adoring gaze. What a sorry sod I was!

Yet I was able to extend myself. My playfulness was matched by her receptive responses. She was bright, and in her own way she was inviting me into her life. Like in the movie *Wuthering Heights*, I was her Heathcliff and she was my Catherine. We created opportunities to be together away from others, where no one could spy on us. We talked about art and music. We drew pictures together. She came to the football games and track meets to watch me play and run. It was just her and me.

So it was that I fell in love with a girl and she returned my affections. During this time I felt that my social conditions in Piedmont were finally bearing the fruit of years of fighting for myself and not backing down. I was becoming comfortable in the slowly developing friendships with my white counterparts through my participation in school sports, art, and music, but my world was about to have a rude awakening.

It seemed that the birth of my baby brother had started to widen the gap between my sister and my mom. Her new child and new husband had detached Mom from her three surviving children with the "Rubio" name. Valerie Joyce and Mom battled. My sister just wanted attention from Mom, as any eleven-and-a-half-year old daughter would want from her mother. Their battles came to a climactic head when Valerie Joyce was removed from the picture by being sent to live with Dad and his new wife in Walnut Creek, was over the Berkeley Hills and far away. Now, Valerie Joyce had always been Dad's little girl, as almost all daughters are to their fathers, so it was deemed a safe move. Except Mom did not take into consideration the infamous "Daddy's daughter and the new stepmother" relationship from the classic fairy tale, *Cinderella*. This was bad juju. So as this big decision about Valerie was being finalized, Mom came to me and said, "Ronnie, you are going to move to your dad's house with Valerie. You are going to protect her."

WHAT? Now hold your horses! I loved my dad, as any physically abused victim loves their tormentor, and yes, I stayed with him in the summers and sometimes I even liked working with him. I wanted to be accepted by him in my odd, sicko way, but Dad did not like me much and he had a mean temper that flared my own mean temper, and this was just not a good idea for my well-being.

"Mom! Dad hates me and he beats me!" I pleaded. "Mom, I am making friends here in Piedmont and I am doing well in school, please Mom!"

"No! Ronnie boy! You must go with your sister to your dad's house to protect her."

"Me, protect her from Dad?"

"Yes, you will protect her. Rubio has a temper. Your older brother will finish high school here and you will go with Valerie Joyce to your dad's. You like going to your dad's house."

"Mom. I like visiting Dad's house but I don't want to *live* there!"

"No! And that is final. Enough now!" Mom gave me the look that demanded obedience.

Silence.

Mom left the room and I was alone.

Pain, anguish, and betrayal rocked me. Mom was doing it again: she was abandoning me again, and this time she was giving me up to a man who hated me and beats me!

I was crushed. I left my body. I was furious and speechless.

Still, I loved my little sister and I would protect her—anytime and anywhere.

My new school was in the same athletic conference as my old one, so I still saw my old Piedmont friends, but only at sporting events. Walnut Creek is so far away from Piedmont. In the 1970s, Walnut Creek was a land of stereotypical rednecks and country kids. This was not seeing "both sides of the fence." No, this was straddling the fence on my ass!

And what about my new love relationship with a girl who actually liked me? A white girl! Dust was in my mouth and in my heart. I told her of my inevitable move, and she was sad with me. I promised to visit her every weekend, taking the bus from Walnut Creek to Oakland, and then catching another bus to Piedmont. I cursed all the gods and goddesses! How could this be happening? Why now? I had to put all this aside because I was going to live with my dad.

I feared for my life. Dad was unpredictable. I would follow my sister to my dad's house, because Mom could not handle her relationship with Valerie Joyce and was booting Valerie out. I was devastated. My woolly mammoth head ached. This was not going to end well...I knew it in my gut. I was going into the Land of Mordor.

"The young manling does have a big heart for a little body," came the voice that prickled Woolly Mammoth Boy to consciousness as he stood dozing in the shade of a gigantic tree that shaded the entire herd of mammoths.

" I was dozing..."

"Yes, and I am talking to you," voiced Thought. *"His life will be in danger."*

"I know, I know...I have observed the behavior of the male who sired him—quite violent and unpredictable," Woolly Mammoth Boy said, now awake as he stared into the searing heat that bathed the vast, open plain before him. *"The lad understands sacrifice; he is willing to go into harm's way for his younger female sibling. I have watched him display this virtue since he was a yearling."*

"The dark journey before him will ask much of him," Thought announced through the chirping of a locust.

Woolly Mammoth Boy released some water from his bladder. *"He will persevere though he may wish to depart his world. For one so born in fragments, he retains the wholeness of the Universe from which he came. This is what gives him the strength, though he is not yet aware of it."*

"He is a peculiar lad. He thinks of others before himself. Others would not give of themselves in this manner." Thought sparkled as a flake of dust before Woolly Mammoth Boy's eyes.

"Yes, he is peculiar in this way, and therefore, unique to his kind. His rites of passage forged this quality into his being. He knows no less, and so he could DO no less than to give of himself for the survival of others. And for this, I believe, he will survive even a saber-toothed tiger's attention."

21. Love Letters and the .22 Caliber Rifle

We fled away from the ambush. As the mammoth herd burst through the circle of hunters unscathed, the Matriarch turned and charged her adversaries. Having foiled the trap she signaled us to flee. She would sacrifice herself for her wards. In my last sight of her she was turning to face her killer.

—Woolly Mammoth Boy Remembers

THE EVENING AIR WAS COOL and carried a sweet fragrance with it. I believe it came from the honeysuckle bushes all around my dad's home in Walnut Creek. I was acutely aware of the danger I was in, and the sweet fragrance that soothed me could not hide the fear coming out of my pores. I knew I would have to be very careful in this new place, my dad's home. Violence would always be close by, lurking behind the façade of calmness, in this dry and open land I was now banished to with my sister.

Step lightly!
Be alert! All senses piqued!
Be prepared for violent actions!
Don't space out!

Only hours before, my younger sister and I were saying our goodbyes to our life in Piedmont, the land of white castles in the clouds. Our older and younger brothers were staying there with Mom, while Valerie Joyce and I were going to a new life in suburban Walnut Creek with Dad and our new stepmother. Nothing was more horrible to me than seeing Mom and Horst pulling out of the driveway that late afternoon to head back to Piedmont after driving us out here to the middle of nowhere.

The first evening in Walnut Creek I walked around outside our new home, but Valerie would not leave her new room. She was distraught. She wanted love from Mom but all she got was the boot. Mom could now focus on her new son in her new life. She kept her firstborn with her in Piedmont. Valerie Joyce and I were out of the house. Did we remind Mom of uglier times in her life? Did we represent "Rubio?" We would never know. Valerie and I were together in a strange house in a strange land. None of it made sense— no rhyme or reason. What was I to do? Mom said I had to leave so I could protect Valerie from "Rubio." How could I possibly protect my sister from my dad's temper and rage? I was a fourteen-year-old young man who was opening his heart to the vast world of Jimi Hendrix's universe of energy, love, and self-awareness; and who was at the same time shutting down his heart from being extremely sensitive to his dad's ridicule, impatience, and angry violence. My heart was opening but Dad would shut it down. His oppressive behavior toward me produced the "easily spooked out" reactions of a jumpy-ass squirrel—I jumped at the sound of a falling leaf. The body-anchored reactions I displayed were no different than when a beaten dog cowers on hearing the loud, abrasive yelling of a human.

I am strong on my own.
I know who I am.
I will survive.

Why was my dad, who I loved so much, so disappointed with me? Dad's energy drained me of my inner joy. My artwork was dark and no poems came out of my head.

Dad and I shared so much that he refused to acknowledge. Maybe my being the sickly, dimwitted son born after the death of Sabrina was a real letdown to him. But I did not understand why Dad and I could not enjoy the type of relationship he shared with his firstborn son, Fred, and his only living daughter, Valerie Joyce. I longed for recognition from him. I wanted to be a shining and proud "Rubio" for him. I was very proud of who I was and what I was capable of doing. Dad expected more from me and he made sure I knew it. It was like being in the movie *The Great Santini*, the portrayal of a family held hostage by a raging ex-Marine father who demanded complete obedience and perfection. Life was very difficult.

The new land around me was very different than the white sidewalks of upper-class Piedmont. In Walnut Creek there were no sidewalks. The streets went on forever with very little traffic on them after certain hours. We lived in a house surrounded by an open field. There were also many one-story ranch-style homes surrounded by large parcels of land. The air smelled differently here. The birds sang different songs. The land was brown and opened to the sky. The night was filled with stars, for the city lights were far away.

The place appealed to the traveling Hobbit in me. By sneaking out my bedroom window and moving as quietly as a mouse in a room filled with hungry cats, I would take nightly walks deep into the dark hours of the early morning. Most every morning I chose to walk the three-plus miles to school. The mornings were special times for me; there was so much to be inspired by in the gullies and dirt trails along the way. I later found the air in spring and summer days to be very warm and comfortable, with the nights cool and fragrant. The new land was constantly calling me to lay down in its meadows of tall, yellow, crackly grass and look heavenward as the white, fluffy clouds streaked by.

This new land was a sanctuary where I mused over my world of exploration and high adventure, of a deep sadness and despair, of visioning a life where I was loved and taken cared of. I realized that, compared to my peers, I had not lived the childhood most of them had experienced. My childhood was filled with physical and emotional trauma, and I was laden with heavy responsibility at an early age. I had experienced violence, an ugly divorce, and living with the underlying vibrancy of responding to the world around me as a kid with undiagnosed learning disabilities—not to mention the telltale behaviors that would later distinguish me as a person on the autism spectrum. At fourteen-going-on-fifteen, my world was as surrealistic as a Bosch painting. The music of Jimi Hendrix and Carlos Santana was the soundtrack to my heart and mind. I was aware I was alive, but I was not enjoying my life.

While all this was happening Valerie also had to deal with our stepmother, who treated Valerie in the same way Dad treated me, and these two adults were our life banes. Later, in my awakened adult life, I would come to understand that without my dad's brutal teachings I would not have grown into the person I am today, but that meant nothing to a young teenager in pain and despair. All I knew was that our life teachers were two people with a mean bully-stick stuck up their you-know-what.

At times they were so mean that their behaviors just baffled Valerie and me. Dad was on me hard, so he backed off his daughter unless Stepmother forced him to get on Valerie's case—often by manipulating him with deceit and lies. Stepmother was on Valerie in a bad way so she stayed off me, and she did not explore or promote any of my artistic talents either—even though she was a high-school dance and drama teacher. Sometimes she did prod me to stand up for myself when speaking to my dad. I tried that, with dismal results.

Stepmother had the lifestyle of a princess in exile. She would ring a small bell she kept near her for my sister to respond to her every whim or desire. "Get my cookies from the cabinet. I want four on a plate. Also a cup of tea."

Valerie answered with a blank stare which meant, "Yes, Missy, Your Royal Highness, Queen of the Queen Bees, Wicked Witch of the North."

"Be careful with those looks. Start dinner in a half hour. Walk the dog now. What did you say? Did I hear you say something under breath? Wait until your dad comes home!"

I was defenseless to help Valerie. Piedmont was so far away, with so little communication from Mom or Horst. It was as if Valerie and I were forgotten by them to survive life with Dad. There was no time or opportunity to wonder why Mom and Horst just vanished from our lives. To me, it was no water off my back; dealing with adversity for so long—since my boyhood days—

made me callous to the void of love in my life. All I could do was fume with Valerie about Stepmother, and plan how to leave together someday and live a happy life. I hated my life and I hated my sister's life of torment, sadness, and helplessness. Valerie and I were living in a world so different from the one my older brother was living in with Mom and my new baby brother. We were not really wanted when we visited on weekends. Valerie and I were just extra bodies in my mom's house. Valerie and I never left our dad's home for summer vacation or holidays to be with Mom, and Mom hardly kept up with us or called us at Dad's home. She wiped her hands of us. It was just Valerie and me. We worked every weekend and after school. Dad was always building something and had his hands in real estate. Stepmother always had some idiotic demeaning job for Valerie Joyce to do. We worked and worked and tried to assimilate to a new and very different world. Very strange times.

During this phase I bought a .22 caliber semi-automatic rifle that I found in an ad in a pennysaver magazine. It had a nineteen-bullet clip that shot fifteen rounds in semi-auto without getting jammed, and to my surprise it was made in the Philippines. I paid for it with my own money I had saved; like I said, I worked a lot. The rifle felt good in my hands. My next-door neighbor, an older kid, would take me to a shooting range every once in a while. I was a very good shot. I took my time and pretended that I was shooting at bad guys: Nazis and mean people. One shot, one kill. I would switch to auto and blast away at the target. I cleaned my rifle like the sacred artifact it was. This rifle was an extension of me—the power I could not reveal or show in my life.

High school was very intense. I was now the "Mexican kid" in class.

"No, I am Filipino."

"What's that? Huh?"

"No, my family comes from a place called the Philippines."

"Huh?"

"No! Not Philadelphia!"

I went out for the track and field team at my new high school, the Las Lomas Knights. My events were the 100-yard dash, 440-yard relay as the first man or the anchor, the long jump, and—mimic my life—I ran the 330-yard low hurdles and the 120-yard high hurdles. I loved it. I showed the world what I could do, but I had no friends at my new school. Sports were my only outlet besides the art and band classes I excelled at. I was fleet on my feet.

Learning the hurdles was a time of dealing with constant open, bleeding scabs on my knees from running into the hurdles, hitting them, tripping, and crashing. I got myself up and continued on. I always finished a race no matter how far behind the pack I was after falling into the hurdles. It was humbling falling in front of a football-stand full of spectators and classmates. I wore thin dress ties as headbands that I would buy at the Salvation Army, and when I bought my first leather sprinter running shoes, they made me feel like I was running barefoot. I saw myself as a Greek Olympian, or more precisely, the Greek messenger who ran the billion miles to Athens to report to the populace of the Greek victory over the Persians at the Battle of Marathon. That poor bastard dropped dead after completing his mission. This was me as well; I was going to drop dead but always finish the race. There were times when I fell badly in a race and wanted to scream, cry, and walk off the track. Thank the Great Spirit I did not resort to that behavior in front of my new classmates and community. I was not that dense. Slow, perhaps, but not too dense at the right time. I later excelled in my running events and started taking first- and second-place finishes.

My dad saw sports as a waste of time that took me away from work; it took me away from his control. He hated sports. He never came to any of my events or anything. Life with Dad was just plain sad and confusing to me. My room was painted in plain and dark colors. My entertainment was a music system fueled by an amplifier Dad gave me that sported old-fashioned glass bulbs and fuses that were all exposed bare and attached to an uncased frame. The amp pushed sound through one big bass speaker. I bought an old 45/33-speed record player and played my growing collection of Hendrix, Santana, Steppenwolf, Cream, and other rock 'n' roll bands. I played my music until late at night as I wrote my love poems.

Like I said, before moving away from Piedmont I had started a courtship with a cute white girl who actually liked me enough to maintain a long-distance relationship. I would take the bus over the Berkeley Hills to Oakland, transfer on a bus to Piedmont, and be there by 10:00 a.m. on a Saturday morning. I did this for months. She was very sweet and nice to me, and I was extremely shy and naïve to romance. We would talk in her living room, take walks to the store, or stroll the empty grounds of the high school I moved away from and that she still went to. We sat in the empty football stands and talked and talked and talked. I would stretch these times out, and then head back on the bus to Hades over the mountains. During our times apart I would write her beautiful, romantic love letters filled with fragrances and the beauty of Romantic love sealed with wax, stamped with the letter of her first name, "E" for Elizabeth.

Well the, "talk and talk and talk" love-ins with Elizabeth came to a head when she wanted to kiss me one evening. I froze and squirmed. I wanted to kiss her so badly, but I just froze. I left my body and floated away. She was within my defenses, my barriers of safety, and I was helpless to respond. Maybe I was in shock that someone really loved me. I froze. I simply froze and went numb. She ended the relationship. It was too frustrating and hard for her to have a boyfriend who was terribly shy and scared. All my ideas and words of love for her were smashed into the hard rocks of reality. She let me go with reluctance. I went spooky in despair and tried to see her on the weekends anyway. Letters and calls to her were left unanswered. I would make the trip to see her and was finally turned away at the door by her mother. The relationship died. No more trips over the hills; the brown lands were where I lived now.

One lonely night a few weeks after my last trip over the hills, I sat at the edge of my bed listening to Hendrix. My newly bought black-light posters glowed eerily out from my bedroom walls. I had my rifle in my hands fully loaded. With despair in my heart and so much pain and sadness raging in my mixed-up mind, I wanted to go now—go and never come back. I wanted to die. The way I dealt with stress, despair, and frustration was modeled after my parents. My dad responded with rage and violence. My mom responded with death and numb departure. Mom always had bottles of "mother's little helpers"—pain meds—near her. I had a loaded rifle.

The rifle felt solid in my hands. It felt reassuring; it would not fail me. It would not lie to me, hurt me, or leave me. This was my rifle. Like holding a flower in my hands, the wood stock felt organic to me. I could smell the rifle cleaning solvents and oils. The clip was fully loaded and the safety was off. I placed the rifle barrel into my mouth, the metallic taste vibrating on my tongue. My right thumb was pressed against the trigger, which had a sensitive and light touch for firing. I knew the trigger did not need a lot of pressure to discharge a round into my brain. I was ready to rock 'n' roll into a painless and loveless release from a life I could not understand or fit into. I was almost fifteen, and the world was just a cruel place to me. Those I wanted love from were unable to sustain any amount of attention for me, or even just recognize me. My sister in the next room was my only concern. I thought I could will my ghost from Purgatory, send it to protect my sister, and haunt the shit out of my stepmother or any other mean person that wanted to hurt Valerie. I sat, not moving for hours. The Hendrix album played and played. The darkest of the morning hours stilled all sounds outside my window and in the house. I was alone, cold and stiff. The rifle was part of me. I knew at any moment if I squeezed just a little bit more on the trigger the rifle would go off and it would be a moment of sweet freedom.

"*Do it, Woolly Mammoth Boy, and you will have to come back and do this life all over again.*"

What was that? The clock showed 4:00 a.m. when I pulled the rifle's barrel out of my mouth. I turned the barrel away from me and put the safety on. I ejected the live round from the chamber and released the loaded clip. The rifle was cleared. I took a breath and started to cry. I hated my weakness. I hated this moment. F*ck it! I had high school to go to and the sun was coming up soon. I was tired and went to sleep with my lights on. Dad did not like that when he woke me up for school two hours later.

The sun glistened brightly off the icy blue glacial waters of the vast landlocked sea. The woolly mammoth herd had settled down before continuing their migration to the fertile southlands.

"He came kinda close on that one," Woolly Mammoth Boy mused to himself as he gazed across the mirror surface of the seemingly endless waters before him.

"Yes, the young manling faced his demons and almost ate his rifle," Thought reflected off the gleaming waters.

"Our last matriarch charged the hunters that would have slain us all at the ambush site. She faced the demons. She sacrificed herself for us all; I saw this with my own eyes," Woolly Mammoth Boy said toward a multicolored dragonfly the size of a small bird that hovered near his head. "This boy has small echoes of me in him. Maybe he will come to feel our strength, the strength that is in him, to continue to persevere himself."

"Come now, my little one..." chuckled Thought. "He faces the demons of his sire and his own. He is besieged by the One that renders flesh from the soul!"

Woolly Mammoth Boy became silent. "Yes, he does face the bare fangs of the spirit-killer," whispered Woolly Mammoth Boy to a passing cloud above him. "He learns through this pain...his pain. Yet, his mammoth spirit will remind him of the bigger picture."

"And what is this 'bigger picture,' my little one?" Thought squawked though a gliding land gull.

"To stand your ground always for the whole Universe to witness!" Woolly Mammoth Boy trumpeted with gusto.

Hearing Woolly Mammoth Boy's sound to battle, the entire woolly mammoth herd awoke in unison and joined him in blaring a symphony of defiance.

22. The Rudgear Estates Boys

Growing up I had four other juvenile mammoths to learn from and get into trouble with. The elders swatted us out of the way when we became a nuisance. The Matriarch allowed the young bull mammoths to teach us. Being the clumsy one, I was treated with harsher measures to learn the basic survival skills needed to be part of the herd. Two of my young peers never made it to maturity. They never had a chance. It was not their time. Their bones lay broken and abandoned in a saber-toothed tiger cave.

—Woolly Mammoth Boy Remembers

"DAMN, IT IS A SCORCHER today!"

"No shit."

"Pass the joint—quit holding on to it!"

The air shimmered off the hot plywood like a desert mirage. It was a typical summer day in "Creektown": 101 degrees in the shade. Hot and dry. My skin was bathed in baby oil. I was dark brown to black in color. My friends were working with me, hired by my dad for the summer building project: a massive home built from excavation to shingled roof—a real project of family joy.

I had been swinging a hammer for almost two and a half years by this time. On this project, I started in the early spring by ripping down or splitting recycled, 20-foot-long 12"x16" beams salvaged from torn-down Victorian mansions in Oakland with a tiny Sears chainsaw. I was cutting them into the dimensions we needed for the main timber framing. I learned to sharpen the dull chainsaw blades with a file, and only took a break when the saw grew too hot to handle. I could work a circular saw without cutting any fingers off. I had the executive skills together enough to understand how to use a measuring tape and calculations to frame a wall. My dad would say something like this to me at the job site before he left for work in San Francisco: "Build a section of wall: a 2-by-4 wall by 8 foot high by 12 foot long with measuring tape and calculations to frame studs at 16 inches on center, with double top plates, single bottom plate, fire blocking, 1-by-4 diagonal bracing cut slotted in to the studs—we will raise the walls when I get home."

The wall was trued and ready to be raised with help. I had done enough building by myself after school, on every weekend and on every school vacation, to be independent on the site. I was taught by Dad who was a carpenter and had instructed me in his self-made, self-taught fashion. There were not so many terms to remember; just the right way to do things, with the proper tools, the right leverage to use, the right force to apply, what nail size was appropriate, and, of course, remembering that most things could be called "goop."

I was fifteen-and-a-half in the summer of '72; I was getting ready for my learner's permit, and I now had friends at Las Lomas High. I excelled at football and track and field. I had no girlfriends and hung out with the group of "Heads." The "Jocks" were kids into sports and the "Heads" were potheads, and then you had the "Nerds and Loners"—the smart kids from art and music class. I fell into all three groups and had friends in all of them. I moved quietly and diplomatically though the school scene. *Watch and learn if you want to survive.*

Life at home was unbearable. I started smoking marijuana—pot or weed we called it—in the fall of '72. My new friend, a fellow artist, track and football athlete, and Head friend, John Wilcox, offered it to me one night after I had snuck out of the house. I had walked two miles from my place to where he lived in the Rudgear Estates area. He saw what the deal was with Dad—that he plastered me with anger, physical bullying, and humiliation on the construction site that summer.

"Ralph, try this, bro, you could use this." "Ralph" as in "Ralph Kalskofski," my nickname from track that stuck, and was the only name I was known by in the various Head circles at school. It was my alter-ego hippie persona. I wore skinny ties as headbands with hiking boots, bell bottoms, and a "Detective Columbo" rain overcoat in the fall. I took my first hit and coughed. I had tried smoking my dad's unfiltered cigarettes and found nothing appealing about them (unlike a lot of my friends who had started smoking). This joint tasted real nice though. It soothed my ragged nerves. It made me feel mellow, and not angry or scared. Smoking pot was a new savior to me. We laughed and ate and laughed more. Getting stoned was nice. It made me happy. Smoking pot opened all my creative juices, and man did they flow. I oil painted, played Latin percussion including the congas, and wrote poetry. Drugs were part of me staying sane. I was self-medicating so I would not kill myself. Speed was another drug I tried. Wow, that stuff made me a jitter at zillion miles a minute. I dropped that quickly. I was already moving through life too fast anyway. The '70s were a time of exploration and personal expression. It was a time of rock 'n' roll, drugs, and, on the East Coast, the beginning of disco.

Valerie helped when she could on the construction site; she was still Stepmother's slave, but she would work with Dad on other projects in the future. Fred Jr. was not around. Even on school breaks he stayed with Mom in Piedmont, and if he was around he would complain and bitch until he got out of work. He refused to visit Dad on the weekends to get out of working. He did put in his two cents on labor though. "The only thing I will pick up is a pen to sign checks. Forget about picking up a hammer!" Fred had a point.

Through those hot summer days we sat in the hot shade of the work site. This was going to be the new home of my dad and stepmother. My friends and I were literally burnt out. Since moving in with Dad, he had trained me to persevere under extreme situations. He pushed and pushed me. He once said to me, "Ron, I am training you to be a captain of men, not a follower." He also said, "Ron, you are only good for me if you can work. You are nothing to me if you cannot work." I was really inspired to excel. (NOT!)

Valerie and I had been living with Dad and Stepmother and things went from unbearable to SNAFU ("Situation Normal, All F*cked Up!"). Valerie found her way of staying sane. She was getting older and sought out friendships in school. I watched her from the outside and knew she would make it all work out for herself. She knew I would be there if she really needed me. I was up to my neck with dealing with my dad and trying to figure out if I should stick around on this crazy planet. I remember on New Year's Eve, 1972, when the new place was closed up but not finished, Dad wanted me to stay at the house to guard the empty space. I was bummed. I wanted to party with my friends.

"No, you stay at the house and guard it. The house is not christened yet, and I want someone there," he said.

Arguing with him was pointless. I packed my sleeping bag, an old army cot, my newly bought stereo with a turntable, my Led Zeppelin, Black Sabbath, and Jimi Hendrix albums, and went to the empty home under construction. Before I left I told a friend where I would be: "I will be at the new house guarding it from f*ck-ups like you." Well, for some unexplained reason, word got around that there was a party at Ralph's new place; so there I was with my lonesome self, listening to Hendrix, when a knock on the door caught my attention. Upon opening the door ten of my friends walked in. The place was unfinished with no railings or proper lights, but hey! My friends were there to keep me company for New Year's, 1973! "Come on in!!!"

There were three girls I knew in the bunch of friends that came in. Beers and hard liquor were out with a lot of weed and loud music. Soon people I did not know started to show up. Suddenly, a buddy came rushing into the room, "Ralph! Your old man is here!" My heart went to my stomach. All the booze, smoke, pipes, and party material went out the second story sliding balcony door. My dad and stepmother appeared at the bedroom door, along with three unknown kids who were just arriving with them. Damn!

"What the goddamn hell is going on here, Ronnie?!?"

"Dad?"

Everybody's stoniness vanished. We were all sober and wide-eyed. The place reeked and Led Zeppelin's *Houses of the Holy* album was playing on the turntable.

"Turn that goddamn thing off!!!"

Music died. I died. My friends died.

Dad lined all my friends up against the bedroom wall and gave a sermon.

"My son has brought bad energy into this new home. This house is not even christened yet!" Dead silence. The smell of booze, cigarette smoke, and pot lingered in the air. "He was not to have anyone here. No one!"

I left my body as I watched my friends sway from being drunk, stoned, or both; they all looked with awe and fear at my dad. They had heard stories of him, but here he was in the flesh: Ralph's Dad.

"Go! All of you go!"

My friends left in a quiet hurry.

A friend whispered in my ear, "Ralph, I threw a lid of smoke out the balcony door. I'll get it tomorrow." Whatever.

Alone in the unfinished bedroom with Dad and Stepmother, we just stared at each other. I did not feel a thing. I floated above my body looking down at it. The single light bulb reminded me of being in an interrogation room.

"Pack your things and get back home, NOW!" His blazing red eyes spoke of things to come.

Upon arriving back at home the house was horribly bright with all the lights turned on. My sister Valerie was awake and looked sick with fear for me.

"GET IN HERE!!!" I remember walking into the bright living room. All was dream like. I floated above my body ready for a beating.

Dad was pacing and smoking his unfiltered cigs.

"We are so ashamed of you, Ronnie," Stepmother said.

"Damn YOU! YOU have disgraced the house and brought bad energy into our new home!" I watched as he came within an inch of my face with that crazed look in his eyes and then struck me. As I hovered above myself, I saw myself trying to defend against his attacks. My sister was screaming at Dad, Stepmother was screaming at Dad, Dad was screaming at me.

"Bring your goddamn stereo in here!"

Upon returning with the stereo, Dad grabbed the stereo cord and with his pocketknife he cut it. "No more goddamn music for you...damn you!"

When Dad went into a rage state his eyes would go "crazy eyes"; he shook with rage and fury. The rest of the night was a blur; my disembodied self dealt with the physical world as I floated above with the angels and heavenly things.

We finally moved into the new home the next year while it was still under construction. One day Dad and I fought at the home/work site. He beat me with a rolled up electrical extension cord. Then my stepmother and dad took off for dinner. This was my final beating. I had had enough.

"You have to leave and never come back," my little sister said to me with determination in her eyes. "Dad is crazy, he'll hurt you...you have to go." Valerie helped me pack my stuff into the newly bought car I paid $400 for—a 1964 Blue VW Squareback, which I named "Eleanor" after a flower that grew in the Land of Gondor (Duh! From *The Lord of the Rings*, of course). We quickly packed all my belongings into Eleanor, knowing Dad would be back soon. Valerie and I were both crying, knowing I was leaving. I would still see Valerie in school, but I was leaving her. My life was at stake.

I left my father's home. I was going to be sixteen years old with my new California driver's license. I was the disgraceful son. I was the sickly, stupid, slow son. He said that I was not even a real Rubio. I was gone. It was a sad and freeing day. My friend John and his family took me in like a mangy alley cat. I was on my own. I knew this was real and there was no turning back. Dad was furious to find me gone and still living in the same town. I was a disgrace to him and a humiliation because I was still living in Walnut Creek. I had left his home, his control, and his hate for me. Life was bizarre and sad. I loved him, but I just could not do anything right. I knew how to survive, and I would. I was still in high school. My sophomore year was halfway through.

I got a job as a dishwasher at night. On school nights I worked and came home smelling like cooked burger meat. I tried to pay rent to Ma Wilcox, John's mother, but she would not accept it. I tried to keep up with all the schoolwork, but I sucked at school except for art, music, and PE. Later, I got a job as a door-to-door salesman after school. "Hi, I am with Webster Dictionary Company," I would say. I had to learn and memorize a thick book of lines and sales pitches. My friends made fun of me as I practiced my lines stoned. I had decided to survive, provide for myself, and still finish high school.

The first night out in the field trying to sell dictionaries went like this: Ring the doorbell. Door opens. Door slams. Ring the doorbell. Door opens. Door slams. Door opens. Door slams. Now, if that did not humble any sorry sod, I do not know what would. Noting like a slamming door in my face to instill more confidence. But I never gave up, and, out of my sales group, I made the first sale in the first week. I made it at a 7-11 convenience store while waiting to buy something to eat before being picked up to head back to headquarters. I got talking to the guy in front of me, he liked what I had to say, and bought the whole dictionary package! I laid out my whole presentation right there on the aisles of the 7-11. Later I received my first-sale congratulatory bottle of Cold Duck, a nonalcoholic champagne. I was still under twenty-one. My shyness disappeared when I had to "perform." I surprised myself. Racism taught me to fear people and stay away from folks, their evil looks, and their raised-chin demeanor. I faced each door slam with a steel heart. Their shit was not going to bring me down. I would survive!

Being out of the house was liberating and my art excelled. I was an oil painter and illustrator. I had taken up the conga drums—I had a few uncles on my mother's side that were hot drummers. Pot smoking freed my shyness and fear, and I fell in love with life. My friends were the "Rudgear Boys," a collection of pot-smoking, gambling, hard drinking, hard-fighting, hard-partying males. We lived on the fringes of Walnut Creek in a housing spread called Rudgear Estates. From my home, the Wilcoxes' house, I was able to jump a fence and be in open pastureland spreading far to the east into the foothills of towering Mt. Diablo. Today, those pasturelands are now cement and square boxes for people to live in, but back then I lived at the brink of adventure and freedom.

On full moon nights I would pack up and take off deep into the foothills until the early morning hours. There was no one around me but the cows, the night birds, and open night sky. Damn, cows looked very weird in the moonlight. I feared nothing and accepted what was in front of me. The world was mine and no one was going to stop me. I was sixteen and free.

The girls associated with the Rudgear Boys were just as tough and easy. The girlfriends of certain Head friends were cute, sensuously beautiful, and into making out. I saw all this from afar because I was the silent, funny-at-times, cover-your-back-in-a-fight guy of the bunch. Though my friends accepted me easily, I was just a very socially awkward person who stayed in the shadows of the group. My romantic view of girls was still lost in the ancient fantasy world of *The Lord of the Rings*, and being a shy brown boy did not help either.

My social skills sucked, big time—girls found me so "nice," and yet, no girl wanted to be my "girlfriend." Try as I may, I was still the "Best Personality" award winner from seventh grade that every girl felt safe with. Boring! They could confide in me their "girlie" troubles with their boyfriends "as easily as I can talk to my best friend." Boring! I was bumming out. So work, art, music, sports, and partying soothed my confused teenaged life.

My senior prom was an example of how big a social loser I was. I could not go with the girl I wanted. At the last moment, I asked a really nice buxom Head friend I kind of knew who was a junior. She would not hold hands with me or give me a kiss or anything. I was just a free ticket to the prom for her.

Later, at the senior dance at the St. Francis Hotel, I was called to the stage by my classmates to play the congas along with the hired band. The night ended with the Rudgear Boys, in oblivion without my date. I forgot at what point she left me.

High school came to a merciful end for me in 1975. I had moved out of the Wilcoxes' the year before, and now lived in an upstairs apartment rented to me by a Head friend's mother. I had also found a job at the local country club, the Round Hill Country Club. This is where all the rich, old, white men gathered. I was a dishwasher and making good money. I paid for all my living expenses and was still attending high school. My friends' parents all thought this very peculiar. One day at the country club I asked the chef, a Frenchman by the name of George Rey, for a raise. Now, Chef Rey had once said to me, "You know Ron, I like Filipinos. You people are good hard workers." So after kicking ass for months I asked for a higher wage.

Approaching the chef I said, "Chef, do you got a moment?"

"Mr. Filipino, what can I do for you"?

"Well, Chef, I have been working hard and would like a raise."

"You do?"

"Yes. I feel that I have been kicking ass and I will be graduating from high school and I live on my own, as you know."

"Yes."

"Yes. So could you give me a raise?"

Chef Rey looked at me intensely and then said, "Follow me." He went back to the dishwashing station, my station, and yelled, "George, can you bring me a box of canned fruit?" "Yes Chef!" George was the line cook, my friend, and an amateur boxer with a baby boy. George retrieved a box of canned fruit from the storage room.

"Place the box right here, George." Chef pointed to the floor in front of the industrial-size dishwasher.

I was thinking, "Damn, Chef is just going to get me working and not talk about the raise."

"Filipino, come here."

"Yes, Chef."

"Stand on this box."

I did so unquestioningly.

"There," Chef Rey said, "There is your raise!"

The kitchen staff broke out in hysterical laughter. Chef was beet-red in the face laughing so hard at me. I was pissed! It was not wise to make fun of a Filipino with so many sharp knives nearby!

"Ah, Filipino...you don't like your raise?"

With a kitchen full of sharp knifes I had visions of a bloodbath of spilled French blood! "Not really, Chef," I answered with contained anger, rage, and embarrassment.

He announced aloud, laughing, "Ah, Filipino does not like his raise!"

"Chef, there is no future in dishwashing!" I tried to hold my ground. The kitchen staff went quiet by this time with the occasional snickering.

"Ah, Filipino..." Chef said, "Okay, I will give you a raise and you will become my apprentice. But, you have to wash dishes still." I was floored! From ridicule to accomplishment.

"Thank you, Chef. I won't let you down."

The kitchen staff were smiling and chuckling before they returned to their workstations.

"Now, Filipino, open the box of fruit and help me prepare the fruit salad."

"Yes, Chef!"

So I got my raise, and I was promoted to Chef's apprentice. Not bad. I went back to school the next day feeling good.

As graduation day drew closer, the principal announced over the intercom one morning that any senior interested in speaking at the graduating ceremonies should talk to the English teacher and the speech committee. I was very interested. I felt the mortality of my high school year experience coming to a close, and I knew I would never see some of these folks again. I knew the whole senior class of 1975. Being a weird, artistic, musical, silent kid, I knew all the loners and quirky artsy kids. Having been a Jock I knew the jock crowd and the "Rah Rahs." And also being a Head, someone who smoked, partied, and hung with the hippies, I literally knew the whole class of seniors. Nothing would be more fitting than for me to speak to all my high school friends at graduation. I went to the English teacher and applied. He pondered my speech, sent me up to the speech committee, and I was approved.

My speech talked about life after the big graduation party and moving forward into our destinies. The class of 1975 grew up during the civil rights movement of the '60s, the winding-down of the Vietnam War in the early '70s, the building up of the Cold War and the threat of nuclear destruction between the United States and Russia, the beginning of eco-awareness ("Save the whales!"), and incredible music. My speech was about how we would make a difference. I drew from my own life story of going to high school, working to pay rent, my car insurance, and all my other life expenses. I was going to speak to my friends for the last time and send them off into the world with my fellow eighteen-year-old words of wisdom.

Soon enough June rolled up and graduation was just days away. A month earlier I started to date a silent artsy girl one grade behind me. She was the sister of a very popular fellow senior who was a varsity cheerleader. Laurie was not at all like her sister. Our courtship was sweet and romantic with dinners on the weekends in San Francisco and hikes in the Berkeley Hills and in deep redwood forests. We held hands and never kissed. I was still way too shy and very much a virgin at eighteen years old. Though I was a rough, tough partier, and a brother of the Rudgear Boys, I was still a very shy, poetry-writing, oil-painting, classical trumpet- and French horn-playing guy living in a romantic action warrior fantasy. Laurie was my gentle princess who I wrote poetry and love letters to expressing my heart's dear feelings. She must have been bored by my shyness, and yet, she went out with me. I was gaining the strength to figure out this crazy world.

On the day of graduation I was taking the last long walk to high school even though I could have driven there in my car. On the way I spied something glittering on the hot country road. When I was close enough I picked up the small aluminum packet. Upon opening it I discovered it contained a nice chunk of strong smelling black hashish. Good omen! The day was going to be a party! I reached the high school and gathered with the rest of the graduating class of 1975. Excitement, sadness, happiness, cockiness, and spaciness filled the air. We got dressed into our gowns and got in formation. Being in the school band I went ahead of the main group with my other band mates to take our place in the "pit" to play "Pomp and Circumstance" for our peers. How fitting. The ceremony was held on the football field with the families seated in the stands. It was packed, and the day was sunny and slightly windy. The music teacher raised his baton and we began to play. My friends began the long walk toward their seats. Flashing lights and cheers went up. I had to focus to keep playing. With all seated the speeches began.

The principal addressed the field and then introduced me: I was the first speaker to begin the ceremonies. Cries of "Ralph Kalskofski" rang out—my Head name, and the only name some knew me by. "Rubio!" others cried out. I smiled to my peers as I walked up to the podium and faced the packed stadium stands of family members with my back to my classmates. I began, "Welcome. My dear seniors and peers I want to wish you..." then a strong gust of wind came up and blew my speech out of my hands! I watched in dismay as the paper flew across the football field toward the opposite end zone. Damn!

The crowd of parents gasped, the seniors laughed, I was stunned. I worked hard not to leave my body. Then I just started to improvise. "I just want to begin by greeting the parents and families of the class of 1975!"

Great cheers and applause! Simple enough. As I looked at the stadium of parents and families, I realized that the seniors, whom my speech was for, were behind me. So I turned myself around on the podium, twisted the microphone to the sound of electrical static, and faced my friends with my back to the parents. I caught the eye of the principal and saw the School Board honchos just looking at me. They were holding their breaths.

"This is better!" The senior class of 1975 roared and laughed.

"Listen, we are going to have a great time tonight...we made it!" another hearty roar. "Our lives begin tomorrow when we wake up with a nice hangover. But what are you going to do when the party is truly over...?" I scanned my whole class of fellow seniors in silence. The rest of my speech talked about life, working hard, and how I made it through high school. Some knew my life, while others had no idea. What I said after that was forgotten in time. I remember my friends applauding and cheering after I finished. My mother said I was stoned up there at the podium and that I was talking nonsense. I wasn't stoned and I hadn't talked nonsense.

Upon walking up to receive my diploma from the principal I remember the whole world around him and me going dim and silent. As I reached out to shake his hand with my right, and reached out with my left to receive my piece of paper, the world stopped. I saw his mouth moving, but he would not let go of my diploma. "Interesting speech, Mr. Rubio." I grabbed the diploma out of his hands and never looked back. It was over. I was a proud C+ graduate of Las Lomas High School's class of 1975.

Two months after graduating I lost a dear friend. Jon Ralph and I ran track together and competed in the high and low hurdles. He was a strapping, tall, blond Apollo and I was a short, muscular, brown boy; the top of my head came up to his sternum. We took first and second in all our hurdle events at track meets. We partied together and were brothers. Jon had the girls, the grades, and the future. He was supposed to go places. During the summer of '75 he was learning how to fly when his single-prop plane took a dive into the Benicia Straits. His body, and that of his flight instructor, could not be retrieved for months. Jon lay at the bottom of the Straits in the cold, dark waters. The thought of him lying there disturbed the Rudgear Boys badly. He was eighteen years old and beautiful. Life went on.

Woolly Mammoth Boy heard the howls of the predators as the last light of dusk and faded to night. The deadly saber-toothed tigers, coming down from their mountainous lairs deep in the high peaks, were on the blood scent of their prey.

His fellow young bull woolly mammoths had created the herd's defensive circle for the night: the young and old in the middle, the fighters out on the rim.

"The boy grows strong. He learns and adapts," Thought sang through the night breeze.

"Yes, he does," Woolly Mammoth Boy answered to a shooting star streaking above his head as he shuffled closer to his brethren to tighten up the perimeter. "I saw that he grows the small tusks, though his fellow young manlings do not see them." He smiled at the thought as he heard a rustle in the dark, and swung his bulk toward that direction.

"You were right, my little one, he is growing strong," a vibration of Thought tingled his trunk. "He stands and holds his ground."

A sudden cry of fear slashed through the darkness. The predators had found a victim and the death song would soon follow. Woolly Mammoth Boy thought of the young sister mammoth taken by a ferocious, full-grown cave bear that had lain in ambush at a narrow mountain pass a few days back.

"Nothing is offered for nothing. The promise of a full life cycle is not guaranteed to any living being," Woolly Mammoth Boy snorted as he scanned futilely into the impregnable darkness, on high alert now. The sounds of savage combat and struggle echoed though the thin night air—the predators were making their kill. An anguished death scream shattered the blackness before his eyes.

"Yes, little one, all that transpires happens in the blinking gleam of a distant star," Thought gestured as a bright firefly landing on one of Woolly Mammoth Boy's long, curved, ivory tusks. "In one moment you could be here, and in the next moment, you could be returned to the Void."

"The young manling now knows this fact. He has caught a glimpse of mortality; the hand that takes away and returns nothing," Woolly Mammoth Boy offered to the starless night that was filled with the sounds of feeding.

23. Bolinas and *In Watermelon Sugar*

The herd stumbled upon the great vastness of the Ocean by sheer luck. Having been driven off course by predators and unforeseen natural obstacles, we came out of the valley and into the expanse before the great waters. Thirsty, we ran toward the crashing waves. The lead mammoth signaled us to stop as she ventured forward alone. A light wind whipped the sand upon which we stood into our eyes as we watched and waited. We saw her go into the crashing waves and drink. She spewed out the water and trumpeted irritably. The waters were undrinkable! It was then that we realized, as the brine caked our eyelashes, that the waters were salt.

–Woolly Mammoth Boy Remembers

BOLINAS WAS, AND STILL IS, a little town blending into the Pacific Ocean about forty miles north of San Francisco, settled after the 1849 Gold Rush. Back then in the late 1800s it took four days of a bumpy carriage ride out of Sausalito, after a ferry from San Francisco, to reach the windswept sand hills where the foundations of the wooden town of Bolinas were embedded.

I was acquainted with the area from my rite-of-passage journey almost six and a half years earlier: the Marin coastal mountain range, Muir Woods, Point Reyes up the road, and Stinson Beach.

One of the many road trips taken by the Rudgear Estates Boys during my high school days was to Bolinas. The two-hour ride in Phil Gangee's 1970s Continental big-boat car was well worth it. Bolinas was as magical then as it is now. The vastness of the Pacific Ocean spread far and wide as one looked from the cliffs above Agate Beach at the end of the Mesa—where soil meets erosion, and where rock meets pounding salt water ocean. There is definitely an ending and a beginning in Bolinas. There is no mistaking it. You never knew when you were standing on solid ground or when you might be swept away at Poseidon's fancy.

After graduating from high school, I moved to Bolinas. I found a job as the night chef at the Gibson House Hotel in town. The Gibson House Hotel was one of the original buildings dating back to the founding of Bolinas in the late 1800s, after the Gold Rush of 1849. The hotel carried a lot of history, and was a watering hole for the peculiar night creatures of the town. I had some cooking skills underneath my belt after working my way up from dishwasher to chef's apprentice at the Round Hill Country Club. I had also been taking cooking classes at night at the local junior college. I bought my first chef blades and was confident and excited about cooking. I was a hard worker and was not afraid to strike out on my own. Before leaving for Bolinas, I had approached the chef where I worked, Chef Rey, and I told him of my desire to move on. He was wary of my plan.

"Filipino, stay a little bit longer and learn a bit more, gain more experience."

"Chef Rey, I want to move out of here, I want to see this world on my own. I want to move to Bolinas. I applied for a night chef position at the local hotel and got it!"

He looked at me and I could tell he was admiring my gusto for life as a young man. He was probably thinking of his own apprenticeships in France. Like my Austrian stepfather Horst had done in his youth, Chef Rey had left home and tried out his own wings. The difference was that these two men actually finished their training and came out masters in their respective culinary fields of expertise. True to my character I decided to act in a fashion that would remain part of me for the rest of my life: impulsively, based on an inner gut desire, and not allowing anything to change my mind. I had burned my hand before and I knew when to take it off the flame. I wanted to live life on my own terms. Trying to understand the logic behind the social world around me was just too confusing. I was going to do this my way. Sometimes this strategy was great, other times it was disastrous. It did not matter, I would learn on my own—like I had always done up to this point in my young life.

My wings were not dry and not developed, but the gusto to try was there. Within a month I was living in Bolinas. I was now eighteen years old. I still had Eleanor, my ocean-blue '64 VW Squareback, and I was able to pack everything I owned into it. My plan was simple: cook at night, and oil paint, write poetry, and play music during the day. I found a room to rent in a home on the Big Mesa. My dream had come true. I was living in a beach town and pursuing my art. Now this is where fiction would meet reality.

Bolinas in the early '70s was hit by a big oil spill. Standard Oil Company paid the yippies and hippies from the streets of Haight-Ashbury, San Francisco, and radical Berkeley to clean up the mess. The funds to clean the beaches eventually went dry, and most of the flower people went back to where they came from, but not all. The ones who stayed lived on the beaches, parks, or, if you left the door open to your house, on your couch.

I had just finished reading a book that really impressed me: *In Watermelon Sugar*, by the late author Richard Brautigan. The little novelette was a tale about the magical town of "iDEATH" and the magical folks who lived there. The love lives and relationships of the town folks revolved around watermelon sugar. The antagonist in the book was named "inBOIL." Bolinas was a reflection of this book to me. There was a leftover yippie from "The Spill" who called himself "Icon." If you were not careful you would find Icon in your home, taking what he wanted and generally causing mischief and trouble for the Bolianians. Icon added to the already-eccentric flair of Bolinas, yet with him came dangerous and dark overtones. He had his followers, who, like him, were not to be trusted. You had to keep an eye out for your personals around Icon. There were times I found him in my home hanging around and eating whatever he wanted. An open door was an open door, and Icon would walk right on through with his followers. Then one day something happened with a young girl or something like that, and Icon's name was mentioned in the story. It was not much later that the town "elders" ran Icon and his hooligans out of Bolinas. I heard about threats and people disappearing without a trace amongst the bluffs. Icon was gone before anyone knew it.

For me, the town graveyard in Bolinas was a favorite place for me to hang when I wanted to be warm, cozy, and alone. A bike ride from the center of town, up and down the Mesa, led to the graveyard that was nestled in a stand of ancient Eucalyptus trees. A quiet place, the souls of the early pioneers of the town and their descendants were all buried there. I was, and still am, attracted to graveyards. The stories of the dead seeped from the cold stones into my heart and mind, like in the book *Spoon River Anthology*. The first time I went there, I was drawn to a particular gravestone. It was dedicated to a young woman, Katherine McMullin, a native of New Jersey who died almost 100 years prior and whose birthday was around the same time of year as mine. We were the same age—give or take 100 years. I imagined her coming to these barren sand hills, and facing the fierce winter storms that came inland off the Pacific Ocean back in the 1870s. I saw her brokenhearted from leaving the East Coast for this foreign and hostile land, falling sick with pneumonia, and dying so far away from her birthplace. Sad. I promised to visit her often and I did. Most of the time I was alone in the graveyard. The warm summer months guaranteed a dry, warm, and quiet place to go, surrounded by tall, pungent-smelling eucalyptus trees and the sounds of huge black crows cawing. Poison ivy strangled a lot of the older gravestones. I noticed a lot of young people buried there. I felt at home. The quietness soothed me.

The days were dry and smelled good, and the nights were filled with fog and spectral spirits. The nights would find me painting until the early morning after working at the Gibson House. I painted on fresh canvas with my turntable nearby. For hours on end I would play the same song and oil paint. As the song came to an end I would turn to the stereo, lift the arm of the phonograph needle, and place it at the beginning of the same song. This would go on for hours. I painted roughly ten paintings in Bolinas.

There were other nights I would rehearse with the Bolinas jazz band as the percussionist. The band was made up by men of all ages, and from all walks of Bolinian life. I was the "young blood" of the band. Once, on the way to a gig in Sausalito, we were driving down Highway 1 along the coast. I stopped my VW at a favorite parking spot so I could look upon Bolinas. What I saw caught my breath. In the distance, Bolinas was bathed with a beam of light coming down from above, or going up to the heavens. I mean it was a true vertical beam of light right on top of Bolinas. There were other cars stopped looking at it, too. I did not care what others said of Bolinas; this town was from another planet, and it was a home to out-of-this-world inhabitants.

In the late summer of '76, my stepfather called me up and asked me if I wanted to drive up to Oregon and scout out a bakery he was interested in. My mother would be coming up with us as well, and I said, "Sure." I was in the frame of mind that it would be cool to learn baking and see what this green state of Oregon was all about. At the time there was a book out called *Ecotopia*. It was about the fictional secession from the union of the states of Washington, Oregon, and the northern part of California, including the San Joaquin Valley. The idea was that this new land, called "Ecotopia"—which had the richest of forests, an abundance of fishing and fresh water, and at the time produced most of the world's produce—could live as a separate entity. Cool! I was sold on going north. The trip was a success: Horst wanted the bakery, and he offered me a job to help take over from the departing owners, the Nogas, and learn some baking skills. Oregon here I come! I was leaving everything behind and going into the unknown.

There was one person I had to say goodbye to—Laurie, back in "Creektown." Even though I lived in Bolinas I would still see her as often as I could. We really liked each other. On the night I was to leave for Oregon I saw her one last time. As I was saying something to her in the garden of her house, she drew me into her and kissed me strongly. I responded with vigor. She placed my hand upon her breast and kissed me deeply. I was happily shocked. Laurie had been wanting this all along from me and I was just too shy and naïve to see it. Well, not anymore. With great regret we parted. I was never to see her again.

It was easy to pick up and leave. It was easy to pack everything I owned into my VW and head out into the unknown. The naïveté of my actions, of my trust in the great wide world, drove me without a second thought. Would there be a time like this again? I had shed my winter fur from the top of my mammoth head. It was time to head north to Oregon.

Once, after the great mammoth migration to fertile feeding grounds, Woolly Mammoth Boy ventured away alone from his foraging brethren to some low-lying hills in the distance. He was now a young bull woolly mammoth: powerful, naïvely strong-willed, and daringly adventurous.

"You and your earthly incarnate share the vitality of youth, and the wisdom of an opening flower: so new, fresh and yet, fragile," Thought tickled his eyelash as a tiny mosquito.

He followed a worn path vaguely visible in the hard soil: the trail of the two-legged ones. The path led into a large cave whose opening allowed his huge mass to enter easily.

Strewn about were the white, dry bones of the two-leggeds' prey. Large circles of dark charcoal lay scattered as well. On the cave walls were drawn figures of animals and the two-legged ones. He recognized the depictions of his kind: the woolly mammoths.

Lines were drawn sticking out of their bodies. Woolly Mammoth Boy had seen how the two-legged animals brought down their prey by throwing sticks at them. Here, he was viewing a hunt. He grunted at the sight of what seemed to be a successful kill of a mammoth.

"They have learned much to survive in their world, as you have done, my little one," Thought breezed through the cave as a gust that stirred the black charcoal at Woolly Mammoth Boy's feet, as he stared angrily at the drawings of the mammoth hunt before him. "Trial and error is the path of evolution, and thus the successful continuation of any living being."

He scanned the walls of drawings, and thought of all that he had learned while surviving the early years in which he grew into the young bull mammoth he was now. Many of his peers of his early youth had fallen prey to the killers, to the dark swamps and the black pits that drew one under to vanish forever.

"I challenged my life so I may become the lead bull mammoth someday," Woolly Mammoth Boy said into the cool, dank cave air.

"Yes, I have witnessed your achievements, and your near-fatal mistakes," Thought validated. "You, like your manling incarnate, have always done it your way—to the irritation of your elders and teachers."

"And why not?" Woolly Mammoth Boy echoed into the cold stone. "Did not my mentors try their 'own' ways to become unique, and thereby show the initiative, creativity, and ingenuity to be leaders?"

"Yes, your mentors did. They carried the wisdom of the ones who came before them as well," Thought answered as bustling red ants scurrying at Woolly Mammoth Boy's feet. "Tried ways are also safe ways."

Woolly Mammoth Boy shook his huge matted head in agitation, his long curved tusks scraping the cave walls to dust. "Yes, tried ways are safe—for lazy followers. I will continue to dare my world as I dare all to try and stop me."

Trumpeting loudly in defiance, Woolly Mammoth Boy exited the cool manling cave, leaving it to wither into the isolated dust from which it came.

He could hear Thought's bellowing laughter in challenging amusement.

24. Croissants and Vampires: The Journey North to Oregon

I saw young Woolly Mammoth Boy, who was now a human once again, as I was once before. I looked down from where I flew above him as Woolly Mammoth Hawk Boy. The Great Universe is an amazing place where we can be in many forms, in many places, and in many different times, at the same instant. Seeing Woolly Mammoth Boy, I could easily discern the energy shape of his woolly mammoth head around his now structurally human head. And me...I was Woolly Mammoth Boy reborn as Woolly Mammoth Hawk Boy. The laws of the Great Universe will not allow me to cross the dimensions of space and time and interact with young Woolly Mammoth Boy, but I can be present to him as Woolly Mammoth Hawk Boy, and observe him as a hawk would a rabbit in the open.

–Woolly Mammoth Boy Remembers

I LOADED ALL THAT I OWNED as a nineteen-year-old man into Eleanor, my 1964 VW Squareback, a quirky little German-made car with a "pancake" engine in the back of the car where the trunk would normally be. I admired the German who designed this car, because he must have been stoned or suffering from shell shock from too many Allied bombings back in World War II to come up with this unique car.

I remember the exciting feeling of being back on the road. Alone, self-sufficient, self-reliant, like being on a quest, like Frodo Baggins—the Hobbit with his life on his back, and venturing into the unknown on his big hairy feet. The journey was heading north into the state of Oregon. I loaded up Eleanor, and left by late afternoon on a hot summer day in July 1976. Mom, Horst, my younger brother Shawn, and some of their friends were driving the U-Haul truck and the family car; they were going to caravan the trip together. I was on my own as the vanguard. I left hours before them.

I drove up the center of the state, through the seemingly vast, open lands of central California, and into the no-man's-land of northern California toward the border of Oregon. Long stretches of brown lands, distant mountains in the east, and small redneck farming towns, with their large numbers of migratory Mexican workers, dotted the lonely landscape. I passed the massive, white peak of Mt. Shasta in the far northern lands during the early night; I could feel its immense, Earthpower in the growing darkness. Climbing the Siskiyou Mountains and through the Siskiyou Pass, I entered the state of Oregon around 10:00 p.m.—driving and driving into newness, passing from all that was into what will be; driving and driving into places of strangeness and tall tress, where the stars were bright.

After almost crashing on the road due to fatigue, Eleanor and I stumbled into the sleepy town of Cottage Grove at 3:00 a.m. I found our new house, parked my VW in front, and fell dead asleep in my cramped seat. Waking brought a foul taste to my morning mouth and the tired, but happy, arrival of the rest of my family. The unpacking happened quickly and then, after a few hours, our friends headed back to California, and we were left to begin our new lives in Oregon.

The summers were hot in Oregon, and this new place was just beautiful. Cottage Grove was a town locked in some type of weird time warp. It was as if the town had stayed in the 1950s. There was one black cop in town, and everyone had a family history or connection with the logging industry that went back for generations. The local lake was just right for fresh-water swimming, and the hills were covered with tall green trees. The place was just beautiful until I saw the raw patches of harvested, clear-cut forest. The rich, green trees had been abruptly cleaned off into huge square patches of stumps and dark soil many square miles wide. It was as if the great gods above had come down and ripped the trees right out of the ground—like they were picking flowers for their heavenly flower vases. What was left were stumps, mangled remnants of trees, and tons of firewood material for anyone who wanted to drive up these lonely logging roads and fill a pickup truck. Later, tree planters would come in and plant tree young'uns to fill in the emptiness where their brethren once grew majestically.

Now, it must be said that the Oregonians are fair and friendly folk; they were also big eaters and thus big folk. Back in 1976, Cottage Grove, like most small Oregon towns, had a healthy population of newly graduated high school-aged married couples with newborns, and life in a small logging town was simple. You either drank cold beer, smoked pot, or did both; you got your girlfriend pregnant and then worked for Weyerehouser, the local monster lumber company. Killing trees was dangerous business. Many stories abounded of loggers losing limbs or dying from runaway chainsaws, snapped metal logging lines taking off a head, bodies crushed by rolling trees and machinery, or gruesome logging truck accidents where fully loaded and harvested trees slammed into the cab, crushing the driver after a sudden stop. That is the way it was and logging folks did not mind it.

Having pulled into this sleepy Oregon lumber town with my black California plates and my handmade Led Zeppelin car stickers pasted on it, I kind of stood out. Being one of the few darker people in town didn't help, either. But to hell with it, I was here to help my stepfather out; we had a bakery to learn about, and were going to ensure a positive transition from the leaving owners, the Nogas. These Nogas were a real bunch of characters. The three baking sons loved to play tricks on me in the wee early baker hours between 1:00 a.m. and sunrise, and that was just the way it was. I was used to this form of relationship from a lifetime of dealing with white folks and working on crews.

Baker hours were the "ghoul-like walking dead" early hours, when most people are sleeping and drooling. In those early hours I had to learn how to make donuts over a hot vat of oil, how to prepare dough for the breads and batter for the cakes, and how to package all the goods for sale. In the furious three-month training from the Nogas, before the bakery ownership was to change hands to my stepfather, we worked hard and long hours.

"Look here and learn," Larry Noga said to me during one morning shift at 2:00 a.m. He stood in front of the vat of boiling oil used for frying up the donut dough. "You got to be real careful working this station," he grinned. Now, when Larry Noga would start grinning, you had to be real careful for any prank he would pull. Larry began a slow, drawling story as I impatiently waited. "There was this guy we hired to work here. One morning he comes on in after a night of drinkin' and starts up the oil vat for the donuts." I had a sick, stupid feeling where this story was heading. "Well, this sorry sod of a baker was not paying attention to his footing and slipped. He fell face first into the vat and melted his face right off." I looked at Larry and his grin widened like he just took a shit in his pants. I looked around and his other two brothers were just grinning at me.

"Thanks, Larry, I'll be careful." And before he turned away I said, "Oh, Larry...by the way...f*ck yourself." The Noga brothers burst out laughing and my hell training continued.

Now, I found nothing wrong with being a baker—except for the vampire hours I had to work. I had to go to sleep at 5:00 p.m., while the sun was still out in the summer hours and darkness came at 9:00 p.m., and then I had to wake up at 12:30 a.m. to be back at the bakery by 1:00 a.m. This madness got out of hand, badly. I have to admit, driving through town at that time in morning was quite peaceful, though it took time for the Cottage Grove cops to get used to me and not stop me every morning the first month. Like— What the hell is wrong with you guys? I am a f*cking baker going to work in the only bakery in this town. It's as if you have such a busy beat you can't figure it out after the first week of stopping me? Damn!

My stepfather Horst was a baker supreme. His buttery croissants were the best a Swiss-trained baker could make. Oregonians in this little town had never seen a croissant before, let alone all the excellent European baked goods he put out. These Cottage Grove folks loved their potato loaf breads and iced, custard-filled donuts. It took time, but finally Horst's great pastries and sweets were a hit. One day, after months of this baking job, and after gaining twenty-plus pounds from eating freshly baked croissants and donuts every day, I told Horst I could not take the vampire hours any longer, gaining all this weight, and starting to look like one of the friggin' locals. The bakery was now under control, we had made the transition from the Nogas successfully, and Horst was doing okay. Horst said "Thank you," and I quit.

The bakery days were over and I was twenty pounds heavier. I quickly found work at the local motor hotel. These motor hotels could be found up and down U.S. Highway 5 at the time. Traveling up and down the northwest by car was the thing to do back then if you were retired and had money. The Village Green in Cottage Grove was a five-star motor hotel in its heyday, and I was accepted as a line cook in the morning and was later switched to dinner cook. I always knew that the cooking trade was a good job to learn. Always out of the elements, eating my fill, and, if I were good enough, I could find work anywhere, anytime.

One day I met one of the grounds maintenance personnel before starting my cooking shift. Her name was Michelle Cahill. She was my age and drove a 1959 wood-sided Chevy station wagon. The year before I had bought a white 1957 Chevy pickup from Larry Noga. Michelle was a big-boned woman, and though not exactly pretty, she had a great smile and a gleam in her eye. She was to become my first full-time lover and girlfriend. Her small-town mentality was sweet and it put me at ease. Life was real mellow and slow. I was learning so much about being in a relationship with a woman.

Yet, true to part of my character, which always enjoyed stimulation and newness, I started to get itchy for change and adventure. I started to get bored with Michelle and small-town life. Our relationship felt like a small mountain stream moving toward the ocean; it could not contain me or make me want to be contained. Desire for newness was in the air. How our relationship was going to develop, or end, was not on my radar.

After leaving the bakery, I had found a small cottage on the edge of town where I could paint and live alone. It was here that I started to finish my hot showers with ice-cold Oregon water right out of the pipes. I had the image of wanting to be purified by water. I think I almost passed out the first time I did this, but I have been doing this ever since. Oregon invited me to newness and freshness. 1976 was coming to a close and I knew that all was well with me.

The sparkling stars glistened in the morning sunlight as Woolly Mammoth Boy spouted fountains of blue-clear water from his long trunk into the air above his woolly head. He was alone and bathing in a large, deep pond that was mountain spring-fed.

He had taken to wandering a little ways from the herd to explore at his own leisure once the herd settled into one place safely. He knew his responsibilities as a young bull mammoth to his herd, and therefore, he was aware of his relationship to them...Woolly Mammoth Boy stayed connected in his independence.

He was now mature enough to attract and mate with the females in the herd if he wished. Yet he found the mammoth social hierarchical rituals for mating to be boring and painfully time-consuming. He knew that as long as he stayed with the herd, he must conform to the laws of the herd as passed down by the first woolly that had trodden this rock.

The cold water he bathed in stung his consciousness to clarity. He was going to be a leader under the Matriarch someday. He knew that, and yet—there had to be more to this life.

"Why so impatient, my little one?" Thought questioned from a tiny fish near his submerged ear.

"I feel a restlessness to be...to be validated that 'I am,'" Woolly Mammoth Boy gurgled, with a mouth full of water.

"You are who you are...this validates you," Thought answered as a falling leaf.

"Your existence is your validation!"

"NO!" Woolly Mammoth Boy spouted to the open sky above him. "I desire to be seen by the others."

"Ah, the cravings of the young," a whisper trickled into his sternum. "Crave then, my little one. Crave until you crave no more."

25. Mushroom Heaven and Nijinsky

There are many deadly poisons upon Gaia. Some are unseen for they are airborne; others are soluble in water and there for the innocent, while others can be inflicted by a bite or fang. Be wary! Yet always remember, a little poison is always needed for the body to strengthen the immune system, for its deadly gift enables you to adjust to the adversities you may encounter.

–The Observations of Woolly Mammoth Boy

IN JANUARY 1977, I BEGAN thinking about finally going to college. I was a year and a half out of high school and the small city just north of Cottage Grove, Eugene, was home to a great junior college as well as a four-year college, the University of Oregon, where the mascot was a duck. Apparently, back in the 1930s Walt Disney allowed the U of O to use the cartoon character Donald Duck as their mascot. Now, coming from California where college mascots were ferocious animals or macho characters like the USC Trojans, UC Bears, or UCLA Bruins, having a duck as a mascot seemed damn near embarrassing. The college just north of Eugene, Oregon State University, had a beaver as a mascot. What the hell! Back in the '60s and '70s a "beaver" was affiliated with the female genitalia, and a duck, well, a duck was a friggin' duck for god's sake! Needless to say I have been a die-hard Ducks fan ever since.

I started up at the Lane County Community College (LCC) in the spring of 1977. Being an artist and musician, my first semester at LCC was 19 credits of art and music classes. Being so involved with college, I moved up to Eugene to be closer to the school. Michelle and small-town Cottage Grove were slowly moving out of my life. Michelle was my first true relationship, and the breaking-up thing was totally unknown to me. I was trying to be nice, which just made it worse. What I did not offer to our relationship was any attempt at trying to understand what her side of our relationship meant to her. I could understand her pain and frustration with me, but I did not understand how to communicate with her. I was causing her pain and I did not know how to just drop her. I had outgrown the relationship, but I could not tell her this. I tried to deceive her with lies, and I was a total failure with that strategy. She finally saw the inevitable, protected herself, and ended the relationship for us. I was relieved and thankful. It was a mess. I did not understand how selfish I had been and I would not learn that lesson for many, many years. My romantic self and my fantasy world got what they wanted, and I was now on to something else. This was a life lesson I was to experience over and over again through my life—the world was not just about me.

    The move to Eugene was made easier when I applied for and got a job at the Valley River Inn, the sister hotel of the Village Green in Cottage Grove, as a cook and banquet cook. I was set for money, which allowed me to focus on school and create a new life in Eugene. Just focusing on what I wanted to study—art and music—was a dream. Academics were too conforming for me. At the time, I was not disciplined enough to do "solid" college courses, but it was a dream come true moving to a college town. I liked being around cool, groovy young folks, and being free. I met some old high school buddies by chance who were going to the U of O. They turned me on to peyote and "shrooms"—psychedelic mushrooms. Carlos Castañeda's books were hitting the bookstands, and peyote and shrooms were the incredible, invaluable, mind-expanding experience that was "in." At that time in Oregon you could pick your own shrooms, for they grew in the farmlands.

    This particular shroom was called the Liberty Cap, and they grew on cow dung. Their life span and window of growth was a delicate balance of morning light, moisture, and a cow-dung host. Too much sunlight burned them and wasted them. Too much moisture drowned them. One had to drive west toward the coast in the early morning, find a farmer's cow pasture fields, jump the barbed-wire fence, and wait for the sun to break the horizon and look for fresh cow dung. Now, you had to be careful of a mushroom that looked just like the Liberty Cap, but made you sicker than a dog. You had to be real careful and not so greedy, so as not to pick too quickly and make the wrong choice, but when did you identify the right shroom, it was a pick-all-you-can-eat kind of thing.

    Peyote buttons were a different beast all together. You had to be super-careful. Peyote has a protective armor you have to be very aware of. It contains a white, bitter alkaloid poison called strychnine—used to poison rats. The trick was to clean off the white furry nodules of strychnine with a blade. You can eat the buttons raw at that point, (they reminded me of dried-up fruit with a leathery consistency), or grind them up and put them in gelatin capsules. In most cases you would get sicker than a dog, throw up, and then get really high. If you drank an acid, like orange juice or something similar, it would balance out the alkaline of the strychnine, and you might get away without getting sick. I never threw up on them. I was twenty years old when I ate my first peyote button. The world turned into bright colors, sounds were magnified, and everything around me was alive with electric vibrancy. The complex world was rendered down to the quietness of an atom—my whole life made sense to me. The confusing social world of lies, bigotry, and the racism of my past were dust to the inner realization that I was One with the Universe, and everything else was just an illusion.

I never hallucinated on peyote or shrooms like others did. One of my friends saw little pink elephants running around in his apartment after I gave him a handful of fresh shrooms.

"Get in here, quickly!!!" He beckoned toward his apartment.

"What?"

"Man, there are little pink elephants running around my apartment!"

I went into his place, sat on the couch beside him, and waited in silence for a sighting.

"There! Look! Right there!" He pointed toward the kitchen.

I could not see what he saw.

"There! Can you see them?"

"Nope…" I left him to his pink elephants and went for a nice long bike ride around Eugene.

Psychedelics had tuned me in to my connection to the subtle flow of energy around me in the form of waves of color and light. It was as if I could go through a wall—I could see the space between the atoms that made up the wall. I swore to myself that I would never let any drug, drink, or anything ever take over my mind. What peyote and mushrooms did for me was to open all the barriers that fear, stress, depression, hatred, and anger had shut down, locked up, and had thrown away the key to. Yet, like anything in my life at the time, my addictive personality took it to the extreme, to where when I was off eating shrooms, the very taste of store-bought mushrooms got me high! After a year of journeying with peyote and shrooms I stopped partaking in them and that was that.

The behavior of addiction is a crippling cross to bear. Addiction devours your psyche and pains your heart as it pleases the physical senses. Later, I would define my addictions as more of perseveration on a thought or behavior, manifested into bodily action, as a character behavior of Asperger syndrome. It is no wonder that Aspies were sometimes described as being "addicted" to computer fantasy game playing in the 1990s. The singleminded focus on one thing, on one object, can be devastating to one's wellbeing.

I was able to wean myself of most of my addictive attentions in my life by, firstly, enjoying the addiction (like my computer fantasy game playing in my 40s!); secondly, coming to awareness that it was destroying life and home; and lastly, quitting. I was not always successful in my timing, though, in quitting before damage was done to my health and mind.

Living in Eugene in the '70s was a special time of waking up to myself. My fantasy view of the world bloomed. The romantic life of the post-Vietnam war, civil rights movement, and the Haight-Ashbury era was coming to a close. The green life of Oregon was awakening me to Earthpower and the nature of life. I moved farther away from the materialistic world and the glitter of "things."

In Eugene, I joined a band called Liso as the percussionist. An experimental jazz/funk improv band, Liso allowed me the musical freedom that I was experiencing in my painting. The artist in me bloomed like wildflowers in an open field. I wrote poetry and oil painted all the time. I jammed on the streets with my congas and held drum parties in my home. Life was good for a young hippie artist in Eugene. During this time I learned to eat tofu, rice cakes, and tahini. I advocated for saving the whales and rode my ten-speed bike everywhere I went, and through all kinds of weather. Oregon rain never stopped me from riding my bike. It was throw on the foul weather gear and off into the pouring rain.

Relationship-wise I had friends, yet loved being alone. Relationships continued to remain a wandering albatross for me—alone and wanting, and wanting to be alone and wanting. I met a few hippie girls. The young women I met taught me about sex, a highly stimulating experience for a romantic, shy person like me; and once I became a lover, I was obsessed. I wanted to be glued at the hip with my lovers; I had dependency and abandonment issues—not a good combo for relationship-building. My jealousy about a lover's independence led to anger and rage. I had so much to learn! I would realize later that it was my social ineptness in close relationships and my immaturity that were the real issues, but I continued to try.

In Eugene I experienced living with a woman for the first time. We were both twenty-one years old and both Pisceans. It was splendid...at first. Then the obsessive, insecure, projecting-my-fears-upon-the-other-person mentality took over. I could not hear or recognize her feelings or opinions. Sadly, I destroyed this nice relationship by sabotaging all the goodness, and then conveniently placing all the blame on myself: "It is me who is all messed up, not you," I would tell her. What a damn chivalrous thing to do, and such a cowardly load of crap at the same time! I drove her away from me, from "us," and shattered our relationship. And then I wanted her back—help me, Mr. Wizard! Help me fix it up! The romantic, brokenhearted me allowed myself to get lost in the deadly spiral of blame, guilt, despair, and thoughts of suicide.

"How can anyone love me?" Me! The Me who had such anger, sadness, and pain embedded in my bones, and who was just so bewildered by my inability to validate someone else in my life.

THEY JUST DON'T UNDERSTAND ME!

ME. ME. ME.

The self-absorbed me...poor me...me...me.

"I am so worthless...worthless..."

Pretty messed up, huh?

This questioning of my self-worth would follow me for a long, long time. The pain and shame drove me back into myself where no one could find me. On the surface, I was so very pleasant, talented, funny, creative, and physically attractive to people. On the inside, I was tormented by shame, guilt, projections of family and social ridicule, conjuring all my past failures, not having a sense of my physical state of being, and distrust in the world around me. What a fake I was, I kept thinking. It was such a destructive cycle of self-directed words of hate and condemnation.

When I was younger it was easy to get away with all my perceived downfalls. During my high school days I could get lost with my close outcast-friends, in drugs and my fantasy world of Tolkien. But now, living as a twenty-year-old young man—being so naïve, projecting my fears, and understanding vulnerability in relationships while seeing the world through the rosy lenses of a pathetic, gullible romanticist—it was a stumbling, fumbling life of controlled chaos. I was surviving pain, be it self-inflicted or not, because I knew how. So I took to the road to release myself into freedom.

Eleanor, my '64 VW Squareback, my dearest of companions, and I drove everywhere. We were gone. We went deep into the backwoods of Oregon, on logging roads that wound through and connected Washington, Idaho, and Northern California. We fled together to get lost and to remove me from the world of social reality, of people and pain. I saw myself as helplessly lost, alone, and confused beyond help. This drove me deeper and deeper into solitude and sadness. It seemed my current life was no different from the life I had been living since birth. Then another tragedy happened.

Eleanor, my love, was murdered. She needed some work done on her, so I took her to a VW mechanic in Eugene. The mechanic said she knew what to do and it was an easy job. Well, this mechanic forgot to replace a very important oil seal when she was putting the engine back together. I got Eleanor back and she was great—at first. We drove fifty miles and then she just froze up and died. Without this important oil seal that the mechanic forgot to put back, Eleanor leaked all her lifeblood, overheated, dried up, and died. Her engine frozen, metal fused together, her heart would not turn over. The mechanic would not take responsibility for her mistake and I had to junk Eleanor for scrap metal. I was devastated. My world had become a dark, angry, and vengeful hell. I hated unfairness. I hated racists. I hated people who cheated. I hated people who lied. I hated people who took advantage of the poor and weak. I hated those who wronged others, smiled, and then walked away. I hated this mechanic. I hated myself.

Thank the Great Spirit I was a hard worker and made good money as a cook. I had taken out a loan for $1,500 to buy a stereo system the year before—big money for a stereo system in 1977—and had paid the loan off quickly, so I took out another loan and bought a 1969 MG Roadster. She was a two-seater racecar, pearl white, with red leather interior, a heavy roll bar, and a black canvas top with silver, 60-spoke wheels. She was a beautiful and elegant sports car, and she purred! I named her Rajada after a waterfall in Oregon.

I saw myself as the character Dustin Hoffman played in the movie *The Graduate*—he drove a similar MG sports car. I remembered the young woman who offered me a ride when I was coming home from Point Reyes, on my self-initiated Rite of Passage journey alone, when I was twelve years old; she drove a white MG Roadster. Rajada was a beautiful MG and she was mine. With a new set of wheels, a large loan out, and the cost of living by myself, I needed more money, so I started to model for my art classes, and that meant in the nude!

Now, the strange part about modeling for figure drawing classes was that I knew all the students in the class; these were my peers and I was a fellow artist. One day I walked into the figure drawing class, greeted my friends and started to disrobe. My friends looked at me, smirked, and prepared for the session. Being naked in front of my peers was real weird, and yet I knew what kind of poses were good for an artist, and I gave them great poses. Being naked in front of others was an out-of-body experience for me. But it wasn't a big deal—to me living life was an out-of-body experience most of the time.

There were moments I would look at myself in the mirror and start talking to myself. The reflection in the mirror showed a brown-skinned, black-haired man, whose mouth was moving. I heard a voice. I could see the mouth moving in the mirror, but I could not connect the voice to the image I was looking at in the mirror. I could not connect to my self. What a strange existence this living as a mortal was. Being out of my body was something I had gotten used to since I was a child. When the screaming and beatings started up, I would just leave my body and float away. Safe and content, I was detached from the chaotic, unsafe, mortal world. I guess I hadn't learned how to come back down into my body yet. I felt the old nubs of my woolly mammoth tusks deep in my human skull. In some sense it was so much easier being a woolly mammoth, but that was a life in my distant past.

Life continued to offer change and transformation to me. When I went out for the college fencing team I did not know it would open a whole new world for me. Since I ran track and went out for football, I was well-built, short, and stocky.

The fencing master said to me one day, "Listen, if you want to gain more balance and center for fencing, take a ballet class."

"Huh?"

"That's right, take a ballet class: you will get stronger in your body's center."

"Ah, okay."

The next day I checked in with the college dance teacher, Niki Crafts. She was beautiful in a goddess kind of way. I was sold. Now, having been an artist all my life, I had a good idea about bodies and dynamic bodies in motion. I was an avid follower of the Marvel comic book illustrator Jack "the King" Kirby. He drew the original characters for *Thor*, *Captain America*, *The Fantastic Four*, and many others. His style was bold in muscularity and exploded with action. I would plant these action body images in my mind, and my body would respond in real time. I could move dynamically in any sport I took up. You see, I was able to picture a movement or view a sport on film or TV, store the information in my mind, and then transfer that information into my muscles and move accordingly. I could do this with very little physical training. Now, my body would only go so far in body action, and then I would hit that "ceiling" where I needed actual training to become more proficient.

Walking into Ms. Crafts's office in the dance department, I asked if I could join her ballet class. She was very enthusiastic about me. I could not figure out why. The first ballet class revealed the reason for her enthusiasm—I was the only male in a class full of gorgeous girls! *Damn! Damn! Damn!* I was shocked. *I am in some sort of Heaven!*

After class Nikki pulled me over and instructed me, "Now Mr. Rubio, you have to buy some dance clothing; your gym shorts won't do."

I was thinking, *"Sure, anything you want!"*

The next day I went to the dance store in town and bought my "gear": black dance tights, a male "dance belt"—which to me looked like a jock strap—and a blue leotard. Ready to go!

On the day of my second ballet class I went into the men's locker room to put on my dance gear. Now, being a former football player and track person I did not know what the hell to make of this dance stuff. I got the part of the "dance belt/jock strap," but the other stuff looked pretty "womanlike" to me. So I put the black "stockings" on next, and then the leotard on top of that. This shit was weird! I felt like I had given myself a mean wedgie, and that I was cross-dressing for a night out on the town. My buddies sitting on the bench next to me gave me tons of ribbing and crap. I waddled uncomfortably into the dance studio, and all the girls turned around and started to laugh hysterically at me. *This was not starting out too good!*

"Whoa! Mr. Rubio, stop!" laughed Nikki. She called her boyfriend over, who so happened to be taking the class, and told him to get me squared away.

Back to the men's locker room we went. The damn leotard was supposed to go over the dance belt, and then the damn stockings went on after that. Ladies reversed the procedure. *Well, FU*K me!* Finally, I was squared away, and after giving my buddies in the locker room another show, I went back into the dance studio with all the adoring female eyes on me. I realized they could see everything about my body, which is the purpose of dance tights. Dance corrections cannot be made if the teacher cannot see your body. Damn! I felt naked...again.

I will tell you this: a ballet class is much harder than any football practice or any sports training I have ever done. Ballet training kicked my butt! I fell in love with dance. I loved the discipline and the attention to detail.

"Mr. Rubio, would you like to be in the spring dance performance in two months?" Nikki asked me.

"Oh, yes!"

Yes, dance was very, very cool, and so I signed up! Dance training was extremely physical. I danced to music, and there was a fine art about it: the costume design, the stage props to be made, and theater characters to be played. Dance was the medium in which I could express everything I was and loved. The ability to keep my body balanced while moving slowly (*adagio*), or quickly (*allegro*), with power, grace, and elegance—while on time with music!—was astounding to me. I found the challenge of dance just right up my alley. Dance combined physical training with fine arts and music!

It was also cool that I was a Piscean, like the famous male danseurs Nijinsky and Nureyev, an auspicious sign for me. It proved to be sexually bountiful as well, for I represented—at this time in the world of dance—a part of the less-than-five-percent of male danseurs who were heterosexual. It was heaven on earth, and I would be hooked for the rest of my mortal life!

In the moonless night, the bunched mass of dark shadows around Woolly Mammoth Boy indicated where his brethren slept or tried to sleep.

He stood firmly rooted, looking around in the blackness on high alert. The small group of mammoths—young strong male bulls—were testing their mettle in a "look-see" mission for the main herd that had stayed safely in the open plain of the deep valley far below them. They had settled in an open notch of a wide mountain plateau that offered a surprising bounty of hardy sweet mountain grass to feed on. A small watering hole trickled nearby. Climbing slowly upward for two days, the party stopped; they were nearing the summit. Green rich valleys lay beyond the craggy peaks.

They had followed a well-worn wide path used by all migrating creatures for centuries. As the rocky path left the valley floor and meandered up the high glacial mountains, the dangers had increased dramatically. For here in the higher altitudes a great and mighty predator held reign.

The Mountain Cave Bear.

The Mountain Cave Bear, standing on its hind legs, could meet a full-grown bull mammoth eye-to-eye. The encounter had taken many a mammoth in this part of the migration route. Their bones lay strewn about, sun-bleached and ominous. All creatures migrating along this path must go through the summit pass, where all were fair game to this gigantic hunting bear.

Woolly Mammoth Boy was up for the night watch. He heard many noises in the high rocky terrain. The wind whistled and rocks fell, crashing from heights in the darkness.

Woolly Mammoth Boy was comfortable and daring for any challenge.

He felt that he had trained hard and learned from his mentors. He was able to bridle his youthful vigor and arrogance in order to excel. He was honored to have been chosen for the scouting party. Now, as he stood guard, his mind wandered for a long second to the memory of one of his peers becoming stuck in the deep black-tar pit.

The juvenile mammoth had charged forward into the death trap, unheeding the trumpeting call of his mentor-handlers. His death was sad and long.

"You have learned much, my young one," a voice whispered in his ear, awakening Woolly Mammoth Boy from his dark reverie.

"Yes, I have. I survived where others did not," he answered silently. "The young manling is not a young manling any longer. He grows his tusks as I have."

"Come to speak about it, he DOES have a lumbering attitude like you," Thought answered as a vibrating wing of a passing firefly. "He tests his skills as you test yours."

Part 4:
Dance, Woolly Mammoth Boy, Dance!

26. Two Suitcases: "Go East, Young Man!"

He told them to go the edge. They were afraid. He told them to go to the edge.

They went to the edge. He told them to leap. They were afraid. He told them to leap. They did and they flew.

—Story retold by Woolly Mammoth Boy

MY FIRST DANCE PERFORMANCES WERE with the Lane County Community College Spring Dance Company of 1977–1978. I loved being onstage; the thrill of performing dance was very different than performing in a musical concert, running sprints in track, or playing a football game. To me a dance performance exhibited the mind, body, and spirit in motion together. Learning to control my body to be so graceful and powerful—while at the same time making it all look effortless—was truly an experience from another world.

I learned the techniques of ballet—the language of dance. Grueling, precise, and unmerciful, ballet embodied the highest caliber of physical training coupled with elegance and lightness. That the ballet swirled around the dance themes of princesses, royalty, and the glittery fairytale world of the bourgeoisie was not lost on my inner-city pedigree. But to my romantic spirit, the art of ballet was a feathery pen writing beautiful physical poetry. It was the dance of porcelain white skin, restrained feelings, and untouchable love. I felt totally at ease with jazz dance. Jazz was black, raw, and filled with unleashed passion and unfettered sexuality. All that funkiness and soul was right up my alley. My ability to sing along with all the R&B and soul/funk masters' tunes—including Earth, Wind, and Fire, Marvin Gaye, James Brown, and any other tune that was played for class—made Nikki, my dance teacher, very jealous of me. It was like reliving my childhood days, listening to those '60s Motown songs on the AM radio and dancing with my streetwise jive friends.

Now, modern dance technique was another matter. Developed mainly by white people, certain modern dance techniques are steeped in psychological interpretations of anthropological and archetypal overtones—the stuff is deep. The founding modern dance/theater techniques of Martha Graham, Lester Horton, and Charles Weidman and Doris Humphries would stretch, bend, and go to the point of breaking the highly disciplined world of ballet. The themes of modern dance/theater works were not the stories of princesses and the "castle dreams come true" of ballet. It was the ritual darkness of Graham, or the Native American mysteries and soul of Horton. Modern dance awakened in me the painful terror and grief I had buried in the poetic parts of me. Dance, and dance theater as a whole, was a perfect way for me to finally understand the myriad nuances that made up the repertoire of possible expressions made by the facial mask and body language that were communicated with every social interaction I encountered. I was getting the social training I never received though my life up to this point.

On my twenty-first birthday I went up to Portland, Oregon to see a New York City-based dance group, the Alvin Ailey American Dance Theater company. It was my first true viewing of a highly polished professional dance ensemble, and this group was a primarily black and mixed-race dance company. I was excited to see dancers of color not dancing Eurocentric prince- and princess-themed dance pieces. The Portland auditorium was immense and grand. People filled every seat and there was excitement in the air. When the tall, elegant curtains drew open what I beheld on stage was magical. My life was captured and forever changed.

The first piece was called "Gazelle." Set on the African plain, the dance depicted the beauty and freedom of a gazelle, the hunt for her by African warriors, and the way of life in an African tribal village. As the house lights dimmed, and the stage lights came up, a wild, free gazelle bounded onto the stage. I was watching a beautiful gazelle leaping and gracefully "grazing." The dancer, Sarita Allen, had morphed into a gazelle. Her lithe, powerful body was sensuous, animal-like, and utterly convincing to me. My heart/body was crying with joy. This was better than sex or anything I had ever experienced at this point in my young life.

The final dance offered that evening, I would later find out, was one of Alvin Ailey's signature pieces. The piece was called, "Revelations." The piece was a brilliant portrayal of Southern black religious beliefs and the journey of freedom from slavery. The piece left me gasping for air. It was as if I had never breathed life or passion until I saw "Revelations." I knew I had to go where this company came from. I had to go to New York City. I had to follow this company to New York City!

My impulsive nature saw no restrictions to the idea, except for the fact that New York was on the other side of America, on the East Coast. I knew nothing of New York City except the TV character played by Telly Savalas, a bald-headed, lollipop-sucking New York cop. I also knew that there were grimy, dirty, and wet streets filled with crime, where sharklike people took you for all you had if you were a soft-hearted fool; I knew that some places on real tourist maps of NYC were marked with a skull and crossbones indicating areas that were not to be trodden by the unwary and the naïvely stupid.

I came back to Eugene from Portland, knowing I had to move away and get ready to head east. It was in the summer of 1978 that I met the sister of my best friend who at the time was an architecture student at the U of O. His sister's name was Jacqueline, and she was sweet and delicate. Her father worked for IBM and was stationed in Tokyo, Japan. She herself lived in New York City. We had an intense beginning and it forged a new "love." She went on her annual summer stay with her parents in Japan, and I moved back down to the San Francisco Bay Area to consolidate my life, see family, and plan how in the hell I was going to get to New York City and study with Alvin Ailey.

By the end of the summer of 1978 I had sold all that I owned in Oregon, except my MG roadster sports car. One night, I strapped my ten-speed bike to the rollbar of the MG, and left Eugene. I would not return to live there until thirty years later. I holed up with friends from my high school days in Walnut Creek and worked on a carpentry crew during the day that my dad hooked me up with. Dad and I were on speaking terms by then, but he still couldn't figure me out; he could not bring me into the fold.

Living in Oregon all this time and being away from my family did not change how they saw me. I was still a mystery to my family. As my brother Fred would say to me during this time, "You do know, Ronald (Fred was the only one that ever called me "Ronald"), I do not talk to people like you. If you were not my brother I would not even bother with you." (I love you too, Fred.) "People like you are just parasites on society." It was great being with my family. Valerie had moved up to Eugene, Oregon and was going to school up there.

Valerie was now a young woman, who being all of five foot and a little more, could kick ass on most dudes no matter what size. She survived high school and the hell of being the "cinder-girl," graduated, and got the hell out of "Creektown." Before I moved back to California from Oregon, Valerie moved up to Oregon to go to the U. We lived together for a few months and it was fun. Later she got her own place. We were still tight and now older. Valerie did her own thing and I was in the periphery of her world now; she was a survivor and needed no one to tell her how to run her life.

My new love for dance was a hard cookie for my family to swallow. Fred asked me if I was gay. Dad was trying to understand how I would make a living out of it. But I had always been an artist—I was an oil painter, poet, and musician. Choosing dance was not a stretch for me. Everyone held me at arm's distance, and that was fine with me. I was not playing by anybody's rules but my own anyway. I guess when one is on the fringe of society it is best to stay out on the fringe. I mean, there were reasons that drove me to the fringe in the first place. I was accountable to no one except myself. I could wear what I wanted to wear, and do what I wanted to do. Of course, I did have to "sleep in the bed I made" too. There was not a lot of money as an artist. I was on food stamps and I did not always have the best roof over my head. Stability was elusive and dangerous at times, and it was more important to have gas in the car than food in the belly.

By September of 1978 I joined a local ballet company, the Contra Costa Ballet, to stay in dance shape. While there I took ballet classes with a male dance teacher named Bryner Mehl. Mr. Mehl had long arms and an even longer neck. His ballet was impeccable and his bodylines were dynamically elegant. He had studied and performed in New York City, and had mastered a style of ballet that was very classical and romantic; it was called Classical Theatrical Dancing (Cecchetti Method). This was the rigorous ballet method developed by the Italian Maestro Cav. Enrico Cecchetti (1850–1928). Challenging, demanding, and a taskmaster, Mr. Mehl continued to shape my still-very-raw dance body. I mean, I had only started dance at the age of nineteen. My body had been shaped and toned by years of playing high school football and running track as a sprinter and hurdler, so my body was still muscular with large thighs, a strong upper body, and flat fleet. He pushed me and I responded. I was trained by beatings to take pain from an early age—this ballet was no sweat. It was with the Contra Costa Ballet that I would perform in my first *Nutcracker*, the traditional Christmas-season ballet. The piece I was to perform in was the "Waltz of the Flowers." This piece was a traditionally an all-female-corps dance piece. Mr. Mehl was to set three male roles for the piece. I was one of the male flowers. Damn! Quirky shit for a quirky world!

During the time of rehearsals Mr. Mehl informed us that a special guest was coming to watch. I was to meet one of the old masters of ballet dance. Having been reading about dance and ballet I knew about the person who was coming. His name was Léonide Massine. He had been with the famous Ballets Russes in the early 1900s, and had been a peer of the ballet legend Vaslav Nijinsky.

Maestro Massine was well into his eighties at the time, but in his eyes I could recognize the brilliance of the "artist" in him. His movements still demonstrated the presence of a danseur in his aged body. He watched the rehearsal and then was gone. Thinking back to that day in 1978, I often wondered what he was thinking as he saw us, such young dancers, many generations past his own generation of legends. His life is now gone, and his

Vaslav Nijinsky

time is history to be brought up on Google. His life was like swirling clouds in the sky; now here, now gone.

In December 1978, *The Nutcracker* was up and running. My family saw me dance and did not have much to say. I was staying in contact with my girlfriend Jackie who was in Japan for the Christmas season.

In love, we wanted to be together. "Do you want to move in with me and live with me in NYC?" she asked over a long distance call.

"Sure, I would love to be with you."

When love calls, you have no choice but to answer. No one in my family had ever been east of the Sierra Nevada mountains, let alone to the Big Apple. I liquidated all of my belongings in California, drove back up to Oregon to say farewell to my mom, Horst, Valerie, and Shawn, and booked a one-way flight out of Portland, Oregon to NYC. I was on a cheap "red-eye" flight that would depart at 10:30 p.m., and arrive at JFK at 6:30 a.m. I arrived on February 2, 1979, my sister's birthday. It was a bitter cold morning and I had two suitcases in my hands: one with art supplies and a few favorite books, and the other filled with clothing.

Go east, young man!

The belly of the beast was waiting for me and slavering with anticipation.

Once, upon his journeys, Woolly Mammoth Boy came upon a stretch of desolate, arid land far from the known country of his kind. He had embarked on the "Rite of Understanding." Every mammoth of the herd, male or female, was granted a period of twelve complete cycles of the moon to sojourn alone, to silence the "wanderings of the heart." The Matriarch only led those who would stay for the herd—those who had satisfied the wanderings of the heart. Others chose to wander the earth alone. Woolly Mammoth Boy's heart had led him to come to this place on the third moon cycle since he had left the herd and the Matriarch.

"Seeking what, are we?" a huge black raven croaked harshly at Woolly Mammoth Boy as he stood breathing slowly and deeply, eyeing this foreign, empty land.

Woolly Mammoth Boy answered ever so quietly, so as not to disturb the dead silence of the land around him: "The Measure of the Wanderers." He continued as if reciting,

"The strange lands.
 The unknown plights and dangers.
The different stars of distant black night skies.
The untasted clear waters of sweetness.
To follow the wanderings of the heart.
To follow until the silence."

A wind started to pick up from the snow-capped eastern mountains far beyond the dry land that confronted him. Something had drawn him to continue on in this direction for weeks. He had forded deep rivers and crossed the long plain, always heading toward the eastern lands where the sun rose.

Woolly Mammoth Boy thought to himself, "I will see this to its end. I will not fail the Matriarch if I choose to return nine moons hence. If I return."

Thought-Raven landed on his broad, matted back. "To seek is to be blind! To seek is to be blind! To seek is to be blind!" it shrilled wildly with its shiny black head turned upward toward the heavens as if baring its throat for sacrifice.

"Be silent and still your words!" Woolly Mammoth Boy grumbled lowly. Ridding himself of the raven with a vigorous shake, he stared at the large Joshua tree before him. Woolly Mammoth Boy's grumbling became deeper and dangerous, "I make my choices and live my choices! The vast world is before me! There will be time-a-plenty to be sated by the consistency of living amongst my kind. The calling beckons me onwards! Now, be off and befuddle another living being!"

27. Year One in NYC

In the end, all that could be done was to watch the whole drama unfold to its finality. Earlier I had watched with awe as a whole herd of small sheep tumbled down a steep-walled chasm. As the leader tried to jump the distance across the canyon, only to fall to its death, the others followed their leader and blindly leapt, sharing their leader's demise. The two-legged ones who had driven these sheep to this trap stared down from the edge of the ravine to the great kill at the chasm's floor, where many sheep lay below. Already other two-legged ones were walking among the dead and killing the injured. As a young bull woolly mammoth now, I learned something simple from this sad event, and that is: do not follow blindly for it may mean your death.

–The Observations of Woolly Mammoth Boy

MY MATTED WOOLLY MAMMOTH FUR could not keep out the intense and bitter Nor'easter wind that blew and howled through the deep canyons of the Upper West Side of Manhattan. Manhattan—and the whole East Coast, actually—was a totally different beast from anything I had experienced before. My flight from Portland, Oregon was my first plane ride ever. During that time that you could still smoke cigarettes on airplanes, which made for a hazy, surrealistic flight across and above the black night of the US continent. Coming from the mellow woods and mountains of Oregon and the peace and love of San Francisco, Manhattan in 1979 was like someone flipping you off and belching a good hot one in your face at the same time.

Calling my first moments in Manhattan a shock would be a real understatement. I was way over-stimulated by smells, sounds, sights, and an energy surge that was present twenty-four hours a day, seven days a week. My behavior and perceptual processing were agitated, pissed-off, and in love all at the same time, with everything that surrounded me.

My girlfriend, Jackie, met me at airport and took me back to the Upper West Side. Though the New York State car plates at the time were yellow like Oregon plates, I was definitely not in Oregon. I was in some place only found in a Salvador Dalí painting. The taxi ride from JFK Airport felt like a crash-car derby; it was a hallucination of sounds and rushing metal. I feared nothing because I was so naïve. I took in the vast world at face value. I was as literal as literal could be. Adopting my *Lord of the Rings* alter ego as the character of

Aragorn, this whole experience was like an adventure to the dark Mines of Moria. I was self-sufficient and the new world was before me. I had enough training from the "school of hard knocks" that I knew I could handle myself in this highly stimulating social jungle, or so I thought.

In retrospect, I believe it is a rare person on the autism spectrum today who could do something like what I did in 1979. For people like me, an undiagnosed, high-functioning autistic person growing up in the '60s and '70s, I had to learn how to adjust and make it, or I would be left by the wayside. There was no knowledge of autism in America back then; it would take another twenty to thirty years—into the 1990s and through the twenty-first century—for that kind of knowledge to become available. Nope, none of that for me. I was learning by the skin of my teeth, and paying the price for all my neurotic and insensible social mistakes with no back-up support.

Dealing with my quirky social behavior, dark depression, and rigid thinking about "my way"; alongside my devastating anger meltdowns, overstimulation to smells, sounds, temperatures, lights, and the myriad of people surrounding me, made every moment in NYC very challenging—whether I liked it or not. I was in the craziest, most dangerous, and most stimulating city in the US of A, if not in the world, at that time. Why in the hell was I in this predicament? Because it was my choice to go to New York, and it always boils down to choice. No one forced my hand. It was my decision to follow my dream and become a dancer. As impulsive or crazy as it may have seemed to those close to me on the West Coast, I chose this path.

It was no wonder that when I left my home everyone thought I was out of my mind. *I was out of my mind.* I was functioning from my heart and what I felt. The world had always seemed untouchable and never made any real sense to me, so why join it now? Well, without knowing about my autism, PTSD, or TBI—not to mention all the other peculiar behaviors that became known to me thirty years later—because all the awareness of what was "wrong" with me really did not matter at all, and it wasn't worth one lousy dime. Once an idea was in my zany head I would become obsessed with it and that was that; don't even try to talk me out of it. It was just the way it was going to be, and this was the way I was going to live my life in the moment. Not by any influences of tomorrow, or by anything that may have happened to me in my past, just me and my decisions.

The apartment Jackie got for us was really just a studio on West 80th and Riverside Drive. It measured twelve feet wide by thirty-five feet long, with twelve-foot ceilings. We had our own full bathroom—other apartments did not have their own toilet—but our place was without a kitchen. A large, lone window looked down into a courtyard garden four floors below. There was nothing on the bare walls, and only a single bed in the middle of the studio to greet me.

We made frantic love to christen our new home. It was another out-of-body experience for me in a long series of experiences that first day. Dressing, we walked down our four flights of stairs and hit the streets. Opening the lobby door I was struck with a lung-freezing, breath-taking 29-degree air, with a wind chill factor that brought it down to 21 degrees. Damn! Where in the hell was I? The canyons of tall apartment buildings seemed to vanish into the horizon line north and south of me as I stood on West End Avenue, looking east. It was like being at the feet of pulsating concrete giants staring at me with countless eyes; and then there were the people—the masses of ant people—moving all around us, streaming up and down the sidewalks of Broadway (often pronounced "B'Way"). There were people of all shapes, sizes, colors, and characters. My head was spinning. I was overwhelmed by the masses. I had never seen that many people before in my meager, stunted life.

I had my first bagel at Humble Bagel on the corner of 80th and Broadway. Jackie and I walked and walked. She took me across town and into Central Park. Trees! They had trees in this madhouse of a city, but they looked tired and beaten up to me; everything looked old and aged in New York. There was trash scattered everywhere I looked. Some people threw their food wrappings, drink cups, and garbage right on the ground as they walked, even though the trash containers were nearby and in view...strange.

New York City was massive, deadly, and dangerous to me. I knew enough to know that I didn't know about the dangers, or the way of the people here. I knew I would have to be careful, but at the same time I felt extremely open, caring, and so very naïve. There was no time to look back and second guess myself. I was in the moment; I was not trained yet to be retrospective and conscious of my actions. That training would come years later.

First things first: work had to be found, money had to start coming in, dance classes had to start up, and I had to begin learning about my live-in girlfriend. How would I be able to pull it all together? I thanked the Great Spirit for my past experience as a carpenter and cook. The executive skills learned from these trades trained my mind to set up priorities; and therefore, a flowchart to help me decipher and catalogue all the information coming in, and put it all in some useful order. In order to make soup, first, you had to take out a pot, then add the desired amount of water, then your stock would go in with herbs and spices, and then...

I found my first job at a Jewish bakery. Before moving to New York City, I did not know what a "Jew" was, but I did know about bakeries. I walked into

Grossinger's Bakery, up on 78th and Columbus Avenue, and asked if there was a job available. Mrs. Grossinger's son interviewed me.

"You got a driver's license?" he asked.

"Yes, sir." I answered. "I also worked in a bakery for a while in Oregon."

"You will not be baking. We need someone behind the counter and driving morning orders around town."

"I can do that."

"Good, come in on Monday at 6:00 a.m. and Maria will train you."

"Thank you."

"Don't be late, Maria doesn't like late people."

"I will be prompt, sir."

As I was leaving the bakery, Mrs. Grossinger came out from the back kitchen, and I saw my first "Jewish mother." She was short, all of five-foot-three, and plump with a round face and body. Her glasses enlarged her buglike eyes. She was eagle-eyed about everything that went down in the bakery. A real taskmaster to the staff, she also cared tremendously for her employees and all the customers. She really did care for everyone, and everyone asked for her when they came in to buy baked goods. Her speech was heavily accented. Later, years spent living in New York would teach me the many accents that thrived in city, but at that point my West Coast upbringing did not prepare me for the wide spectrum of European, African, South American, Caribbean Islander, Puerto Rican, Cubano, and the myriad other accents that bombarded my ears—not to mention the local accents from the Bronx, Brooklyn, Queens, Long Island, and so on and so on. It all sounded like gibberish to me.

I left the bakery, and now the time had come time to check out ballet classes. My ballet teacher out west referred me to a Cecchetti ballet teacher down near the World Trade Center, in downtown, but I needed someone closer. Back then most of the dance masters had great big lofts to teach out of. Later, Starbucks and Barnes and Noble would kick them out of these places, but for now on the Upper West Side there were three or four big-time ballet masters teaching. I found one near my apartment, and his name was Finis Jhung, with his second-in-command, Liane Plane. They were to be my first NYC-grade dance teachers who would help shape me into a NYC dancer. His dance center taught only ballet, and all his students were highly motivated and disciplined. This was New York City: the capital of dance.

"You need to start from scratch," Mr. Jhung told me after watching my first ballet class. "Your muscles are too tight, your flexibility needs to be established. You are raw."

No news here, I thought. "Thank you, Mr. Jhung."

"You can begin with Liane's beginner's ballet classes. You can start on Monday afternoon if you wish." So everything was set to start on Monday: Training at Grossinger's Bakery in the morning, and ballet classes in the afternoon. Slowly my New York life was taking shape.

I got back to the apartment and Jackie wanted to head downtown for dinner. We had to go by train, and I didn't even know what that meant. We were to catch the train at 79th and B'Way—the No. 1 IRT local. As I walked down the grimy, old, chewing-gum-caked steps to the underground train, I felt like I was descending into the Underworld of Nordic mythology. The platform was packed with people. The smells were of things decaying, and the overhead platform lights shined an off-yellow, like an aged and faded envelope. Then came the sound of the train. It was a roaring No. 2 express train riding on the middle track. The only warning was a blast of dead air rushing in my face; then came the dim eyes of an underground beast, followed by the screeching, scraping, high-pitched, and blasting-blur of the express train crashing and speeding by. I held my hands to my ears to the embarrassment of Jackie; others on the platform looked at me with the knowing glance of veterans. I may have screamed in astonishment. Then the train was gone and there was no sound. I was devastated, and splintered into pieces.

Our train came and we boarded. Inside our car was a mishmash of humanity colliding from the many outer worlds of distant galaxies. I stared naïvely until a sharp elbow from Jackie stunned me and broke the child-like awe distracting me from what the hell I was doing. I later learned that looking at others indiscreetly on a New York train could evoke a sharp word, or a challenge to a fight. There was so much to learn. The rest of the night seemed like a blur.

Monday morning arrived. I bundled up to deal with the 26-degree weather and headed for the bakery. It was 5:30 a.m. and I walked briskly through the vacant, early morning streets. Upon arriving at the bakery, I rapped on the glass door, which brought out the baker who was already there. He grunted at my morning greeting and yelled for Maria. From the back kitchen bounded a dark brown, black-haired young woman who looked me over for a second, and ordered me to grab an apron. She said something to me that I did not get; she was speaking too fast, and with a heavy accent that I later learned to be Puerto Rican. She repeated her direction again with agitation and was off. I believed I was supposed to wipe down the glass display counters.

Focused on the task, I heard someone yell at me, *"YO!"* My head jerked to the voice. "Yo! Come here."

I replied, "My name is Ron."

Maria looked at me like I was stupid. "Yo! Follow me."

Once again I said, "My name is Ron."

In a tone that was too kind to be nice, Maria repeated, "Yo! Follow me. I got a lot of setup before we open!"

I realized then that "YO" was some kind of call-to-attention. I snapped out of my confusion and followed. The rest of my training shift went easily, and I got out of there with directions to come back in the next couple of days. I got the job.

Damn, there was so much to learn in this city. They spoke too fast here, and in a slang-talk muffled with foreign accents that I was not familiar with at all. Growing up in inner-city San Francisco made me street-smart to the ghetto-jive, black-fueled way of speaking, but this shit was way too foreign. It was like being in another country far from America. This was New York City in 1979, and I had to stop being so naïve and instead rely on my street instincts.

I went back to the apartment and gathered my dance clothing for my first NYC ballet class. I walked downtown on B'Way toward the ballet school. Opening the glass doors, I climbed the well-worn steps to the front desk. Signing in and paying the dues, I went to get dressed. In the men's dressing room were posters of male NYC ballet dancers in graceful poses. Posters of ballet gods and goddess adorned the simple walls. Dressed, I went into Studio A. The class was full of dancers of many shapes; this was a beginner's class. Liane entered and introduced herself to me. Very gracious and elegant in all her movements, she started class. The pianist got her cue from Liane and began to accompany her. As we went though the paces of Liane's teachings, I was struck by the fine-tuning she was applying to myself and the other students. Fine adjustments, hands-on placement of limbs, torsos, heads, shoulders, feet, pelvises, and hands. Damn! This was the beginning of my transformation into a ballet dancer from my raw body of muscles and bones.

I was in love. My physical "self" was being made known to me. I was discovering and learning where my body ended and space began. This was spatial awareness: upstage, downstage, stage right, stage left, upstage stage right, downstage stage right. I had learned a lot about stage placement during my college dance experience, but learning it in New York City came with a different spin. This was where I was going to make the grade or not, so I "emptied" my mind and started from scratch. Learning spatial awareness, where one is in physical space, is so important in social situations when amongst a mass of people so as not to bump into others, and so on. For me and those on the autism spectrum, not understanding where you ended and space—the space of others— begins can curtail any opportunity to meet and be comfortable around people. If you are standing too close to someone you are talking to, for instance, and not aware of the socially accepted distance between two adults talking, well, you are not going to make that person you are talking to feel safe or comfortable. Result: that person will try to avoid you like you are the plague.

Learning to be NYC streetwise took time. In my neighborhood in the W. 80th Street block between West End Avenue and Riverside Drive, there were three brownstone buildings that served as housing for welfare compensation folks. Basically, they were very low income and very low functioning people. One old black guy always sat on the steps of his building, and greeted me every chance he got.

"Hey, Youngblood!" he would yell.

"Good morning, Charlie Brown!" I yelled in return. If his name was really "Charlie Brown," I did not know. This was the name he had offered me with a strong, smelly handshake.

"Got a dime, Youngblood?"

"No, but I got a dollar." My giving West Coast-spirit always came through. Since a dime back in '79 could buy you a phone call, a buck was 7/8ths closer to buying a cheap bottle of wine.

"Thank you, Youngblood."

He took the buck out of my hand with a smile and we parted. This happened almost every morning.

My upstairs neighbor, friend, and frisbee mentor Mel, a strongly built black man whose job as a bike messenger kept him trim like a panther, said to me one day after I told him about Charlie Brown and all the "Good Samaritan" deeds I had done, "Rubio Filipino..."—I did not understand why I was always given nicknames with the word "Filipino" in them—"You got to stop handing money to all them poor folks you meet on the streets, there is a shit of them and you'll go broke soon enough, mon!" Mel lectured me over a joint. "You're too friendly for the mean streets, Filipino." Damn, I never figured I was too friendly. I cared for people, and maybe I was too gullible and naïve for the mean streets of NYC. Mel's words would ring true in the near future, but for now this was who I was.

The season moved from winter to spring, though not before I experienced more Nor'easters—those kick-ass winter storms that dumped heavy snows and howled with Siberian-like angry winds. I remember standing in the middle of West End Avenue in the dead of night during one Nor'easter snowstorm. Wrapped in thick wool clothing, I found the avenue vacant and void of all humanity—neither cars nor people were visible for many blocks, in both uptown and downtown directions. I watched as the ghostly, lonely traffic lights turned from green to yellow to red in a long succession for many blocks. The snow fell in thick sheets with the wind demons whipping it all around, spiraling snow upward into the sides of the canyonlike walls of the bordering tall cement buildings.

I was alone and mesmerized by the ferocity and raw power of the winter storm. It made me feel very alive and calm. I loved it. It was the beginning of my love affair with the four seasons of life on the East Coast. The sun and mellowness of San Franciscan and Northern Californian weather was out; this was in! The seasons were life changing and I had to adapt and change with them; stagnation was out of the question. Unknowingly, this external environmental experience was helping me learn ideas about flexibility and adaptation. I was unconsciously learning to come to terms with my rigidity in thinking and developing an "open mind." It was just the beginning. Very tiny, tiny steps toward self-awareness.

My first spring in NYC was magical. Trees and flowers bloomed. Birds sang and the buried, winter bodies of dead, frozen, homeless people were revealed in the receding snow-covered streets and alleyways. Spring was here, and the down jackets and heavy clothing were replaced with spring fashions only New Yorkers can parade. People were happy and smiling with pale skins and winter-worn faces; it was a truly magical time in the city. There was a freak, late April snowstorm that forced early-morning subway riders into wearing their heavy winter jackets again, only to faint from overheating in the stuffy, still-heated subway cars as the afternoon sun came out and temperatures soared back into the 60s. *I must continue to adjust. I must be ready to adjust with what I am given in the moment.*

My ballet classes were making a big difference in the development of my core—my "center" of strength and physical balance. I added ballet classes from Cecchetti's with Diana Byers, down on Chambers Street and up the street from the World Trade Center. Just as my ballet teacher in Walnut Creek, Bryner Mehl, had told me, the Italian classical ballet technique introduced me to the romantic classic gestures and "shadings" of all the ballet positions. Harder than shit, my Cecchetti ballet classes were demanding, and had to be executed with precision and detail (as in all ballet techniques); this could only be accomplished from a vigilantly maintained body-centered awareness, and an extremely strong and confident connection to the wooden floor upon which I stood. Double and triple *pirouettes*, or turns, were accomplished now with confidence and strength. Once again, ballet training kept my usual spaced-out mind "in" my body. I became coordinated and more aware of the space around me, my childhood clumsiness and dorkiness was gone. I was an elegant, graceful, brown-skinned prince in dance tights.

Now, there is something to be said about dance tights. Most "Aspies" (a name people with Asperger syndrome gave themselves in the early '90s) can hardly tell where their bodies end and the space around them starts; they have a hard time recognizing where their world ends and the "live" social and physical worlds begin. Ever since I was a kid I have enjoyed wearing close-fitted clothing. For example, the many-buttoned black underfrock altar boys wore fit me like a cocoon once it was all buttoned up, and I loved it. Other Aspies love feeling weight, like a heavy blanket, against their bodies, but others can't stand the constriction of tight clothing. I myself loved tight or heavy clothes, and dance tights made me feel like a finely tuned jungle panther. (Not to mention that in all the Marvel comics I read in the '60s, all the characters were outfitted with some type of tight-fitting clothing—Spiderman, The Daredevil, The Fantastic Four, and Thor all wore tights!) It was so natural for me to put on dance tights and feel myself move through space like a superhero. The dance tights allowed me to feel contained as one entity, and not spewing all over the place like The Blob. It made me feel sleek, and powerfully graceful like the Marvel character, The Silver Surfer. My body was changing from a bulky, squat, football player/track sprinter to a well-defined and stretched-out male dancer. Just turning 22 years old that spring, I was awakening to the physical me.

The months before the summer of 1979 were filled with long hours at the bakery, but I still tried to get more work. I found a job as a waiter at a Steak and Brew on the Upper East Side. Steak and Brew was a chain of burger joints that could be found all over the city. One night a young couple, about my age, walked in. As they sat in my section they told me they were celebrating. I was just getting into my dance classes and was pumped up with dance energy and enthusiasm.

"What are you two celebrating?" I asked with a huge smile, for I was infected by their joy.

"Timmy is having major knee surgery tomorrow." The young lady said.

I was confused. "I hope all goes well. So are you celebrating the expected success of the surgery?" I asked smiling.

"I blew out my knee dancing, and now I can move out of New York City and continue with my life," the young man said, looking at me with a sad, resigned look in his eyes.

"I just moved to New York City to start my career in dance," I said before I could catch myself. Sometimes I spoke what was on my mind at the most awkward of times. It was something I had done most of my young life. There was dead silence. They looked at me and I looked at them. We were standing at a crossroads in our young lives. His dance career was over, and mine was just starting. They ordered their food and left a nice tip. Their celebration feast was a success. That was weird. Was this some strange omen? Screw that! That was his story, not mine! I quit Steak and Brew shortly afterward.

Relationship-wise, living with Jackie had its ups and downs. My temper flare-ups, resulting from projecting my own fears onto Jackie, wreaked havoc on our relationship. If I became too anxious and overstimulated by the environment around me, or frustrated by my still-fragile confidence in my dancing, I could not stop myself from hurting the genuine love she felt for me by picking and bickering over nothing to judge and criticize her. I was extremely jealous of her past loves, which she remained in contact with. To me, it was more that I was comparing myself to her being white, and me being brown, and that I was not really good enough for her. Her family was wealthy and I felt very underclassed. I was sabotaging her love for me with my made-up fears. Though I could be extremely loving and giving, it seemed my unpredictable emotional swings were getting the best of me. With Jackie's annual trip to visit her dad and mom in Japan coming up, we thought that might be a good way to fire up the relationship. She suggested that I come to Japan with her for the summer. We would leave in June and be back by the end of August.

I got the summer off from the bakery, and they said my job would be waiting for me when I got back. I talked to my dance teachers and Mr. Jhung was not pleased, but he understood: I was a young, impulsive man and the opportunity to live in Tokyo for a summer was very appealing. I had worked a lot to make the money, but I was sure about going. My itinerary included going to Tokyo first, then visiting the Philippines for the first time in my life (to see my mother's oldest sister's family), then making a quick trip to Hong Kong, spending a few days in Hawaii, and then finally coming back to NYC.

This would be my second time flying in my life, and it was going to be a long one. The smoking section was in the back of the plane, but cigarette smoke filtered throughout the whole cabin. The flight to Tokyo went nonstop from JFK, but it still seemed like an eternity. Jackie and I got it on in the bathroom and then tried to sleep the best we could. The vast Pacific Ocean below us was shimmering in the moonlight, and I was thinking that, if this metal bird went down, we would all be lost in the watery vastness, becoming fish food never to be found, like Amelia Earhart. After four thousand years and a headache from the cigarette smoke, we landed in Narita Airport, Japan, almost twenty-three hours later.

If NYC was an anthill, then Tokyo was an ant universe; there were

Japanese people packed all over the place, and tiny little cars that fit down alleyways as wide as double doors back home in the States! Jackie's family's IBM-paid three-story home was down the street from the US Embassy in the Rappongi District of Tokyo. It was located in the lush, exotic "Red Light" part of town. Her mother set me up downstairs and Jackie upstairs. Her folks were leery of the brown country-bumpkin boy their daughter brought home for the summer. They treated me cordially and I did the same. For a Filipino boy like me racism was strong everywhere in Japan; they knew I was not Japanese and they let me know it. Some of the younger folks were cool, but others were just outright rude. I was already used to this behavior from back home, so it was no sweat off my back.

Japan and all of East Asia is hot and humid during the summer months. Hot wet air, and hot wet rain. Anything you wore stuck to your skin and that was that, but most Japanese in Tokyo wore suits and stayed wrapped up in layers of clothing anyway. In the countryside life was different, but here in the anthill supreme it was social mayhem. The stimulation of the neon lights, blaring sounds, and tons of odd, beautiful-looking Japanese people, was incredible. Once in a while, I would catch sight of a mountain of a sumo wrestler walking down the street. These guys were like movie stars, and were often surrounded by their entourage of *geisha* girls and "homies." These sumo dudes were big, very big. You made room for them. When they moved through the streets, normal-sized Japanese people looked like shrimp in the wake of a passing whale. You could also catch sight of a rich Japanese playboy with his two buxom blonde *gaijin*, one on each arm, and his *yakuza* "gangsta" bodyguards trailing. I read *Shogun*, the epic Japanese fiction book set in medieval times on the way over on the plane, and knew a few Japanese words. I got around by pointing and smiling.

It was in Japan that I started smoking cigarettes. There I was, a childhood asthmatic with weak lungs, starting to smoke. My dad was a smoker of unfiltered cigs, a habit he had picked up as an enterprising nine-year-old Filipino working the black markets of Japanese-occupied Manila during World War II. Growing up, his cigarette smoke was everywhere—in the family car, the home, and on the work sites. Jackie also smoked when I was around her, so one day I was sitting in my room with a pack of Seven Star Japanese cigarettes, and I lit up and took a long drag. Damn! I got so high off the nicotine I was flying! I had the strongest urge to take a crap while feeling incredible wobbly on my legs. I looked out my window and saw a tall building nearby swaying like a bamboo tree in the wind. I thought I was beginning to hallucinate like I was on shrooms or something. Then I realized I was in an earthquake! The quake passed just as quickly as it had come. I would later learn that the Japanese built their skyscrapers to "sway" with a jolting earthquake, rather than be rigid, break, and crumble. There was something for me to learn here. So my first experience with cigarettes was a success, and my addictive behavior was ripe for a smoking habit. What a relationship born in hell, and I was comfortable with it.

Having taught English every summer she was there, Jackie got me a job with the company she had worked for the summer before. My new job as an English teacher found me all over Tokyo. My clients ranged from a Japanese family of six to a rich Japanese tycoon's son who only wanted to practice English at his favorite restaurant downing beers and smoking Seven Star cigarettes. Most of my clients were grateful and very kind to me. It also helped that I got paid some good *yen*. After work I would go to an arcade café and order heavily sugared iced coffees, smoke tons of cigs, and play a new game that had yet to hit Europe or America called Space Invaders. The game featured a pulsing, beeping sound that got faster and faster as the enemy space invaders got nearer to defeating your sorry butt. This was a highly addictive game, and, coupled with a multitude of caffeine drinks and cigarettes, really got a person's heart racing. The hot, humid Japanese nights, hours of Space Invaders, drinking tons of iced coffees, and smoking cigs burnt me out.

Jackie and I would hit the discotheques once in a while and that was a blast, but our relationship was dying. At a certain point she just stayed away from me, even though we lived in her family home. She was too busy to talk to me about things, so one night in great despair, messed up in the head from hours of playing, smoking, and a racing heart, I threw myself, fully clothed, into the compound pool to end my life. I had tried suicide when I was thirteen, and I had a tendency to lean toward deep melancholy and dark depression when confused about life. I will tell you now it's hard to drown yourself if you are not knocked out, or tied up wearing cement boots. There is a natural reflex to take a breath and not to breathe in water; thus, filling your lungs with water is hard to do. After floating face down and holding my breath for a few long minutes, I just couldn't breathe in the water, and so I swallowed the water until I puked instead. I finally got out of the pool feeling worse than I did when first threw myself in. I went back to the house soaked, shoes and all. Jackie was awake and saw me come in. I explained what happened and she just looked at me and then turned away.

As my days in Japan drew to a close in early August, the US Embassy instructed all US citizens in Tokyo to carry identification because the police were going to monitor all pedestrian traffic. The major world leaders were in town for an economic summit, including then-President Jimmy Carter, and the Tokyo police were going to impress by being very strict. No problem. I was going to carry my US passport; I was thinking, "Just try to mess with me, I am a citizen of the US of A!"

After a heavy night of drinking and playing Space Invaders, I was making my way home through the short cuts and dark alleyways of Rappongi, when I heard the dreaded, curt command to hold, "HOO!"

I froze. Three samurai-looking Tokyo tactical cops came out of the shadows. These guys looked like they came out of the book *Shogun*. They were dressed in black, and all wore identical, highly polished wooden or padded plates of black armor across their chests, thick shin and forearm guards, and samurai-looking headgear with ear flaps. They also carried medium-length, black bamboo riot sticks. These guys had a "kick-ass and take names later" aura to them. I almost peed in my pants out of fear.

"PASSPOORT!" One yelled at me in a heavy Japanese accent. I could not understand them at first.

"PASSPOORT!" He yelled at me again, more menacingly this time, as the lead cop took one small step toward me.

I had a bad feeling about this as I reached for the sky. "Gaijin" (foreigner), I said. A low grunt came out of the lead dark shadow.

"PASSPOORT!"

"I am reaching for my passport in my pocket," I said very slowly and deliberately.

The three dark samurai went into a battle stance as I reached in my pants pocket. I thought I was going to be beaten and thrown into a dark alley to die.

I could not find my passport anywhere. I think I let out a small whimper. My hand came out of my pants pocket empty handed. A growling grunt came from the dark shadow in front of me. Two shadows behind him detached themselves, and were on either side of me in a flash. I was held in a harsh vice grip. They led me to an armored command car around the corner from where we were. The sharp lights of the interior blinded me. The electronic battle chatter from the radio operator's station sounded like something out of *Star Wars*. A senior cop came to me from a group of cops looking me over.

"No passport?" he sternly said,

"*Hai*, I mean, Yes, I do not have my passport on me."

"*Namu?*"

"Ron Rubio, USA citizen."

"Here..." He handed me a paper. I wrote my name.

He called the American embassy and an officer from the embassy was dispatched from down the street. A short time later, the armored car door opened and a white man exited.

"Mr. Rubio?" this fresh looking American officer asked me.

"Yes, sir."

"Come with me." He spoke to the senior Japanese cop and whisked me away.

As I left I said to the senior cop, *"Domo arigato."*

He looked at me, grunted, and turned away.

The US embassy officer said I was lucky I wasn't just thrown in jail to sweat it out. I thanked my all ancestors, and hurried to get back to the family compound. Upon arriving home, I saw my passport on top of my dresser. Dope! I was to leave two days later.

I left Japan without Jackie; we were to meet back in Hawaii in one week's time. First, I flew to Hong Kong, which was still under British rule. I remembered walking the grimy, sweaty back alleys by myself to absorb the heart of the people and their city. It was like being in a '60s James Bond movie—on a secret mission in an exotic Asian city with bustling people speaking a sing-song language. When I walked into a Chinese restaurant, men in white tank tops gave me stares from around a large, round table in the back. Because the menu was written in a Chinese dialect, all I could do was point to an item, and then to the guys in the back of the restaurant. The waitress smiled at me and disappeared. She came back with a plate of food and a large bowl of soup. It was great! I was lucky.

Later that week, Hong Kong was hit by a typhoon that came roaring in off the China Sea. All of us in the hotel were hunkered down in the lobby, drinking and partying, as the winds howled and waters raged outside the barricaded windows and doors of the hotel. The next morning, after the typhoon had passed, I went outside and found a huge ship sitting on the docks outside of the water. It was as if the water gods had picked the ship up from its moorings, and placed it on the docks whole and undamaged. Barnacles and sea life clung to the exposed hull, and were drying out in the hot summer sun. The ship was at least three stories above my head. I was stunned, and in awe of nature's might. The next day I flew to the Philippines.

My visit to the Philippines was the first trip ever to my native homeland. I had one uncle from my mother's side still living in Manila, while the rest of the family had migrated to the United States in the late 1950s. My arrival at Manila International Airport reminded me of the stereotypical image of a third-world military presence—small-headed Filipinos wearing large, outdated American steel helmets, toting large rifles, and giving me the stare down. I was a very tall and broad-shouldered Filipino American. They knew I was Filipino, but my blue jeans and physical size said I was very different. My uncle and two cousins, "Pinky" and "Girlie," met me at the airport. (Filipinos are given nicknames when they are very young, and your nickname is how you are known from then on. I still do not know my cousin's real names; they were always Pinky and Girly to me.) Martial law was in effect at the time and there was tension in the air. The airport smelled of fish and smoke. I was home.

In the Philippines in 1979, there was no middle class. You either had *pesos* or you did not. My relatives had money. High cement walls enclosed their home in a sea of corrugated, steel-roofed, small, and dilapidated shacks that surrounded them. The very hot and humid Philippine summer was still and wet. Upon arriving, my uncle told me my maid would clean my clothes and see to my every need. Now, coming from the USA, I felt very uncomfortable having my own maid, but my uncle explained that being a maid meant having a job, and at the equivalent of 30 US cents a month, the maid was happy to be working at all. I still did not ask her to do anything for me, though she took my dirty clothes, hand-washed them, and folded them for me without being told.

As Uncle and I talked in our first meeting, he ordered some freshly cut avocado, with milk and sprinkled sugar, to be served to me. Yummy!

"Listen, nephew, when you go out tonight with your cousins, be careful," he said in his heavily Filipino-accented English.

"Of what, Uncle?"

"Of the security people who will be questioning you."

"What do you mean, Uncle?"

"You know we are in martial law, right?" I nodded my head as I ate the sugared avocado. "The agents of Marcos will want to know what a Filipino American is doing here." Damn, I was thinking to myself.

"Be careful what you say, be very careful, nephew. They will be wondering if you came here from the US to raise trouble against Marcos."

"Yes, Uncle." He looked long and hard at me; it would be a drag if a visiting relative from the USA got kidnapped and disappeared without a trace.

Later that evening at a discotheque in Manila I went to have a drink at the bar. The incredibly loud music and annoying strobe lights were really making me nauseous and agitated. I was sipping a gin and tonic when two Filipino men sat down on either side of me. My radar went up, and I felt endangered.

"Ooh, you habbing a good time?" the one on my right asked.

"Sure."

"Ooh, you like it here in the Pilipinas?" the one on my left asked.

My head swiveled to answer him. "Sure."

"You American?" Mr. Right asked.

"Yep."

"Bisiting pamily, here?" Mr. Left asked. Filipinos can't pronounce the letters "F" or "V" very well.

"Yep."

They became quiet and just stared at me. I looked at the mirror behind the bar and saw my cousins staring at my back and talking amongst themselves.

"What do you think of Marcos?" Mr. Left asked suddenly.

"Marcos who?" I knew full well that Marcos was their dictator-president for life, and ruled the Philippines with an iron hand. My Dada hated him.

"President Marcos of the Pilipinas," said Mr. Right.

"Don't know anything about him," I answered into my drink.

"You do not know President Ferdinand Marcos?"

I looked into the eyes of Mr. Right as he glared at me, "That is what I said, I do not know anything about your President Marcos. I have a lot to think about my own president back home in America."

Mr. Right and I had a mini-staredown. I felt Mr. Left adjust his bar stool behind me. From the corner of my eye I saw in the bar mirror my cousins heading in my direction.

"Can I buy you two gentlemen a drink?" I asked breaking the silent stare down between Mr. Right and me.

"No," said Mr. Left at my back.

"Be carepull on your trip here, some blacess are not sape," said Mr. Right, as he and Mr. Left got up to leave.

"Thanks," I said as I downed my drink. My cousins were at my side a second later. They gave me a worried stare.

"Let's go home," I said quietly.

"Yes, cousin. Let's go home now," they almost said in unison.

A few days later I left for Hawaii to hook up with Jackie, but I knew I would be back to the *Pilipinas* someday. This was the place my whole family came from. I was a first-generation Filipino American and this is where it all began—here in the "Pilipinas," not the "Philippines" as the Westerners spelled it. Yes, I knew in my heart I was going to be back here. When the time was right I would return.

When Jackie and I met in Hawaii we knew our relationship was over. It was all too strange and bitter for me. Relationships are just weird. I just could not get out of my own way. I was too possessive and fearful, and lacked any self-confidence in relationships.

I had a very strange experience with the natives there in Hawaii. I was wearing a New York Yankees baseball hat. Two brown-skinned "brahs" walked up and asked me where I got the hat.

"I live in New York. I bought it there," I answered honestly.

"You lie!" one scowled at me. "Where did you buy the hat?"

"Yo, I bought it in New York City."

"You lie! You live here—give it up, brah!" Gesturing to the hat.

Now, I had no intention of giving up my baseball hat to these two island boys.

"Back off..." My newfound New York City toughness was bubbling up through my veins.

"Give me the hat, man!" said the bigger of the two.

"If you want to get f*cked up for this hat, *then let's go...*" I said not taking my eyes off the bigger brown boy. These homies thought I was an island boy like them, and trying to brag that I live in the Big Apple, off the island. One reached straight for my hat still on my head, but I slapped his hand away.

"Yo, dudes...I ain't jiving." I said going into my inner-city slang tone.

A little more posturing from them both, and then they backed off their yapping threats, walking off down the beach kicking sand as they went. I smiled inwardly and laid out in the sun. I don't really think I could have hurt them; I had never fought as an adult. Playground battles were far from finesse.

On the plane ride back to NYC, Jackie said she was not going to be there for us, that I could take over the lease of the apartment studio we lived in, and she was going to move uptown to 92nd and Broadway. There was nothing I could say. You could only say "sorry" so many times. "Fine," I said. "Thank you for the apartment."

It was a long, quiet plane ride back to the mainland. We reached NYC not looking at each other. Strange.

Woolly Mammoth Boy could not get the high screeching sound out of his head. He closed his eyes from the sharp pain that started from the back of his head to above his eyes. He saw in his mind two bright lights, like twin suns, bearing down on him—rushing toward him. He was confused and disoriented.

Suddenly he heard the trumpeting call of warning...ward!!!!

Woolly Mammoth Boy opened his eyes in time to see a huge long-horned woolly rhinoceros charging at him from three hundred paces! In his pain and delirium, he had blundered too close to a mother rhino and her calf that had been grazing nearby. He quickly retreated and the rhino stopped her charge.

"Ho, awake my boy!" Thought called out as a mockingbird from a nearby bush. "You crossed into your human life for a second."

"Where was I?" Woolly Mammoth Boy asked the mockingbird now preening itself on his back.

"I believe the place you were standing was a 'subway platform,' in a place called a 'subway station.' The '79th Street and Broadway stop on the IRT line,' to be exact." The Thought-mockingbird crunched a ripe tick off his matted back.

"The place of my human self is a mad world! It is a place of confusion and mayhem!" Woolly Mammoth Boy said, still shaking off the shock.

"Yes, my boy. Your human reflection-self is now a man. He learns and changes. He lives though his world bombarded by all that could harm the whole of him."

Woolly Mammoth Boy called to the departing mockingbird, "He must be careful; there are many hazards in his journey."

"Stay awake, my little one. Your path and his are crossing. This is a time for great awareness!" laughed the mockingbird, jesting from the shade of a nearby tree.

"Stay awake!"

28. "Once a Dancer, Always a Dancer."

I faced the Mountain Cave Bear without hesitation, for my life depended on it. The sow had been sleeping in the bush when her cubs ran off between my feet. I had been grazing nearby, not knowing of their presence until it was too late. Now I was between the sow and her cubs. I had once seen a Mountain Cave Bear sow take down a charging Woolly Rhinoceros in a similar situation. The sow ripped the eyes out of the rhino before breaking its neck with two powerful swats from her huge paws.

I knew I was in deep trouble. I tried to back away, but the cubs had grown scared and hid in the bush behind me. The sow eyed me for death. She charged. I was almost a fully-grown bull mammoth. I swatted powerfully at her with my tusks, which threw her into the bushes. She charged again. This time I met her face on. Lifting her high in the air, I threw her into the bushes where her cubs lay hidden. With one slap of her flailing paw she cut me, and opened a deep gash that ran from the top of my head to the side of my mouth. She nearly took out an eye. Blood spurted into my eye impairing my vision. The sow stood upon her two hind legs and roared. She was as tall as my head. She was near her cubs and I was now a good distance away. We both retreated and went off our own ways. I knew from that point on that I could take care of myself. It took many weeks for the wound to heal, but finally it did.

–Woolly Mammoth Boy Remembers

SEPTEMBER 1979 CAME MERCIFULLY FOR my lonely, broken heart. Sure, it was I who had sabotaged another nice relationship with a fine lady, but who was counting? This was going to be my first fall season on the East Coast, and in New York City. Winter in Manhattan was like a scene right out of the 1965 movie *Dr. Zhivago*, which takes place in a frozen Russia during the revolution. I had heard about fall colors and the changing leaves and all, but to experience it "live" was going to be a really incredible experience for me.

Having ironed out my kinks in the first seven months of living in NYC, I was starting to become a real, newly minted New Yorker. September found me living on my own, making some cash to take care of my rent, which was $190/month in a rent-controlled building, and getting my job back with Mrs. Grossinger and her bakery up on 77th and Columbus Avenue after a summer in Tokyo. As before, I was working the morning shift, 6:00 a.m. – 9:00 a.m. at the bakery, and then the afternoons were for dance classes. I got right back into my intense ballet training schedule with classes taught by Finis Jhung ballet on 77th and Broadway, and my Cecchetti classical Italian ballet classes with Diana Banks, down on Chambers Street near the World Trade Center.

One day, an audition notice went up on the dance bulletin board in Finis Jhung's studio: "Auditions for Full Scholarships with the Alvin Ailey School of American Dance Theater – December 28, 1979 – Minskoff Theater on West 44th and Broadway, NYC. Sign-in begins at 9:00 a.m." This was it! This was the dance company I had moved to New York City for in the first place! Not a relationship, not a counter job at a Jewish bakery, not to learn how to say "Yo!" with *cojones*; no, this audition notice was my calling. The Alvin Ailey dance company was having auditions for full-scholarship positions—all classes and tuition paid for! I told my ballet master Finis Jhung about the audition notice.

"They are real good, Mr. Rubio." He said to me without blinking.

"Yes sir, Mr. Jhung, I know. It's the reason I moved to New York in the first place."

"Well, it seems you've got your work cut out for you, Mr. Rubio."

"Yes sir, Mr. Jhung."

My body was still changing into a dancer's body from an athlete's body. My thighs were still square in shape and strong. My feet were slowly building an arch, and I was gaining the skill to point them. My coordination was improving, but was still quite raw. My ability to put together dance combinations was good, though, and my ballet lines were nice and steady. Up to this point I had four months of true NYC ballet training, two years of college-level dance training and performance experience, and one *Nutcracker* performance under my dance belt, so to speak. It was going to be tough, but I had a fighting chance. I had all of September, October, November, and most of December to get ready. I knew nothing of real NYC-grade modern dance classes, but I knew I might be able to succeed at the jazz dance part of the audition because I had street jive in my inner-city-Motown-music-listening bones.

I worked like a dog in my ballet classes—four of them a day. Having a real purpose in my life kept my loneliness and depression at bay. I focused my obsessive behavior on dance training, and reading about dance history. My upstairs neighbor friend, Mel, who was from a small Caribbean island, provided some pot when I needed to mellow out. I was still very anxious and hyper. Mel was older and NYC streetwise. He was strong and in shape from being a bike messenger; he lived in a room the size of a large closet, and shared a kitchen and a bathroom with two other people on the fifth floor. Mel lived right above me and we fought at times about the loud music I played on my "ghetto blaster." We had a real older brother–younger brother relationship.

My first fall season in NYC was splendid. Bright oranges and reds mixed with brilliant yellow leaves; all left a sweet fragrance in the air. Folks on the street were a tiny bit nicer to each other, and the ladies were looking real fine in their soft sweaters and fall wardrobe. Being a delivery driver for Mrs. Grossinger's bakery, as well as being the counter person, enabled me to see a lot of Manhattan on my wee-early-morning delivery runs. I learned to race with the crazy, aggressive, yellow-checkered cabs driven by hellborn taxi drivers; I matched their daring and risky pace as they timed their runs to hit all the green lights while heading downtown on Park Avenue at breakneck speeds. Learning to drive in Manhattan would serve me well once I hit the mayhem of Boston's streets years later.

Driving and living in Manhattan meant forging a way of living so unlike growing up on the West Coast. The saying "If you can make it in New York City, you can make it anywhere" is true. I was toughening up my slushy, easily-pushed-around, West-Coast-love-beads personality. I was becoming a real go-getter. Being around people from all over the world, with so many accents, was a really exciting eye-opener, too.

One beautiful afternoon I decided to look for additional work to supplement my bakery job. I walked into Dobson's—a restaurant that catered to the theater crowd and the large gay community that was established on the Upper West Side. A godlike Apollo-looking man met me at the door.

"Yes?" he said. I could not make out the inflection in his voice. I had never met a gay man before.

"Hi, I am looking for kitchen work," I said with the eagerness of a puppy. He looked me up and down.

"Wait a moment, I will get the chef." Apollo gracefully glided into the kitchen. Out came a burly chef.

"Yes?" His accent was Italian and not inflected like Apollo's.

"Chef, I am looking for some work. I am good with the knife and can do prep work or anything."

"Well, my friend, there are no work openings in my kitchen, but there is an opening for a busboy."

"Sure."

Chef signaled for a dapper-looking man sitting nearby. "Michael, this young man is looking for work. Is that busboy opening still available?"

"Yes, Chef." Michael answered with an inflection in his speech similar to Apollo's. I was trying to figure what country this "accent" was coming from.

"Your name?" Michael inquired.

"Ron Rubio."

"Well, Mr. Rubio, have you ever bussed a table before?"

"Yes."

Michael led me to a table and asked a nicely groomed waiter to set a table for six. After the table was set, Michael says to me, "Please, bus this table."

Now, I had never bussed a table in my life. I just remembered a story my dad told us kids once about a job he had as a busboy when he was a young man. The story goes something like this: when Dad bussed a table not a sound of clashing plates or clinking silver was ever heard. The maître d' noticed how my dad bussed the table compared to the mayhem unleashed by the other busboys, and he promoted my dad on the spot. So that was my plan—I would be quiet as a mouse, not clash any plates, or clink any utensils.

I began bussing the table, stacking the plates one on top of another; quiet and efficient, I thought. With the plates placed quietly into the bus tray, I was done. The chef and the maître d' were watching me, smiling. The gathered waiters were grinning.

"You've never bused a table in your life," said the maître d'.

"Sir, you are right. I was a kitchen man." I answered.

"Look here, Mr. Rubio, you were very quiet and you look trainable. Come back tonight and Pierre will train you. The pay is $50.00 a shift, $250 a week, cash. Sound okay?"

"Thank you, sir."

"Be back at 5:00 p.m. Wear black pants and a white shirt, with a black tie." With that he turned on his heels and was gone. The gathered waiters snickered at me in a peculiar way and vanished quietly.

The chef lingered and said, "Good show. You were quiet in your work and very focused." He belched out a hearty laugh. "Good luck and welcome aboard."

That night I was to learn how to carry plates lined on one arm, and bus wine glasses without breaking them. By the end of the night I was a New York-trained busboy, and, I would later find out, working in an upscale Upper West Side restaurant. I was given a Monday-through-Friday night schedule, and I was to make $250 cash. That was a lot of money for 1979, especially for a dancer paying a $190/month rent. This would leave me with a lot of spare cash per month. I was really settling in to living and making it in New York City.

As the months passed, I worked in the early mornings at the bakery, trained ballet all day, and bussed tables at night. I was getting stronger and more confident in my ballet technique. I walked with confidence on the streets and had a New York swagger in my demeanor. That is to say, I had a look that said, "Don't mess with me or else you will make my day!"

The days got colder and winter arrived with a blast. I was alone and obsessed with getting really good at my ballet. I was sparse and frugal with how I fed myself. I only liked certain foods and did not cook; my hotplate was good for boiling water. I did the best I could. Soon the weeks counted down and I spent my first Christmas alone in NYC. I worked at Dobson's during the December holidays. I was also introduced to the holiday of Hanukkah at the Jewish bakery. Mrs. Grossinger was very jovial, and surprisingly generous with all the Jewish baked goods that packed our display counters. She handed out treats to certain kids and families that came in to wish a Happy Hanukkah. I did not know anything about Jews, or Jewish culture, before moving to New York City. It was great. I was learning a lot about the vast world, and all the cultures and people that made it up.

The day of the Alvin Ailey auditions, December 28, had finally arrived. I took my ritual morning hot water/cold water shower with a sense of purpose. The hot water opened my body up and the ice-cold New York tap water sealed my pores. It was a form of purification I would later learn ancient warriors had done. The hot/cold shower felt familiar to me. It felt like something a warrior would do before battle. I had read as a child the story of the elite Spartan warriors bathing before the Battle of Thermopylae that would, in the end, take all their lives.

I had the jitters like I was getting ready for a high school track meet or football game. The bright New York City day was sharp and cold when I hit the streets. I gave myself enough time to walk the thirty-six blocks right down Broadway toward Times Square and to the Minksoff Theater. The air was cold and brittle, and the people were all bundled up. I started my walk whistling and soon got lost in my head with thoughts of comparing Oregon trees to the tall buildings lining the long avenues.

I arrived at the theater around 8:30 a.m. (I always made it a point to show up early in life—I was kind of obsessed with this habit). Having arrived early, I was at the front of the line when the other dancers started to appear. The whole line circled around the long New York City block. I was told later that for the ten male scholarship openings, two hundred-plus men showed, and for the ten women openings around three hundred and fifty-plus women showed. This day would provide odd, unexpected opportunities of fortune sprinkled throughout the very significant experiences unfolding in front of me.

Upon signing in, I was given the number 49. I was told where the men's dressing room was and headed for it. As I walked down the storied hallways of this acclaimed dance company, I saw the walls were lined with posters of the famous black Alvin Ailey dance logo shown in a variety of colored backgrounds. As I began to realize I was in the training studios of a world-class dance company my focus got real spacey and my mind lightheaded. The dressing room was filled with men of all shades of black and brown, with a sprinkle of white. I started to feel comfortable. I dressed slowly, with great care and deliberation, as if I were going into battle. I wore all-black dance tights. My fantasy mind started to take over and reality started to drift. I started to feel a change in my perception as soon as I felt the tight-fitting dance clothing cling to every contour of my body. I felt sleek like a panther, like a superhero. I began moving with the grace of a galactic sun—powerful and charged with energy. I was the Silver Surfer! I was floating above the ground. I was a little out of my body. I woke up to the calling for all men to proceed to Studio A.

"YO! Get a grip Rubio!" I told myself as I moved with the mass of men. "This is real time!"

Studio A was a cavernous space with thirty-foot ceilings, and tall, rectangular floor-to-ceiling windows. Very breathtaking! Hundreds of male dancers mingled and jostled for space. Some knew each other and a jive-banter filled with nervous laughs could be heard. The crush of bodies was overwhelming me; it was way too stimulating and suffocating. I quickly found a quiet corner and began to stretch. I took a wide horse stance with my feet turned out, placed my hands on my bent knees, and started to stretch like a big, predatory black panther. I slowly scanned the entire room looking at and studying the other dancers. Some performed incredible triple pirouettes; others did standing leg stretches with one leg held high—almost vertical in the air and close to their bodies. Others did incredible splits on the ground with seemingly great ease. I stayed in my stretch position and barely moved. I watched and observed.

A tall black man entered the room with glasses hanging on the tip of his nose; he bellowed, "Everyone gather close!"

"My name is Mr. Stevens. I will be managing the audition today. The auditions will be in three parts—ballet, modern, and jazz. All of you have numbers and will be called by that number. Is there a number 49?"

"Yes," I answered.

"Come forward, Number 49." Mr. Stevens said.

The crowd of men parted to let me through. As I stood before Mr. Stevens he looked down at me and said, "There was a mix-up at the sign-in desk. Your number was given twice. You will now be 49A." He reached over, and drew a capital *A* on the number pinned to my chest with a black marking pen.

"Sir." I backed off into the crowd and noticed the other male dancers staring at me. I heard whispers:

"Bad shit. His number was changed. It is not even a number...it is '49A.'"
I took a breath and wondered how this day would turn out. Mr. Stevens continued.

"We got three hundred-plus women in Studio B, and we are going to join up with them. So what we are going to do right now is quickly break everyone into groups." He paused and scanned our dead, quiet studio. "We will begin by making four groups according to your ballet experience. Four years or more of ballet experience in Group One, three years or more in Group Two, two years or more in Group Three, and one year to beginner in Group Four. So form up, now!"

Now, this is where I made an impulsive decision. Technically, I had seven months of professional-grade NYC ballet training under my belt, with a combined total of a year of college ballet classes and a three-month season with a semiprofessional ballet company for a *Nutcracker* performance. That put my total ballet experience at two years, maybe. So, as I looked at the forming groups, I said to myself, "If I am going to go down today, I am going down with the best." So, I boldly and calmly strode over to the group with four or more years of experience. This group was comprised of the dancers who, during warm-ups, were doing multiple turns, showing off outrageous stretches, and stood around with veteran ballet swagger. I thought nothing of it. "To hell with it!"

With all the male dancers squared away into our four groups, Mr. Stevens said, "All right dancers, I want Group One to go into Studio B, next door—now!" As my group moved next door we passed a multitude of women dancers streaming into Studio A. The women dancers were all shapes, colors, and beauties. It was like being in an exotic human zoo.

The openness of Studio B was refreshing. Studio B was about 200 feet deep by 300 feet long, or so it seemed. The thirty-foot floor-to-ceiling windows faced and overlooked West 45th Street, and a busy Broadway theater across the way. The theater's front was lined with white bulbs that highlighted the feature show. It looked like something out of a movie. There were about forty-plus men in my group. Standing there to meet us were about seventy-plus women from their Group One. We were told to face the front of the studio, into a wall of six-foot-tall mirrors. Lining the mirrored walls were the seated gods and goddesses of Alvin Ailey's first company dancers and senior teachers. Group One, comprised of one hundred and ten-plus dancers, men and women, were going to audition before them. This was going to be the first cut.

A majestic, small, light-skinned black woman got up from her chair and stood before us. "I am Dolores Brown. I will be conducting the ballet section." The pianist was a white guy with a wool cap on. She turned to an assistant and requested that Group One be broken down into four groups. I was in Group Three.

We all backed up as Ms. Brown had a senior teacher demonstrate a ballet combination. The senior teacher was midnight black in skin color, lithe, supple, and strong, with an elegant and sensuous air to her; she was beautiful. The combination was surprisingly short and sweet—a series that showcased lateral movement, with leaps and turns, to be finished with a balanced pose. I watched as the first two groups of mixed women and men went before me. The staff and Ms. Brown wanted each group to rotate and do the combination twice, so front people moved to the back and back people came forward. As my group's turn came up I went to position myself at the front. I was thinking, "First impressions." I felt confident that my hard work during the last four months at Finis Jhung ballet, and learning the grueling Chechetti Italian ballet techniques, had made me strong, sharp, and balanced. Where some dancers executed triple pirouettes, I calmly performed clean doubles. The movement before the final balance pose was a series of leaps; I stopped and balanced on a dime.

After all groups did the combination, the examiners conferred amongst themselves and asked for some dancers to repeat the movement. Numbers were called out: "15, 19, 24, 29, 49A, 52..." I heard my number! I stepped forward again with a mix of other dancers. The same combination was called, and once again I nailed it.

"Dancers, please move back while we confer," said a senior teacher.

We moved back into a large group. There was small talk and nervous nail biting. I stared out the window at the theater lights across the street that had been turned on for the matinee show.

"When you hear your number please step forward and move to your right." Mr. Stevens then called out: "6, 7, 11, 49A, 52, 54..." I heard my number and stepped up and moved to the right with the other dancers. Finally, when all the numbers were called, we heard, "Those dancers whose numbers were called please proceed to Studio A. The remaining dancers please hand in your numbers and talk to Mr. Stevens. Thank you for your time." End of the first cut. The guillotine had dropped and heads flew! But not mine. Group One was down to sixty dancers from the one hundred and ten who entered Studio B. We moved into Studio A.

Studio A held a large group of dancers that numbered around one hundred and fifty; they were the remnants of the three other groups that had been whittled down. My Group A was added to the lot. I was thinking, "Damn, the school only wants ten men and ten women." We numbered about two hundred and ten-plus dancers. Mr. Stevens joined us.

"We will now start the second part of the auditions: modern dance. You will remain in your four groups. Each group will be broken down into smaller groups for viewing. Please take a very short water break." As we filed out of Studio A to the water faucets, the senior teachers and first company dancers filed in. They looked at us as front-line warriors might look at their replacements. We were all wannabes, and they were the gods and goddesses of the first company dancers, and our future dance drill sergeants—for those of us who made it that day, anyway.

Upon returning after a short break we listened to instructions: "Ms. Denise will now do a Martha Graham floor warm-up, followed by a combination. Everyone find a place on the floor." As a mass the dancers spread out and found a place on the wood floor. "Watch, do not do," was the command Ms. Denise gave in a curt, no-nonsense tone. As soon as Ms. Denise started to demonstrate half of the dancers started to follow. Ms. Denise barked out loud, "I said watch, do not do. Do you understand?" There was dead silence. I looked at the seated examiners; they were grinning and shaking their heads. Once again, Ms. Denise started to demonstrate, and a quarter of the dancers followed. This time Ms. Denise stood up off the floor and yelled, "The next dancer that doesn't follow my instruction is cut and out of here! Do you understand: *watch, do not do!*" The mass of dancers nodded their heads. Ms. Denise started again with no distraction this time. Whew!

After the Martha Graham floor warm-up, we were asked to stand for an across-the-floor combination. First, we were broken into groups within our four main groups. I was in the first group of Group A. Our accompanist was the same pianist from the ballet cut.

I had only taken three semesters of modern dance, but, as Ms. Denise performed the combination, I recognized the triplet step with turns and some other movements I had done in college, except now there was a flurry of new arm movements and balancing positions I had never seen before. Thankfully, I was gifted with a photographic memory, and, having drawn action poses from comic books for years as a kid, I was able to recognize some of these poses in the dance combination. I was in the first group to go across the floor and perform the movement. We were to go as pairs. My partner was a young black woman who looked like me—all dressed in black tights and filled with panther energy. When it was our turn to go, we took off. In that moment I was relying on something more than myself. Everything came together: the rhythm of the music, the mental images of the movements, and my peripheral vision of my partner. We nailed it.

After all groups did the routine, we were informed, "Please, dancers, move back and rest as we confer." And then again, "Dancers, when your number is called, please stand forward and move to your right." Dead silence. "2, 5, 31, 34, 45, 49A, 52…" I moved forward and to my right. Again, when all the numbers were called, we heard, "Those dancers whose numbers were called please proceed to Studio B. Remaining dancers please hand in your numbers and talk to Mr. Stevens. Thank you for your time." I had made the second cut. The guillotine blade was bloody; more heads flew and our numbers were lessened. The group entering Studio B was down to seventy from more than two hundred and ten.

It was now late afternoon. The last part of the audition would be jazz dance. As I walked into Studio B I noticed it had started to snow outside. Big, white flakes slowly descended from a dark grey sky. The white theater lights sparkled brightly in relay succession beckoning attention for the upcoming evening performances. It was magical. I once saw the same sight in a black-and-white movie about Broadway; the song about the "lights are shining bright on Broadway" came to mind. It was a sight I never dreamed I would see.

"Okay, dancers, this is the last section of the auditions. This will be the jazz dance section led by Mr. Alvin McDuffie," Mr. Stevens bellowed, waking me from my spacey attraction to the theater lights across the street. I saw that the accompanists were two conga drummers. I was going to like this part.

Alvin McDuffie was a slim and muscular black man whose aura spoke of funkiness and jive. He wore a bandana and had a goatee. He looked like a slim Eldridge Cleaver, a radical Black Panther member from the civil rights days of the 1960s. He said, "Dancers, I will do a short warm-up with you," but first he acknowledged the seated company dancers and senior teachers with a wink; then he counted out the drummers to a funky 6/8 rhythm, and we were off across the floor following him.

He had us do a walking combination toward the mirror where the seated examiners and first company members were sitting. It was a combination where your feet were keeping time as your hips and pelvis did another isolation movement, and your hands were doing something else all together. I was in the first group and rocked out. This was cake. It was like dancing in San Francisco as a kid to some Motown 45 vinyl records! I finished with my group and went off to the side to hang out as four other groups went through the routine. I looked toward the large, tall window. The snowflakes were falling heavily now, and the early evening darkness made the Broadway theater lights seem so magical. Their lights seemed suspended in a sea of white flakes...out of the dim space came a voice...a calling out...a repeating call...getting louder and louder...

"49A...49A...49A!" I emerged from my space out with a dancer elbowing me and yelling my number, "49A! Mr. Ailey wants you to do the combination!"

I turned to see the wide-eyed and frantic look of the dancer getting in my face. I looked around and everyone was staring at me. The drummers had stopped, and in the middle of the dance floor stood a big, burly, bearlike person with his hands on his hips staring at me with intensity. I hurried up to the front as the dancers cleared a space for me. I did not see that Mr. Ailey, *as in Alvin Ailey*, had walked into the studio and was watching this last section of the auditions. I stood before him. Every sound in the studio, and everybody in the studio, vanished from my periphery. It was the tunnel vision on the bear-man in front of me that mattered. This was Mr. Ailey!

He faced me at about arms distance, and clicked out the rhythm for the conga drummers with his fingers—he sounded like two sticks striking. "One! Two! Three! and..." We took off! Mr. Ailey was walking backward, and I forward. He snapped his big bear-paw fingers at my hips, looking only at my hips for five measures of four as I did the jazz combination.

Then he stopped on a dime. The drummers stopped on a dime. He turned on his heels and left the room. I was left breathless; frozen where I had stopped dancing. The vacuum left by his departure had taken all our breaths. I looked at the examiners; they were grinning at me and shaking their heads. The auditions were done.

As before we heard, "Please, dancers, move back, and stand down as we confer." And once again, "Dancers, when your number is called, please stand forward and move to Studio A." Dead silence. "5, 7, 15, 17, 21, 26, 31, 49A, 52, 58, 61..." I moved back to Studio A. I was still in shock, as were the others in my group. That was Mr. Ailey! I looked at my group. It was a mishmash of dancers. I knew some of them were really good, and others looked really raw. After seeing the previous cuts, I did not know where I stood. I had seen some really talented dancers cut early on. Mr. Stevens walked in.

"Okay, dancers, thank you for your time today. Please leave your numbers at the desk." My heart sank. I heard others gasp and sigh. The auditions had lasted almost eight hours and we were all tired. To go this far and not make it! Mr. Stevens started to leave, but then turned to face us and looked at his clipboard seeming preoccupied. "Oh, dancers. Classes start at 9:00 a.m. on Monday, so please be here to set up time to talk to Ms. Jefferson about your class assignments. Congratulations." Then he turned and walked out the door.

We were the twenty new scholarship students of the Alvin Ailey School of American Dance Theater, Class of 1979. We stood looking at each other and started yelling and jumping around. Someone suggested we go have coffee and chill. After we all got changed, we met in the lobby and walked around the corner to 8th Avenue to a diner. The snow was coming down and the air was surprisingly comfortable. We had all been indoors for almost eight hours. We were all exhausted and filled with energy.

"You know, Rubio, I knew you were going ace the audition," said a dancer sitting next to me at the diner.

"Yeah, me too. You just had that look about you," said another sitting across from me.

The group was looking at me now, and they all chattered at once about Mr. Ailey calling me out when I was spacin', staring out the window, and not responding.

"Yo, Holmes! You didn't see the Man walk in?"

"No," I said, laughing.

"We were all shittin' in our pants when Mr. Ailey called your number and you were spacin' out," the dancer next to me said, pointing to his head.

"Damn, I knew you were going to nail it, bro," said the dancer sitting across from me.

"Me too," said another dancer sitting next to him.

"How did you know?" I asked.

"Damn, when I saw you warming-up before the auditions started with all those dancers in Studio B, damn it, it was the way you were so...so..." The dancer paused.

"So what?" I asked.

"You were so calm and cool. While the others were struttin' their shit, you were just stretchin' and being really...blank...you were not showing anything that gave away nothin'!" he answered, grinning.

"It was like you had something on all of us and you were not going to show it until you had to...like you was playin' poker or something," added another dancer from across the table.

"Oh, well, I don't play poker. I was just studying the scene," I said.

"Yo, whatever man, you nailed that shit down!"

We hung out for a little while longer and then parted. I walked toward B'Way and hit Times Square. The place was hopping and packed with the post-Christmas tourists crowding the sidewalks. Times Square was lit up and bursting with energy; snow was falling and all the store lights were blinking brightly. I finally realized that I had accomplished what I moved to New York from Oregon for. I let loose a rebel scream and started to go berserk right then and there on the crowded Times Square sidewalk. People parted for me as I went bonkers. I danced in circles, twirling my dance bag around me, yelping and laughing like a crazy fool!

The crowd parted like the Red Sea did for Moses in the Bible. *There is this guy going crazy on the streets of New York. Give the man room!* I danced all the way home from the West 40s to my studio on 80th Street. I was now a New York City dancer!

The lone male mammoth eyed Woolly Mammoth Boy, who stood before him on the battle glade, with exhaustion and sharp pain. He felt the broken bones in his body. Not fatal but significant, his injuries would hamper his abilities once healed.

From across the short distance of a hundred paces away, Woolly Mammoth Boy could plainly see the damage he had done on his herd-mate and rival. The charging and rib-bashing contest was over, and he was now one notch higher on the social ladder. Slowly, he watched as the mammoth across from him breathed heavily as it sank to its knees.

"I am now a bull mammoth for the herd," Woolly Mammoth Boy silently acknowledged to himself. He looked over to the side of the battle glade where the elders and his mentors stood in a line facing him. The Matriarch stood alone in quiet fortitude, holding the truth of what she had witnessed.

One gained for one lost.

Woolly Mammoth Boy left the glade and moved toward the small mountain-fed pond of clear blue water. His body ached. His left tusk was loose. One eye was swollen shut. He walked into the cold, numbing water and submerged himself.

"I survived."

"Yes, you did!" cawed a black crow flying in circles above his head. "Yes, you did!"

29. Elevators and Bagels: NYC

Severe trauma, once charged into the blood and bones of the Mind and Body of a living being, is forever anchored there in each and every vibrating cell. Like a haunting, whispering breeze moving through tall summer grass, it first appears here, and then there. As hard as one may try to disregard the deeply embedded tremors and screams of that which had scarred the living breath, the trauma remains quite alive to remind the slumbering one.

–Woolly Mammoth Boy Speaks

UPON RECEIVING THE FULL SCHOLARSHIP with the Alvin Ailey School of American Dance Theater on December 28, 1979, I got out of New York City for a couple of days before classes started up. My younger sister was visiting from Oregon to see her new boyfriend who lived upstate in a college town called New Paltz, about a two hour train or bus ride north of Manhattan. I took the train that followed the Hudson River north. It was my first time seeing the East Coast outside of NYC. The winter season was here, and snow was everywhere. I hitchhiked from the train station in Poughkeepsie, NY to New Paltz.

New Paltz started as a French Huguenot outpost in the early 1600s. It was set in the fertile Hudson Valley with the Mohonk Mountain ridge ("The Gunks") due west. There were beautiful freshwater lakes and cool watering holes for hot, humid, summer dog days. The former world boxing champion, Mr. Floyd Patterson, made his home in New Paltz. SUNY New Paltz lent to the town a young college crowd and a hippy-dippy scene. I would visit New Paltz for the next ten years while dancing in Manhattan. New Paltz was my getaway place from the hustle, bustle, and craziness of NYC. That first weekend I had a great time with my sister, and even made some new friends. I saw the 1980s, a whole new decade, ushered in with a big snowstorm. After the new year I went back down to NYC to start my classes at the Alvin Ailey Dance School.

Life for me in Manhattan was now scheduled and laid out; it made me feel safe. Time had clear boundaries for me, and I was not just flailing in the wind waiting for things to happen. Things were *happening*, and I was proactive in their manifestation. My depression and tendency toward deadly procrastination did not get the better of me. There was purpose in my life; I chose to make my life worth living. I was going to be twenty-three years old.

I held on to my job at Grossinger's Bakery in the early morning, then grabbed the No. 1 local IRT from West 79th Street to 42nd Street. I started dance classes at 9:00 a.m. and finished by 3:00 p.m. I had been assigned four classes a day: Modern 1 (Graham), Ballet for Men, Jazz 1a, and an Afro/Dunham class. I was also assigned numerous special workshops held at the school. One was for a Brazilian martial art called *capoeira*. It was part dance and all martial arts. It was the first martial arts class I ever took, and this started a lifelong interest in the martial arts for me. After a full day of dance classes, I headed back uptown to Dobson's, up on West 77th and Columbus Avenue, and worked a night shift bussing tables. These were packed New York City days and nights.

I would get to my apartment by midnight, bone tired, and still having to mend and wash my dance tights. One night I had just gotten to bed when I heard a mad ruckus in the hallway outside my apartment, and then a crazy pounding on my door. There was a screaming woman's voice and a man yelling in English with a heavy Russian accent. Jumping out of bed, I rushed to the door butt naked. I unlocked all three locks on my door—the chain lock, bolt lock, and finally the bar lock—and flung the door open.

Standing in the dimly lit hallway right in front of my door was my equally naked Russian neighbor, whom I hardly saw, holding off a partially dressed, black-haired woman screaming in Spanish and waving a bloody knife. She turned to me pointing the freshly blood-stained knife at my bare chest and yelling in Spanish. As I kept my eyes on the knife waving in front of my face, my neighbor continued yelling in Russian.

"Yo! Stop yelling! Silencio por favor!" (This was the only Spanish I ever picked up from our high school Spanish class teacher who would yell at our unruly Spanish classmates so many times!) "YO! YO! YO!" I yelled. They both shut up for a second, and then both yelled at the same time.

"He would not pay me!" she said in Spanglish.

"She steal my money!" my neighbor said in Russinglish.

"Please give me the knife," I said to the Spanish knife lady. She quickly jabbed the knife into my face.

"No! Not unless he lets me go right now!" she threatened.

"No, she give back money!" my Russian neighbor yelled at me while looking at her.

With the bloody knife waving in my face, and both my neighbor and I butt naked, I had to put an end to this deadly situation. I reached out like a cobra and grabbed the knife out of the lady's hands, and then stepped in front of my neighbor with my back to him and yelled to the lady, "Go! Get out of here! NOW!" As I blocked my neighbor's way, the Spanish lady ran down the stairs and into the winter night. I turned to face my neighbor.

"You are bleeding, man," I said as I saw a red, bloody slash near his ribs. He looked down at his chest and saw the blood. Then he staggered back into his room. I do not think he knew he had been cut that bad. He closed his door and I was left naked holding a bloody knife in my hand. It was 3:30 in the morning. I went into my apartment and washed up and fell into a cold bed. The next morning I saw my upstairs neighbor, Mel, as he was heading off to his messenger job, and I was going to class after calling in sick to the bakery; I was too tired to go to work at 6:00 a.m. that morning.

"Filipino, what happened last night?" Mel asked in his Caribbean Island accent.

"Yo, you mean this morning! Yo, this lady slashed my neighbor over money. I guess he did not get the service he paid for and was holding back the money. She grabbed a knife and slashed him. I woke up, intervened, and took the knife from her and she took off. Damn Mel, I was butt naked when I answered the door!"

Mel looked at me with anger. "Filipino! Don't you ever do that again! Don't you open your door in the dead of night for anybody! Man, you could have gotten stabbed yourself!" He stared at me and looked as if he was going to throttle me. "You too nice, Filipino! Mon, this is not San Francisco! Don't do that again!" With that, we parted to start our day.

Damn. Was I wrong? I had heard that, in the 1960s in Manhattan, a woman was screaming for her life as a man raped and stabbed her. Many people heard her pleas as she ran from door to door, but no one did a thing. The man chased her down and stabbed her to death while people watched and listened. It really shocked the nation that so many people had heard the woman cry, but no one helped her. It gave NYC a real ugly reputation as an uncaring city. Mel may have had a point. New York City violence back in the late '70s and early '80s was unpredictable and deadly, but I was not one to stand around when someone is in need. So screw all those nondoers. I was not going to allow the Big Apple to turn me into a heartless, stone cold, uncaring human being. I decided there and then I would never turn my back on anyone. I was not a martial artist, and I knew it was crazy to jump in on something going down on the street. A deadly knife or a cheap gun could appear out of nowhere, and shit may go down real ugly, real fast. But that was a chance I was willing to take. I was no hero, but I was no standby person either. Never. Ever.

My dance schedule was intense, and it was exciting. The Ailey School drew people from all over the world. The morning hours, when students were signing in, was like viewing an exotic zoo of beautiful men and women of all shades, colors, and of most races, except there were very few

Asians. A heterosexual male dancer was a real find in the dance world for women dancers. I made up a population of around 5% that were not gay, and the women knew it. The gay male dancers were chiseled, gorgeous, and untouchable to the women. I was getting hit upon by both men and women. After a while the gay dancers knew I was not interested, and just played around with me like I was their cute cousin. The real "queens" were absolutely funnier than hell to me, and they all knew it. The way their long, colorful scarves wisped behind them as they danced down the hallways was delightful. The Latin gay dancers were a real crack-up with their overly exaggerated gay accents and mannerisms that drew cheers all around. It was a very lively place to be.

I had my choice of the many women who were interested in me. It was not like I was an Adonis- or Apollo-looking young man; I was just another exotic animal in a very international human zoo filled with other beautiful exotic animals. Hooking up was the way a dancer, who worked his or her tail off surrounded by gorgeous bodies all day, could indulge in the sensuality of it all; it was a way of letting off steam and getting some relief. Plus, most of the dancers at the school were far from home, living packed like sardines in some real funky spaces with perfect strangers. When word got out amongst the women that I lived in my own place on the Upper West Side I became a very attractive catch.

It was so surreal, and I learned quickly that beauty truly was only skin deep. At first, the studio was an overwhelming, constant sensory overload of sexuality and sensuality. Beautiful black women, brown women, and white women were always ready for a night out. What I did not experience as a teenager with girls because of racism and being a weirdo loner in high school, was erased as a dancer at the Alvin Ailey dance school. I remember my social trysts becoming so overwhelming that I started to forget names and who I was supposed to be with that night. At first, all the exhilarating excitement of exotic flesh and sensuous beauty—to be so easily enamored by the scent of a woman—was a heaven on earth for me. But I was soon so burnt out and overstimulated that I withdrew because it started to feel hollow. Sensation without meaning. Form without substance. I knew there was a "heart" piece missing from this whole physical madness. I had to remember that all the women were my age, early twenties, and on their own like me. It was all new and exciting, but flesh for flesh's sake was cheap, I soon realized. It was just another stimulant in the dance capital of the world. New York City: The city of stimulation.

Being an Asian with Latin features, I was given the opportunity to make my mark in the company—if I could excel in my training. That first couple of months of my scholarship was really going well. I was honing in on the Ailey dance style, and working hard in all my classes. There were three companies under Mr. Alvin Ailey's directorship. The first company was the world touring company; the second company—the Repertory company—did national tours; and the third company—the Workshop company—did colleges and local events. You climbed up the companies until you reached the top company; or, if you were hot, you went straight to the top. I was making my way up toward the third company.

Then, disaster struck in April 1980: I injured my knee. I had been pushing hard in my dance classes, and it was the last class of a very long day—Afro/Dunham class with Ms. Peters. I loved the class. I went up for a high kick leap and landed on a buckling left knee. The medial collateral ligament went out. I fell to the ground. I dragged myself off the dance floor so as to not stop the class. Ms. Peters checked up on me. I could not stand on my leg. I was pissed. Back in college I had a similar accident in modern dance class. I made it home and mellowed out.

The next morning my knee felt good enough wrapped up to go to work at the bakery. Dance classes were out though. I had a talk with my advisor, Ms. Jefferson, about what happened. She said to take a couple of weeks off. My scholarship would stay intact.

"Mr. Rubio, heal yourself and get back into your dance schedule," Ms. Jefferson said to me in her office.

"Thank you." I left the school.

I had a good amount of money saved up, so I asked for some time off work to heal my knee. I got the go-ahead from my bakery and the restaurant job for the time off. At the time there were some really groundbreaking injury rehabilitation programs just for dancers being developed in NYC. One program was the precursor to what would become Pilates, and involved those innovative, room-filling wood machines with the pulleys and levers; these machines worked the injured parts of your body while putting very little stress on the rest of you. It was expensive as hell, and I only had a couple of sessions.

Around the same time my friend Adele, whom I met in New York at a friend's party, got a piano-playing gig at a hotel on the French/Dutch island of St. Maarten in the Caribbean. She invited me down there to work my knee out in the salt water and sand, and I jumped on it. Adele and I were friends and I liked that about us. It was a relief for me. We were very comfortable in each other's presence without needing the messiness of becoming intimate. It was late April in NYC, and the cold and snow still gripped the Northeast, so island sun sounded great. I took off for two weeks, and it was just what the doctor ordered. Food was free, my friend housed me, and we had a blast in the sand and salt water. My knee healed with nature. No machines, no gimmicks, just sand, salt water, and simple exercises.

I had one incident while I was there that illustrated my youthful perception of mortality. Having been in the surf and water all day drinking tequila sunrises, I drove back to my friend's house. The island had curvy, sharp-turning coastal roads; I was driving like I had nothing to lose and feeling pretty loose from the alcohol, speeding around up and down these dangerous, narrow island roads. I went zooming up a hill and flew—right off the top of the hill—and when I landed on the other side, the road wasn't there anymore; it curved drastically to the right! As I headed toward the edge of the cliff into the crashing sea below, I jammed the brakes and pulled a James Bond driving maneuver that got me swirling around, sending the dirt and dust flying all around me. A car coming up the opposite side of the road stopped at the bottom of the hill and watched. Back and forth I swerved to the right, then back to the edge of the cliff, until finally the car stopped, enveloped in a cloud of dirt and dust. I was facing in the right direction; I was intact and so was car. I let out a hysterical, laughing scream, and then continued on my way as if nothing happened. As I passed the car at the bottom of the hill, the occupants were laughing and pointing at me. So what? I made it and that was that. I was not meant to die that day. I was young and fearless. I left St. Maarten in one piece the following day.

I got back to NYC with a healed knee. I returned to my full dance schedule a little gun-shy, so I had to jump right in and continue with gusto to get back into it. Bussing tables was getting old, and I had overheard that Mr. Ailey wanted to paint the entire school. I went to Mr. Stevens and asked if he would hire me for the painting job. He said yes, and I went into my restaurant and quit the bussing job. It was a little impulsive, but that was the way I was in my brain (people with Asperger syndrome can be real impulsive at times; jump first and ask questions later). I knew how to paint commercially, so I put in a bid that would do me right, buy all the paint for the job, plus a little bit more. I was told I could paint after my dance classes and when the dance center was closed on weekends. The money would last for a while, so I took the chance and moved on from the restaurant.

One day, as I was prepping the first company's warm-up room, I witnessed what would be the beginning of the end of Mr. Alvin Ailey. At the time the room was lined with posters of the black Alvin Ailey dance logo in different colors, roughly twenty of them. Mr. Ailey came in with his assistant following close by.

"Take all these posters down! Throw them all away!" Mr. Ailey yelled, gesturing at the posters with a jabbing, accusing finger. "Get them out of my sight!" The room was filled with first company members when it fell deathly silent. The assistant tried to calm Mr. Ailey. He stormed around the room and then fled like a raging bull.

Within a year, Mr. Ailey made newspaper headlines about an incident that included erratic, violent behavior, and involved a student of the school. I could relate to the madness that had gripped Mr. Ailey's mind. It is a madness that consumes you when you are pushed to a place where reality and darkness meet. It's a place where emotions and confused feelings merge into a volatile mixture of white-hot rage and uncontrollable thoughts of violence that are unmercifully pointed inwardly toward the self. I felt real bad for Mr. Ailey. I recalled that as a child, when I was being misunderstood, not validated, and beaten, the reality of my world of fairness and right would clash with the world of my tormentor, the racist and bigot, or my dad. Cornering a wounded animal is asking for death by a berserker.

Painting the entire Ailey School, including all the dressing rooms, bathrooms, and large dance studios, took me almost a month—but it was a job I accomplished well and it made me some good cash. My dance buddies had a good laugh at my expense. I was the painting dancer. All dancers had to do real odd jobs to make living in NYC work. Some of my friends did really weird and dangerous dance jobs at sleazy bars. I had an experience or two with those sleazy dance-for-money jobs, and I choose to bury those memories. I reminded my dance buddies that I had my own place, and did not have to share a small East Village studio with six other dancers from Brazil or Kansas. That shut them up quick!

About this time I got my first cat ever. I named her Lúthien Tinúveal. Lúthien was from Tolkien's *The Lord of the Rings*. In the book she was an elf maiden who had given up her immortality for her love of a mortal man, Beren the Half-Hand. Lúthien was a black and brown tortoiseshell cat. A friend's mother from school had set her up for adoption. Lúthien would greet me when I came home from work at night, and sit on my lap while I smoked a unfiltered Turkish cigarette to decompress from a long day. I built her a porch outside my window so she could sit outside while I was gone. Her porch was at treetop level so the birds would give her hell all day. She was great company for me.

The building where I lived became a haven for bachelors. There were sixteen apartments, and twelve bachelors lived there. We had floor parties in each other's apartments, and became a family of brothers. We were dancers, actors, composers, bike messengers, printers, musicians, student lawyers, and holders of jobs you asked no questions about. About those secret jobs:

when I asked what they did, they told me it would be best for me not to know. "Let's us just party." Fair enough. No questions out of me. It was truly amazing to have other men to confide in about your daily fears and joys, to party with, and to make sense of the crazy life living in New York City.

The summer of 1980 came in hot and humid. It was my first summer in the city, since the year before I had been in Japan and Asia. It reminded me of Japan, hot and humid, except for the smell of sour milk and urine down near Times Square and other places in the city. NYC pulsed differently in the summer; there was a looseness to people's struts. The subways were unbearable, though I was now accustomed to the shrieking metal and screaming trains. This is when I started to ride in between the trains. As my train pulled into the station I jumped the chain guard between the cars, and stood on the ledge at the end of a car. There would be others like me, who, not wanting to be in the stuffy overcrowded cars, rode outside in between them. Some would be smoking pot, and others listening to their Walkman tape players. It was risky riding in between the cars because the express train really cooked down the tracks slamming the cars side to side; you really had to hold on or you might lose your footing, fall in between the cars, and get crushed or run over. Crazy and surreal, it was an experience that woke you up or really mellowed you out. It was just another part of living in NYC, where everything you did involved taking a chance, but you were young and only had one shot at this life, so what the hell?

I got my first dance-teaching job that same summer. I was down in Washington Square Park in the West Village, near New York University, when I walked into the day care center looking for more work. There I was offered a position teaching a creative movement class for two- to five-year-olds. I said "Sure." I loved being around those little ones.

Later in life I would be involved with NYC-sponsored summer movement and art classes for inner-city youths. I would be sent to places in Harlem, Far Rockaway, and Queens. To see this gritty side of NYC was always an eye-opener for me. It was a great social service, and all these teaching opportunities gave me tools and strategies to deal with the challenging behaviors of the wide spectrum of kids I would work with for the next thirty years. I related so easily to their dismal plights, and the savage ways they communicated their anger and grief. They came from broken homes triggered by violent, criminal deaths, drug addiction, and the random challenges of just being in the city. Many of their parents were in prison doing time, or dead from doing drugs. I fell right in with them and they accepted me as a kindred spirit. This gave them the boundaries and guidance they sought after, and this was the glue that made our relationship work. My supervisors marveled at how I worked with these kids; and the word went to other agencies out that I was a "fire jumper," to be placed where the kids were the worst. I welcomed it tremendously.

Getting these extra jobs helps a lot when you are budding artist in the biggest shark-city in the world. NYC would eat you up if you were not on your toes, and I was learning quickly. I also started modeling for art classes at The New School on 5th Avenue, and Parson's School of the Arts. All the hustling around for work allowed me to continue my full schedule of classes at the Ailey School, still pay rent, buy food for my cat, and eat. I no longer worked at the bakery or the restaurant, and at times money was real tight. The local diner, the 79th St. Diner on the corner of Broadway, knew me well. I remember coming back from classes one night; starving, I walked into the diner and sat down, the waiter recognized me easily. I was up front.

"Good evening, my friend." He greeted me with cheer. In most diners in the city, the waiters or counter people would greet you with, "Hi, my friend!" in Greek, Spanish, Chinese, or some accent other than English.

"Good evening. I need to be honest, I have no money and I am starving."

The waiter knew me, looked at me for a brief second, and said, "I will keep a tab, my friend. Pay when you can. I trust you."

I was so grateful I must have blurted out "thank you" a million times. He got the point and took my order. I would pay my tab after a few weeks and then start another. It was the way the city worked after it got used to you, and people knew you were going to stick around.

Life in the Upper West Side was very different from other parts of the city. The Upper West had budding families, a mixture of races, and big loft spaces where most of the ballet masters rented for cheap and had taught for years. My particular section of 80th Street between Riverside Drive and Broadway had four or five welfare recipient hotels and housing units. My friend, Charlie Brown, lived in one that was right across the street from my building. Charlie Brown was an older black man with snowy white hair and eyebrows. He reminded me of the character Uncle Tom from the early white movies that depicted the stereotypical "old black slave." The specialty food store Zabar's was on the corner of 80th and Broadway, and above their store was one of these welfare hotels.

One late fall day, I heard Charlie Brown ranting and raving on the steps of his building. I crossed the street to see if I could calm him down.

"Damn! Youngblood! They are kicking us out!" he yelled with rage.

"Who is 'they'?"

"They the landlord bastards! Youngblood, they are moving us all the way uptown! Damn, I have no money for the train to come downtown to get my welfare checks or meds!"

"Shit, Charlie Brown! When are they moving you guys out?"

"End of the month! Damn, Youngblood! They are clearing us all out of here. All the hotels on this block, all the way up to Broadway!"

"I am sorry, Charlie Brown..."

He looked at me with sorrow and confusion. "Youngblood, got a dollar?"

"Sure." I gave him three for a cheap bottle of wine. I knew that would soothe him.

By the end of November all the welfare hotels were cleared and vacant. The landlords were going to remodel them into expensive condos. I know it was their property to do with what they would, but being a person for the people, I was angry and frustrated that those who had naught were at the whim of those who had. The welfare folks above Zabar's were going to fight for their right to stay. The local paper, *The Village Voice*, wrote articles on their plight, and about fighting the "big sharks" with money. I was going to watch this closely.

At this time my dancing at the Ailey School was once again doing well. The Martha Graham dance techniques included a very tough series of exercises done on the floor. For some men the exercises were very challenging. You needed to have really loose hip joints or your knees would take a real beating, and I had tight hip joints. Having started my dance training when I was nineteen years old instead of twelve years old, I was really playing catch-up. Though I was getting better with the Graham modern technique, my knees were sore. I kept up my rigorous training four classes a day, plus working modeling jobs, a couple of sleazy club dancing gigs, and other odd jobs. It was tough living.

That winter, I was dating a dancer from Sweden, and she and I were in bed hanging out listening to some jazz on the FM radio, when a news flash interrupted the program.

"This is an important news flash: Ex-Beatle John Lennon was shot and killed in front of his residency at The Dakota on 72nd and Central Park West! He was shot five times..."

I jumped out of bed, and my friend followed me as we rushed out of my apartment on West 80th and ran down to 72nd Street to The Dakota where John Lennon had lived. A small crowd was already there. The snow was coming down lightly, and we were all in shock. People were in anguish. People were crying, moaning, and huddled together. Cops were everywhere; news lights turned the night street into day.

This was John Lennon who was killed. John Lennon of The Beatles. I was numb and confused. My heart was all over the place. I left my body. My friend held onto to me and was crying. John Lennon was dead! What was the world coming to? My friend and I headed back uptown to my place as the area in front of The Dakota became packed with news crews and onlookers. We slept that night holding each other tight as if the world was not going to exist the next morning.

In the days after John Lennon's murder the city continued on its crazy pace, but with a heavy heart. The winter came in with cold temperatures and snow. One night before Christmas Day, a crew of thugs came in and threw all the folks who lived in the hotel above Zabar's out onto the streets amidst the cold snow. The newspapers caught whiff of this, and photos of the poor people and their belongings strewn all over the snow-covered sidewalks of West 80th and Broadway filled the morning pages. Nothing could be done, and the incident was just the beginning of the gentrification of the Upper West Side and other neighborhoods throughout Manhattan. Soon all the great ballet masters would lose their dance studios. Barnes and Nobles and other shops would fill in the vacancies. Zabar's expanded their food specialty store to the second floor; where once the poor folks lived, shiny cookware now lined the new shelves. I would never step into that store again. I would boycott Zabar's as long as I lived in Manhattan.

The world had changed. The passing of John Lennon was the passing of an era of reason and the loss of a voice of truth. This was just the beginning. There was more to come. The New Year was uneventful and I was alone with Lúthien in my apartment. The snow fell outside my window, and the world was hushed by the thick, falling whiteness.

For me, 1981 started out with auditions for the Alvin Ailey dance school again. This time it was different. My class had received the last scholarships given directly by the Ailey School. In 1981 the school began accepting BEOG (Basic Educational Opportunity Grant) applicants, and the standards of student quality was not so stringently kept. Anyone could apply for a BEOG, and upon receiving a grant, be eligible for the Ailey School. Like most dance companies in NYC, the national economy was pretty hard on them, so the major schools tried to receive federal monies to help them survive. The 1980s represented the decline of New York City, which, in my mind, could no longer hold the title of "Dance Capital of the World." Most top dance companies were losing the dance homes they had held for decades. Ballet masters were losing their places to teach, and New York City was not making it easy on the dance world it had sought to own as part of its "Big Apple" prestige. Like the saying goes, "All that glitters is not gold."

The halls of the Ailey School were no longer beholden to the strict traditional dress codes of the year before. Now the hallways were a kaleidoscope of color and visual distraction. The strict dress code had allowed the teachers to see the students' body lines and help them make corrections, but now it must have been like looking at some glimmering rainbow fish in motion to the teachers. The quality of the student dancers was definitely below grade. Most of them were out of shape and undisciplined. It seemed the whole dance world was changing. Mr. Ailey's behavior was becoming more erratic and unpredictable. The dance world was becoming a bargain sale with more for less—cheap thrills and gaudy, flashy dancing was everywhere. Audiences were actually clapping and hooting at dancer's multiple turns and high leaps as if the dancers on stage were performing circus tricks. Traditional dance manners meant saving your applause for the end of a performance; dance was not a gymnastics meet to be applauded for exciting and well-executed movements.

    I started to feel empty. The mentality of Americans was too simplistic and easily stimulated; maybe this was because Ronald Reagan was elected president the year before, and the Age of "Reaganomics" had begun. Credit cards and buying beyond your means were the rallying cry. Buy on credit! Art was being sold out for cheap. The rich got richer and the poor got poorer. I knew I had to focus on what was in front of my face and leave the rest alone, because the whole world was just too much for me. Living in New York City was enough just in itself. I focused on my dance training.

    My body continued to change with all the training. I was becoming leaner and less square. My muscles were long and stretched. I held my body with great elegance and grace. Being in my body helped me from becoming spacey and depressed. Interactions with fellow dancers kept me on my toes; they also helped me understand the social nuances of the performing arts business. By observing my fellow dancers' social behaviors and body language—the subtle nuances of emotional and physical expression—I slowly started to develop my personal expressions of how I wanted to present myself to the social world. In my physical carriage, or in the way I stood at the bank line, or sat at a restaurant, or walked down 5th Avenue, I presented my newly developing physical image to the public.

    I also started to get involved with more dance theater study. Theater taught me how to put on different facial masks for different characters; dance theater created the communicative body that spoke without language. In a world without words, dance theater was a fertile ground where I slowly developed my bodily and facial language. I began to "see" the quick and seamless way people "spoke" volumes without speaking verbally. For instance, while at cast parties and gatherings like dance galas, where political and social statuses are built and maintained, I would observe how small physical gestures produced powerful reactions and understanding.

During my lunch breaks at the Ailey School, I would sit on the steps of the public library at 42nd and 5th Avenue, and watch all the folks walk by. I studied their facial masks and their walking habits, noting all the theater games being played out in real time between people and perfect strangers. I got pretty good at identifying people's true intentions by how they stood, sat, walked, looked at you, or spoke. It became really easy to see people playing their games, but I was too naïve in so many ways to utilize all that I was learning.

All of this was essential for the creative trade I was in, and living in highly stimulating and sensual Manhattan, this training helped me in the theater of real life as well. It was so rewarding. For you see, I had not learned the social nuances of body language and facial expressions one learns at an early age—on the playground, or in social games and circles. I was oblivious to the social subtleties around me, and frankly I did not care. I was too involved with my little world to care about others. Theater allowed me to understand what the hell was going on at parties and other social events.

Though I was getting to be New York City-tough, I was still soft and gullible in my heart. There was still so much to learn. I stumbled and fumbled along with dating women who were not always shiny and beautiful. I had numerous short relationships with dancers who were just as quiet and lost as I was. Just being with a woman, and all that was "woman," attracted me. Later in life, when I worked with young men with Asperger syndrome, I came to understand that there was one characteristic among many others related to Asperger syndrome: often having a single, obsessive attraction to one thing and one thing only. That one "thing" might be an intense interest in all there is to know about trains, microwaves, maps, action figurines, vintage electronics, or any object under the sun; Aspies would do anything to have or be around that one thing that stimulated their focus.

As an undiagnosed Aspie, I had an obsessive focus on the stimulation I received from "Love and Woman." I wasn't a stalker or driven to be in relationships, I just wanted to be around women and explore all there was to know about them. The fact that I was a rigid thinker and had anger meltdowns (my rigid thinking of "Do it my way or the highway!" inevitably led to fights), that I would close up emotionally when I was confused and would leave my body when driven into a corner (the infamous "spacing out"), and that I had my own limited ideas of what defined "relationships"—all this added up to create major roadblocks on my life journey with women. With every failure, I would put another Band-Aid on my heart by numbly apologizing for the agony, guilt, and shame I caused, and thus take the "blame" for the demise of the relationship. I had left countless women bewildered and hurt, and then moved on—hopefully with more wisdom. I was not proud of the burning wrecks I left in my path, but I kept trying to understand "love" and not give up.

In the spring of 1981, I started a one-man carpentry business called Lothlorien Woodworks, which specialized in "space-creating" for lofts, small kitchens, and tight little New York studios and apartments. "Lothlorien" was the Elven woodland kingdom from Tolkien's *The Lord of the Rings*. I bought some cheap Black and Decker tools, and started doing small weekend jobs so as not to interfere with my dance classes during the week. I got a few good-paying jobs. I learned a lot of from my mistakes—how to get lumber from the lumber store to the actual job site, or how to get all that material up four flights of narrow New York stairwells, for example. I saw that New York City was the place to live out the American dream of capitalist free enterprise and out-of-the-box moneymaking schemes. I did very well for a dancer-artist living in the city.

My color and race meant nothing to the average New Yorker, because the average New Yorker was of many races. Things could be different in the snobbish Upper East Side or in the other small enclaves of rich white folks—certain areas of Park Avenue and the like. But I had no trouble in Black or Spanish Harlem, crazy Hell's Kitchen, or Alphabet City on the Lower East Side. If you walked with the New York strut and put out the energy that you were partially insane enough to not give a damn, people left you alone most of the time. Even the crazies let you be, because you were crazy like them, walking on the "wrong" side of town.

In March, I was approached by one of my Ailey teachers and asked if I wanted to be the choreographer for the Miss Greater New York beauty contest to be held at the Beacon Theater on Broadway on the Upper West Side. I took the job with a smile. This opportunity was my first chance to explore the art of creating a dance piece.

I walked into the dark Beacon Theater and beheld the big stage filled with beauty contestants of all colors and shapes. I walked up the steps and introduced myself as the choreographer who was going to teach them how to walk down the runway and perform the opening dance piece. I was not wholly impressed with the contestants. They were all beginner dancers who had the basic "lets-get-down-and-dance" energy any person growing up in the city was surrounded by, but they just had no stage knowledge. My first choreographed piece was simple and easy to learn. It moved the contestants around the stage and showed off their elegance and smoothness. I really liked the role of chorographer, and I also liked working with the light and costume designers. I saw how things ran backstage and off on the wings; I got an overview of how to put it "all" together. The job lasted three months. It was a great experience, and one that put a desire in my veins to have more opportunities like that one.

One day in early summer, after my modern dance class at the Ailey School, my knee was aching pretty badly. I couldn't do what I wanted to on the dance floor. I became gun-shy about certain movements. Though I had the potential to climb the ladder up through the companies of the Ailey world, my body was telling me different. I pushed through the pain until, early that summer, my knee just pooped out on me. I was instructed to watch all classes while attending rehab. I knew something was coming to a head, to a critical mass. By early summer it was evident that I needed to seriously address my knee if I was going to move forward with my dance career. Once again, I was asked to heal myself and come back in a couple of months for a re-evaluation. So I left the Alvin Ailey School again.

I got a summer job at a sleepaway camp for Jewish kids; it was two months in the Berkshire Mountains of Massachusetts as a dance teacher and counselor. There I met counselors from England, Scotland, and France. I healed my knee and had some typical summer flings. The newness of the Berkshires was beautiful and brought me back to my days in Oregon. Nature was powerful; the summer nights were magical and filled with fireflies and night wanderings. I made enough money to figure out what I was going to do with my life in NYC, but in the middle of everything I was offered an opportunity to drive across the USA with two British dudes.

What a journey! From NYC to LA, transporting a car for a person who was making a coast-to-coast move, it was one adventure after another. Most of the time I wanted to be alone, but I talked too much because I did not understand the importance of silence in a group. My British friends told me to shut my mouth often. I learned to keep my thoughts to myself, though I did not understand why this was important. We had a great time. The US of A is a great big country, and driving west meant you would always be following the sun. I would make this cross-country journey three more times in my life, but the first time is always special, or so I am told.

Upon returning to NYC in September 1981, I got work with a construction crew working on an abandoned building right down the street from my apartment on West End Avenue and 80th Street. I needed money, and I was still trying to figure out what to do with my knee and my scholarship with Alvin Ailey. Working on a construction crew in NYC is the experience of a lifetime. For the first time in my life I worked with metal studding to build walls instead of with wood, as I had done with my construction crews in the west. It was fun working on a crew with other guys again; I did miss dancing at the Ailey School, but being around a crew was a blast. The guys on the crew were teaching me how to talk and be more confident in the madhouse of New York City. Having worked on cooking crews and construction crews in the west, working with a New York City construction crew was still real new and extremely funny to me. My crew chief, or lead carpenter, was a Korean and Vietnam War Marine veteran from Brooklyn. I had crewmates from all over the boroughs, and all with distinct mannerisms and accents. Their jokes were real crack-ups. It was surreal to me that people actually talked like they did in the movies I saw about New York City. There were four other crews working on this eight-story, crapped-out building that was being turned into plush condos. It was here I saw my second death up close. (My first experience with death was my older cousin's death in the 1960s.)

On a beautiful, crisp, November morning I was working as I had been for the last month and a half. That day I met a new addition to the demolition crew. The Kid had just moved to NYC from Jamaica; he was twenty-one years old. He was beautiful with clear white eyes and smooth black skin. It was payday Friday, and during the mid-morning break I went to the corner for a bagel. The Kid had never eaten a bagel before, so I bought him his first one. Now, on this construction site all the wasted material and demo debris was dumped down a chute on the fourth floor. The only working elevator was a derelict elevator car whose doors did not shut and did not have working controls. I remember my first briefing on the job from my crew chief, the Vet.

"Ears alert and listen up, ladies. The only elevator we have on this site is a temperamental S.O.B. The elevator doors do not close. So, if you must ride the car, step in and keep your hands close to yourself. Press the button and hold down, and release when you reach your desired floor. Now ladies, sometimes this elevator has a mind of its own. Sometimes it will rise on its own. Should this occur, ride it to the next floor and walk out or stay in until it stops. The car will stop on the top floor always. Understood?"

"Yep!" "Yo!" "Yeah!" "Sure!" came our answers. The Vet continued.

"Secondly, there is no return or call button to the elevator. If someone from another crew calls for the elevator, they will yell for it through the elevator shaft, and if you are the one who used it last, you have to bring it down or up depending on how many floors they are calling from. Most of the time everyone will walk to the floor where the elevator is. If you can use the stairs do so. Okay, end of speech." Every crew on the site got a similar speech from their crew foreman or chief.

On that beautiful November morning, after a satisfying break and with our paychecks in our pockets, all the crews were back at their separate jobs working on different floors of the building. The Kid and I were on the sixth floor, having ridden the elevator up, when someone on the third floor yelled for the elevator.

"Yo, I'll take it down," I said turning to The Kid.

"No, mon, I'll take it down," The Kid looked at me with a smile.

"Yo, whatever. I can do it," I repeated my offer.

"No, mon, it's no sweat." And off The Kid went, taking the car down to the third floor.

It was one of his mates on the demo crew that called for the elevator to take it up to the fourth floor to dump a load of debris down the chute. I was working not more than ten minutes after morning break when a horrible scream was heard and the power throughout the building was shut off. There was frantic yelling from down below.

"GODDAMN! HELP! HE IS STUCK!"

I looked down the dark elevator shaft to where the elevator was two floors below me. More screaming and horrible crying could be heard. I ran frantically down the dangerous, narrow stairs, tools flying out of my tool bag as I leapt down the final steps. I reached the floor where the elevator was stopped—halfway between the third and fourth floor. I could hear crying and someone going crazy on the third floor below me. I jumped into the open, dark, unlit elevator car; I could barely see in the dim light that The Kid was lying on the floor of the car. A mere second later, the Vet was next to me. We both got on our knees. He took out a small flashlight, which revealed The Kid lying on the floor of the elevator; I started to reach for him as the Vet trained his flashlight upon the Kid's body. One arm and one leg were visible. One half of his body was in the car; the other half had been sucked into the shaft and was wedged between the car and the wall of the elevator shaft. I stood up quickly, aghast at the sight of The Kid's body; I was in shock.

The Vet stood up slowly, sighed, and said, "He's dead." His voice emotionless and empty, like a deep, dank, cold cave. I got myself together and went down the stairs to the third floor where all the crews were assembled. I could see the wall above the header of the third floor elevator opening bulging inward: the other half of The Kid's body was wedged in there tightly.

His demo crewmate was hysterical, repeating his story to everyone around him. He was screaming and crying, "The dude brought the car down and I was going to roll the wheelbarrow in when the car started to rise on its own! The motherf*cking thing was rising on its f*cking own! I told him to stay in the car. The kid started to walk out of the car, and then he got scared and tried to go back into the car! The f*cking thing was still rising and the kid's foot gets caught on the header and he is pulled into the shaft. The dude screams once and then is silent! Motherf*cker! It happened so fast." He continued mumbling in shock. The other guys tried to comfort him.

"Everybody pack your tools and all your shit! The EMTs will be here and the place will be packed with cops and personnel," my crew chief yells to all the carpenters. Other crew chiefs tell their people to get their gear in order and out to the street. The building was dark because the emergency power breakers had shut off the electricity. Soon four EMTs were on site with about twelve cops and firemen. All were men except one female EMT. I watched as they took the wall apart above the third floor elevator shaft and freed The Kid's body. They laid his body on the floor at my feet. The Kid was wearing work overalls; you couldn't see the damage to his crushed body. No blood, no gore.

As he lay there bubbles start to form in his mouth. "He is still alive!" I exclaimed.

"Naw, that's the spent air in his lungs coming out," said the Vet who was standing next to me. I watched as the EMTs wrapped The Kid's body in some type of white canvas. His feet and head hung out unceremoniously. The Kid was a tall, beautiful young man. I watched as the men on the EMT crew, alongside the cops and firemen, strutted around, laughing loudly, putting on a show for the lone female EMT, who seemed to enjoy all the attention she was getting. I was in shock and could not understand their callous behavior in light of the fresh death of The Kid.

"Rubio, get down to the street with the rest of the crew," Vet ordered. I started down the dark flight of stairs to the bright morning light that bathed West End Avenue.

It was only 11:30 a.m. A little over an hour ago The Kid had been eating his first bagel, which I had bought for him: one hour ago this young man was smiling with his paycheck in his pocket. The bright morning sun was hurting my eyes. I held my four-foot level in one hand with my tool bag draped over my other shoulder.

I turned as the EMTs carried The Kid's body out to the ambulance. His head and feet hung out, dangling and swaying in the all-too-short canvas body bag that carried him. I went crazy at the sight of disrespect to his body. I dropped my tool bag and took my four-foot level in my two hands. Later my crewmates told me I had started to head for the EMTs and cops, cursing them. I do not remember that part too well, but I do remember vaguely being held back as the cops faced me with their hands reaching for their sidearms. I knew I wanted to strike them all down. I heard a voice from a distant place yelling at them: How could they be so disrespectful? My crewmates held me tightly. The next thing I knew, I saw the Vet screaming in my face and telling me to stand down. It was like a weird dream. The sun was shining bright, and the dead kid's body was being hauled around like a broken mannequin ready to be thrown away. I left my body. I floated above the circus.

I heard a command from the Vet, "Everyone go home. We will call you later. I doubt there will be any work here on Monday. The OSHA investigation will take time."

The Vet looked at me. "Rubio, get home in one piece." Moving like I was in a dense fog, I turned the corner of West End Avenue onto 80th Street to go to my apartment less than a hundred yards away. My apartment felt like a prison. My clothing was caked with dust and dirt. My tools were in disarray in my tool belt. I was going crazy. I felt my body raging with emotions I did not understand. I had to call someone; I had to hear a voice. I called my dad in California.

"Hello," My dad answered.

"Dad?"

"Ron? You okay?"

"Dad, I just saw someone die on the work site I was on..."

Silence. Pause.

"Ron, son..."

"Dad, this kid was crushed in a elevator accident. I was there..."

"Ron, I am sorry..."

"Dad, I am going crazy!"

"Ron, be cool...is there anyone you can talk to over there where you are?"

"Dad, there is no one I can be with. The crew chief sent us all home." I think I was screaming into the phone, but I couldn't tell. "Dad, the job site is just around the block from me."

"Ron, be cool...be cool, Ron." Dad was lost as to what to say to me.

"Dad, this just happened this morning." I was forgetting the three-hour time difference meant it was only nine in the morning in California.

"Dad, I got to go...my apartment is too small. I am going crazy!"

"Ron, you be cool now...don't do anything crazy."

"Goodbye, Dad."

"Ron..."

I hung up.

I rushed out of my apartment and hit the bright street. I walked past the work site. I would have to walk past that place every day. The place was vacant: everything was chained up, and no one was around. I took the train uptown to my ex-girlfriend's apartment.

The intercom crackled on. "Yes?"

"Jackie, its me...Ron."

"What do you want?" The voice was hesitant.

"Please let me in."

"Why?"

"There was an accident on the work site I was on...someone was killed..."

Silence. The buzzer startled me. I opened the door and ran up three flights of stairs. I knocked on her door.

"Ron?" Jackie said through a cracked door.

"Jackie, I did not know what to do. The kid was killed in an elevator accident."

She looked at me and kept the door slightly ajar.

"Ron, I am sorry."

"Jackie..." I was pleading.

"Ron, I am not here for you. I told you I would not be..."

"Jackie?"

She looked at me and slowly closed the door.

I slid down the wall outside her door and started to cry and cry. The world seemed distant. My body seemed transparent. My consciousness drifted. I spiralled down...

I got up to leave the building and walked back downtown somewhere.

So this is the big city! Death and brightness...a glorious day. Payday Friday! Blue skies and the air filled with the fragrance of late fall. I started to see white rage. Alone. I was alone. The city continued to hustle and bustle. All those smiling faces around me didn't know that a beautiful young man died a horrible death. Leave me be! Get away from me! You all don't know!

I got back to my place and collapsed. I tried to sleep and sleep. Nothing mattered. All this shit just didn't matter! Whatever...

Monday rolled around and the job site was shut down, thick chains upon the doors, blackness from the vacant windows. It would be this way for months. I headed downtown to look for work, into the West Village on the No. 1 local IRT train to Christopher Street and 7th Avenue where life was bustling. Restaurants lined the avenue. Crossing west off 7th Avenue, you were in the gay community of NYC. I walked into the Limelight restaurant; the place was next to the famous Buffalo Roadhouse, and up the street from the jazz place, Sweet Basil.

The owner was a big, rough-hewn Irish man. "Can I help you?" he greeted me in heavy Irish brogue.

"I am looking for work. In the kitchen or on the floor, sir."

"You done this work before?"

"Yes, sir."

He looked me over and said, "Come back tonight and trail a waiter. Might have a couple of lunch and brunch openings. Okay?"

"Thank you, sir."

"Come back around 5:00 p.m. and help set up."

"Thank you."

I would wait tables there for a year. The Limelight was a hopping place; it was a watering hole for the owner's cocaine friends. At the Limelight, the waiting crew was tight. Like most crews or teams I had been in, the camaraderie was loose and fun. Since I had kitchen experience I got along well with the temperamental head chef and his prima donna cooks. On the weekends cheap tippers from New Jersey came in and were a real pain in the ass. Back in the early 1980s in world of NYC waitering, tourists from France were nicknamed "Frogs," and they were a pain in the butt, too. They asked for a lot and tipped little. I remember one French couple walking in on a busy Saturday night. Us waiters saw they were French and we flipped a coin to see who would serve them; we all knew they would be a pain in the ass and nobody wanted them. I lost the coin toss, and the "Frog couple" was seated in my section.

No matter what I did, the Frogman was a pain. The Frogwoman was all raised chin and pretentious. "Yo!" I was thinking, "Yo, this is New York City. We are some of the best waiters around and we know how to serve." When the couple got up to leave I noticed their tip on a $175 tab was a few quarters and two pennies thrown in. Two pennies!

Now, something has to be said about Asperger syndrome. Aspies tend to speak what is on their minds, unnerved and unmoved by the possible consequences. Our actions may be described as "impulsive" and sometimes we may come off as rude. Well, seeing the pennies got to me. The other waiters were laughing at me—we knew about Frog people and their infamous lack of tipping skills, and we all knew this was coming. But two pennies? Here is a lesson for all you people who go out to eat in restaurants: be cheap if you want to—what goes around comes around—but never leave pennies! NEVER!

As I watched them leave the restaurant, I tracked them both in the crosshairs of my vision, like a panther tracking its prey. The Irish night manager saw me watching them leave. "Now now, Mr. Rubio. Leave them be."

"You saw the two pennies. You saw the service I gave them."

"Leave them be...they are not worth it," he said to me, while trying not to smirk.

The blood went into my head and, without saying a word to the manager, I rushed out the door after them. The night manager tried to follow me out into the street to call me back, but he was not authorized to leave the restaurant. I caught up to the Frog couple at the street corner of 9th and Broadway, which was filled with the Saturday night crowd.

"YO!" I yelled at their backs. They turned.

"Take your cheap tip! This doesn't even buy a subway token!" I hurled the 52-cent tip into the astounded Frogman's chest. "Try not to be cheap at your next restaurant stop!"

I walked back to the Limelight with my back held straight. Some people who were in the surrounding crowd must have been off-shift waiters and waitresses, because they applauded me wildly. In typical New York fashion, the restaurant people in the crowd started to hoot and badger the Frog couple. I got back to the Limelight a few yards away, where the night manager was waiting for me. He witnessed the whole affair.

"Okay, Mr. Rubio, none of that again." He was trying to be serious.

"Yo, you saw how the crowd responded. Enough said." I went back to the welcoming arms of my fellow waiters. New York City was teaching me how to stand up for myself, and to fight for my beliefs and rights. You do not cut a person off in line in New York City, and you certainly do not leave a lousy tip on a hardworking New York waiter. If you do, you best be prepared to defend your decision and take the lumps, for they will surely come.

It seemed that, back in the early 1980s, white people in New York City did not mess with people of color, be they black, brown, yellow, or red. I guess white people knew anything could happen on the streets of NYC, and the privileged knew they could act their uppity way in their guarded-gate world, but not on the streets. Now, if a person of color headed out into the racist white areas of Queens or Brooklyn, well, that was just plain stupid. Racism was alive and well in the '80s in the northern United States, but Manhattan was just a cool place to be if you were a person of color. As a brown man I was taken for many different races. The black folks let me be; the many types of Hispanic people saw me as one of them; the Chinatown crowd, the Asians, accepted me. The only part of Manhattan that could be a little weird was Little Italy, but even in that small part of Manhattan there was a sense of tolerance.

By late fall of 1981, my knee was strong enough and I had enough money to take a few ballet classes. I had heard of a brilliant master ballet teacher who had developed a series of exercises that were done on your back. The exercises relieved pressure on your joints and also strengthened you to recover from (or prevent) dance injuries. They were called Floor-Barre exercises. The master teacher was Madame Zena Rommett.

I took the elevator up to the fourth floor of a tall building at 20 West 20th

Street, between 5th and 6th Avenues. The building was the home of the Zena Rommett Ballet Studios (4th floor), the Joyce Trisler Dance Company, under the direction of former Ailey dancer Milton Myers (6th floor), and the Erick Hawkins Dance Theater Company (3rd floor). The building was always a buzz of dancers going to different floors for their classes. Erick Hawkins was a contemporary of Martha Graham, and had danced in her company. He was a real pioneer in dance theater. Joyce Trisler was one of Alvin Ailey's dancers. A quicksilver of a dancer, she was one of the few white dancers in the early Ailey Company of the 1950s. The Horton-based modern dance technique of the Ailey School was taught under the direction of Milton Myers, but I was at 20 West 20th Street for Zena Rommett.

I walked into the loft, and saw a large studio with many carpets laid out on the wooden floors. Madame Rommett was about to begin a 10:00 a.m. advanced Floor-Barre and ballet class. Her daughter, Camilla, met me and gave me the rundown of the classes. There was no viewing of her class allowed. I was told if I was interested in her classes I would have to start with the 6:30 p.m. beginner's class. No problem. I felt like the 1970s TV show character Steve Austin from *The Six Million Dollar Man*. Steve was an Air Force pilot who got mangled in a jet plane accident. As Steve Austin lay on the operating table all messed up, the doctors looked at him and said to each other, "We can rebuild him." I was putting my money on Madame Rommett to rebuild me.

Madame Rommett's loft was a typical, big, downtown open space. Maybe 50 by 150 feet in dimension, the loft had aged wood floors and pillars. The floor exercises called for eight or so 20-by-15-foot rolls of carpet section to be laid out for dancers to lie on. Sometimes there would be six dancers per carpet. The floor barre exercises lasted for about 45 minutes to one hour. The exercises consisted of ballet movements usually done standing up, but instead were done isolated, lying down on your back, so you could really focus on the "core" of each movement. This type of training was extremely tough and unforgiving on your center. You were building core body strength, and in doing so, you were strengthening the flexibility and fluidity of all the movements of your body. The floor barre exercises were followed by a one-hour regular ballet class taught by Madame Rommett, where you would then stand and execute ballet movements with strength and control. Most dancers taking her classes were doing so for injury prevention, or like me, rehabilitation from injury. The 10:00 a.m. class was comprised mostly of the top dancers from various dance companies in New York City. It was inspiring for me to witness what these professionals did to keep in tip-top shape. It was also amazing to see the top ballerinas, danseurs, modern dancers, and jazz dancers all taking Madame Rommett's morning class. It would take me two years to get into the 10:00 a.m. class from the 6:30 p.m. class.

I was offered a work scholarship there, which I took without question and with great gratitude. My job was to lay out all the carpets before class and vacuum all the carpets after class. I also cleaned the dressing rooms and bathrooms, and painted if needed. I soon started to read and learn about kinesiology and physiology. I wanted to learn what had happened to me, why it happened, and how to heal myself. Not having a lot of money, I could not afford to see doctors. My readings started to include energy healing, color and sound healing, medicinal herbs, and tea usage. I had this idea of being as self-sufficient as possible. No one was around to take care of me, and I had no money for any type of medical care. My whole life had been a study in looking out for myself and making a world for myself, because I certainly did not fit into this one.

Madame Rommett's classes were showing me how to stand tall and move in safe ways while conserving energy. I marveled at what I was beginning to learn. For so many years I had been so disconnected and out of my body, and had not cared much about it. I looked back at my younger life and wondered how in the hell I made it out of those tumultuous years of trauma, despair, and anger. What I was involved with now was changing me and my whole life for the better.

One day in late December, I took the elevator up from Madame Rommett's loft to check out the Joyce Trisler Dance Company, and the Horton classes being taught there by former Alvin Ailey dancer Milton Myers. I talked to him after class and he suggested I take part in his classes while I was rehabbing my knee. I was thrilled to be moving in a modern class and be around Ailey people again. As December came to a close, I visited Ms. Jefferson at the Ailey School, and talked about my scholarship. It had been two years now since being awarded a full scholarship. It was time for a re-evaluation.

"Come in, Mr. Rubio."

"Thank you, Ms. Jefferson."

"So, Mr. Rubio, your scholarship is up. If you want to continue here you have to re-audition, and sign up for a part-time work scholarship as well," Ms. Jefferson said as she looked over my dance class records. "How is the injury?"

"I am over at Madame Zena Rommett's, and all goes well. I also started taking the Horton floor exercises with Milton Myers at Joyce Trisler's."

"Good." Ms. Jefferson knew Milton Myers, of course, as he was still performing with the Ailey Company. "Can you come back?"

"Ms. Jefferson, my knee is not strong enough, and I am working hard to get back into shape, but I am not sure if I can audition next week."

"Well, Mr. Rubio, you just continue to get better. I do have to close up your scholarship, though. I know this is tough news, but the program here is strenuous, and it seems you need to take care of your injury."

Silence.

"Thank you, Ms. Jefferson, for your time and for talking with me." I stood up and we shook hands. I left the Ailey School for the last time. I had come to New York City almost three years prior from the West Coast to be with this company, and had accomplished part of my dream. I was bummed out and crestfallen, though I knew I had given it my all—and after all, I did make the 1979 Alvin Ailey dance auditions! But now I was on a path of recovery, getting stronger and learning to dance more intelligently. I understood my body in a way I never imagined I could in the past; I was okay. Everything was going to be okay.

I flew back to San Francisco to see my family for the holidays. Mom came down from Oregon and stayed with my brother. I went to my dad's house. Dad was not happy to see me; he was angry that I had not saved my money and stayed in New York, and had instead wasted it to see my family. Being around my family had always been a sad and disappointing experience for me. It was no wonder I lived on the other side of the USA. They all wanted something else for me. Here I was, the only person in the family who lived on the other side of the nation, in the most expensive city in the country, trying to be a dancer. It was bewilderment, pity, concern, shame, or ridicule that I got from my family. I guess I had been odd since birth: so unwanted by my Dad, so sensitive and high maintenance for Mom, so weird and embarrassing for my brother, and pitied by my loving sister. I realized the farther I was away from them, my family, the safer it would be for me to grow.

A week later, I was arriving in New York City on a red-eye flight from San Francisco on New Year's Day 1982. Welcome back, Filipino!

The woolly mammoth shook the snow from its thick hide. All around the city there seemed to be noise, light, and vibration.

It was an energy that seemed always there, always vibrating.

See! See the coffee mug trembling on the table? See the newspaper trembling in the man's hands? Did the undercurrent wake the baby again? Or soothe it to sleep?

There is a constant humming in my mammoth bones—bones the two-leggeds will dig up someday. There are no woolly mammoths around this area...not here in Manhattan. I know. Distant cousins lived up north in the Hudson Valley, some mastodons I believe.

I can feel this vibration if I am awake or asleep; it is like an echo of the earth shifting from deep down below. When I am walking the streets, the vibration seems to come from below the sidewalk, or above from the vast sky. People around me hum. The tall cement buildings hum. The lovers hum after screaming and moaning.

My woolly mammoth senses are overwhelmed. It is certainly not like being near the glaciers of distant pasts. Then, all had been still and vast, despite multitudes of lifeforms evolving, dying out, or being created. The front of the massive glacier wall was miles high, and at its feet was lush life. From its crushing weight and receding coldness sprung life of all shapes and forms. A world still young and yet so old.

Here in the city all is evolving, but to what? Superficial and materialistic madness. Hunters and predators all around me. I saw a saber-toothed tiger the other day in a tuxedo, eyeing out his next meal. Scary! To his left was a woolly rhinoceros sorting garbage from a trash can, looking for something tasty to eat. To her right, a mountain cave bear was about to have an argument with a cop.

I best make my way back to Central Park, which is where I left the herd.

Part 5: Life Dancing

30. Boston Tea Party

For a person who is a rigid thinker, life can be a black-and-white world, filled with extreme opposites—it is challenging to see "the grey"—the middle way. This "shutter-vision" thinking produces an uncompromising behavior that brings grief and pain to himself and those around him. Destructive and unmerciful, this polarized thinking takes no prisoners, while asking for forgiveness for all the havoc and sadness it creates. Please show mercy to the poor soul who is trapped in this hell.

–The Queries of Woolly Mammoth Boy

THE NEW YORK WINTERS WERE cold and extremely bitter at times, and the winter of 1982 was no different. January, the dead of winter, brought cold winds that howled down the wide, vacant avenues; the steam radiators in my apartment overheated and dried my place so badly I became prone to nosebleeds. The winter nights made me feel very lonely. Maybe it was the fact that all around me people scurried off the streets to get out of the cold. Maybe it was the fact that it was freezing-ass cold outside, and the ground was covered with white, slippery, ice-packed snow. I would put on my gear and walk in the winter night. It was like when I was a teenager in Walnut Creek, California, taking midnight hikes up into the foothills of Mt. Diablo. To me there was something special about being alone in the elements and in nature, especially at nighttime.

Bundled up I would walk down to Riverside Park, or down to the 79th Street Boat Basin. No one was around, and the snow would pile high on the sidewalks making narrow corridor trails. I did not fear the dark paths where no one walked. I liked it that way. It was like being on an adventure—like Bilbo Baggins in *The Hobbit*. It was all in my head and I played it out in real time.

The seasons kept you honest about the changing world around you, and seasonal changes were something that really resonated in my bones. Maybe it was because I had been a woolly mammoth in a past life and a mountain puma in another that the ancient animal in me felt at home with the shifting New York City seasons, but New York City in the winter was a very different place than New York City in the fall or spring. It was a tough world of coldness and death, of retraction and introspection, of deep sleep in a dark cave or burrow. The winter season was tough.

My world was an adventure of Life and Death. Every moment was a thrill. Damn, I never felt comfortable in this world anyway, and the people who were supposed to take care of me when I was young had made it a very dangerous place. The racism and the hate-fear that I experienced in the social world around me had made me very weary. It made me more daring, more eager to live in my peculiar manner, a manner that not too many people understood or cared for. This was how I saw my life—on my terms, right or wrong. That is why I hated simple things like transitions. I liked making my own schedule and not being at the whim of someone else's fickle change in plans. I liked structure. Structure made me safe. The world overwhelmed me, but the four seasons were a different type of transition I could handle. The seasonal changes were transitions that were organic to this earth; they were part of *Gaia*. Humans in the social world were unpredictable and dangerous to my sanity. Humans pushed against the rigid structure that I had created to be safe.

Many years later, I would learn that most of my anxieties, fears, anger rages, sleep deprivations, lack of confidence and social skills, immaturity, and obsessive and risky behaviors could be attributed to Asperger syndrome, post-traumatic stress disorder, and traumatic brain injury. But those insights were too far ahead in my future to help me or guide me now. 1982 was fresh and I was a young man in New York City in the dead of winter.

That winter, when I returned from California, I went back to work at a restaurant as a waiter. My friends there were great, and being in the funky West Village was fun. My dance classes at Madame Zena Rommett studio were going great too. My body was getting stronger and felt more under my control. Madame Rommett allowed me to move into the intermediate class at 1:00 p.m., and my classes with Milton Myers were also doing well. Keeping up with the Lester Horton technique and the Alvin Ailey tradition was solid. One day in Zena's class, a dancer I knew asked if I would check out a modern dance class with a former Martha Graham dancer named Dan Wagoner. I walked into his packed class just down the street from 20 West 20th Street.

Dan Wagoner's teaching and choreography was humble and technically challenging. Quirky, it had a down-to-earth kind of feeling. Mr. Wagoner's people came from West Virginia and the Appalachian Mountains, so his dance and style just felt very *Americana*. It was very different from my city-boy rhythm and Motown/R&B background. After his class Mr. Wagoner invited me to be an apprentice at the company. I appreciated his dance lines and the heart energy in his choreography. I took up the opportunity to be inspired by him. Why not? I was in New York to dance and learn. I was the only person of color in his class, but I did not mind; I was used to it. Back in the '80s, the ballet world was mainly white, except for companies like the

Dance Theater of Harlem, Alvin Ailey, and a few others.

My dance world was really exciting and full of challenges and new relationships. I met a woman in a ballet class who was from a small town in Kansas. She was taller than me, and very engaged by the smaller things in life, as I was. She liked quiet poems and small pictures of landscapes in small frames. Our passionate short-term relationship kept us laughing and questioning during those winter nights and days. It was very easy to be with her. Yet, I was still trying to understand how to express myself in relationships and this was still a very difficult, elusive thing for my heart to learn. I realized after a few months I did not really know what I wanted from a woman. Physical passion and sensual connection was never a problem; that part of being in a relationship with a woman was like swimming in calm, blue waters for me. My passion for the physical expression of love was like painting—using a palette of vibrant colors, the smells of turpentine and lush, rich oil paints, filled with bold strokes and light touch—but expressing emotions, and the day-to-day experience of living with someone, confused me. (I had stopped painting a year before, only producing one painting the whole time I was in NYC. Dance was using a different type of paint.)

I expected to be understood and forgiven, but I could not offer the same in return. I would allow my raging anger to rear its self-righteous head; I would scream and say things meant to hurt my partner. I realized I was creating chaos out of serenity. Then came the apologies—"Please forgive me!"—it was like I could not believe I could be loved, that someone could actually accept me. I feared abandonment and being alone. I protected myself by blowing up on the ones who loved me. I wanted to abandon them before they could abandon me. My relationships ended as they began: with intense passion and fury as if the day would end too soon. Looking back, it seemed that this was the dynamic way my life transpired up to that point. All my experiences seemed to be tinged with intense emotion and high vibration.

One day I was walking past the building at the corner of West End Avenue and 80th Street where I had worked and witnessed the death of the Jamaican kid the year before. I stood looking at the building when a gentleman walked out and came up to me. He lived there, and I asked him if he liked it. He said "yes," and we spoke about the building, which was now a set of beautiful condo-apartments. He asked me if I did carpentry. I said, "Yes."

"I need shutters to be installed on all the windows, about nine double windows, for my apartment," he said.

"My name is Ron Rubio." I took my hand out of my glove and offered a handshake.

"My name is Nicholas Azerbandian. Call me Nick."

"Thanks, Nick. I can install shutters for your apartment," I answered. I needed the money and it was the dead of winter. The offer for work came out of nowhere, unplanned, but that was the way New York City could be—opportunities springing from nowhere.

"I live down the street on West 80th near Riverside Drive. What floor do you live on, Nick?" I asked nervously, thinking of the day when The Kid was killed in the building.

"I live on the fourth floor. Right off the elevator," he answered.

My heart froze and I lost my breath. The Kid was crushed in the elevator shaft between the third and fourth floor.

"You okay?" he asked. In that split second he had seen something in my glazed eyes.

"Yes, thank you. I just was thinking of something for a second."

"Why don't you come by my apartment and take some measurements," he offered.

"Sure."

"How about tomorrow? Say around 6:00 p.m.? I am in apartment 4C, facing West End Avenue."

"Okay. Thank you. I will see you then." We shook hands and parted.

I was amazed that life offered me an opportunity to make some money in the same building I had witnessed death. Amazing! I figured I could do the carpentry job on the days I wasn't working in the restaurant, and between my dance classes.

The next day I stood before the row of buzzers next to the apartment numbers. 4C. I saw the well-lit and carpeted lobby through the clear glass doors. Part of me could see the split image of the lobby just as I remembered it—a gritty, dark work site filled with the ghosts of work crews long gone, and that kid walking silently by. I took a deep breath and buzzed.

"Yes?" a voice crackled from the little speaker on the wall.

"Hello? It's the carpenter, Ron Rubio."

"Please, come on up." The door buzzed and I pushed through.

The lobby smelled of new carpets and freshly painted walls. The hallways to either side of me, that ran north and south, were lit with bright fixtures. I walked up to the elevator, and paused at the elevator door. In my mind I could hear the voices of ghosts, of work crews—male voices shouting, a scream, and then dead silence. I looked and saw a new staircase beside the elevator. The old staircase was buried behind the new walls. Just then the elevator's polished steel doors opened with a ringing chime, inviting me in.

I backed away from the brightly lit elevator car, seeing myself in the mirror attached to the elevator car's far wall. Nope. I took the stairs to the fourth floor

I arrived at the fourth floor and stood looking at the closed, highly polished steel elevator doors. I expected to see the elevator doors open, revealing The Kid's crushed body lying on the floor of the elevator car. I awoke to the sound of apartment 4C's door opening.

"Welcome." Nick stood at the door. His hand extended. I turned to face him and took his hand.

I took the measurements and saw it was at least four weeks of work, and consisted of buying the shutters, painting them white, and then installing them. The logistics ran through my head—getting the material to my apartment through the snow-packed sidewalks from the lumber yard; spray painting all the individual shutters, getting them to Nick's apartment, and installing them. I knew I would have to deal with going into the building, and I knew I could not walk all the material up four flights of stairs. I would have to take the elevator. As I walked down the stairs to the lobby, I told myself I would cross that bridge when I got there.

In my life up that point I had to face so many dark places alone. It was something I was trained to do. My dad was a hard-ass and treated me with the tenderness of a predator cat playing with a mouse. He taught me to be tough and get over it. He hated when I cried and he hated weak, stupid people, which I was. He'd beat me, and would scream into my dreams, into my fears and hatred for him. To know he was training me to be a leader of men was tough to keep up with, as a clumsy slow-in-the-head child and teen. "I am not training you to be a sergeant, I am training you to be a captain!" Okay, I get it!

Life was, and had been, a great mystery filled with social landmines, racism, and the struggle of trying to be accepted; of trying to obtain the American dream as a first-generation Filipino American; and now I was faced with working in a ghost building and the trauma of a horrendous death. I could do it. The "why and how" were not questions for me to ponder. I needed the money and that was that. I was alone and that was that. I wasn't going to be able to click my heels and make all my dreams come true. Nope, it was my destiny to take the hard road. Why? Someday it would all make sense.

I went numb re-experiencing the trauma of death in the building, but I would finish the shutter job for Nick. I took the elevator to the fourth floor; the first couple of times I found myself holding my breath while in the elevator car. Painting the window shutters ended up being a complete clusterf*ck. Moving around all that material in the snow-clogged sidewalks and wind-whipped wintry streets was tough and frustrating. In the end, I finished the job; I got the money and received complete customer satisfaction. It was all in the training. Damn you, Dad! And thank you.

As the winter continued I would take the train up to New Paltz to visit my new friends on weekends. My friend, Danny, always received me without question and I was grateful. I remember on one trip I asked to borrow a friend's car, and took a drive up to Lake Awosting during a snowstorm. I parked the car near the road so it would not get stuck, and I hiked three miles or so to Lake Awosting in heavy snow. I was safe in my waterproof clothing, and I had ample food. The snow was coming down hard and the skies were dark. I loved it. I was alone and feeling oneness with the elements. The pain of being around people and feeling alone was gone. I was totally at peace.

When I arrived at the lake the surface was frozen solid. With the heavy snow coming down, I went to the lake's edge and tested the surface—solid as a steel slate. I walked to the middle of the lake without fear. There was not a human soul for miles. I sang a few songs and danced on the frozen lake. I screamed into the cold wind; I tasted the moment with joy and contentment. I imagined that if I were to fall through the ice, no one would ever know. My cold body would sink to the bottom. Frozen and at peace. But, naw! I would have to go back to the world of men and continue my life to whatever ends I was meant to manifest. I was only twenty-five years old.

Stu Kohler up in New Paltz wanted me to meet his buddy Stewart Lerman from college, who was starting up a band in New York City. They needed a percussionist. I got Stew's phone number and called.

"Hi, Stewart Lerman? Hi. I am a friend of Stu Kohler up in New Paltz."

"Hey, what's up?"

"My name is Ron, and I hear you are starting up a band and looking for a percussionist."

"Yo, we are. Why don't you come up to our studio on 30th and 8th Avenue—8th floor, studio number 4."

"Cool, what time?"

"Tomorrow at 8:00 p.m. You got your drums?"

"I have a set of bongos. Thank you, Stew. See you then."

Now, I didn't actually have any drums. I had sold them all in Oregon when I moved out to New York City back in 1979, so I went down to the music store section of Times Square. I viewed an assortment of Latin drums at different stores, and settled on a nice set of bongos, not to be confused with the larger congas. I arrived at 30th Street and 8th Avenue early to find the building. It was not hard to find. It seemed there were whole buildings nestled in the Fashion District that were devoted to rehearsal spaces for musicians. From the street you could hear many different bands practicing at full volume—rock bands, punk bands, soul, R&B, and everything in between. I entered the building and got into an elevator packed with band members who wore spiked hair and black leather, glossy clothes, and large Afros, or the large winged collars sported by professional studio musicians in the 1980s. It was a circus of smells and sights. At each floor the elevator door would open to a blast of sounds and screeching, electrical chords, booming bass, and screaming vocals. The elevator door would close, and then an odd silence emerged until the next floor. I arrived at my floor and pounded on the studio door. I was invited in with a yell: "Yo! Come in!"

I entered and was greeted by two women and three men. One of the women had short, cropped blonde hair, and the other was tall with short-styled brown hair and a beautiful smile. A man with curly hair sat behind a drum set. Another guy with a handlebar mustache sat behind a beaten-up piano. A small, dark-bearded man walked up to greet me holding an electric guitar.

"Ron?" he shook my hand. "Stew Lerman. That's Hope Fisher," pointing to the close-cropped blonde-haired woman. "She is the bass player. That's Mike behind the drums." Mike pointed at me. "Marty Balin is the piano man." Marty tilted his head in my direction. "Judy Whitfield is the lead singer." Stew bowed to the tall woman with the beautiful smile; she held an acoustic guitar. "Here brother, have a seat." I sat and looked at the band. Everyone was distinct in looks and body language. They each held their instrument like one holds a security blanket. Mike was twirling his drumsticks. Marty was plinking on the piano.

"Yo, tune your bongos up. You got congas?" Stew asks me.

"I'll be getting some soon." Lie.

"Welcome Ron," Judy said to me with a smile. Hope was quiet and working out some fingering on her bass. I tuned up the bongos and was ready to go.

"We were thinking we would play something and you just come in when you think about coming in." Stew said, seeing me ready. "Sounds okay?"

"Sure," I replied quietly.

They started to play a song, and I easily found where to come in. I checked in with everyone with a glance. Judy was grooving and smiling at me. Stew was bobbing his head to my beat. Marty was looking at his keys. Mike was locked in on me and was smiling. Hope was staring at me with a glazed look. The song finished.

"Nice touch," Judy said first, and started in with another tune; the band followed her in. This time she sang. I followed Judy's sweet voice, the song, and then came in tastefully. The song finished. I ended with the band on time.

"I like your playing," Stew said smiling.

"Nice groove, man," Mike was pumping his fist. Marty looked up from his piano and smiled with a nod. Hope looked at me, and smiled with white teeth. Judy smiled and said, "Welcome to the Millionaires!"

This began a yearlong relationship with five people who would become my family. I moved in with Stew, who lived downtown near the West Village. I subletted my Uptown apartment and offered my cat, Lúthien, to a friend because Stew was allergic to them. My friend renamed Lúthien "Cat," and I bought a set of congas and many percussive toys. We sounded great: a smooth, mellow rock-funk band. Our band motto was, "The Millionaires: We sound like a million bucks!" We played many cool gigs all over the city and into New Jersey. Judy was the main songwriter and had a great voice. Hope, the bass player, sang with an angelic voice, too. I loved watching Hope's long fingers playing her bass strings like it was a harp. Hope, Marty, the drummer, and I were the rhythm section. We would set up next to each other at gigs, and were constantly looking at and playing off each other. I loved being on stage and playing congas; my dad fooled around as a self-taught conga drummer, and two uncles on my mother's side were real hot conga players, too. Drumming was in my blood. I had been playing congas since high school and had a knack for anything musical.

Playing in a band in the 1980s brought me in contact with the drug scene associated with long hours and hard practicing. Cocaine was the drug of musicians. Like many before me in the music trade, cocaine gave me the zing for long hours in the studio or long hours on a gig. It was a really cool feeling doing lines of cocaine before a gig and going before the crowd. Unfortunately, I did not respect my addictive pull toward stimulation and touching euphoria. As with all drugs I did earlier in life I thought I was always in control, though really I might have been out-of-control.

I experienced cocaine as a sharp-edged high that expressed the exhilarating energy of the "anything goes...just do it!" culture of the time. A savage *carpe diem!* Cocaine was the engine that powered living in New York City throughout the 1980s, until the deadly killer of crack emerged later on. Cocaine was everywhere: there was music for it, and it seemed like everyone was snorting it or smoking it. Cocaine went well with the shiny, glittering lights that illuminated the senseless spending on spellbinding high thrills. All of this madness was just a reflection of the state of the American culture of the 1980s. Americans were the young and restless, free-spending, pleasure-seeking teenagers to the rest of the world. Cocaine-fueled lifestyles were very cool and pretentious. Cocaine was a drug that could kill you easily. After the nosebleeds started up and sleepless nights piled on, I stopped and never returned to it. Lesson learned and that was that. I never needed the drug—I never had craved cocaine, so it was easy for me to let it go.

Being in a tight band was very delicate at times. Passion flared up between Judy and me, but that did not go anywhere. Hope and I were cool with each other and became lovers and kept it relaxed. I also started to see her roommate. Again, I saw these relationships as experiences of sensuality. My romantic, almost-fantastical, age-of-chivalry perspective of the "woman and man" relationship was one fit for the clouds. My dreamlike expectations only developed into disappointments for me and frustration for my partners. I continued to be open to women, seeking their companionship and the opportunity to be lovers. But to what end? There was so much to learn and understand. A big part of me just wanted to find the "one", to be happily married and in love "forever." I did not want to end up divorced like my parents—a life of separated homes, with children going from place to place and being the objects of child support payments—no, I would do it right in my time.

Spring in New York City was amazing again. The snow melted and the thawing bodies of the street people who did not find shelter during the winter were found. The people shed their winter skins and heavy coats. Women started wearing refreshing clothing that summoned men to their "rutting" rituals. Lovers appeared, and the trees and flowers began to blossom. The Millionaires were busy and the dance floors were packed. Life was exciting and the streets were busy with lively people blessed to have survived yet another winter in Manhattan! The outdoor cafés down in the Village were hopping. I enjoyed meeting friends for dark, rich coffee, smoking some unfiltered Turkish cigarettes, and doing some serious "people watching" deep into the night.

A friend told me about a treasure of a spot called the The Cloisters at the top of Manhattan Island. "Yo, take the A train all the way up past 190th Street. You will be up in Washington Heights. Walk through Fort Tyron Park and you will see the tower of The Cloisters." I followed his directions on a Wednesday morning. No one was up there. I had the whole park to myself. The Cloisters is a collection of other cloisters, other 12th- to 14th-century buildings moved to New York, stone by stone, from Europe. The artwork presented was beautiful, and the incredible Unicorn Tapestries are there. The outside gardens are splendid. At the northern tip of Manhattan Island, the cliffs of the Palisades rise across the wide Hudson River in New Jersey. The place turned into my sacred sanctuary in New York City. I would go there through the years when my heart would ache for Oregon or nature. The churchlike atmosphere silenced the "city crazies," and when I would visit during the middle of the week, the place was quiet and empty of people. It is so important to find a bit of paradise in a place of chaos.

I was working hard enough in my dance classes that I was now allowed into the 10:00 a.m. advanced ballet class with Madame Rommett. Back in shape, I could go out for dance auditions again. When you are auditioning a lot, you see the same dancers at different auditions, and I would go out with some of them afterward if we were not picked. It was the '80s and Reaganomics—the state of the national economy named after the president of that time. Ronald Reagan, whose son just so happened to be a dancer, was cutting budgets everywhere. The dance world was hit hard and dance work was tough to find.

I was still an apprentice with Dan Wagoner and loving it, but his company was tight and there was no room for advancement. That was okay. I was learning a lot. I got some small dance gigs that only paid a little, but gave me precious performing experience. I was grateful and worked hard. Thank the Great Spirit for my job as a waiter. It was no wonder most dancers, actors, and musicians during those times found themselves in the service industry. Not bad—you eat, you're out of the elements, and you get a paycheck with a cut of the tips.

Before long the dog days of summer returned. I rode a bike in the warm season now, like I did in my days in Oregon. Riding a bike in New York City was an adventure back then. There were no bike lanes, and motorists barely realized they had to share the streets with you. Many friends of mine were daring bike messengers. Not me—that job was a bit too crazy even by New York City standards. One hot summer day in late June, I was walking on West 14th Street in the Village pushing my bike in front of me by the seat, a common way to walk a bike when not riding, when I bumped into a guy in front of me by accident. The guy actually stepped right in front of me too quickly, and I could not stop in time. He turned and glared at me. He was a white guy, slightly balding, and in his early thirties.

"I am sorry, man." I said quickly and continued. He stopped and let me go by.

"Yo! Asshole, you bumped me with your bike!" he yelled at me.

I turned and with a little attitude said, "Yo! I said I was sorry."

"F*ck you! You yellow-skinned chink f*ck!"

I was stunned that this stranger was revving up so quickly. I turned again and looked at him without taking off my sunglasses. "Yo, mellow out! I said I was sorry." I turned and kept walking. He continued to follow while spewing filth at me.

"F*ck you, you f*cking chink gook bastard!" He yelled all the racist garbage he could think of. "Go back where you came from, you wetback greasy Mexican!" I kept walking. By this time a crowd of Hispanics were following this white guy, but he just could not stop yelling racist crap at me, a black-haired, brown-skinned man.

I started to yell at him without turning. "F*ck dude, I said I was sorry. F*ck you!"

This went on for several yards down a hot, New York City sidewalk in the heart of a mostly Hispanic crowd. I became real fiery with rage. I was no longer a little boy that was abused by racist bullies. I was now a young man with a large New York chip on his shoulder and a "kick-ass and take names later" mentality.

"You f*cking Chinese gook bastard! Go back to your gook land. You slimy greasy wetback motherf*cker!" He stopped and entered a store.

F*ck him! I went into the store after him. The huge, slavering, Hispanic crowd waited outside. I was right behind yelling at him when he turned and struck me in the face! I was the fool who wanted to fight, but I did not have the brains to take off my sunglasses first. *What a doofus!* The sunglasses smashed into my nose, drawing blood. I jumped him and took him to the ground. I started to pound on his hand-covered face. I thought I was hitting hard, but I wasn't. From the corner of my eye, I saw the store guard rushing over with his nightstick ready for a clubbing. I figured I would be the first to get hit, so I got off the guy and made for the door. Out on the street, the crowd was waiting, and began to cheer as they caught sight of me. Someone offered me a cloth to wipe the blood off my face.

"Yo, brother. You want us to finish off that white trash bastard?!" A voice yelled from the salivating, angry crowd of brown-skinned, black-haired people.

I looked into the crowd. The mob wanted to mess this white man up badly. The heat was frying the cement streets, the humidity was thick, and people were hot and bothered. These people heard all the racist crap this man had been yelling at me. They wanted revenge for the belittling and shaming they had received from the White Man.

"Yo! Leave that dude alone. He'll get his shit someday. Leave him be. Thank you, brothers!" I walked away. I heard muttering from the crowd; they were waiting in front of the store for the white guy to come out. I made my way home to wash up. I had a gig that night. Let the crowd do what it wanted.

I realized I could have hit that man hard and busted him up, but this was not a schoolyard fight. I was not yet trained in the martial arts; I was searing mad at this guy but I could not physically hurt him. It seemed that the crazies I felt and the physical rage that I could unleash as a boy/teenager were very different as an adult. It was almost like a unconscious override in my mind–body to reduce my physical strength by 40% so as not to hurt the man. I was swinging hard, I thought, yet striking the man felt like I was hitting a pillow—soft and safe. I was puzzled by the whole experience.

The next day a tap dancing friend from New Paltz called me up. He invited me to be his accompanist at a dance venue called Dance New England (DNE). This was an organization of many small chapters in New England that sponsored creative, improvisational, weekend dance jams. They were putting up a one-week summer camp in Vermont. It sounded great. My band did not have a gig, I got time off from the restaurant, and I didn't have any other dance responsibilities, so I said I would do it.

My buddy picked me up along with my drums. I was going to play percussion for him. During this time in the 1980s contact improvisation was big and all types of groovy people showed up for DNE events. Vermont was glorious and there was a beautiful freshwater lake to swim in. Movement to all kinds of music was explored. A typical recorded tape produced for the event included a mishmash of rock, classical, bluegrass, country, R&B, funk songs, and everything in between mixed into one long dance jam. You danced by yourself, in large groups, in pairs, or in any social configuration you wanted or found yourself in. This was not the pick-up scene found in an urban discotheque or club. This was dancing—just moving to what you felt inside. Should you hook up with someone—cool; if not—cool. It was so liberating to be free of ego, the pick-up scene, and how you looked. It was just dancing and playing. During the day I accompanied my friend to his contact improvisation class, and at night I danced for hours. This went on for a whole week. Vegetarian food, clean water, and clean air were on the schedule. I made a lot of great friends, and I returned to New York City with a new head on my shoulders.

I got back to New York in time for an end of summer eco- and energy awareness concert at the foot of the World Trade Center. I remember the bright sun reflecting off the sides of these two majestic towers; these two symbols of financial power and American might, which also symbolized energy usage. The whole city seemed to feed these two towers immense amounts of energy. Thousands of people surrounded me as we heard speeches on energy conservation, alternative energy innovations, and wasting energy and our natural resources. The twin towers appeared to look down on us mere mortals with royal arrogance and vibrant potency. I felt very small. I looked at all the other ants surrounding me.

It wasn't a bad life for a young man living in New York City. I was in a working rock band, an apprentice for a modern dance company taking classes with top-notch teachers, and working at a nice restaurant making good money. All was well, I thought. In the fall I moved out of Stew's place and found a new spot in the East Village at 9th Street and 2nd Avenue. I was into wearing all-black clothing, and had my hair cut to where I had long tiny braids but no sideburns. I was dancing for small, modern companies all over the city. I even had an opportunity to dance in Stockholm, Sweden or Munich, West Germany, that December. My tendency toward depression was coming back, and I found myself not wanting to do too much; it was those dark, cold nights. The band started to crack at the seams from egos flying. As the percussionist I was on the outside as the song writers tugged at each other. The band broke up a short time later.

My never-ending explorations into relationships with women were stressing me out. I did not want to be alone, but it seemed I could not handle the neurotic energies of dancers, actors, and theater women. Was I cursed to be alone? Was I cursed to have, but not have? Was my perception of "woman" too perfect? Was I not willing to see the mortality of beauty? Why was I, on the one hand, willing to be so naïvely open to the "first-kiss-we-are-lovers-forever" dream and, on the other, willing to sabotage and destroy the very thing I aimed to create? The realization of this paradox in my social life threatened me with deep depression once again.

That winter I was reading a lot of the German writer Hermann Hesse. I had read *Siddhartha* and *Steppenwolf* while in Oregon, but here in the East Village it was his fictional, introspective writings on human existence and the frailty of human love that added to my dark moods. I was feeling, like other animals, the need to hoard away food, and create a large cache that would be well hidden and prepared in a safe winter burrow. However, being in a human body in this lifetime and living in bustling New York City, I felt I had to accomplish something like all the other sorry sods around me. I had to be somebody. I was feeling anxious and edgy. I hated the feeling of being like one of the sheep people—following the dazed person in front of me as we all fell off the edge of the cliff in blind obedience to social correctness.

Help!

It was late November, and my diet had deteriorated to consisting mostly of butter, sugar, cookies, and potato chips. Training hard and dancing long hours, I thought my body was doing fine as my mind went down the drain. I began to isolate myself more and more as my depression become darker and darker. My thinking was rigid. "Don't want to go forward. Don't want to go backward." I didn't want to reach out; there were no calls for help coming from me to anyone. The cold air bit hard, and I began to cough a lung-rattling cough. My breathing was short and wheezy. The air became colder and colder. The wilted, spent leaves from the glorious fall season flew off the trees driven by the brisk, cold winds. The feeling of death loomed in the air. The strong ones would survive, and the weak ones would succumb to death. It seemed that the coming of winter began the process of thinning the herd. I pushed myself harder to do nothing and everything at the same time.

I began to read *Lord of the Rings*—my teddy bear from the past—for the hundredth time. I retreated to my single, bed-sized, rented room and read until late. My room was cold, and the single-pane window rattled in the freezing night temperatures. One morning in mid-December, I woke up unable to breathe. I got my butt to St. Vincent's Hospital Emergency room across town on the West Side. I was found too fit to be admitted, so they gave me a steroid inhaler and sent me home. The inhaler worked, but I was getting worse. The cough was pretty raw and it rattled my insides.

My dark moods continued to seclude me. I was talking less and less to my former bandmates, or to anyone for that matter. It was almost like the recurring nightmare I had as a child: the dream of a freshly butchered chunk of meat hanging from a large hook, and from it suspends, by a length of thread-thin, white, glossy sinew, a second, larger piece of freshly butchered meat. The dread and suspense came from waiting for the thread-thin sinew to break. The second piece of meat swayed and stressed the very thin sinew, but the sinew wouldn't break. Just snap damn it! Just f*cking break! It doesn't...

I woke up the day before Christmas, 1982, unable to breathe at all. I imagined my airways swollen and restricting all air flow. My brain was barely getting enough oxygen to put my body into motion and get my clothing on. I was all black from head to toe. I stumbled down to the street corner, not telling my roommates, no one, and hailed a cab. The cabbie rushed me to St. Vincent's ER. Once there I was rushed in and pumped up with oxygen and liquids. I had totally deprived myself of water. My lungs were dry and inflexible; my body was running on empty, and my lungs were totally shot. I was diagnosed with asthmatic pneumonia.

For the next four and a half weeks I was in the hospital. What had started as a prognosis of a week to stabilize ended being a trip down health Hell. I was first placed in the intensive care unit (ICU) because there were no beds on the maintenance ward where I belonged. Not a good sign. My ICU bedmates had some very severe cases. The guy to my right was a tourist from Italy whose throat was cut ear-to-ear—even after he gave the thieves all they had asked for. The guy to my left was a drug dealer who had half of his face blasted away with a shotgun to his face; he turned at the last second, and only half of his face was destroyed instead of his whole head. The guy next to him was an open-heart surgery patient with major complications. The guy across from me was another knife-in-the-heart-and-lung victim. Then there was me—a guy with a chiseled dancer's body, no visible injuries except oxygen tubes in my nose, and an IV in his arm. The ICU room was a wall of stimulation that bombarded me. The sounds of clicking machines, pumps, beeping oxygen controls, emergency alarms going off chaotically at all hours; the moans, groans, complaints, and angry, crying outbursts from the patients enveloped me. I was awakened early every morning for blood tests. I was going insane. The heat drove me to shed all my clothes and sleep with the sheets barely covering me. The food was inedible. The ICU nurses were hoping I would get out of there quickly, or hoped I would be placed in the correct ward soon. I was praying for a savior.

On the fourth day after Christmas I made a call to my former bandmates. I let them know where I was. They were shocked. I called my dance teachers; they had no idea I was in such a dire health condition that warranted me going to a hospital. I hid it from everyone. I never called my family. I saw myself as the stoic man on the mountaintop dealing with the hardships on my own. What a fool I was!

One morning the nurses told me I had to cover up my nakedness. I told them I was overheating and couldn't handle the temperature in the room. They proposed moving me to the corner of the ICU ward toward the window and near the air conditioner. I said, "Right on." Blasted Half-Face complained through half a mouth that I was getting preferred treatment. Slashed Throat followed the actions with his eyes. Heart Man moaned. The nurses moved my bed. I actually had curtains that could close off my little corner from the rest of the ICU! I woke the next morning for a blood draw with a view of the bright rays of early sunrise reflecting off the twin towers of the World Trade Center. The sight inspired beautiful hope.

I woke every night to the purgatory of darkness and fear. I would look at my IV to find it bone dry. I pressed the call button. A nurse would come in and deal with it. This went on for days on end. After two weeks I was still in the intensive care ward. I was told that there were no beds available on the ward they wanted me in. I was still discovering my IV bone dry during the night. Then came the day the head doctor did a check of the ICU unit. He came to my bed and looked at my charts.

"Nurse!" he bellowed. Scurrying feet. A nurse at his elbow.

"What is going on with this man? It appears he has not shown any improvement and his numbers are off," he questioned with a stern face.

Great! Someone noticed me!

"What is he doing in this ward?" he continued. Mumbling from the nurse. "What is going on here?"

"Sir?" I perked up. He turned to me. "Sir, there are times I wake up at night, and my IV is bone dry. When am I getting out of here?" He looked at me, and then turned slowly to the nurse. I turned away and looked out the window to see the Twin Towers in the distance.

"Follow me out, nurse...now!"

After almost two and a half weeks, that afternoon I was finally moved out of the intensive care unit and moved to a ward where I was the only patient in a room full of empty beds! It seemed that since I did not look messed up I was not paid much attention to. My irregular IV servicing prevented my numbers from stabilizing for two and a half weeks. Now I was the only patient in a empty ward for the nurses to pay attention to. Damn! Only in New York City!

As I started to stabilize, I became able to get out of bed and walk around, but I was still very weak and had lost weight. I was told there was a little chapel buried deep in the maze of floors and wards. I found the chapel, and it was truly a sacred place. The stained glass windows received natural light from a shaft that illuminated the chapel. The hospital had been built around this chapel, and I would visit it everyday. I had a fondness for stained glass and churches. The peace and quiet calmed me, and the absence of people made it better. There was a certain smell in old churches—a mixed fragrance of wood and incense—and this chapel had that smell. I felt safe, and protected by an invisible force field. My world revolved around remembered smells, sounds, and images. I could be lost in a world of remembrance triggered by a certain smell or fragrance no matter how faint or strong. For me this chapel had it all; it was like a time machine. I was back at St. Kevin's in Bernal Heights, San Francisco. Amidst all the chaos of the hospital I was safe. As I walked the empty halls of my ward I would stand by the window and look on to the street below. I realized the world outside the hospital walls was still in motion; it was still turning and had never stopped, even though my world had. In my hospital gown it seemed like the snowy world outside my window would kill me. I felt threatened. I moved away and made my way back to my bed in the empty ward.

"You will be able to leave tomorrow," the nurse was telling me after breakfast one morning. The idea of leaving scared me. After almost four and a half weeks off the streets, I was going to leave this safe womb. That night I was imagining what it would be like entering the world of men. Lights, sounds, and smells—all those people not knowing where I had been all this time. The hospital had been a place of low stimulation, a place I could handle. The next morning they brought my clothes. A white garbage bag contained my black underwear, black t-shirt, black pants, black-collared long-sleeved shirt, black socks, black shoes, and black overcoat. I dressed very slowly like a warrior preparing for battle. Each button had meaning. Each piece of garment I placed on my body was a shield against the world outside I was about to re-enter.

"Mr. Rubio, sign here," a black nurse said behind a plastic partition. A piece of paper slid toward me through a slot. The nurse was shielded from the outside world I was returning to. The pen felt foreign in my fingers. I signed it and slid the paper back to her.

"Good day, Mr. Rubio." She looked at the paper. "Next!"

The sliding glass doors opened with a "swoosh," and two black security guards eyed me as I left the hospital grounds. It was a new year. I had been in the hospital through New Year's Day, 1983. The cold January air was biting into my brittle, newly healed lungs. The sun burned strongly and brightly on 7th Avenue and 11th Street. Once again, I was amidst the world of men. The overwhelming stimulations started up immediately upon walking through the hospital doors—honking car horns, crowded sidewalks filled with fast walking people, the sweet, bitter, and sharp city smells, reflecting lights off building windows, and blue-black exhaust blasting out of buses and cars.

I walked downtown on 7th Avenue to the restaurant to check on my job. All was well, I was told by the manager. I left the Limelight with a smile, and walked all the way across town to my place on 2nd Avenue and 9th Street. The cement felt hard and harsh on my feet and legs, which had barely moved in the four and half weeks in the hospital. The next day I awoke with painful shin splints.

As my health improved, I got back into to my dance schedule and all my dance classes. I had a dance performance a month later with one of the three small modern companies I was with. The life of a dancer can be really tough. You train seven days a week, rehearsing maybe three to four days a week, and then your performance run lasts for a weekend, maybe two. Often your pay is not great (unless you are in a top-tier dance company, in which case your compensation could be much better). Most second- and third-tier dance companies, however, were struggling in the 1980s, but the more I danced the more I could put on my résumé. My knee was fine, and I was in the advanced ballet classes and steadily becoming more proficient in my modern classes.

I often found myself up at my city sanctuary, The Cloisters Museum, in Washington Heights at the top of the island. I went up to New Paltz as much as I could to see my friends. Being in rural upstate New York was great; the connection with nature, the rocks, trees, water, and land were healing and kept me grounded. My relationships were still fleeting, and were often a touch-and-go phenomenon. The essence of being a human and a man eluded me. As a son of Filipino immigrants, I had absorbed inherent Eastern (Asian) values and viewpoints that left me at odds with the Western, Eurocentric values that surrounded me. The white-skinned women's beauty and attractiveness had created a desire that was quite illusory; the world of materialism and pace of the urban life were all false goals. The sensitive balance of spirituality with the physical world was a tightrope walk out-of-sync, and it rendered me a self-destructive, confused, and seeking man.

My dancing friend Danny, who was living up in New Paltz, moved to Boston, Massachusetts in February 1983. "Ron, come and visit me here in Boston," he invited me over a phone call. My birthday was coming up in March, and the invite sounded tempting since I had never been to Boston or Massachusetts. I knew Boston from history as a place where the American Revolution was fought actively, and as a major Northern city during the Civil War. It was a place of freedom, or so I thought. Not having any money, I decided to hitchhike to Boston. I took a train to New Paltz and started from there. It was a long day of traveling getting to Boston via the Massachusetts Turnpike. By the 1980s hitchhiking had become a rare way to travel, but my rides were generous—yet quizzical—of me. It seemed like my rides fancied being a part of a dying culture in America—the days of hitchhikers and train jumping went out in the 1970s.

My friend met me in Harvard Square, which was a central transportation stop for the famed Harvard University. My buddy shared a large Victorian home with four other young folks our age. The next evening was a Dance New England night in a small place outside of Boston proper called Watertown. I was looking forward to meeting some cool people, and enjoying a night of "free dancing." We arrived at the large dance hall, and the place was already starting to get full. After we paid I walked onto the dance floor and saw a beautiful woman with long legs stretching out. Her pointed feet accentuated her strength and caught my eye. I was checking her out when she looked up at me; her large, dark, doelike eyes were mesmerizing. I smiled a big smile and she responded. The lights went down and the music started. I lost sight of her as the crowd of dancing bodies filled the wooden floor. Once we danced together and then we floated away. I caught sight of her long hair and made my way toward her as the dance finished for the evening.

"Hi. It was nice dancing with you. My name is Ron."

"Hi. My name is Jennifer."

"Well, I am visiting a friend in Boston for my birthday. I live in New York City."

"I live out in Watertown and I work in the Back Bay of Boston. I am a waitress."

"Jennifer, it would be nice to get together with you, that is, if you're not busy?"

"I work tomorrow at the Top of the Hub on the top floor of the Prudential Building in Boston."

"Well, my friend and I are going to Hull. Do you know where that is?"

"Yes, it's out on the coast. When I get off work, I can take the train to meet you."

I was excited and stunned. Jennifer was willing to take a train to meet me. I did not even know where Hull was in relationship to Boston.

"Where is Hull?" I asked her.

"It's south of Boston," she answered sweetly. Her voice was light and her eyes held me.

"You don't need to take the train. I can see you when I get back to Boston," I offered.

"No, that's okay. I do not mind seeing you in Hull. It would be nice to get out of Boston." I gave her my friend's number, and she said she would call me once she got to Hull train station.

"I am looking forward to seeing you out there tomorrow," I started to fumble.

"I am looking forward to seeing you as well," she answered.

We shook hands and parted.

My friend was happy for me, but a bit surprised.

"Moving a bit fast, Ralph." He was using my high school nickname I had told him about. We got back to his house and partied the rest of the night—it was my birthday weekend.

The next day Jennifer came out to Hull on the train after work like she said she would. Jennifer and I walked the beach and wrote in the sand. She told me her dad was Irish and her mom was Puerto Rican. Her last name was Mitchell. We talked about dance and being young in a crazy world. We both waited tables for a living, loved to dance, and were very attracted to each other. The night wore on and my hosts, Russell and Erin, cooked a birthday dinner for me. We had a great time. When it came time for Jennifer to go back to Boston, Russell suggested that she stay the night and leave in the morning. He said she could share the living room with me. Sure! I would sleep on the couch, and she could sleep on the mattress they had provided for me. Uhmm, right...

When Jennifer and I were set up in the living room—me on the couch, her on the mattress in front of the lit fireplace—Jennifer and I started talking while the rest of the house slept.

"Ron, would you like to join me here?" She opened her blankets to me. I looked at her from the couch, as the fireplace behind her created a fiery halo around her silhouette. I was drawn into her embrace. We floated for hours together, staring into each other's eyes, with the fire crackling and blazing through the night and into morning. We whispered to each other as if we were in an enchanted place of magic.

The morning found us in a deep embrace. Russell and Erin came down stairs and told us we could use their bed to get some sleep. They laughed; Jennifer and I laughed. We headed upstairs to a still warm, vacated bed. In a quiet moment, lying on top of Jennifer and looking down at her into her deep eyes, I was taken by the inspiration of love.

"Jennifer..." I paused. I was taken by what I wanted to say to her.

"Yes...Ron?" She whispered to me.

"Jennifer...will you marry me?" There, I said it.

Without a pause she answered, "Yes, I will, Ron." There, she answered me!

We looked at each other and begin to laugh and hold each other tightly.

In less than 24 hours of knowing each other, I had proposed marriage and she had accepted. We were both twenty-six years old. Well, I had just turned 26 that very weekend. We told the household; they were astonished, and we partied and rejoiced. It was a Haley's Comet love. A kind of love that comes once in a lifetime and then is gone.

We decided I would move to Boston and get married on July 4 in the Boston Rose Gardens. I left Jennifer to go back to New York City. Once there I began the process of tying up all my business with dance, the restaurant, and subletting my place. Then I got a call that Jennifer's parents wanted to meet me. Oh, yeah, I had forgotten about that part. It seemed right that I meet her parents and ask her dad's permission for his daughter's hand in marriage. This was part of my Filipino and Spanish etiquette; it was a respect I understood. I had also seen this in movies I watched as a child. I made plans to fly out and meet her parents a few weeks later.

Jennifer and I understood what we were doing, or at least we were on the same page: Fantastical love! We knew it seemed totally crazy to everyone around us, but that was totally okay with us. We knew something was happening—there was a mystery to our love, and we had to go with it.

In the meantime I had to find a way to buy the wedding rings. I talked to my chef at the Limelight. He was a burly Italian named Caesar. We met in his office, and I asked him for a loan so I could buy the wedding rings.

"Do you love her?" he asked me.

"Yes, Chef." I answered with a surety and conviction I had never felt before. (Well, it was similar to the conviction I felt about moving to New York City to study with Alvin Ailey four years prior.)

"Well then, how much are the rings?" he smiled.

"About four to five hundred dollars, Chef."

"You want cash or do you want me come with you and pay by card?" he questioned me.

I looked at him with deep gratitude and humbleness. Here was a man that knew me, but didn't *know* me, and he was willing to lend me up to five hundred dollars with no hesitation.

"Chef, you know I will pay you back completely?"

"I do not worry about it...I am Italian. I will hunt you down if you jilt on the loan," he said to me with a deadpan, expressionless look on his face. "Just kidding!" I did not doubt he would hunt me down, but I had every intention of repaying him and he knew it. The next day I was off to buy the wedding rings with the cash I borrowed from Chef, and that weekend I flew up to Boston to meet Jennifer's parents. Jennifer met me at Boston's Logan Airport. After time away from her, our meeting was filled with the passion and joy that only time apart can generate. We settled into our new relationship and our upcoming marriage-to-be with ease and confidence. Where the world around us saw only chaotic, love-struck, "shoot-from-the-hip" actions, we saw this was about us and not about "them." We knew the world would have its opinions, but for right or for wrong, we were along for the ride.

"Yes, Mr. Mitchell, I will be moving to Boston." Jennifer's father sat across from me in one chair and her mother sat in another. We were seated in the living room of their modest Boston home.

"So, what will you do here in Boston?" he asked quietly.

"I will probably work at a restaurant at first, and then develop my dance teaching and performing. I have worked as a cook, chef, and waiter," I answered, looking right into his eyes. I had prepared myself for this moment by reminding myself to look right into their eyes and speak from my heart with truth and clarity. I was not nervous because I was comfortable about how I felt about Jennifer and me. This was our moment.

"Your parents are Filipino?" her mother asked me.

"Yes, Mrs. Mitchell. Both were born in the Philippines. I am a first-generation Filipino American born in San Francisco." She looked at me, studying my features.

"My parents are Puerto Rican. Mr. Mitchell's are Irish/English." She paused. "When are you two getting married?" Silence. The clock ticking on the mantle was loud and sharp. I looked at Jennifer. She stared at me.

"We thought in July in the Boston Rose Gardens," I answered. Jennifer and I felt it would be beautiful to be amongst roses on our wedding day, which was only three months away.

The rest of our time together was relaxed and comfortable. Their questions were light and non-invasive. We left to stay at Jennifer's place out near Watertown. That night we talked long, and held nothing back. We understood what we were doing. Confidence and strength were vibrant in us. We both wanted the same thing: a marriage that would last a lifetime. The next day I left for NYC to get back to work. Jennifer wanted to see my place in New York City, and we decided she would come stay with me a few weeks later. I got back to work and continued to close up all my loose ends. I doubled up my time at Madame Rommett's studio, and worked hard with all my other dance teachers. I also added more time at the restaurant, and saved money. I understood I was leaving New York City—and my dance training. I felt I could always drop down from Boston and take classes in New York City if I needed to. I knew nothing about the dance scene in the Boston area, but I knew I could kick ass if need be. I had been grueling it out in New York for almost four years, and I was feeling confident I could make it anywhere else.

Despite my upcoming marriage, my family was very distant. My older brother gave nothing, but my sister offered to fly out and be my "best man." My dad, well, he wasn't too happy or supportive at all. My mother gave me motherly advice about my "Rubio anger" and asked me to wait. Mom gave me the same advice any time I talked about having a girlfriend: to be wary of my explosive anger. She likened my anger meltdowns to Dad's. I took it all in stride. My family had always seen me as the odd one out, so why should things change now? For right or for wrong this was my life, and that was that.

Before long all was ready for me to make the move to Boston. Jennifer had found us a place in Watertown, and I sent her money to help secure the spot. By the middle of June I was settled in our new place. The summer days in New England were cleaner and had more open sky than New York. Jennifer and I were getting to know each other; we were still new to each other in so many ways, but we were fearless and in love. We knew there would be work to do to make our relationship what we wanted it to be.

On our wedding day Jennifer prepared at her parents' home. My sister Valerie flew in from San Francisco. She, and not my older brother, was going to be my best man; she planned to wear a tie and a beautiful red vest for the service. It was the Fourth of July, and it was hot and humid with clear blue skies. The day and night before the rain had come down heavy, and the sky was dark and low, but on the day of our wedding the Boston Rose Garden was ablaze with vibrant reds, yellows, and whites, and the air was perfumed with the fragrance of hundreds of blooming roses. Jennifer and I were blessed. A small contingent of Jennifer's family was present, but my sister was the only one representing my side of the family. I was saddened by this lack of family support and acknowledgement, but I was used to this from my family. It still hurt, though.

The ceremony was simple; the rings were placed upon our fingers and finished with the sacred words "until death do us part." I realized that I could love this person, and this person would love me *forever*. I was raised on a marriage that resembled nothing that I saw in the movies when I was growing up. I was going to be the Man for Jennifer. I was not going to go down the same path of destruction with my wife as Dad did with Mom. That divorce was the outcome of his failings to the marriage—to Mom. I was going to do this right. Jennifer and I were now man and wife.

In the weeks after our marriage Jennifer and I looked for a new place to live. We wanted a fresh new place, closer to our work and downtown Boston. I found cooking work at the same restaurant where Jennifer was a waitress. To me, life was moving in the right direction—in how I had envisioned it, and in the way that Jennifer and I had planned. The gold ring glowed on my finger as I watched Jennifer walk into our new apartment in the Back Bay section of Boston. She had just come back from having her hair cut, and her long golden brown hair was now closely cropped on her head. I was stunned. My mind saw one thing and it became set in stone; like a minted metal now cooling, the cast had been set. Change was not something I handled too easily from those close to me. What happened in life concerning myself was one thing, of course, but where life concerned another person and a relationship, well, that was a different matter. My only teachers about relationships were my dad and mother's disastrous relationships, and the only role model I had about how a man was supposed to function in a relationship was from my rigid thinking, and my angry, harmony-destroying, belittling, and demanding dad. So when Jennifer walked through the door with her hair cut real short, I was speechless.

"Well?"

"It is new..."

"I know it is short, Ron. I have always wanted my hair short." Her big doe-eyes looking into mine for approval.

"Baby, it's short..." I came to her side and ran my fingers through her short hair. Parts of me were imagining her long hair running through my fingers. "It's a nice cut, Jennifer, I will get used to it." She stared at me.

"Baby, I liked your long hair…" I must have looked dumbstruck. "Jennifer, it is hot and humid like hell, and your haircut is perfect." I reached out and held her tightly to me, more for my sake than hers.

It took me a great amount of restraint to keep from blowing a fuse. I did not like surprises or sudden unannounced changes of plans or transitions in life. Jennifer's haircut blew my mind. She looked different from what had attracted me to her in a childish way—her long hair. Yet I was mindful enough, at first, to be aware to support her move toward personal freedom, expression, and change. So, I sucked it up and shut up! Her happiness was very important to me.

Our relationship continued to grow. I found cooking at the restaurant we both worked at, The Top of the Hub, sufficient. The restaurant was on top of one of the tallest buildings in Boston, and we had a 360-degree view of the surrounding land. I sent my first paychecks back to Chef in New York City to pay back the loan for our wedding rings. As with other work crews in my past, I soon created a boisterous and fun atmosphere in the kitchen. My crewmates on the line were mostly student musicians and art students. We had a real hoot and kept the job pace hot, fast, and loose. In situations like this I allowed the creative, imaginative, and zany "me" to let go and have fun in the mundane, mortal drone of life that I had to sustain in the moment.

My life was different in Boston than in New York City. I found parts of Boston to be very racist and intolerant of others, which amazed me. I thought this was the hub of American Revolution fervor, and freedom. I was reminded how the American constitution was written by a bunch of white men with lofty ideas, who held slaves and were not forthcoming about giving their power up. It is hard for Americans to change laws that are truly outdated and no longer relevant. From my background, I was born to fight for the underdog, and always wanted to right the wrongs of others. Racists were at the top of my list of people to stand up to, and in this Boston surprised me. A fellow cook from Georgia told me he saw racist things he never saw down south.

As I settled in I started to find dance work and teaching at a place called the Joy of Movement in Central Square. Having been trained in New York City, the local dance scene was just okay. But, like my Alvin Ailey ballet teacher once told me, "Once a dancer, always a dancer!"—and I was going to make any dance class work for me. No matter what, I would always get something out of a class. Hell, I was paying for it, so I better get something out of it, or I shouldn't take the damn class!

I was a go-getter, because that was the way I survived when I was a teenager, and no matter what other challenges I may have had, emotional or cognitive, I had worked my way through some tough times and had learned a lot about feeding myself. Well, now I was married, and I had a wife to think about. I guess that as an American husband in the 1980's, I was supposed to be the breadwinner of the family, but the thinking of the women's movement, which had been picking up a lot of steam in the last decade, challenged this "breadwinner" mentality. It was truly a mixed-up time for men. For someone who had been trying to figure out social skills for most of his life, being married was putting everything on the line.

Growing up in an insecure family environment filled with violence and abandonment, having to struggle with low-esteem, poor self-confidence, and all the other diagnoses I would later learn about—I just never felt comfortable in my own skin. I never felt comfortable in the world that I was born into; it all seemed too confusing. Why was loving someone so damn hard to do? Was it because I could not trust she would want me if I showed her my demons and depression? Would she leave me? Why couldn't I read what was happening in the relationship before it blew up in my face? Was I always looking for a new and forgiving situation, where all was oh-so-passionate and exciting?

When I thought about it, it appeared that I was being very chivalrous in my behavior toward Jennifer with thoughtful, loving, and caring expressions one moment, then being a rigid, self-absorbed, "me-me-me" asshole the next. At least I was being more pro-active in resolving my issues before I went too far.

One night, Jennifer told me she wanted to find new work away from the Hub. She wanted to try her hand in the kitchen and get off the "floor."

"Right on! Go for it, Jennifer!"

"A new restaurant is opening up called Annie B's right across from the Hancock Building. It is real nice. I applied for a prep-person. They may need a second chef. I thought you might check it out, too."

The next day I checked out this new place called Annie B's. The chef was a Brazilian named Kayo. He looked like a skinny, bearded, escaped convict from some island prison colony. His humor was rich and his handshake was solid. Annie of Annie B's was a very friendly and warm person. Her brother, John, worked as an assistant manager. He was a mild, quiet man. Kayo interviewed me with Annie. He liked Filipinos. Damn, what is not to like about Filipinos? Annie seemed pleased with Kayo's assessment of me, and I was hired. Jennifer and I both quit the Hub and started working in the new kitchen.

The New England seasons came and went, and by early winter Jennifer and I were struggling. Our inability to communicate was tiring to the both of us. Bickering was common, and the little fights and long anguished moments of silence between us started the slow moving apart from each other. I found life challenging without the inspiration of dance. Though I was teaching and taking dance classes in Central Square, it was not the same as with the dance classes in New York City—I was not inspired, though I loved the teachers. I took classes to stay in physical shape. Musically, I was playing congas in a jazz funk quartet that featured a violinist. The work at the new restaurant was exciting and challenging enough to keep my interest, but I was unhappy with love, marriage, and myself.

I knew I was creating this sadness and distance; it was like sliding down a familiar, muddy chute. I tried and tried to stop myself, but the slide continued. The repeated "I am sorry, Jennifer"s hurt her and killed me. Seeing Jennifer distant made my stomach ache with a guilt-laced concern. One day I left my wedding ring at home, though I had never taken it off before. I stood near the living room window with the warm morning sun upon my face, feeling utterly bewildered and defeated about Jennifer and me. I felt that I was not being the husband I had thought I would be in marriage. Jennifer was a wonderfully beautiful and talented woman and devoted wife. The symbol of the gold ring seemed tarnished. I pulled the ring off my finger to clean the slate—to "re-boot," and I planned to put it back on once I got myself squared away for Jennifer, for us. That night I came home from work to find Jennifer crying; our place had been ransacked and burglarized, and my wedding ring was gone. Bad omen. I felt like death had breathed on me. My heart was cold and still. Did I bring this upon myself, upon my home, upon my wife? Jennifer was broken by the incident of our home being violated and by me forgetting my wedding ring; she did not recover.

By early February 1984, I had taken to living on my friend Danny's couch near Harvard Square. After the burglary of our home, Jennifer took another shift so we were on two different time schedules. She was strong and resilient and took care of herself by staying active. She started practicing soccer with John from the restaurant and meeting new folks. One cold morning I went back to our place in the Back Bay, and I noticed John's car parked up front. Knowing he was up there with Jennifer broke my heart, and yet, I thought, did I not create this mayhem? Did I not create the distance between us? I went up to the apartment like a fool to catch them in bed together. I knew the pain was there, and I knew the anger would rise and release would occur. What a selfish bastard I was. It would have been compassionate of me to release her to be happy and free, but in my selfish agony, I wanted her to be in pain. Like a child who never grew up I wanted to hurt both of them. After getting what I deserved, I turned from the door of "our" apartment, and walked away like a man who saw his own death. I filed the divorce papers, and went through the hell of "becoming" my dad and mom. I thought I was going to do what had not been done in my family: successfully marry without getting divorced.

Shitty idea...nice dreaming...I had a lot of work to do on myself.

A month later I found a nice place in Little Italy through a connection. He was Italian and said he had made the "rounds" and told the neighbors I was a very nice man. I was allowed into the neighborhood, and I started putting my life together again. Living in Little Italy was real nice. My neighbors were folks from the Old Country; they were very nice and smiled when I walked by. Normally, people of color were not allowed in the neighborhood. If I were black, I don't think I could have moved into the area at all.

I found work with a children's dance company called Peanut Butter and Jelly Dance Theater. It was fun and I made some money. I applied for numerous positions with afterschool programs at the local elementary school, and got them all. I was teaching theater, dance, and stage production. I even wrote a play, *The Story Purple*. It was a simple story of two races, blues and reds, and how they had been fighting for centuries about the color of their skin until a magical person came and showed them that, by combining their two colors, a new color was created: purple. Parents loved it, the school loved it, and the kids were great. The school had never seen anyone work with so many kids by himself and manage it all without killing a parent or child. To me it was a sign I was healing.

Slowly and painfully, my life became grounded once again. I was still cooking at Annie B's, so I was fed and making steady money, but it was a sad pain to see Jennifer. She had quit the restaurant and was happily seeing John, who still worked at Annie B's as the manager. We kept our distance. At Annie B's we had dishwashers from Vietnam and Cambodia. One day, one of the dishwashers came in really upset. I could not understand him. He took me out to his car parked in front of the restaurant. All over, racist graffiti had been sprayed. "F*ck-off gook! Slant eyed gook!" and more. I became incensed. I got Chef to check it out.

"Kayo, I am going to clean this up for him," I said, barely able to contain my anger to right this wrong.

"Filipino, go to it," Chef looked grim. "I'll cover the line."

A busboy and I scrubbed the best we could to get most of the graffiti off. Passersby gawked and commented. "Shut up and help or just leave, you hypocrites!" I wanted to yell at them. The dishwasher lived in Dorchester, which was a pretty mean Irish part of town. Racist bastards! The dishwasher was extremely grateful. I was sorry I could not do more.

Most days I was introspective about life and trying to piece together how I had allowed love to leave my marriage, how I had destroyed what I wanted so much. I went to the library and investigated my astrological make-up. Generally speaking, I am a triple Piscean with Leo rising, and my head in your anus (Uranus). Yeah, I got it: sensitive, destructive, lover of fantasy, and a dreamer of the highest caliber. I was a strong-willed lion with an anger to match. Low self-esteem; projecting fear into my life. Yeah, yeah, yeah, okay, what now?

Back in 1981, a friend in New York had treated me to an accomplished psychic reader. The reader told me I was a warrior in many lifetimes, a leader of men, all looked up to me, and women dug me. I had not done so well with the money aspect in former lives; I had suffered much and served many. I was told to study and bring the Goddess Athena into my life. After the marriage ended, I started to put some of these pieces together again: What made me tick? How could I do better next time? I felt cursed. I called it the "Rubio Curse": The curse of violent anger and the domineering, rigid, and abusive behavior I got from my father and his bloodline. I hated the curse. I guess that was why I felt like killing myself anytime I hurt anyone's heart or destroyed someone's harmony. I wanted to love, and I wanted to share love and have children. But how?

Work, work, work! Presto.

Her name was Andrea Pastorella. She was a new waitress at Annie B's, and had a beautiful smile and lovely olive-brown skin, which I guessed came from her Sicilian/Italian side. Bashful at first, I went up to talk to her. She had already heard the complete lowdown on the "Ron and Jennifer Show" and wanted no part of it. I did not blame her, but she was really cute and I was really lonely and in need of a woman's smile. Finally, I was able to see her outside of the restaurant. I guess I had badgered her enough with small talk and about her interest in dance that she gave me a chance. Though she was wary of me, I had felt drawn to try to get to know her because I saw her as just another young person like me, going through life learning and fumbling. We had so much of our lives in front of us. I liked her. Andrea made me smile. We went out to a place she knew in Central Square, the Star and Plough—a neutral, safe place. Though I hated beer, I liked stouts and Guinness. So for hours we downed pints of Guinness, smoked cigarettes, and laughed and laughed. Our humor was in sync, and I found out she was an aspiring dancer. Ages ago she had been a samba dancer in San Francisco and was now living in Little Italy, too. I did not want to get physical or anything like that with her. I just wanted to hang with a beautiful woman and get to know her. Andrea was very cool.

I was dancing a lot to stay in shape, playing music, and teaching dance classes. At home I wrote poetry and kept quiet. One night, sitting at home in my cozy little pad writing, I was jostled out of my silence and introspection by someone yelling, or at least I thought I could hear someone yelling.

"Ron!" I did hear a voice, and it was screaming my name!

"Ron Rubio!!!" Damn! My neighbors! It was late; what would the neighbors think? I opened my window from my fourth floor apartment and looked down to the street. It was Andrea Pastorella! Yelling my name and laughing!

"Shhhh!!!" I said and gestured to her.

"Let me up!" she whisper-yelled. Damn! I saw her face glowing and gleaming. I rushed down four flights to let her in. I opened the front door.

She was beaming. "Can I come in? Am I disturbing you?" She was swaying.

"Yes…I mean no, you are not disturbing me…you are disturbing my neighbors."

"Oh, them…" she started to giggle, and then started to laugh. I couldn't help but laugh with her. "Well? Can I come up to your place?" Her eyes were playful.

"Sure, please, come in, Andrea." I was not sure what to do. I liked her and I wanted to have some quiet time, but here was a beautiful woman who had come to visit me.

"I had a few glasses of wine at the restaurant at the end of my shift…" she started giggling.

"I figured," I grabbed some glasses and a bottle of red wine.

We talked into the night, and then the time came when I really wanted to sleep.

"You can stay the evening here if you wish. It will be cool. No pressure or anything," I offered her.

"Sure. I would like to stay with you tonight." She looked into my eyes unwavering. I led her into my very small bedroom. I undressed but left my underwear on. She took off her clothes, and we lay together for the first time. We snuggled and I held her. We fell asleep.

The early days of that summer were pleasant. Andrea and I would go to Singing Beach up the coast from Boston. It was nice, but I still kept my distance, as did she. I had my emotional antennas up and wanted to make the right decisions and stay damn awake! This woman was beautiful, sexy, made me laugh, and wanted to be a dancer. I would stay at her place on the other side of Little Italy sometimes. As time went on we grew tighter, and I allowed myself to fall for Andrea. In time we became intimate as lovers. It was a big turning point; once again I opened the door in myself to be close to someone, and let Andrea close to the vulnerable places in my heart. I knew what I had done in my marriage with Jennifer, and I knew I wanted to do the right thing with Andrea. I would stay vigilant this time around. Later that summer, I made fifty copies of a collection of poetry I had been writing for a year, and gave it to friends. It was called *Singing Beach*, and it was dedicated to Andrea Pastorella. What a romantic spud I was!

By end of the summer my divorce date was up. On that day I met Jennifer on the courthouse steps. We looked at each other and felt the sadness of our distance.

"Is this it, Jennifer?"

"Yes, Ron. Let's finish this."

We sat in the waiting room making small talk. Our docket number was called and we entered the Judge's chambers. The whole procedure was simple, and the judge asked us individually if this was our final decision to divorce.

"Yes, your honor."

"Yes, your honor."

"The State of Massachusetts hereby declares your marriage voided as of this day."

Later, on the courthouse steps, the sun was shining brightly. We hugged, cried, and bid each other goodbye.

"Ron, I will be keeping the Rubio name. I hated 'Mitchell.'"

"I wish you would not do that, but do what you want. I cannot stop you."

We stared at each other for another second, and then we parted.

Well, that was marriage number one.

Andrea really wanted to get her dance career going, but her body was pretty rough and untrained and I was finding the dance options in Boston uninspiring.

"Andrea, would you like to move to New York City with me? You could get some really great dance training and I can get back into my dance career," I asked her one night over dinner.

"Yeah! Doing it in New York City would be really great! Where would we live? My friend Cathy wants to dance as well. What about her?"

"Well, we could move into my studio on the Upper West Side. Cathy can live with us until she finds her way. My place in Manhattan is small, but it will be okay for awhile for all three of us." I had been smart enough to sublet my loft to a friend all this time I was in Boston. I would give him ample notice, and it would be cool.

"Great! Can I call her to let her know?" Andrea gave me a big hug.

"Sure, you can call her. Let's figure we leave by October. That will give the person who is subletting my place two months to find a new place."

The plan was set, and the Wheel of Life began to revolve toward the manifestation of our plans. Damn, back to New York City! It was about time. I had moved to Boston, gotten married, gotten divorced, and was now moving on with a new woman in my life. I had taught dance and performed in Boston, and had written a small play and staged it. I had been in a band, I had lived a real full life in New England, but in September with the beginning of fall approaching, there was one more circle I had to close. Chef Kayo pulled me over after the shift one night.

"Ron, can I talk to you for a moment?"

"Sure, Kayo. What's up?"

"Annie's brother, John, is in the hospital. He has been in for a couple of weeks."

"I am so sorry to hear that, Kayo," John had quit the restaurant after I walked in on him and Jennifer. I had not seen him for months. "What do you want from me?"

"Can you go in to see him? I know he feels real bad about what happened." Silence. Kayo looked at me and I nodded. I got the information for the hospital and his room. I figured he was caught in the crossfire and was collateral damage. He was a gentle soul, so I felt he deserved to be released from any feelings about me. To me what had happened with Jennifer and me was over, and I wanted him to move on with his life. I went to see him the next day.

It was making decisions like this that allowed me to reinforce positive social thinking, of being aware of someone else rather than the world according to "ME," and more compassionate instead of releasing vengefulness and anger. In the past this was not my way of thinking, and my relationships with men were just as strange as they were with women. The sense of betrayal was always present: that sense that the men close to me in my life would betray me as my dad did. It seemed like all the relationships in my life were just an ever-changing process of trying to figure things out and learn. For many people like me both deep and shallow relationships were a minefield, a scattered environment filled with misunderstanding, miscommunication, and projections of personal fears upon other people—a total misreading of the whole damn thing!

So there I was: taking the elevator to John's floor where he was in for a bleeding ulcer and some persistent lung weakness. I found his room and

Annie B was standing outside his door.

"Ron?" she looked at me completely surprised.

"Annie B." I looked at her calmly and hugged her.

"Why...what...why are you here?" she stammered quietly. Her eyes watering up.

"Annie, Kayo told me about John. I did not know. I came in to wish him well. Is that okay?"

"Why, of course. It will mean a lot to him."

"Annie, it will be okay." I took her hand and give her a confident squeeze.

I took the time to clean the slate of my emotions from the past, and imagined the day John and I first met. We were two young men making our way through a big bad world. I smiled to myself and entered his hospital room.

"John, you look like shit!" I said as he turned his head toward me, and away from the window as he heard me walk up to his bedside. I noticed one of Jennifer's books on his bedside table.

He stared at me as if seeing a specter. Was I there to smother him, like the hospital scene from *Godfather II*, and take advantage of his helplessness?

"Ron?" His voice was quivering. He just stared at me.

I walked closer to him and reached out to run my fingers through his chaotic hair.

"Damn it, John, you got to get better and get the hell out of here." His eyes watered up as he looked into mine. I continued to soothe him by running my fingers through his hair. I felt his body relax. I heard him take deep breaths. He was crying quietly.

"You really look like horseshit warmed over! Shit John, don't you take showers anymore?" I got him to crack a smile and a laugh. "Listen brother, everything is okay," I said to him quietly and with great compassion.

"Ron..." he began but stopped.

I took his hand in mine.

"Look brother, you don't need to say nothing. No apologies, nothing. What happened...happened. Understand? John, you are a good man. Get well, get the hell out of here and move on."

I heard footsteps behind me. I turned coming face to face with Jennifer.

"Hi, Jennifer."

"Hi, Ron. Nice for you to visit."

"Yeah, I wanted come by and say 'hi' to John. I did not know he was in the hospital." I turned to John; he was calmer in the face, and we were still holding hands.

"Look, John, I will be on my way. I came as soon as I heard you were in. I did not know." I squeezed his hand strongly. "Everything is okay now, and you get well and get out of here."

John and I looked into each other's eyes for a moment and then I turned to leave.

"Be well, Jennifer. Good-bye." I left the room. I would never see her again.

Outside John's room, Annie was in the hallway and had been standing near the door; she had been watching. "Thank you Ron. Thank you so much."

"I know he will get better and be out soon. I will see you at work, Annie."

One month later, Andrea, Cathy, and I were in New York City. My life in Boston was now behind me, and New York City once again demanded my full attention.

Okay, Miss Big Apple, I am back and I am real hungry!

Woolly Mammoth Boy was silently foraging and eating, far apart from the main herd.

"Impulsive, the Man-boy is," sang a blue-feathered bird into my ear.

"Why do you call him a 'Man-boy'?" I replied to the bird.

A large, orange and purple Thought-lizard croaked nearby, "He moves like the wind when inspired, and strikes like lighting in his actions, fueled by impulsive behavior more associated with a young unfettered boy, though he is in a man's body." Zipping to the top of a rock, the lizard continued, "His exuberance is to be admired and his good intentions to be noted. Note as well, though, the collateral damage of his explorations."

"Yes, I agree. Man-boy is appropriate for him," I mumbled as I ate. "He pains others and belittles himself as he learns about being with the female of his kind. He seeks solace and oneness in these illusive relationships he creates."

"The Man-boy will learn as he burns and rises each time from the devastation he wrecks and the beauty he sows," a red-tailed hawk whistled above me.

I looked out into the simmering southern savannah where the mammoth herd had migrated for the winter. In the air before me transpired a wavy mirage vision of the Man-boy packing his belongings and talking to his female. I trumpeted out loud, surprising all around me. Bellowing a fair warning...

"Be alert Man-boy, the lessons continue!"

31. Rajada Falls and the Sacred Circle

Once the visionary mind of an individual who is a gifted berserker gets whirling, deadly erratic creative bolts of inspiration begin to fly around unchecked. The once impulsive and obsessive tendencies are now utilized as assets rather than the detrimental behaviors they would normally be. For it is better to have the enthusiasm of a madman, with abandonment from all sound reasoning and plain logic, when in the throes of creative birthing!

—The Queries of Woolly Mammoth Boy

"MY PLACE IS TOO SMALL for the three of us," I said, looking at Andrea while having a quiet moment in my Upper West Side studio apartment. It was the beginning of December 1984, and we had been living in my small apartment for about two months since moving from Boston. Andrea and Kathy had been looking into different dance classes while I got back into Zena Rommett ballet and my Horton modern classes. I picked up work as a cook at a cool take-out/eat-in place called Allison's on Broadway and 8th Street, a neighborhood where things were hopping. I first helped as a carpenter building Allison's, and then, once it opened for business, I got a job in the kitchen. No more waiting and dealing with customers. Nope. Back into the kitchen to work and have fun. The kitchen job accommodated my full schedule of dance classes. I had also completed a couple of dance auditions as soon as I got back into New York, and got into two small modern companies. One was as an apprentice, and the other as a dance member. Cool.

My apartment was small and when we first moved it worked with the three of us, but now stress was building at the seams. Kathy was getting too depressed; she was from a Midwestern state, and New York City was just too much for her. She was overwhelmed by the power and energy of the Big Apple, and her dance teachers were killing her for her lack of training. This was New York City, not Kansas! Andrea was holding her own ground by taking beginner ballet classes, and had discovered modern dance with the legendary Mary Anthony, whose work was based on Martha Graham's style. Ms. Anthony was holding scholarships for her dance theater school and Andrea, as well as Kathy, were working toward auditioning. But Kathy was just not getting it—you had to get into a New York City *thing* and really grab the tiger by the tail and jump into the mouth of the dragon fearlessly, or least pretend you were fearless. New York City took no prisoners!

"I know. Kathy has been crying a lot after classes lately. Mary has been really on her case in class," Andrea said, between bites of dinner. "I hope she can hang in there."

"Andrea, Kathy hasn't experienced anything yet! This is just the beginning."

"I know, Ron." There was a somber pause. It could happen to the best of us. "Oh, by the way I found a job at the Lone Star Café downtown," she shared.

"Not bad, babe. That place pulls in great tips. You'll do great, Andrea."

"I know. Ron, the scholarship auditions are coming up at Mary Anthony's."

"You will rock, Andrea. Stay strong with the ballet classes. That will give you the core strength." I looked at her feeling proud that she was really strong and moving with confidence through the pulse of the city. Only time would tell if she could do it, but I did not doubt her ability.

A few weeks later I came home to Andrea and Kathy talking quietly. Kathy had been crying, again.

"Ron, I have decided to move back home." Kathy looked at me as I sat near them.

"The city is just too hard and I don't feel comfortable here."

"Kathy, I am sorry. The city is tough, and it does take time to really get into the swing of things. I am sorry that it did not work out. Keep dancing wherever you go."

A few days later Kathy moved out and went back home. Andrea and I now had the whole apartment to ourselves. We were in love and our relationship began to build a connection and trust that allowed for our deeper personalities to surface. We squabbled over little stuff. For me, rigid thinking and my intolerance to change how *I* did things, reared its head again. I unconsciously demanded I "lead" the way; I knew better, I had lived in the city before; I had lived through the turmoil of adversity in my early childhood and knew how to survive. Yikes! The little things grew into bigger things. I maintained a good line of communication with Andrea, but I started to stumble on "my way or the highway" thinking. As much was I was aware of my poor social skills with someone intimate, it was too challenging to change. I was a considerate man with a loving heart, but I had learned some very bad ways of thinking about relationships, and they were embedded in me from an early age. I just had to keep trying harder, I kept telling myself.

After rehearsal one night, I found myself on a crowded train platform during rush hour surrounded by thousands of city minions heading uptown. I was thinking about love and the "whys" and the "why nots" of staying in

New York: Why didn't I just become a baldheaded monk, live in a desolate cave someplace in downtown Newark, New Jersey, and forget all this mumbo jumbo about love and people? The jostling and close proximity of people always gave me pause, and alerted me to anxiety and danger. People, I had learned, were just too unpredictable in the City, and tonight the platform was packed like cattle waiting to be slaughtered; the mindless herd. I heard the train coming and the herd got tighter. The #2 Uptown Express rumbled into the station. The first couple of cars were packed, but then an empty car stopped right in front of me. The herd pushed me from behind into the car. I quickly grabbed a seat and zoned out. By the next stop all the folks were gone, and I was the only one left sitting in the empty car. Then the smell hit me. It was the sweet smell of death and decay. At the far end of the car was a huddled body. The smell got stronger and drove me to the other end of the car. At the next stop I got out and walked the rest of the thirty-three blocks back home. I needed to air the smell of death off myself and my clothes. New York City was not merciful when winter came. This homeless person had just gotten warm enough to die in an underground train car. It is said there are a million stories in New York City. Now it was a million, minus one.

By January 1985 I was dancing a lot again. I was back with Zena Rommett taking classes and reconnecting with dance friends. I had been dancing for six years and been married once. New York City was no longer a big scary place. Though death was close and the distractions were many, I was still heading toward my dream. That year saw a free-spending mentality spread throughout the nation while President Ronald Reagan was kicking ass on the middle and lower classes of society. There was a disease called AIDS killing the gay people, and on the streets was a deadly drug called crack cocaine, ruining lives and killing anyone in its path. I was around a lot of people who had their own dance companies, or who were in struggling dance companies.

I was reading a lot about the state of dance in America, about the state of the economy, and how art and social services were the first programs to be cut. President Reagan thought we were all living the good life, and that we should spend money with credit cards while at the same time cutting programs and services the poor and disabled people needed. Something smelled fishy. What I started to see in most choreography performances did not appeal to me. It seemed that dance companies were putting out dances for the knee-jerk reaction of approval; there was not much substance in them. I guessed dance companies were doing this in order to attract attention for grant money and dwindling art funding. The dance world was throwing out glitter and shiny things to attract the easily stimulated minds of the "sheep people." I started thinking about creating my own dance company. It seemed a natural course for me. Why do something that did not resonate with my soul? I had always, up to this point in life, lived my life in my own way and danced to my own music. I was not much of a follower. I did not want to be one of the sheep in the crowd or just be content with the status quo. So for right or wrong, regardless of what anyone thought, I was going to start my own dance company.

I began the arduous process of getting a 501(c) not-for-profit status for my dance company. I buckled down and corralled my rebellious "anti-anything-structured-about-money" attitude. I worked with the very little money I had to manifest my dream. I chose the dance company name "Rajada Falls." Rajada Falls was a beautiful park in Oregon just outside of Cottage Grove. The full name of the company was The Rajada Falls Dance Theatre. I connected with my music buddy Adele Dinerstein to be my musical director and to develop original music for my dance pieces. I hired a lighting designer, and I involved myself in the costume making, stage design, music composition, and choreography. This company would be where I would allow the voices of the dancers to be part of the creative process. I was a very idealistic dreamer and a socialist. I wanted to be the chief and share the wealth with all. It was a way of thinking I got from the 1960s and early '70s. It was a daring experiment: I was a risk-taker and this was not any different from how I had been living my whole life. I invited dancers I knew to join Rajada Falls, and Andrea was one of them.

Then, in late January 1985, I got a call from my sister back in California. Dada, my maternal grandfather, was in the hospital and not doing so well. I did not have the money to fly back to see him, but I had heard the whole extended Ponciano clan was gathering around Dada. This man had been a real rock for my family after my parents divorced back in 1963. He was someone I really looked up to growing up. He instilled in me a sense of pride for being an American, and most importantly, for being a Filipino American. His wartime stories of being captured by the cruel Japanese and surviving horrendous conditions were empowering to me. My Dada's duty to America as the first Filipino officer in the United States Navy, serving in the Navy during World War I and II, stuck in my heart, but now the Wheel of Life had finally had caught up with Dada and his time had come.

Unfortunately, I was busy with dance rehearsals and working in the kitchen, and I could not fly back to see him because I had no money. I was just too far away following my dream! I was too busy staying alive in New York City to be thinking about life in the west. Then, on February 5, the call came to tell me that Dada had passed away. I was terribly depressed and mad. Mad that I could not be there for my grandfather. Depressed that

Dada was no longer here on this earthly plane for me to see, talk to, and be around. Dada was just plain-ass gone. He no longer existed on the mortal plane. It would be almost twenty-five years before I saw his gravestone. I was told he would be buried at the Golden Gate National Cemetery with full military honors. I would have been honored to have played "Taps" on trumpet for Dada, but life in New York City called; the world kept turning despite all the pain and sorrow. I moved on.

Dance, Dance, Dance!

Andrea and I were working hard on our dance. Andrea now had a scholarship, and she was getting her behind kicked by the keen-eyed Ms. Anthony. Mary Anthony was a true master of the craft of choreography. She was from the old school; her training in dance theater and the art of choreography had come from Martha Graham, and her work with the German dance theater master Anna Sokolow in the early part of the twentieth century. At a public relations showing of my dance work at the DanceSpace rehearsal spot on 19th Street off of 7th Avenue, I met a former student, and now choreographer, of Anna Sokolow who was familiar with the Native American theme I was developing for one of my dances. His name was Henry Smith, and after the show he came up to speak with me.

"Mr. Rubio, I am Henry Smith." The former Penn State linebacker turned dancer extended his hand. "I like the piece you put together based on Native American ideas."

"Yes, I am developing it for a performance in the near future." Henry was very engaging and showed interest. "Would you do me the honor and check out a rehearsal?"

"Sure," he answered. We exchanged contact information and set a time for him to see my company. We were to meet the following week. Upon seeing my work Henry was very helpful and suggested many cool ideas. He came off as very eccentric and odd, but with an energy that would draw you in and mesmerize you with his stories and tales. He asked if I wanted to check out his company. I agreed, and he invited both Andrea and me. Henry's dance company was called Solaris Dance Theater. The choreography was full of leaps, diving toward the hard ground, and rolling to a standing position. His work featured whirling, circular movements and contact improvisation. There were great opportunities to experiment with theater character development. His work had strong warrior themes and mythical tales woven throughout. After showing his stuff he invited Andrea and me to join his company. We both joined up.

In our relationship, Andrea and I had been having our ups and downs. Her work at the Lone Star Café was good and kept her busy along with her packed dance schedule. Men were always after her and I tried not to be jealous, but I was an insecure man with a big roar. Though I could be a big-hearted Leo that could conquer the world of men, I was hamstrung by self-doubts and self-hatred. Fear crushed me and left me gasping; I repressed my soul damage like a pain-driven animal, stimulated by the strength that came from anger and shame, but not the softness of love.

Andrea and I had our "tit for tat" fights over things. I was always thinking I knew better about living in New York City, and made sure she knew that. She was a fiery woman and wanted no part of my domineering, insecure personality. My anger meltdowns did not help either. Being the director of a dance company and having the responsibility of being with two other companies was stressing me out. My self-importance was killing me. I did not know how to delegate the work of my company to others—especially since there was no one to delegate work to! I would stress out and bring it home to Andrea. The fact that I felt Andrea was a little slow about things fed the fire. My dad had taught me to despise slowness in others. Of course, my intolerance of the mistakes of others was very hypocritical, and made me one big, fat, pain-in-the-butt to those close to me. I was a perfectionist that could not tolerate deviation in my direction or requests.

Andrea was very tired of my trumped-up charges of her inadequacies. I was feeling angry with myself that once again I was causing disharmony in my home and in my relationship. It was the classic image of the snake devouring itself by its tail first. I was very busy with a dance company to direct, and with my responsibilities to be present for others. I was not taking care of myself, nor was I taking the time to focus myself and bring my frantic, anxious energy back to earth. I took it for granted that our relationship would weather the storm as best as it could. It did not help that it was another snowy winter in New York, and I was aware that the lack of sunlight and cold weather was hard on me physically and spiritually. I was aware, but disregarded the warning signs. Andrea knew I loved her dearly and she loved me just the same, but stress was stress and that was plain and simple. We endured through the winter but continued to build our separate lives, even as we danced in Rajada Falls and Solaris together. The bitter cold of winter made our relationship frozen in a dance of loving sadness.

Breathe.
Someday I will make it better.
Someday I will be a better man.

One day in late January, Henry wanted to talk to me after a Solaris rehearsal of a program of theater dances called *Bushido,* which means "Way of the Warrior" in Japanese.

"So, Mr. Rubio..." he said with a theatric flair, "Do you like the martial art sections of *Bushido's* choreography?"

"Yes, Henry. It is real nice."

"Well, the movements come from the martial art *aikido*. It is a Japanese martial art."

"Nice."

"Why don't you try a class? The aikido dojo is on 18th Street and 7th Avenue."

"Sure." I made a mental note to stop by if I was in the area in the near future. I knew the area well. I would walk there sometimes going to and from dance classes. There was a place in the area around 6th Avenue and 12th Street that original sold artwork. I had noticed one artist was being featured a lot, and his paintings were of samurai-inspired themes. The art pieces were large in dimension and executed in great, rich, oil paints—the medium I had painted in as well. The painting that caught my eye depicted the dramatic action between two samurai—two Japanese medieval warriors preparing to duel. I would stand for long minutes admiring this artist's work, and now I was getting the invitation to check out a Japanese martial art. I had once participated in a capoeira workshop at the Alvin Ailey Dance School. Capoeira was very dancelike and included high-flying kicks, sweeping leg movements, and smooth-moving floor work. It was the first and only martial art I had ever studied. Being Asian-looking, it was always presumed that I practiced the martial arts. Ah, stereotyping! It was like presuming that all black people play basketball and all black people are great dancers—not!

One evening I found myself with time off, and I was near the aikido dojo's vicinity. The *dojo*, or training hall, was above a parking garage. I walked up some very narrow stairs and found myself in a very open space with people working out. Some wore blue or black skirtlike things, and others wore all white with white belts. The instructor was a very big, impressive, and solid man who reminded me of the actor Charles Bronson with a Fu Manchu-like mustache. I watched in awe as people were being thrown around, doing the rolls I had learned in Henry's choreography, except they were doing rolls on mats and I was doing my rolls on dance floors or cement! Then, as everyone knelt down on the sides of the dojo, this woman, in one of those skirts, was called up and thrown by the Charles Bronson-like instructor. She flew in the air, with feet up, and landed with grace, bouncing back up to standing. Damn! This stuff looked pretty cool. I realized the ones wearing the skirtlike things looked like samurai.

After the class was over, I went over to the dojo's office counter to talk to someone about signing up for classes, and what was above the counter?

A framed copy of the dueling samurai painting I so admired in the art store window on 6th Avenue.

"Nice painting!" I said to the guy in a white *gi*, or practice uniform, who was giving me information about aikido classes.

"Yes, that's Sensei Harvey Konigsberg's work," he said, looking up at it and admiring it with me.

"You mean the person who painted that painting teaches here?" I said with great surprise.

"Yes, he is standing behind you," the fellow answered.

I turned and saw the same teacher I had been watching teach class standing a few paces from me. A circle of fawning women who seemed to be waiting their turn to give him a good-bye kiss surrounded him.

Damn! I walked over to him after the ladies left, and introduced myself.

"Hi, I am Ron Rubio." His light eyes pierced into mine, "I am a dancer with Henry Smith and he told me to check out an aikido class."

"Oh, that Henry!" he laughed a hearty laugh with his eyes sparkling. "Welcome."

"I was told you painted the samurai painting. I have been admiring your work at the art store on 6th Avenue for some time."

"Thank you. I'm Harvey Konigsberg."

"Thank you, Mr. Konigsberg."

"Just call me Harvey."

We shook hands and I left. I started taking aikido classes the following week. Aikido was going to change my life in a big way. I just did not know it at the time. My aikido home became the New York Aikikai school under Yoshimitsu Yamada Sensei. Like anything that I liked, I became obsessed with the need to do it all-or-nothing. I started to take as many aikido classes as I could. A 6:45 a.m. class was a great fit.

"RUBIO! THIS IS NOT A DANCE CLASS!" yelled one of my morning teachers, the late Phil Oseke. "Quit dancing around! THIS IS A MARTIAL ART!"

I was trying my best, but I was a dancer. Learning aikido was easy. It was like learning new choreography. Watching the feet was the secret; forget about the hands, just watch the feet and move. I just had to stop adding my dance flourish at the end of an aikido exercise. By April I accomplished my fifth *kyu* test: the first rung on the white belt ladder toward black belt. This was going to be a cool thing. Aikido had flowing movement, powerful circular throws, and grounded stances. What amazed me the most was the breath part of aikido. I walked into the aikido dressing room one day, and noticed the guys I really admired all had big beer bellies. I was to find out later that these beer bellies were actually a development of breathing from the belly, and dropping your energy to that part of the body instead of using the upper part of the body.

I was never taught to breathe in dance. It was never discussed. In, fact breathing was barely covered in aikido, but being my classic, obsessive self I started reading all I could get my hands on about aikido. In texts about "O Sensei," the creator of modern-day aikido, it was clear that he saw breath as the foundation of life. I realized the breath was essential in my own life. From childhood I had been born with weak lungs, and now I was getting involved with a way of living that focused on breathing. Studying dance had focused me on my flat feet, feet that I thought would never matter to me in my life, but now I was pointing my feet and had actually built arches in them. Dance helped me with my physical presence, and aikido was going to help me build an internal presence.

I soon started to read about Taoism, Shinto Buddhism, and the chakra system; the energy points in our body, acupressure points, trigger point muscle therapy, energy healing, healing using color, and healthy eating. My years of training with Madame Zena Rommett and being a dancer made me quite aware of body alignment and posture. Now I was developing a martial aspect in my life. I would become a warrior-healer, and not the berserker who maimed and destroyed. I had always wanted to help others. My vision of wanting to be a helpful doctor started when I saw commercials of the *USS Hope*—the hospital ship that went all over the world helping others—as a kid in the 1960s. Yep, this was the path I wanted to take. Dance, movement, and now the martial arts were going to be a big part of my dream of being of service to others.

My life was excited by these new discoveries. I knew I lacked many things in life—social skills, an understanding of money and the materialistic world, how to love others without hurting them, or how to receive love without the fear of abandonment. I felt like the character Lenny in John Steinbeck's *Of Mice and Men* who crushed others because he was ignorant of his strength and lacked social awareness. Oh, yes, I lacked things, *and* I was growing and learning.

Maybe someday I will understand what love is about...

The spring was a busy time; Andrea and I were dancing with Solaris and working hard on Rajada Fall's upcoming opening performance at St. Mark's Church on the Lower East Side. Our relationship was going up and down, but barely holding on. The Solaris performances kept us both busy. Henry was a good man, an okay choreographer, and a lousy company manager. Our dance performances took us all over the Tri-State area and pay was hard to come by, but it did come eventually. We all complained about Henry and we all loved him at the same time. His collaborative work with the Native Americans dancers and drummers—mainly the Lakota Sioux of North Dakota—was great. We were slated to have a big performance in the spring of 1986 with them. He got work, and that was important for a dancer.

Henry also was involved in the men's movement that had sprung up in the '80s, which had emerged in response to the women's movement that had been going strong for decades, but most especially since the 1970s. Henry held warrior workshops, and he invited me to get involved. I found myself at weekend retreats in some plush, upstate New Age center, which was filled mainly with groups of confused white men in their late 30s to early 60s. These guys did not have a clue what was real and what was an illusion in this world of materialistic, superficial glitter and bait. Their views of women were patronizing and chauvinistic. They feared other men and especially men of color. Henry's workshops allowed them to get to know their bodies and showed them how to ground their energies. I had little faith that the work would last any amount of time. Their handshakes were not real. The workshops paid money, and I got to get out of the city on weekends.

One of the Solaris performers, Irvin Faust, was also an aikidoist and a karate man, He opened my eyes to aikido weapons training, and we became good friends for life. Irv and I had the same birthday, March 10. We joked about having the same mother but different fathers. Irv was a tall, black, and lean Vietnam veteran who had served in the US Air Force. He reminded me of an elegant Zulu warrior. Before shows he would practice his sword *katas* off in the stage wings. Since aikido was based on the sword, I took to sword training with enthusiasm. I read books on Japanese sword training, and, most especially, the legendary Japanese sword master Miyamoto Musashi.

It seemed there was a direct connection between the sword and the breath. I repeated a basic sword-training motto: "One cut—one breath." This became a way of thinking and seeing life for me.

"One cut—one breath…One moment to live."

For most of my life I had struggled to understand how to live in the world of men. This world was oh-so-confusing; this world where I suffered the pains of being mortal, and where I was so out of place with others. I realized I was a person with much love and appreciation for people, but I could also cause sadness and disharmony. My self-loathing and disconnection to others would leave me empty, and impotent to live my life fully.

"One cut—one breath…One moment to live." This simple vision and collection of powerful words allowed me to begin to understand that the only time I could live and be free from pain and suffering was in the moment of a single breath—in a single moment; not in the past, nor in the future, but right now in the present. Living with such anguish and suffering for most of my life, I had built a high threshold to physical and emotional pain, and I believed I had found something that would change me. Heck, I was a young man of twenty-seven years and I wanted to change for the better or die in the attempt. But Andrea was not going to wait for me to change. By early summer she wanted out of the relationship. I could not blame her, though I was bitter about her decision.

My world of dance and artistic successes seemed so empty compared to my social difficulties and relationship failures, and here was that heart/soul pain again. I had failed to adjust and implement all that I knew about my social deficiencies from past relationship experiences. Once again, a beautiful woman was leaving me. My anger meltdowns and inability to be accommodating once again suffocated my truer intentions of love and compassion for another. If I just could figure it out—I knew I *could* figure it out, but I did not know how to implement my revelations. Whatever the reasons may have been, Andrea was leaving me, but she still wanted to participate in Rajada Falls and we would be still dancing with Solaris. I would have to deal with it. I braced myself once again to be alone.

Choreographing, designing lighting schemes and costumes, and helping compose the music for my dance company ate up lots of time and kept me very busy. Solaris dance rehearsals and summer performances kept me on my feet as well. The hot and humid summer days drove me out of the city in my spare time. I went out to Far Rockaway beach when I could, and that meant taking the A train in the other direction, out of the city and toward the Atlantic Ocean. There the beach was empty and dry. I met a beautiful woman on the train ride back on one occasion. Striking up conversation, we found each other very funny and lighthearted. We hung out together for the summer. She owned a clothing store in the East Village I would visit when I was through with dance classes. It was weird that her name was Jennifer. Our summer relationship was fun, but empty. Jennifer was very nice, and yet, I was vacant about my emotions and my feelings toward her. I was still seeing Andrea in rehearsals, and it was like putting a pie in my face every time. I was starting to realize thorough the years that I could attract women, but I did not know what to do with them once I was with them. Yikes!

The city was filled with too many distractions, and I was way too busy. I had created a chaos of my own making. I started to escape back up to New Paltz when I could, and back to the haven of solid mountains and clear-water swimming holes. I was there one weekend when I saw an advertisement for a rental space. It was my opportunity to put together a movement class based on the "mind–body" ideas I had been playing with since starting aikido classes. I felt that the physical human body was limited, whereas the human mind was expansive and unlimited. This was not a new thought, but I did not see it implemented in the fitness or heath fields at the time. So I offered a class I called BodyKi, meaning "BodyBreath," in the summer of 1985 in New Paltz. The class was a combination of breathing and visualization exercises to see one's body movement before actually moving, and developing positive language to replace old detrimental thinking patterns.

My first class drew one student. That was okay because the path of BodyKi had started. I would teach every weekend for two months. It was great. I knew I was onto something, and once again my creative mind took over and used the sad, depressed energy of my break-up with Andrea as a furious catalyst for "thinking outside the box." I was putting together all my experiences with dance, art, alignment, aikido, energy healing, and peak performance into a presentable teachable package. BodyKi was a holistic fitness system.

I had previously tried my hand as a fitness trainer for a couple of weeks in the city, but I grew despondent and disillusioned with the lack of soul in my clients. I made their bodies beautiful and lean; but it was their limited, hypocritical, judging fear of others—just their plain mean attitudes to people—that I could not be around. I wanted to help change the entire human being. I wanted to be a light to a higher level of personal evolution, and I saw the healthy, aligned, and graceful body as the product of a focused mind and fearless heart. BodyKi was the beginning of what would be my personal mission as a teacher and, later, as a mentor.

With this bright, creative light burning in my heart I continued to grow. However, my poor understanding of intimate relationships, lack of basic communication skills with those I loved, and low tolerance for people's feelings and thoughts created a paradoxical dilemma for me. How could I teach the beautiful concepts of personal empowerment through self-discovery and self-evaluation if I could not apply them to myself? What the hell was wrong with me? I had to "walk my talk," or I was destined to see myself as a farce, a charlatan! Time would tell, I prayed.

I had burned and destroyed many beautiful relationships. I had meant to do so well, to be a great man, a lover, provider, friend, and companion to the woman in my life. I had thought my first marriage was going to be my one and only.

What the hell is wrong with me? Am I cursed? Am I to die unfulfilled in experiencing true love?

WHAT THE HELL IS WRONG WITH ME?

Pause. Breathe. Pause...

In the beginning of September, I saw an audition notice for a position with the National Dance Institute (NDI) under former New York City Ballet great Jacques d'Amboise. I had seen pictures of him and another former New York City Ballet great, Edward Villella, around the city. These two men were the first Grade A male ballet *danseurs* that were American-bred and not from Europe. They really were an inspiration to me. Jacques d'Amboise's dance project of teaching dance to inner-city children was nationally known, and I jumped on the chance to be a part of his organization. The auditions went well and he asked me to stay afterward, where he hired me on the spot. I was the only male on his NDI teams at the time. He assigned me to lead his Spanish Harlem team.

"Mr. Rubio, I am giving you the hardest kids. They are a rough bunch of middle-school-aged kids. You start next week," he told me straight up over coffee.

"Mr. D'Amboise, give me the toughest, and the more the merrier!" I said, looking at him unflinching.

"I like it! I like your confidence, Mr. Rubio! Do you have an accompanist you could recommend?"

"Sure, her name is Adele Dinerstein."

"Great, I want her number. You start Monday. You will learn our basic choreography, and then you will add your own, okay?" he said, with a nice big smile. "The project will be performed at our annual performance at Madison Square Garden next year in June 1986, with all the other NDI teams from the five boroughs."

"Anytime you're ready, Mr. D'Amboise, I am ready."

"Good, we begin setting the general choreography this week. Oh, you get paid every week. Stop by the NDI offices, fill out the papers, and then you're set."

"Thank you, sir."

"Thank you, Mr. Rubio."

We shook hands, a solid handshake that I liked, and I was on my way out the studio to hit the sunny streets. Working with children and teens was easy. I could effortlessly put myself into their shoes and into their lives. The kids I worked with had tough upbringings and lived in a pretty tough part of town. This was Spanish Harlem. Some had parents who were killed by drug deals gone bad, or from taking bad drugs like the new and highly addictive one called crack cocaine. Others had parents who had died from AIDS. I knew I could reach into the heart of any child who was put before me, I guess because I was still a damaged child in my heart. There were parts of me that were frozen in different times in my life. There was "battered toddler" me, "abused awkward child" me, or "frozen invalidated teenager" me. In different stages of my life existed a different survivor of me. It was because of this survival phenomenon that I was able to understand the most traumatized, abused, left-for-dead humans who came across my path. These kids up in Spanish Harlem would be cake.

I walked into the middle school on W. 134 Street in Spanish Harlem on a bright September morning. I checked into the caged front office and was directed to a large gym by a big security guard where my kids were having their morning recess. I walked into a world of barely controlled chaos. In one corner I watched a teacher play dodgeball with kids, nailing them in their backs with a rubber ball at point-blank range with his entire adult might. Kids were fighting, screaming, and running around. The teachers gathered to one side in a circle and talked amongst themselves. I watched as a *Lord of the Flies* scenario of survival of the strongest and smartest was being played out in the gym. A metal bell rang out coldly and blaringly.

"LINE UP, NOW!" yelled one teacher at the top of her lungs. Another blew a whistle. The unruly mass of children slowly moved toward one wall amidst the pushing, swearing, and laughing. A teacher noticed me and walked over to me.

"You the NDI instructor?" He held out a hand.

"Yes I am, Ron Rubio." I reached out and shook his outstretched hand. His grip was unsurprisingly strong and confident.

"The kids you will be working with are those kids," he gestured to the kids behind him with a thumb. "They have all been chosen by their teachers for the NDI project. Most know it is a special opportunity. You got a bunch of hardcores in the group. The hope is that they will not blow this opportunity. Where do you want them?"

"You got a theater stage we can work out of?" I asked the teacher.

"Yes, sure. I'll have them brought there."

"Great. Thank you."

"You want some teachers to hang and provide security?" The teacher asked.

"Yes, for the first day. Let's see how I am received by the kids."

"Fine." He turned on his heels. "YO, LISTEN UP! THE KIDS WITH THE NDI DANCE PROJECT ARE GOING TO THE THEATER. LINE UP, FOLLOW, AND STAY TOGETHER!" the teacher instructed the kids. He filed them out, and we all headed for the school theater. The theater was large and well lit. I asked the kids to get on stage and sit down. I told the teachers to sit down in the audience seating. I walked up the stairs, onto the wooden-floored stage, and took my place in front of the kids. The kids were talkative and fidgeting.

"Good morning dancers!" I said to them.

"GOOD MORNING!" they yelled back.

"Please settle down. My name is Ron Rubio and I will be your NDI dance teacher and choreographer for the next few months," I said as I looked into every child's eyes. "I want to get something straight before we start." Two boys were making funny fart sounds and cracking up the rest of the kids. I waited quietly until it all stopped, and all eyes were on me in the dead silence.

"I am going to get this straight: what I am going to say, I am going to say once. You ready?" I asked the almost fifty-plus kids on the stage. Their attention was caught.

"We have a performance in six months in Madison Square Garden." There was lots of excited talking and noise. Madison Square Garden was where the big New York City sports teams played and famous concerts were performed. Most New Yorkers have heard of the world-famous Madison Square Garden.

"I will hold auditions today for those who want to be in it." That was a lie: all these kids were chosen for the NDI project. More noise and commotion.

"This is how it is. This is how it is going to be. I am not your parent or your uncle. I am not your teacher, a relative of yours, or anyone you have ever met before. I am definitely not a babysitter. *I AM A PROFESSIONAL DANCER AND CHOREOGRAPHER!* I am here to have a great time with you, and get you ready to perform on one of the biggest stages in New York City. You don't waste my time; I won't waste yours."

Dead silence.

"Any questions?" I asked my dancers.

Dead silence.

"I will first teach you about the directions of the stage. This is important."

The same two boys started joking and pushing each other again.

I focused my energy in their direction, and said calmly, yet hinting danger, "Excuse me, you two boys stand up right now...*NOW!*" The two boys stood up in a flash, not expecting my intensity. All eyes were on these two boys. "You know the game of baseball?"

"Yeah, sure," one boy answered me.

"That is a 'Yes, Mr. Rubio,'" I corrected him with a cold stare.

"Yes, Mr. Rubio," he answered humbly—no more mister tough guy.

"How about you?" I directed my attention to the other boy.

"Yes, Mr. Rubio," the other boy answered.

"Good. Both of you have one strike. There are only *two* strikes, and then you are out in my rules of baseball...do you understand me?"

Silence.

"Answer me please..." I said to them both.

"Yes, Mr. Rubio," they said in unison.

"Good. Now sit down and listen up, there is a lot to teach you. Everyone come down to me and sit here," I beckoned to the dancers-to-be. They all walked to the edge of the stage facing the audience seating. The seated teachers were there looking up at them. The kids were now all awake, attentive, and *appreciative*. I walked away from them to the big curtain behind them.

"Now, everyone, please turn around." They turned and faced away from the audience. I pointed my thumb toward the back curtain.

"Learn the direction and placement of the great stage! Directly back, all the way back from the edge of the stage in front of the audience, is known as 'upstage.' I am standing *upstage* from you. You dancers are sitting *downstage* from me..." Thus began their training, and I never had trouble with any of the kids after that first day. They all saw I was "real," and honestly there for them, and with them. They experienced my sincere respect from them, and I was rewarded with their honest respect in return. I never talked down to them or patronized them. These were inner-city kids and they could sense B.S. blocks away. I was raised an inner-city kid, and I knew all their ropes and tricks. I told the teachers that they did not have to stay, but they all hung around to observe how I handled fifty-plus kids singlehandedly with no stress.

My dancers were the oldest and toughest of all the kids in the NDI program that year, and Mr. D'Amboise had chosen me for the mission on purpose. I would not fail him or my dancers. In my mind this was going to be cake. You see, once my mind was set on something, a plan, a vision, I would set the wheels in motion and you better not be in the way, or you might just get run over! It was a bull-headed way to do things at times, but that was how my dad did things—it was also an attribute of my own rigid thinking. It was how I thought I should live my life at the time. It might seem too rigid a way of achieving things in life, but what the hell! I had made it this far in my life on my own, and I knew how to survive.

I began to teach my young charges the art of performing onstage, the art of dance, and the concept of being 100% in tune with yourself and all those around you. I taught my students awareness of the spatial world around them. I knew I had to gain their respect, and I planned to make this the best experience of their lives. In six months I was going to mold them into a tight dance team, and we were going to be the brightest and hottest NDI group in the five boroughs!

The uptown train ride to Spanish Harlem from my place was a long one, so I used the time to write a series of journals I kept. I had written down my thoughts, poems, and stories since my lonely high school days. Reading the poems and thoughts of Jimi Hendrix in his *Rainbow Bridge* and *Electric Ladyland* albums had inspired me to write with freedom and creative abandonment. My reading interests as an adult at the time included books on Eastern philosophy, Taoism, Shinto Buddhism, and the spiritual aspects of martial arts training. This material channeled my creative writings into a paradigm for personal introspection on healing and empowerment. I filled five or so blank English composition books with honest, self-evaluating thoughts, forgiving affirmations, and healing visions concerning the heart-and-soul trauma of my breakup with Andrea. Quietness and softness settled around my heart. In my teaching work, my creative, artistic drive and compassionate drill-sergeant mentoring approach were filled with power and clarity.

The cooking work at Allison's was going okay—it paid the bills—but one day an old dance buddy walked in. He asked me if I wanted to work at a new French restaurant in the Lower East Side. He was the night chef, and there was an opening. It sounded very intriguing, and trying something new sounded nice. So sure, I took the job; I gave proper notice and moved on.

Madeline's was a small hole-in-the-wall restaurant that already had a notable clientele. I learned new dishes and dealt with French people from another angle. Nice people, except when they were tourists who tipped poorly! The place rocked and I had tons of fun. It was a great place to decompress from all the dancing and sweating I did on the wooden floors. I was the *garde manger*. My responsibilities included preparing the salads, specialty cold dishes, hot appetizers, and desserts. The escargot dish I had to prepare did not make my personal list of foods to eat. There was something about eating a snail that did not grab me. It was a big seller in the restaurant, though.

Madeline's was one of the many restaurants and high-end catering companies I had worked at while living in New York City and supporting myself as a dancer. Some I worked at for weeks, and others for months or years. I loved to be in the kitchen because I was always guaranteed food, and I worked with a crew and got a paycheck, rain or shine. Working the floor as a waiter was tough. My social skills were tested by having to deal with the inconsistent, demanding, and sometimes rude customers. But being a waiter was like a character I had to play—put on the costume and play the role of "server." No matter where I worked as a waiter, a dump of a restaurant or a real nice place, I would always put myself in character before my shift, and

I would see myself as a butler or server in one of those movies where they served royalty. I would be my most elegant and efficient self. Being a waiter, or working any job in the food service industry for that matter, was just like playing a theater character—except when playing these characters I actually had real training to back up my performance.

As another New York City summer ended, the upcoming world premiere of my own dance company in October, Rajada Falls Dance Theater, was also settling in fine. I had drawn the dance company logo, typed up the programs notes, sent out tons of PR invitations, and hung tons of announcement flyers all over town. I had been successful in obtaining my nonprofit status for Rajada Falls. Everything was in order. It was going to be an exciting four-night run of performances; it was all I could afford. The performances were to be at St. Mark's Church on 2nd Avenue and 10th Street. My thing with churches again! It must be my love for stained glass.

One night on my way to the train station I was whistling loudly, as was my habit living in the city, and running over in my head the list of things to finish before my dance company's opening night, when I looked up and saw in the distance the silhouette of another man. This guy had something familiar about him; something in his outline had perked up my interest. I kept whistling, looking at him as we approached each other from the opposite sides of the street. Then I saw it. I saw what was familiar about this guy—it was his hairstyle. I took a chance and called out.

"Yo! Anthony!" Clearly I was shouting in the dark.

"Rubio?" came an incredible answer!

"Anthony!" I crossed over to the other side. He did the same.

We met in the middle of a deserted street.

"Brother!"

"Brother!"

We hugged each other strongly. We were both Alvin Ailey Scholarship recipients and dance brothers from the class of 1979. We had been two of the ten men who made it out of a couple of hundred who had auditioned for full scholarships six-and-a-half years before.

"I cannot believe it is you, Rubio."

"Damn, brother! It was the outline of your hair that gave you away!" I told him. We laughed like two madmen. Anthony was a black man with a unique Afro cut. His hair was shaped like the world champion heavyweight boxer Mr. Floyd Patterson of New Paltz, New York. His hair was cut like the bow of a ship in the front and flat on top. *Classic.*

After a good laugh he said, "Damn, Rubio. I said to myself there is only person I knew who would whistle like that in this whole damn city. It had to be Rubio." We laughed some more and then we checked in with each other. Surprisingly enough, as we stood in the middle of the street not one single car or taxi disturbed our meeting. Not one person was out walking. It was just Anthony and me in the middle of a New York City street talking at night. Time stood still. We were alone.

"Well brother, how is the dancing these days?" I asked him. Anthony used to wear women's pointe shoes during the men's ballet class to work his sorry-sod flat feet.

"I am not dancing…" he said and trailed off. "Things got hard and I could not make it anymore. I went back to school and graduated as a history major. And you?"

"I am still dancing. In fact, my dance company is premiering next month at St. Mark's Church," I said, trying not to sound too proud.

Silence. We just looked at each other.

"Damn, Rubio, you still twinkle-toeing! Damn Brother! Best of luck!" He said to me, recovering a little bit.

"Brother, why don't you come as my guest!" I offered.

"Naw, brother I don't see much dance these days. I have a lot of studying on my plate. I started a master's program."

"Oh…oh, okay. That's all right, Anthony. I can imagine you must be really busy."

"Yo, that's right. Look, Rubio, I got to get to Brooklyn." He extended a hand and we shook strongly.

"Brother, best of luck to you and your life," I said to him and then we parted.

I crossed over to the side of the street he had been walking on, and he crossed over to mine. As we both turned to look at each and offer one last wave, a bright yellow checkered cab drove by. The city came alive once again and covered all the tracks of our meeting. Another small vignette had just played out and was gone forever. Strange. A very small moment in time and space that was custom-made for Anthony and me by the Great Powers that be.

October came fast, and the opening night of my company's first performance arrived. The company was as tight as it could be. My dancers were ready. My choreographical skills were okay; not great, just okay. It was the whole project that was showcasing. The dancing, lighting, costumes, music, flyers, and the not-for-profit status; the whole thing was going to perform. My own piece was a solo dance. Totally improvisational in structure, my solo was artistically dangerous and just perfect for my taste. I had a pattern of living kind of dangerously and taking chances—for good or for bad.

Andrea was going to perform with the other dancers. Not a couple any longer, Andrea and I were professional enough to be in each other's space with respect (and curtness) during rehearsals. She was seeing someone else by this time, and that made my stomach feel empty. I was not angry or sad. I was settled into a heart space, and I understood it was my doing that drove her away in the first place, so I could not blame her for being happy and with someone else. I knew I would continue to heal the pain of loss, and continue to persevere and live on.

Opening night arrived, and we actually had reservations. Soon the time had come to open the church doors and the space started to fill with people. It was a cold October night and I was grateful that peopled showed up. Period. We had a band playing live music behind the curtains before we came on. Then it was show time. To perform and to be on stage, to put it all on the line, was the only way to live for some people. It was the only way for me to live. The lights, costumes, and music created the ambiance for a story told by bodies without words. I was once told by my teachers at the Ailey School that the job of a dancer, or any performer, was to take the world the audience knew—a world of office calls, stress, trying to make it frantically across town for meetings, and the mundane functions of living life—and put it all aside for them, to take them away to a world of your making. For a dancer, it is a world of movement in which you, the dancer, could be transformed into an animal, a mythical creature, a god or goddess; changed into a destroyer of worlds or a creator of paradise, to be a prince or a princess; you are the vehicle of a story that will take the audience somewhere far away, or somewhere very dangerously and deliciously close to their heart.

The four-night run of the Rajada Falls Dance Theatre was what it was meant to be: an introduction to the world of performance dance for my company. I got great reviews, and also critiques of "...what the heck was the choreographer trying to say?" For a small dance company in a time of major financial restrictions for all dance companies, first tier or third, my company was praised for presenting live music, beautiful costumes, and staging. I felt this was just the beginning, but money was a big issue. On the last night of our performances, I paid all my dancers, musicians, and professionals connected to the project. I swept the church down alone and closed the doors. Andrea went off with her new boyfriend after the last performance. I had a pint of Guinness at an Irish pub alone and called it a night. I understood the path of an artist, and it was fine for me. The pint of Guinness tasted great.

There was more dancing to do. There was the NDI dance project with my kids in Spanish Harlem to focus on, and there were the Solaris performances to get ready for. At the same time, I was an apprentice for one dance company and preparing to perform with another one in December. My feet were dancing, and they were not going to stop. Yet that day was done, and the time to wash and hang-dry my dance tights for the next day was upon me.

From the darkened heights where he stood in stoic observation, Woolly Mammoth Boy looked down into the fire-bright ravine. He had wandered off after setting the herd security for that evening with the other young bull males. Below him, some human hunters had built a firepit, and were moving frantically around the huge bonfire, their shadows dancing upon the ravine walls. He did know that the human hunters were performing a hunting ritual dance for the next day. He watched as they jumped with loud screams, twirling and turning wildly while wearing the skins and hides of those they hunted and killed. Woolly Mammoth Boy saw that one hunter wore a fur cape of mammoth hide. These images blended with that of the Man-boy's moving and turning movements, which Woolly Mammoth Boy had seen him do.

"They prepare to hunt your kind at sun-break. They perform a warrior's ritual for death and kill...they evoke their ancestors and totems for success," a nighthawk Thought called to me.

The image of the hunters—the "two-legged ones"—in their frenzied dance of death fascinated me. "The Man-boy practices rituals as well. I have seen him. He trains hard. Does he evoke his ancestors and totems?"

"The Man-boy creates rituals that evoke power and awareness in others. I have seen that he trains young ones. He communicates well with the young ones. He finds great satisfaction in his teachings to them," Thought gestured as a single leaf fluttering on a lonesome twig in the cool night breeze.

"He seems more comfortable and at peace around the young ones he teaches, than in the intimate relationships he has tried to foster with the females of his kind," I answered as the flickering light of the huge bonfire below sparkled in my eyes.

"Yes, for there vibrates within the Man-boy a common resonance with those he teaches and serves," Thought communicated as a shooting star in

the night sky. "He identifies with pain and sorrow in others. He soothes and builds strength in the young ones. The young ones see him as kindred spirit. He is truly a 'Man-boy.'"

32. Return to the West

The Buddhists have a view that all of one's life, all of one's experiences and conceptual perceptions, are like swirling clouds passing in the sky. That is to say that all human experiences and perceptions of this world are just illusions of what might seem concrete to the fettered mind. While in fact all that a person processes in this world of stimulation and distraction is in constant change and constant flux. So, answer me this: what does "I love you forever" truly mean?

—Woolly Mammoth Boy Speaks

Maitraya under an apple tree. Author's photo.

"DID YOU HEAR THE NEWS?" I was working an extra morning shift in the kitchen of Madeline's doing some prep work when the day chef came in. "Yo, the *Challenger* just blew up after takeoff! Check it out, Rubio!" I ran into the bar where the TV was on. The owner, Madeline, the day manager, and bartender were looking up at the TV screen. It showed a the smoke trail billowing from the rocket carrying the space shuttle. The trail ended in a large ball of white smoke, and then divided in two.

"My God!" Madeline exclaimed. "That poor teacher was on board."

I was thinking of all the schoolchildren around the world watching the takeoff of the first space flight that included civilians, and especially the elementary school teacher who was amongst the crew when the space shuttle exploded horrifically before ever reaching the outer atmosphere of Earth.

Damn! I went outside to the sidewalk to look up at the morning sky. The Lower East Side street was clamped down in hard snow and shiny ice. The cold January winter froze my nose hairs. The day was clear and sky blue. Those poor souls in the *Challenger* were strapped down with nowhere to go. How long did they live knowing something terrible had happened to their ship? How long did they survive in the contained, undamaged section of their shattered ship as they fell out to of the sky? *Karma.*

Karma: The cause and effect of all our lives—previous and current.

I went back to work in the quiet kitchen thinking about my life and what it was all about. Being without Andrea seemed bearable as long as I remembered why we had broken up in the first place. As in previous relationships, it was my inability to be flexible and trusting—trusting enough to allow another person to live her life and make her own decisions. Andrea and I saw each other in dance rehearsals and that was hard. The new year of 1986 found us apart with her living down in Soho, and me on the Upper West Side. Since being apart from her, I had been writing down my thoughts and learning to forgive myself. It was an every-moment practice of staying in tune with what I was doing and why at all times. Andrea was gone because I drove her out of my life. She was gone because I lacked social skills. My lack of self-confidence and unpredictable mood swings caused by anxiety and stress had wreaked havoc in our relationship. I had self-sabotaged my life with her.

Cause and effect...Karma.

I spent most of my free time writing in the quiet seclusion of the Cloisters Museum. Putting down my thoughts and musings onto paper allowed me the opportunity to "see" my thoughts on paper and get them out of my head—where all the wild things lived. Introspecting on one's own actions is a very hard task to do, but very important to accomplish. After the divorce of my first wife, and the destruction of the numerous relationships I had had, it was not easy to look at myself and tear down all the safe, self-centered behaviors I had held on to for such a long time. But it was only after such heartache and pain that I was able to face my own actions. I felt like I did after a good beating from Dad: Laying in my dark, cool bedroom crying, trying to catch my breath, and all the while trying to figure out what the hell I did to catch a beating—except that my dad's beatings really had no rhyme or reason.

I came to realize, during this time of introspection writing, that my painfully peculiar and rigid thinking in my intimate relationships had destroyed the joyful and compassionate love I could so easily conjure at the same time. For me, the paradoxical Piscean symbol was true: two fish swimming in opposite directions yet coexisting as "one."

In relationships, my mind and heart tried so valiantly and honestly to be an honorable and loving person to my partner. Breaking my partner's heart and disturbing her harmony was not something I ever wanted to do. I just wanted to love and be loved. Relationships for me were almost like the Great White Whale in *Moby Dick*. Except unlike Captain Ahab, I searched for love not to destroy it, but to experience it. Though the Great White Whale might kill me and send me to the bottom of the dark ocean where Poseidon dwells, it was my life's quest, and I would not turn away no matter what adversity I might face—including adversities of my own making.

Being alone in New York City in the wintertime could be very depressing. I was busy with the NDI rehearsals with the Spanish Harlem kids, working on my next dance company project, and rehearsing with Solaris and two other small modern companies. I was also taking tons of dance classes and studying aikido almost every day. The quiet times were lonely and cold. Andrea was out of sight and out of mind. I had to keep a real distance even though I saw her almost every other day. I was in life training and this was how life goes down sometimes. I had been there before, and so I lived and learned.

Up next was a road trip with Solaris dance theater to Alaska. We were going to participate in the annual Native American Dance Festival. Henry had choreographed many dance theater works that included live Native American drumming, singers, and dancers. Solaris was to meet up with a contingent of Lakota Sioux dancers, singers and drummers, a pair of Mandan dancers in Minnesota, and then collectively fly to Fairbanks, Alaska. I would be celebrating my birthday in the land of the aurora borealis and freezing-butt temperatures.

Now, Henry's history with organizing road trips was notorious. Murphy's Law always seemed to be part of the mix and the company members always tried to plan for the "unlooked for," but stuff always seemed to happen anyway. I guess the Harpies of Chaos flew around Henry all the time. Travelling from New York would be Henry, Andrea, me, and another dancer, a woman. We would be the modern dancers. A musician and percussionist were also going. Henry would be dancing and the company spokesman. The trip had many logistical headaches, but that was the way the ball was going to bounce.

We left New York in a snowstorm, and flew west to Minneapolis where we met our Native American counterparts. This was when I saw up close the remnants of a once proud people. The drummers and singers were great, but the Lakota tribe and the Mandan tribe were not friendly with each other. The men were addicted to junk food, smoking cigs, and drinking hard. The only native woman, a Fancy Dancer, was elegant and had a love for Cokes and McDonald's. All of the natives had scars. I remembered noticing how most of the kids I grew up with in San Francisco, including myself, had "battle scars." Most adults I knew from any metro ghetto had these battle scars too: head cuts, cigarette burns, or car lighter burns. The scars were long and glassy, or raised and conspicuous. Some of the Native drummers and singers were marked. I could tell some of the facial scars were healed knife slashes.

The Solaris Dance Company was on "White Man's" time, and the natives were on "Native time." We learned to take this into account. Henry knew of this from previous performances with the natives and had planned for this. "They will get there when they do. They always get there," was the answer he gave us when asked when the Native dancers, drummers, and singers would be arriving for rehearsal or performance. So the ball bounced...

Fairbanks, Alaska was cold and white. The festival drew native dancers from all over the Arctic region and the continental United States, but most came from the Northern Alaskan tribes as far north as one mile from the Arctic Circle. Their dances were of hunting, life in the coldest places, the ferocity of polar bears, and the cunning of animals living in places not meant for living in. The Native Alaskans' large, round skin drums were mesmerizing in the Arctic *OM* sounds they made. The Lakota and Mandan dancers were out in splendor when it came time for their performance. There was the Chicken Dancer, Grass Dancer, Hoop Dancer, and our Fancy Dancer. Once dressed in their handmade costumes of many colors and feathers, they were all transformed into something from a much older and ancient time than the McDonald's burgers they ate. Their proud, elegant, and native energies came forth, and I was held in awe by their majesty. Then, later, the ugliness of the White Man's food, alcohol, and habits would appear. It was a strange paradox to witness.

We had one performance scheduled at the Fairbanks correctional facility in front of sixty inmates—all Natives, and not one white face amongst them—but our lead drummer/singer got plastered on booze and did not show up on time. The Native inmates got really upset and started to mumble. I was looking at our group dressed in friggin' NYC dance tights, and did not feel too confident with only four guards in the room. Then, just in time, our lead drummer/singer stumbled in, but it was plain to everyone that this native brother was in no shape to stand, let alone sing or drum. We had to change our performance a bit, and got out of there in one piece. Murphy was in the room and loving all the chaos.

Andrea and I slept in different rooms, of course, and hardly spoke to each other. We would perform and then busy ourselves with company things to do. It was lonely and weird for me. On the cold black nights in Alaska, I witnessed the beautiful aurora borealis in the heavens. Shapeshifting in eerie greens and blues, the aurora borealis was as intangible as my heart, a constant flow of shapeless light and magic. It was an odd feeling in my stomach, in my center. It was like the ground was not there and I floated in the Great Universe.

On my birthday night I had a drink at the bar, alone, and went to bed. Next thing I knew, there was pounding on the walls and loud voices awakening me. There was a fight going on next door amongst the natives. I put some clothes on and went next door. The two Mandan brothers were just leaving the room of one of the Lakota drummers. The Lakota was on the floor. Whole bunches of his long, black hair were pulled from the roots and out of his scalp. His face was a bloody, puffy mess. It seemed that in their drinking craziness a fight started up and the two Mandans beat the Lakota to a pulp...literally. As the lone Lakota lay on the ground knocked out, the two Mandan brothers continued to beat and kick him. I slowly came to his side and helped wash him up. His scalp was bald in a number of places. I was going to call a doctor, but he told me to just lay him on his bed and shut off the light.

The next morning he was on his way back home to Minneapolis. His face was doubled in size and his eyes were swollen shut. His dark sunglasses hid little. His whole body screamed pain and ache; he could barely walk. As I accompanied him to the waiting airport taxi, he shook my hand and thanked me for cleaning him up and taking care of him. He gave me his worn-down pair of moccasins. I saw it as my lone and belated birthday gift. He left and was gone. The two Mandans did not even remember what happened. Strange. Both were elegant dancers; the Hoop and Grass Dancers. How could such beauty mingle with such brutality? How could both energies reside in a person's soul so easily? Now I saw that the destroyer and the creator were part of us all just like our heart and lungs. Without death and life we would not be who we are—mortal.

The trip home from Alaska was long and tiring. Like a mist, the experience was here and then gone. I had a pair of worn-out moccasins in my travel bag as evidence that it really happened. Back in New York, I was feeling ready to move out of the city. Seven years had passed, and I had grown into being a real New Yorker. My easygoing West Coast upbringing was now honed into a tough, determined, and "not to be messed with" New

Yorker from the Big Apple. I had experienced some amazing stuff fit for a book of fiction—weird, unlooked for, not-of-this-reality experiences that only living in New York could offer. I was now in my late twenties and ready to take what I learned into the bigger world. The saying "If you can make it in New York, you can make it anywhere" rang true. I decided I would leave Manhattan on my terms, and not run away because I could not hack it. I felt I was ready. I was single, and I was an accomplished dancer, teacher, and choreographer. My martial art studies, combined with my dance training, helped me to create BodyKi—a mind–body fitness and well-being training program—but New York was wearing on my spirits. I was not after the Wall Street mentality. I was not looking for the dog-eat-dog life. Though I learned a lot from New York, I was still a very emotional and sensitive person with too much heart for applying the *coup de grâce* on anyone. Soon I would leave New York City, and be a big fish in a little pond somewhere.

After returning from Alaska, I got a new job as a cook on the line at the 5th Avenue Grill. This was a place to see and be seen. The kitchen was one of the first to be open to the public; customers could see it openly standing on the floor. This brought the usual mayhem of the kitchen down considerably because now the whole kitchen staff could be seen and heard. The money from cooking helped me consolidate what I was making with my dance gigs and teaching. I knew my life was moving toward a critical mass—a point of change. The Spanish Harlem kids from my NDI group and a few hundred kids from the other NDI borough sites would be performing as one big show at Madison Square Garden in June. Henry and Solaris also had a real cool dance theater show date in a Soho Art Gallery. In this performance I was to act/dance the character "the Chattering Mind"; how appropriate! When all the shows were over I was looking into Portland, Maine as a place to move to. I wanted to stay on the East Coast.

During this lull I continued to meet a few women, and that was nice. I thought of Andrea and knew she was with someone so I stayed clear of her. The women I was meeting were delightful and fun to be around. The process of meeting women was always a unique experience of discreet flirtation and naïveté. I could not understand how much to say or not say (people on the autism spectrum can be real motormouths and tell it like it is). Though my remarks had been more of the "off-the-cuff" and not-thinking-before-speaking category, I naïvely thought that speaking what I truly felt from my heart to a person was showing trustful honesty from me. That particular communication strategy of mine did not go well at times, especially on the second or third date. The fallout just left me bewildered and questioning. So I just went with it. I knew they appreciated my exotic looks and that I was a dancer, which was funny because I still had no real connection to how I physically looked. I only had a sense that I wanted to carry myself with elegance, grace, and strength. But to "see" how I looked was a different matter. As a dancer—looking at myself in a mirror for hours on end—gave a different sense of knowing how I "appeared." So when it came to women, I was more in awe of them and the fact they would be interested in me at all.

Ever since my early years in NYC, I had felt out of place in bars and loud places, but I became acutely aware of body language and the facial masks worn by those around me. I could always sense the frantic sex appeal and sensual darts that were flying around. It was so superficial. I was bored of it all. I recalled a very short relationship with a gorgeous and sexy model. What stood out was how she never allowed me to see her without makeup on; or how, when she walked around without shoes, she would still walk as if she had heels on. Weird. I will say this over and over, "All that glitters is not gold." So being around women was a real experience for me—just being accepted by them as a lover or partner. I knew it was at the point where a casual relationship evolved into an intimate one that I would mess up. So with these ladies I was meeting during this time, I kept things pretty light and casual. I still wanted something that would last. I just did not understand how to be successful at that.

Now, I am not sure how it happened, and you will probably get another story from her, but I called up Andrea to let her know that I was going to move out of the city. She and I agreed to meet and talk. We picked a very safe public place during the day to meet. It was a great seeing her, and I felt like a fool for losing her. Our conversation led to an invitation to see her Soho studio where she lived. It was nice to be around her again. We laughed and joked like we always did, and we made another date to meet. I was very happy but cautious with my feelings around her. Our months apart had been an opportunity to clear my head and heart. I saw where I had lost it before, and I knew where I wanted to go now. Again, Andrea and I met, and again, it felt different and fun. The next time we saw each other, I was invited to stay with her down in Soho. It was so tender and fragile. Our intimacy was like a newly released butterfly from the chrysalis. With wet wings and trembling sensitivity we held each other. We knew we wanted to get back together and live together. Later, we decided that Andrea would live with me back in the Upper West Side.

Damn! Another chance! Andrea had said she did not give the men she broke up with second chances. I counted myself blessed, and I kept my antennae up for any signs my past behavior would rear its ugly head. I knew I wanted to make this second chance work, and I knew I could do it. All I knew was that in that present moment I was awake and vigilant, and I would do my damn best.

The spring of 1986 was beautiful in Manhattan. The world was bright once again with love back in my life, and softness and sensuality soothing my soul. All the performances went well. My NDI kids from Spanish Harlem kicked some serious booty! Being the oldest and toughest kids in the whole NDI program, they shined, and in the process brought me acclaim and recognition from the director, Jacques d'Amboise. It was truly an honor and a privilege to be with my kids, watching them on a big, big stage in front of thousands and performing like stars!

Andrea was also doing well with her dance studies and work with Mary Anthony. She was also still at the Lone Star Café, and surrounded by loud bands and filthy, smoky air. Then one day in late May Andrea told me she did not feel well. She started to look yellow in her skin and felt weak. A doctor's appointment revealed that her liver was shot with jaundice. She became sicker and sicker. We feared for her health and life. She sought different health solutions, and settled on a man who had developed a real cleansing way of living and eating. It was a real ball-buster of a health program that involved doing something, or eating something, every two hours on the dot. This highly disciplined program required eating raw vegetables, avoiding all salts and sugars, taking cold showers at ungodly hours, indulging in highly *anticipated* coffee-ground enemas, taking high dosages of supplements like vitamin C, and drinking mudlike herbal teas that tasted ferociously bitter and nauseating.

"Ron, you have to do this program with me," Andrea said to me one evening after a meeting with this healer, who wore a triple scorpion pendant and looked like Sammy Davis, Jr.

"Andrea, this program is heavy duty. I work in a restaurant and I am dancing pretty heavily, and..."

"Ron! You need to do this with me! I need you to do this with me. It will make it easier for me. I need you..."

Well, that was all the lady had to say. She needed me and I was her man. I loved her and she loved me. She was my world and that was that.

"Well, you know, Andrea, I will have to quit eating potato chips! I love potato chips!"

"Yes, I know, Ron," Andrea said with a smile.

"And I have to give up drinking coffee, though I will be shoving it up my ass, and I will be giving up eating meat and..."

"I know, Ron," she beamed at me.

"I will have to eat onions and greens things called 'vegetables' with no dressing. And no salt, for goddess's sake!"

"Yes, I know, Ron. It will be you and me doing this together."

I looked at her and we burst out laughing.

"What the hell, Andrea. I am in!" I promised her. I felt the brightness of our love during times of stress and challenge, once again allowing me to come out of the self-absorbed conditioning of my brain. It was so very gratifying to me as we faced Andrea's crisis as one. Moments like this reminded me why I would not give up trying to understand how to be in a healthy and loving monogamous relationship, no matter how I stumbled and fumbled my attempts.

The early weeks of being on this radical health program was pure delight *if* you came from the grey land of Hades! The every-two-hour schedule meant that wherever I was, I had to be eating or drinking something. Andrea and I started our program so we could shower at two in the morning and do a coffee enema while still at home before going off and living our "real world" life. Raw nuts here and a bunch of ripe bananas there; a handful of vitamins at 1:00 p.m. and deathly herbal tea at 3:00 p.m., and so on and so on.

I was still training hard and I was not getting enough food into my body, but I stuck with the program. On my shifts at the restaurant, my fellow cooks watched me as I ate a plain salad with tons of raw onions and garlic—with no dressing or salt. I could use a little pepper on it. Yippee! Well, I could use a little dressing—oil and a tinge of vinegar—yum, so good.

The cleansing program was making Andrea stronger and her yellow skin went away in two months. The healer that we were working with was talented but had a questionable character, as he preyed on the young women who could not afford his rates and asked for some type of compensation. He gave me the creeps. Andrea told me later when I was not around he would come by for a "house visit" and try to gain sexual favors from her. Had I known this I would have crushed him. So as Andrea continued to gain strength and stability in her health, we decided to move to San Francisco and start a dance company there and live healthy. We were going to start anew and live a life of dance, art, and love. I would leave before her, and then she would follow.

As the summer drew to high noon, the date to move to the west was set. I would leave in the beginning of September, and prepare the way: get a house, car, and job, and Andrea would follow in October. My family was open to me moving back to the West Coast. My dad even offered his place for a couple of weeks as I got my act together in San Francisco. There was an initial construction job available that my dad set up for me. Thanks, Dad.

I felt this was the right move. The west was going to be a small pond in which I was going to be a big fish. I had trained hard and acquired the skills of a proficient dancer, choreographer, and teacher. I had become a man of worldly tastes and travel. I had learned hard lessons from the streets of New York. I had experienced death and vibrant life. I had survived some bitter winter storms and hot, unbearably humid summers. Living with the natural cycles of four very distinct seasons in the Northeast had trained me to adjust, evolve, and adapt to an ever-changing natural environment. The West Coast would only offer seasons of rain and sun. Life would be different and that was okay. I wanted Andrea and me to live healthfully and easily. I closed up my connections, and made sure I had the contact information for certain friends. I had no regrets leaving New York City. I came to New York to be with the Alvin Ailey Company and had accomplished part of that objective.

About one month before leaving for the west, Andrea and I were walking down in the East Village heading to see a dance performance. On the corner of 2nd Avenue and 4th Street in front of a bakery was a discarded cardboard box. People were passing by when Andrea and I looked inside. There, tucked in the corner of the box, almost blending in with the tan color, was a kitten. I don't believe it meowed or made a sound. Andrea picked it up; it was the scrawniest little thing I have ever seen.

She said something like, "Oh, look at this poor thing..."

"Andrea, not now."

"Ron, it is so cute." The thing looked half-dead and listless.

"Andrea, we got a show to catch. If the thing is still here when the show is over we'll check it out."

Well. I'll be damned if that scrawny little thing wasn't still in the box. As Andrea looked at this little kitten, I went inside to inquire about it.

"Yes, the kitten is free to anyone," said the person behind the counter.

"Andrea, the kitten is free to anyone."

"Oh, Ron, can we have it?" Andrea looked at me with those big eyes of hers and *damn!*

"Andrea, I am leaving in a month. You have a full plate with the health program and getting things packed before you move." All I was saying fell on deaf ears.

"Ron, I will be lonely and this kitten needs a home."

Damn!

"Yo! Yo! Yo!!! Andrea, this is crazy!"

"*Please, Ron!*" Andrea pleaded.

Damn and triple damn!

"Okay, babe," I gave in. I had felt my old circuitry of rigid thinking clicking "on," but I had chosen in that moment to be flexible—and to accommodate

Andrea's wanting something that was not my own planning was joyful. The happiness that Andrea beamed as she held that kitten was well worth it. Hey, this being "flexible" thing was not so bad. My ability to be aware to extend flexibility made those around me happy; Andrea was happy and not sad. A couple of lightbulbs blinked on! Lesson learned. Now, I only had to remember to remember to be aware. Yikes.

We took this little scrawny thing back uptown in a cab. The little thing did not make a sound. I was figuring this kitten would die overnight or have a weird disease and die on Andrea while I was on the West Coast.

Needless to say this kitten made it through the night and was frisky the next morning. It was all tan and had a tail as long as its body; it looked like a puma.

"Let's call it Norton." Andrea said as she cuddled up with it.

"You mean Norton from the TV show *The Honeymooners*?" Norton was the sidekick of Jackie Gleason's character on the comedy show.

"Norton? Umm..." I looked at this little guy, who was quite alive and playing with Andrea. "Sure." And that is how Norton entered our lives. Norton would hold down the fort with Andrea when I moved. That was settled and now we could focus on the move. Soon enough the day came for me to go to the airport to fly west to San Francisco. Andrea and I solidified any loose ends about our plans. I would set things up for her and she would come to me, with Norton, and we would all be together in a new place, and start a new era of our relationship. Life was good.

The woolly mammoth herd was on the move again, migrating to greener pastures safe from the predators and the hunters. Soon the mating season would be upon them and they would procreate to sustain the strength of the herd. New ones would be born to replace those who were killed or had perished on the long journey over the high mountain passes.

I watched as the young bulls vied for the attentions of the matured, available mammoth cows. From a distance, I watched the spectacle.

"Hoy! The time is upon you, my boy! Enter the fray and be chosen by one of the cows," snickered a lone coyote from the shade of a thorny brambly bush.

"Leave me be, Thought! My intention is to remain unspent, so I may be chosen as the 'Guardian of the Herd' by the Matriarch," I grumbled at the

annoying coyote.

"*Ah, the 'lone one' is it?*" *laughed Thought-coyote.* "*You are a very promising catch for the right cow!*"

"*You keep it up and I will squash you!*" *I trumpeted.* "*I have witnessed the follies of mating with available cows. A bull loses the edge for battle.*"

"*You are amazing, my boy! You come of age and you choose the path of solitude,*" *Thought-coyote continued to snicker at Woolly Mammoth Boy.* "*I must commend you on your idealistic and youthful ideas of self-importance!*"

With that, I charged into the thorny bush to mash the coyote into dust. Thought easily skirted the threat and landed on my sensitive eyelid as a huge horsefly.

"*Enjoy this path of yours.*"

With that said, Thought-horsefly took a nice chomp into the tender flesh of my eyelid.

I bellowed in annoyance and pain. As I regained my composure, I saw the youngest of the available cows leave her sisters and slowly make her way toward where I stood.

I watched as she began to deliberately sway her hindquarters in a mesmerizing ritual dance of invitation to mate. Before I could muster any resistance, I found himself in a hypnotic trance, following her into a shaded and isolated area away from the herd.

"*Your fortitude toward your temptations is astounding!*" *laughed Thought-coyote hysterically from the shade of a thorny bush nearby.*

33. San Francisco—Again

There exist in the Great Universe life cycles that transcend both time and space. At times, it may seem as if you are living a former life pattern all over again whether you remember that pattern from the previous time or not. These repeating life cycles, if you are lucky enough to be aware of reliving them, create an opportunity to redeem yourself from your previous life's follies, or to damn yourself once again to having to be reborn all over. For are you not reborn to discover the resolution to evolve from the karmic debt you had gained from your past and former lives, and therefore be freed of having to be reborn as a human, and once again suffering, living a mortal life on earth?

—Woolly Mammoth Boy Speaks

POISON IVY ITCHED EVERYWHERE ON my body. Living back in California was very different from life in Manhattan. Clearing some wooded property for my dad rewarded me with a poison ivy rash on almost 65% of my body. I laid submerged in a cool bath of slippery elm and Epsom salt to ease the itching and to dry up the poison ivy. The late summer smells in the California hills were not tainted by the spoiled-milk odor of the New York City subway. The California summer sprouted golden grass landscapes that stretched for miles into the blistering and wavering mirages of the dry lands. I had been staying at my dad's house outside of San Francisco while I prepared the way for Andrea's arrival at the end of October. Dad had provided me some work to get going, and it was hard, hot work. It kept my mind from missing Andrea. The days were hard and the nights long. Andrea and I talked on the phone for hours; I would hear of tales of our kitten, Norton, and how Andrea was getting stronger every day. We were missing each other so much we decided she would fly out to see me in September. Until then I needed to stay focused and prepare the way for our new lives in the golden state of California.

Since leaving the west in 1979, there had been a huge migration of New Yorkers to San Francisco during the mid-1980s, and then into the '90s. I felt the laid-back feeling of the west was somehow being replaced with a "get out of my way you fool" feeling. The quick service in restaurants that New Yorkers were so used to had been replaced with a slip-slide West Coast casualness that drove the imports crazy. The people seemed less polite, and more anxious and impatient. Strange.

San Francisco—Again

I was heading into San Francisco frequently to look for a new place to live for Andrea, Norton, and me, and also to find jobs teaching dance. The determination and personal drive I had learned in New York City were coming in handy though I could not avoid feeling like I wanted to slink into a dark hole sometimes, and hide or procrastinate the enormity of the tasks ahead of me. And yet it was the stress of it all that got me moving. It was like running on automatic. The new stimulations in San Francisco were exciting. Like an addict, I wanted more, and I would take on way too much. This led me to feeling nervous, filled with fearful of thoughts of failure, or trying to figure out if I was doing the right thing. The more I searched for the answers, the more I became wound up with the doubtful chattering in my head. Damn, I had seen this pattern before! Where? Damn! The "where" did not matter; it was "in the now" that I was aware of the pattern and I had better do something about it. *So stay awake, fool!*

Andrea's quick visit in September came at just the right time. We were inseparable for three days. Our future in San Francisco became easier for me to see with her there by my side. Then, like a beautiful dream, she was gone and headed back to New York for one more month. Energetically charged once again, I continued to work and put together the logistical components of living in a new land. After some diligent hunting, I found a used car and a place in San Francisco down in the Mission District. The landlady said I could trade some rent for carpentry work. I also found a place I could study aikido and capoeira, both in Berkeley. I kept the fires of my focus hot, as I knew soon enough Andrea would be by my side, with our kitten Norton, and we were going to rock the world!

By the time Andrea came in October, the house I had found for us was ready to receive her. The area was not the greatest, but it would suffice. San Francisco's cold, grey nights took some getting used to. The air had the fragrance of the Pacific Ocean. Norton kept himself hidden in the boxes for days after he arrived. Andrea was looking good, and her health was now under control. She wanted to study at a local massage school and that was fine with me. I was making some good money, and I could provide for the both of us. Life was good.

One night Andrea said to me, "Ron, I have something to share with you."

"Babe, what is it?" I was hanging up some posters, and setting up my new office space.

"Ron, come over to me," she said to me in that voice I could not resist. We snuggled in bed and she held me tight. "Ron, I think I am pregnant."

"What?"

"I missed my period and I believe I am pregnant."

I sat up in bed and looked at her. " Babe..."

"Ron, I want to keep this baby." She looked into my eyes unblinking.

I started to get lightheaded, a precursor to leaving my body. "Babe?"

"Ron, I want to keep this baby, I want this child," Andrea said again. I could not think at first. It all seemed like a dream or something that had happened before. Then I remembered. I remember saying something really crazy at the dinner table once in front of my family when I was nine or ten years old. It was that I would have a child of my own by the time I was thirty years old. My family thought I was crazy, and a real space-cadet dreamer. And there I was, sitting on the bed with Andrea, at twenty-nine years old. This child would be born when I turned thirty. Life was strange. My vision as ten-year-old kid was becoming reality.

"Well, Ron, what do you think?" Andrea asked me quietly.

"Andrea, if you want to keep this baby, and I am the father, there is no question. I will support you as you prepare for this baby," I said from another part of the universe.

"Oh, Ron!" We hugged and kissed and held each other tight. Norton came out of his hiding place and jumped on the bed.

That night I could not sleep. I knew I had to shift gears. I had to get a real tight job to make sure our home was secured, and that we would be safe. Andrea was going to massage school and I would be the sole provider. The dreams of a dance company started to disappear. I knew I wanted to be a good father, and I was scared shitless! My dad was not the best role model. I knew I could do it, but I was scared...real scared. I had to get my act together and throw all my whining out the window. My woman was pregnant with our child and I was going to do the right thing. The next morning I would get heavy on looking for more work. Carpentry was what I liked to do and it made more money than cooking, and offered steadier employment than teaching dance.

Becoming an expectant father was a feeling of great joy and a feeling of ominous dread. I loved children: playing with children, teaching them, telling them stories, and protecting them, but my dad left a bitter taste in my life about being a father. I was denied a childhood of safety and validation. Of all his children I was the one to have the mark of "being like Rubio"—having his anger and rage. I must admit that my anger issues were deadly, and had wrought destruction in my previous relationships. Though I never beat on anyone innocent, once the rage kicked in my berserker energy was hard to contain. With all this in my mind I dove into being a good provider, and I was determined to not repeat my father's path.

Answering an ad in the paper, I got a job as a carpenter working for an outfit renovating old Victorian San Francisco homes that specialized in troubleshooting hard-to-resolve home repairs. The job included driving a company truck and staying in constant communication with the boss through a walkie-talkie. I was given as many hours as I could handle. I also started to do side carpentry jobs to really stack up on funds. I was building a nest, and I was going to do this right. My creative ways of troubleshooting and solving hard home-repair problems got me raises and promotions. I was working a lot and making good money.

My dancing, either teaching or training, went to almost zero. My martial art training thrived in aikido and capoeira, because I found a place to practice the martial arts, and the martial arts were the perfect vehicle to keep me disciplined and focused on the task at hand.

My relationship with Andrea was working because I was busy with work, and she was busy being a full-time student at massage school and preparing her body for our baby. I still had anger fits and issues with rigid thinking that were a point of contention when I could not deal with the stress. I tried to keep it together, but I was stressing out from the amount of responsibilities. That did not stop Andrea's belly from getting bigger and bigger with our baby, though. We started to work with a midwife and go to birthing classes. It was a life of getting ready for the coming of our baby.

Our home on Shotwell and 15th Street in the Mission was manageable and cheap. I was doing work for my landlady to take some money off the rent. One day I was working on a rear stairwell that connected all four floors of our building. Norton had grown from a sickly and quiet kitten into a rambunctious furball of mayhem; he was getting into a lot of trouble. I had told Andrea to close the window that opened to the rear stairwell because Norton might fall out of it chasing a fly or something. I was on a ladder on the second floor landing, facing away from the stairwell, when I felt and saw a falling blur from the corner of my eye. I knew right away it was Norton. He must have fallen out of the window. At the bottom of the stairwell was a stack of old and rusty pipes, standing on end with sharp edges facing upward. As I ran down the stairwell I was imagining Norton sliced to pieces from falling on top of the upward facing pipes. As I reached the bottom of the stairs, I heard and saw nothing. Then I started to look into the pipes; some of them were sixteen inches or so in diameter. I saw no blood splatters or decapitated cat head. As I frantically called Norton's name I heard a slight meow. Inside and at the bottom of one of the upturned pipes there was Norton looking up at me from the shadows. He had fallen four flights right into one of the upturned pipes, missing the rusty edges, without a scratch. Andrea heard the fuss and was at the back door of our flat as I brought

Norton back up. Relieved, Andrea and I both cried and laughed as Norton scattered to a comfy, dark place to take one more life from his quota of nine. I figured Norton was down to seven lives now—if I took one life off for saving his sorry gluteus maximus from a gloomy fate, abandoned in a empty cardboard box on a Lower East Side street corner.

With Andrea pregnant, I wanted us to be a married couple. I wanted this baby to grow with the love of a mother and father. Andrea agreed, and we prepared to have a ceremony to validate our lives together. It was not to be a legal marriage in the eyes of the State of California, but rather a declaration of our union. I was married once before, and knew a piece of paper meant nothing compared to the love between two people. So with a baby-filled belly showing under her beautiful, handmade, white wedding dress from Ethiopia, Andrea and I were married, and witnessed by our family members and dear friends.

Andrea's massage classes were going well. One of her teachers, Bill Teeter, was a real sweet-hearted gay man who appreciated Andrea and me. He helped with the chronic compound headaches I had had since I was fifteen years old, and introduced me to homeopathy. Andrea had surrounded us with good people, and it was comforting to be building a network of cool friends. Some of them were people Andrea knew from her short time in San Francisco years before. At the time I had few friends since I was working a lot, and did not have time to create new friendships. Andrea was my life and my family. I found making friends to be challenging. My autonomy from the social world was just fine for me. My focus was clear and simple—to be a good father and husband.

I was meeting people in my martial art classes but those friendships did not go anywhere, and I did not want them to go anywhere. I just did not have the energy to spread around. Looking at Andrea's belly kept me on my toes. The day Andrea introduced me to my baby's kicking and pushing made it all too real. I was going to be a father someday soon. We talked to the baby inside constantly. Life was growing. If it was a girl her name would be Josephine Maria; Andrea would call her Josie. For a boy, Vicente would be his name after my grandfather.

At the beginning of May all was ready for the baby. Andrea was doing well; going to massage school and riding her bike around, she remained very active. For me working was keeping me focused and positive about being a father. By June, Andrea was very big. The problem with her liver did not re-emerge or affect the pregnancy. As Andrea's due date approached my job scene changed. A coworker at the carpentry company we both worked for quit to take over a major renovation at his father-in-law's law office. He called me one night to offer me the position as his lead carpenter.

"Name your price, Ron," John said to me. Like most of the older guys I knew back then, John was a Vietnam veteran. "You are the guy I want. Your work is great and you always have great ideas. Name your price."

"Okay, John. Twenty-five dollars an hour, cash." Now, for 1987 that was good money, very good money.

"Sure," he said without a pause.

"Cash, John. Cash."

"Sure," he answered. "Can you give notice to Ernie and start soon?" Ernie was another Vietnam veteran, Coast Guard, and he was my boss. John was a Marine.

"Look John, I am going to do the right thing and give Ernie two weeks notice. He has been good to me," I said slowly.

"Okay, okay. I will start the project as soon as you are free from Ernie."

"That's right, brother." And just like that I had a great paying job. It would allow me to support Andrea while she finished massage school, and take care of our baby. The new carpentry job allowed me to be my own boss, and I could work all the hours I wanted, and be paid in cash. Not bad at all.

One day coming home from work Andrea was filling me in on her weekly checkup with her OB.

"Today, Ron, the doctor was noticing that the baby's weight had not changed. She was not concerned, but she will keep an eye on this. She wants me coming in a bit more now," Andrea was telling me over dinner.

"Andrea, how do you feel?" I asked her.

"I feel fine, Ron. I am not worried." She saw the concern on my face.

"Andrea, I am sorry that I am so busy. Keep me informed about all this stuff, please."

By the second week of June, it became evident that our baby's placenta was not working as well as it should be. The baby was not gaining weight at the rate the OB wanted. The concern was starting to build.

"Ron, the doctor wants me to come next week and possibly induce labor." Andrea and I were talking after dinner following her appointment with the OB. "The baby is not getting enough to eat."

Silence. I looked at her for guidance and reassurance. Andrea looked at me for strength.

"Well, babe, whatever needs to happen just let me know so I can get time off from work. I will be there all the way and I will be by your side." I reached out and held her hand firmly. "Babe, I love you so much. I do not want anything to happen to you or the baby."

"Ron, everything will be okay. We have it all set up. If we need to go in, I have a room at Mt. Zion hospital. My midwife will be there, and my friends as well. I know I will be safe."

"Okay, Andrea."

By June 15, it was decided that Andrea would go in. The baby's weight was unchanged from the last check-up. I got time off from work. Arrangements were made with the hospital and Andrea's support crew was gathered. By June 17 we were at the hospital. Her room was bright and settled; Andrea's friends had made it a beautiful place. By afternoon Andrea's hair was braided, and she looked relaxed and ready for the birthing journey. The doctor induced labor. The breathing exercises began, and all the commotions of birthing became a hard reality. With so many of her friends in the room I was quiet, and allowed Andrea's crew to help her. But something was amiss. Andrea was in great shape, but she was not dilating; she was not opening up to let our baby go, or maybe the baby did not want to come out. For many hours the excruciating procedure continued. Taking small breaks, I would go to the waiting room and take a breather. There, other expectant fathers were waiting for their own big moment. We all shook hands and shared the excitement of this incredible moment in our male lives, and in our relationships with our women. A sense of camaraderie was strong amongst strangers. Returning to her room, I saw Andrea was exhausted and nothing was really moving; I was exhausted from seeing her in so much pain and frustration. By midnight I was told to go home; I would be called if anything happened, and Andrea's closest friends would stand by. So I left to go home and rest.

Upon returning the next morning to the hospital, I learned Andrea had rested through the night, and she dilated a little. The doctors believed this would be the big day, June 18, but by early afternoon nothing was happening. The doctors were now concerned about all the stress that Andrea and the baby were taking. They were both getting beaten up pretty good. It was now almost thirty hours since labor was induced. The head doctor called me out to the hallway for a "man to man" talk.

"Mr. Rubio, I have to be frank with you," he began. "Andrea has been in labor for a long time. The baby's heartbeat is starting to drop with each push and each contraction."

Silence.

The bright, artificial hallway lights were hurting my eyes. There was a hum in my ears that was annoying me. There was an odd smell in the air that was making me antsy. The doctor continued after seeing me take in the dire situation of Andrea and our baby.

"Mr. Rubio, this is a very crucial time. I cannot say how much more the baby's heart can take the stress or your wife's..." He stared into my eyes with intense concern. "Mr. Rubio, you may have to make a decision."

What the hell was he talking about? Where was that humming sound coming from? What the hell was going on here? I could barely feel my feet.

"Mr. Rubio, if anything happens in that room, do you want your wife to come through or the child?"

What the *f*ck* was he saying to me? I couldn't grasp what he was saying to me. I felt like screaming. I did not understand! What is the smell? Those lights were driving me crazy!

Help me! I do not understand!

"Mr. Rubio, do you understand what I am saying to you? The life of your wife, and that of your baby, is at a critical state. I cannot guarantee what could happen in that room in the next minutes. What is your decision?"

I could not breathe. I had to talk to Andrea. I wanted my baby to be born.

Damn! Help me!

"Doctor, if anything needs to happen in that room, my wife is coming out of this in one piece. My wife will live through all this. Understand?" I was almost whispering, but screaming. I was not sure if he could hear me.

"I understand, Mr. Rubio. Your wife's life will be secured. I have the birthing room ready for anything. I have an ICU team unit ready for anything, as well. Let's go!"

We shook hands firmly and went back into Andrea's room.

There was a frantic energy in the room. All of Andrea's friends had worried and worn looks on their faces. I asked for a moment alone with Andrea. Her eyes were closed in pain, and she was breathing hard. Everyone left quickly. I sat at the head of Andrea's bed, and begin to massage her head.

"Andrea, Andrea, can you hear me?" She opened her eyes and looked up at me. I unconsciously begin to unbraid her hair. "Love, the doctor said that the baby's heart is stressing too much with each contraction." Andrea became clear-eyed as she listened to me. "Whatever needs to happen has to happen soon." Andrea heard me and nodded. "Love, whatever happens, you are coming out of this...do you hear me?" I pleaded.

I finished unbraiding her hair. We kissed. I was at peace.

Within minutes Andrea dilated completely, surprising the hell out of everyone. The doctor yelled to suit up and get into the birthing room—*now!* I was helped into my hospital greens and we were off to the races. Once we were set up, the real hard pushing began in earnest. The baby's cord was wrapped around its neck, and then the baby's crown popped out! "I will have to use forceps to help the baby out," the doctor said calmly.

Push! Push! Push!

Then the baby was out! Deep purple in hue, it was held by its feet and smacked to begin crying; it meowed like a small kitten.

"It's a girl!" She was rushed to a separate table to have her passages cleared and stabilized. She weighed four pounds, four ounces. She was so very tiny. She was crying and meowing; I called to her as I hovered over the nurse, "Josie, baby girl, Josie, baby girl, everything is okay, you are safe." Josie opened her eyes and stopped crying. Her eyes were deep blue-on-blue. We made eye contact, my daughter and I, and then she began crying again. Cry on baby! Breathe the life, and let this damn world know you are here to stay! You have arrived, Josie-girl!

Josie was brought to Andrea and she rested on Andrea's chest. She was so very small. Andrea was so happy, exhausted, and bleeding heavily. "The baby has to go up to the ICU floor, because of her weight. She will be observed. Mr. Rubio, please take her and follow me," said the head nurse. She took Josie and wrapped her in a blanket and placed a cap on her head. Josie looked like a little burrito—so small! I didn't know how to hold her. She fit between the palm of my hand and the inside of my elbow. Josie fell asleep. The nurse, Josie, and I left the birthing room. We entered the hallway to Andrea's friends cheering and crying. I was smiling dumbly, grinning, and holding my new daughter. The head nurse and I entered the elevator. Josie felt weightless in my arms. I was afraid I would drop her, so I held her tightly to my chest; you are not going anywhere, baby girl!

Upon reaching the ICU unit for little babies I was struck by all the little ones in the ward. I was told some of the babies had been there for months. Born prematurely, they were nursed and cared to health. Josie was in good company. I placed Josie in an incubator with warm lights and covered her with a plastic shield. Bye for now, my princess. Upon leaving the ICU ward I took a long breath and cried. I went down to the waiting room where the other expectant fathers were. I was met by two beaming fathers. Another sat in the corner crying; his baby had died from complications. My joy was dampened. *I was close too, Brother. I am so sorry for you.* I went home to sleep after checking in with Andrea. Peace.

The next day I arrived back to find Josie with Andrea. Josie was strong enough to leave the ICU and be with Andrea. Great! She nursed and slept. A nurse came in and told us we needed to fill out the papers; our baby's name was to be written down for the records, and the time of her birth recorded.

"Andrea, let us change Josie's name by switching the 'a' and 'e.' So instead of 'Josephine Maria,' her name will be 'Josephina Marie.'" Andrea agreed and so it was recorded. At 6:48 p.m. on June 18, 1987, Josephina Marie Pastorella-Rubio was born in the city of San Francisco, California. Josie and Andrea came home the next day. I was now a father. The questions and fears rose from the shadows. How would I be? How would I teach my daughter she was a second-generation Filipino American? She would grow up a woman of color in a white man's world. How would I teach her to be strong against all that was out in the world? How would I protect her? Would I be a good husband? Would I carry on the "Rubio curse" of violence and anger? Josie was the first grandchild and niece in my family. I swore to do this right, but I was so untrained. I had no role models. I knew something was different about me: Compared to people around me, and my own family, I was not right somehow. I believed something was wrong with me, but what? Slow down, Holmes! One step at a time was all I could do.

I played the Steely Dan song "Josie" when I carried Josie into our home in the Mission. Norton fled into some dark hole until the new crying thing could be understood. Josie was colicky and had jaundice. My baby was yellow-orange. We laid Josie in the morning sun, and she started to normalize. Her colic led to crying and sleepless nights. One late night, I took Josie from Andrea so she could catch some sleep. Josie was just crying and crying. I walked to the other side of our flat. In the living room I walked and walked. Josie cried and cried. It started to dig into my nerves. I had to be at work in a few hours at daybreak, and Josie would not stop crying. Suddenly, I held Josie in one hand and raised the other to strike her.

My spirit froze. My hand froze in mid-air. Josie kept crying and crying.

My god! I was going to strike my week-old baby daughter! My heart shattered. My mind exploded. I quickly went back to the bedroom and placed Josie next to Andrea. I retreated to the living room in disbelief. I wanted to do harm to my daughter. I was lost in feelings of self-hatred. So I *did* have the "Rubio curse." I was truly my father's son, no matter how much he hated me and disowned me, I was his son. *I told you I was your son, Dad.* I sought a therapist the next day. I did not tell Andrea about what had happened the night before. Andrea would not take this from me—who in the hell would? I did not want to harm my woman or my baby daughter. I did not want to hurt anyone. I did not want to die like this, to die with so much anger and sadness in my heart. I wanted to cut out all that was destructive about me. I knew I was capable of being a loving, caring human. People knew me as a giving and good man. I knew there was something salvageable in me. I wanted to make my world safe for Andrea and my daughter. I had to try everything and anything.

My sister turned me on to a book by a woman named Louise Hays. The book was one of the many self-help books that came out of the age of self-awareness in the 1980s. Her book spoke of forgiveness and change, by changing your language and the image that you had of yourself, to know you were doing your best and you were worth all that the Universe had to offer. The book helped tremendously. I saw my therapist every week.

I started to find more balance in life by taking time to do more martial arts to decompress from the stress. Andrea and I took classes together. I started to teach dance again, and I still worked as a carpenter. Yet being a father still brought out the demons in me. It was a vicious cycle of harming the harmony of my family, and then apologizing and feeling like shit with guilt. Once forgiven, I was great for a short time, and then exploded again. It was as if the more I wanted to do right, the more I would do wrong. I saw my father in me too much. My dad did not show joy or pride in his first grandchild. That disappointed me so much.

I realized I missed Andrea. She was a mother, and a beautiful one at that. Her attention was all to Josie, and why not? But I missed her. I did not think I was jealous of my daughter. I just missed Andrea a lot. Funny, I grieved for the loss of a woman in my life, while I rejoiced in the beauty of my daughter. Anger was my destructive mode of communication, but I just did not know how to change. I hated myself and I did not want to leave my daughter or Andrea, but I saw myself as a detrimental and dangerous element in their lives. I was disturbing their life and their harmony. I had to keep working on myself and knowing that I could change, and that I had the power to be a different person.

We moved into a bigger place in my old childhood neighborhood of Bernal Heights. The significance was not lost on me. It was weird to be back in the stomping grounds where so many ghosts of my childhood walked. From my back porch I could see Paul Revere Elementary. I was about ten blocks from my childhood home where real demons lived. I could see the Heights where the Old Witch's house once stood and had burned down so mysteriously. The circle was completing itself. I was going to be a father in the same neighborhood where I was destroyed and gutted by my own father. Strange.

It took time for Josie to grow out of being colicky. Andrea and I were working on building a family and strengthening our relationship. We found that living on the West Coast was different from our lives in New York. The seasons just did not exist in the west. As Andrea got stronger, she and I started to work together on developing a dance duet piece. It was a way for us to work together and do something with our passion for dance. We also did capoeira together. It was a wonderful time to see each other outside of the new mother-father, husband-wife roles. We were moving together and dancing together. Josie was dragged everywhere Andrea and I rehearsed or took class. We had our arguments during rehearsals—or, I should say, "I argued" during rehearsals because I was "Mister Choreographer." Well, in fact Andrea was better, because she was mentored and taught by one of the best in art choreographing in New York City—Mary Anthony. I enjoyed these times, though I may have sometimes been an asshole.

I worked hard enough to get to the first level of capoeira ranking. It was a baptismal in which my *mestre* gave me a capoeira name. My baptismal name was first *Angoro*, like the cat, for my catlike movement and grace. My *mestre* then changed my name to *Agoro*, to express my being "now," as in being right with him during the marital movements I had to do with him. So I was *Agoro*. I also took my next rank in aikido.

As I started to reclaim myself from overworking as a carpenter, I was dancing more and getting dance work. I was asked to dance and help choreograph the martial movement for the play called *Roosters*, which was about the dynamics of a Chicano family and their father's job as a trainer of fighting roosters. I played the father's prize-fighting rooster, Zapata. It was great to perform again, and to be on stage. Then I was asked to join a dance company that would represent the United States at the 1987 World Expo in Brisbane, Australia. Traveling and being away from Andrea and Josie was hard, but I knew it was good for them to have a breather from me. I could be a loving and fun father and husband to be around, as well as a loud and domineering annoyance. Josie and Andrea were tight, and time away from me would be pleasant and peaceful for them.

Why does distance soften the heart? Why did I feel comfortable being alone and depressed without the ones I loved near me at the same time? Was I a selfish person who wanted everything and surrendered nothing? My life confused me. How could I break the curse of being my father's son?

The flight over the vast Pacific Ocean to Australia was like cleaning a slate and starting over. But what an illusion of strength and awareness "starting over" could be. The Pacific Ocean was vast and deep. I felt the depth of the green vastness. I wanted to jump out of the plane and sink to the bottom and join Poseidon's watery world, devoid of humans and love. What the hell was love anyway? I knew Josie was my heart and life. I knew I wanted Andrea in my life, and to be "happy ever after," but how?

Upon my return I found a dance school, The Dance Space, in San Francisco where I took ballet classes, and where I could teach a jazz dance class and a BodyKi class. Being back after Australia was a charge for me, and I felt better about being a family man, husband, and father. The joy of dance and my family was my heartbeat. So I kept on dancing. One day I was taking a ballet class before teaching when the director of the ballet studio came in and announced a special guest would be taking the class. Cool, I thought. I knew the Paris Ballet was in town for a series of performances. He pointed to my ballet barre, and so I made space for our guest. In walked Rudolf Nureyev! I was floored. A ballet dance god in the flesh. A fellow Piscean, one I had read about, and had posters of on my New York City studio walls when I was in intense training years ago. Here he was standing next to me. Though past his prime he was nevertheless a dance god in the flesh. The room went silent and we tried not to stare. We went through a ballet barre for warm up. Everyone was raising his or her legs a bit higher, standing a bit taller. Hell, he was standing right behind me, so when we turned around to do the other side I was looking at him. After a couple of exercises he thanked us all, and with great elegance and grace he left the room. It was like my Alvin Ailey dance teachers always said to us many years ago, "Once a dancer, always a dancer." After he left, we all exhaled and laughed a nervous laugh and finished class. Now that was a dance god in the flesh!

One dance job led to another. I was contacted to teach dance to theater students at the School of Performing Arts in San Francisco. Nice gig. Then I made a connection with the National Dance Institute's (NDI) West Coast operations. Having been with the NDI mother ship back in New York City, and having been hand-picked by Director Jacques d'Amboise himself, I was well received. I was given two schools to work with, which gave me about seventy-five kids in total. One of the schools was my old elementary school, Paul Revere. Talk about coming full circle! I walked into my childhood school where my principal, Mr. Soso, would roam the marble-floored halls back in '64. I could not believe how small everything looked. I was now a giant. I walked into the room where I would meet my kids, and there I was met by an Asian teacher with grey hair and glasses.

"Ron Rubio?" she said to me.

"Ms. Sit?" I said, startled. This was the young substitute teacher who had taken over my classes when our third-grade teacher, Mrs. Ford, died back in '65. Ms. Sit had to be in her sixties by now.

We shook hands and laughed at each other.

"It has been a long time, Mr. Rubio," she said with a gleaming a smile I remembered from so many years ago.

"Please, Ms. Sit, call me Ron."

"So you will be the NDI dance teacher? When I saw your name I recognized it immediately, but to find out it belonged to the same 'Ron Rubio' from so many years ago was a pleasant surprise." We talked for a bit, and soon next year's NDI participants flooded the room. She smiled and left the class. I watched her leave and could not help but wonder: What were the chances we would meet again so many years later? Life truly is a wonderful and mysterious ride through time and space.

By December Josie was crawling. What a complete joy she was! Andrea and I were working on our relationship, and we made some great headway and had some disastrous blowouts. There was an element of New York life we were both missing—an edge of doing anything with intention and vitality. The changing seasons of the Northeast were missed too—including the snow and sleet. California was nice and all, but a bit too laid-back for us. I was making great money as a carpenter and dance teacher, but I still felt frustrated. Part of my personality thrived on change and newness. I was selfishly looking at the "greener side of the fence" sometimes. However, this saying usually applies to people looking for a distraction from boredom rather than those working at a relationship. This was not the case for me. There was a balance missing between my career and my family life. Andrea was different as a mother, but also somehow the same. We were funny together, and still had adventures when we could plan them, but at times being parents was stressful and tiring.

Child-raising methods are always a place of possible contention between parents. Being from different racial backgrounds made things particularly sticky for us. Filipinos were "tough love" parents; strict, uncompromising, and devoted people. Filipinos do not take lightly to back-talking, second-guessing their commands, or any hesitation to obey from their children. I was a first-generation Filipino American raised by a strict, Spanish-Colonial, God-fearing Catholic, lower caste father with a fourth-grade education. I had a mother who lived in rich splendor raised by four maids. I did the best I could, but it was tough.

Andrea and I started to talk about moving back east. We both missed the New York dance scene, and I missed the aikido training of the New York Aikikai and Yamada Sensei. But we felt moving back into the city was not an option while raising Josie. I had heard Woodstock, New York was a cool art town. Also, one of my favorite teachers, Harvey Konigsberg Sensei of the New York Aikikai, had a dojo in Woodstock. So we planned an exploratory trip to visit Woodstock, and to my old stomping grounds in New Paltz.

We made the trip the following year, and it turned out to be the place we were looking for. A feasible distance from New York City by bus or train, Woodstock offered a beautiful hamlet nestled in the Catskill Mountains. Andrea and I decided this was the place to move to. I would start by generating carpentry work, and then teach dance. I knew I would be starting from scratch again, but it felt right and it was a new place where Andrea and I could raise our daughter. Andrea had graduated from massage school and would find work as a massage therapist. The plan was that Andrea and Josie would leave in late spring and find a place for us to live. I would finish my teaching obligations and drive across the United States with our belongings in June. With a plan in hand we began closing our lives in San Francisco.

Before leaving the west our lives were touched deeply by the illness of Andrea's massage teacher, Bill Teeter. By the late 1980s, the newly surfaced and deadly disease called AIDS was devastating the gay communities throughout the USA. In later years, AIDS would spread throughout the world affecting heterosexuals and those engaged in at-risk lifestyles such as drug users who shared needles. After a persistent lung sickness, Bill Teeter was diagnosed with AIDS.

By the spring of 1989 he was in the hospital. His once-beautiful, muscled body had shriveled into skin and bones. Andrea and I, along with several others, came to the hospital every day in shifts to look after him as his caregivers. I made it a point to be with him often. He was my wife's dear teacher, and he became a friend and healer. Our time together, when I would visit, was filled with Bill talking about what he would do when he got well: the new business he was going to create with his partner, and his life-to-be. I did any errand he wished me to. I had seen death up close. I had missed being near my grandfather in his final days, so there was nothing I was going to deny Bill. As his health slowly ebbed away his large blue eyes became the most prominent feature on his face.

In the early years of its appearance AIDS had a very high mortality rate, but Bill's dreams of life after AIDS only grew bigger and bigger. I would always agree and brainstorm with him. All his caregivers had a call-list of all his other caregivers. After leaving him one day and upon arriving home, Andrea and I got a call that Bill was not doing well. Andrea took care of Josie as I went back to the hospital hours later after getting some food in my belly. I arrived at the hospital to find an empty room with an empty bed. He was gone. He had died. I felt his bed; it was slightly warm, and his body had just been removed. I remembered just looking at this now empty bed and seeing his gaunt face staring at me, his bright blue eyes ablaze. Bill was gone and that was that.

Andrea and I went to a service for him and said our goodbyes. Bill became a guardian angel to our daughter Josie. We felt his presence around her. We were blessed by our short time with him, but his death weighed heavy on my heart for a while. The reality of Life and Death, the mortality of all living creatures, and the fragile balance of now-here and now-gone forced its prominence to the forefront of my poor mortal mind. I became aware that if I wanted to accomplish what I wanted to do in my life I had best do it now, and not later. I realized that death truly was the great equalizer. When your time was up, no matter how it may appear to your mind, your perceived strengths or your weaknesses meant nothing. You either lived your life or you did not. It would come to a close someway or another. *Peace, Bill.*

Andrea and Josie flew out to Woodstock, New York in April. Our saved monies would help her find us a place there. I missed Josie and Andrea tremendously. My dance obligations were over by the end of June, at which point I packed up our stuff and drove a U-Haul truck across the USA back to New York. My family thought it unwise for me to leave my well-paying jobs, moderate California weather, and closeness of family. Besides my Mom and Horst, and my younger brother Shawn up in Cottage Grove, Oregon, most of my family was in the Bay Area. My sister Valerie had moved back into San Francisco during this time, and spent time at our home with her niece Josie as much as she could. My brother Fred was down in the San Jose area doing well in commercial real estate, and Dad and Stepmother were in Orinda, on the other side of the Berkeley Hills. Trying to explain the "whys" of our move was pointless because my reasons made no sense to them. That was okay. Our time in San Francisco and the West Coast had come to a close. Andrea and I started out as a couple, came west as a trio with Norton, and now would return to the East Coast as quartet with our beautiful daughter Josie.

The torrential downpour ceased as quickly as it had appeared on the vast savannah where the woolly mammoth herd and other Ice Age creatures foraged and rested.

"The Man-boy has fathered a child with his female mate. And with this phenomenon of creativity, the newborn has stirred the demons of fear in his heart," croaked a huge, black Thought-raven that stood near my front right foot.

"Yes, I have seen his offspring...she almost did not enter the world of the living. The mother too was threatened by the birthing," I answered, now fully grown. "I have seen stillbirths among our breeding females. Why is this so?"

"Maybe the living and growing ones in the womb were not ready to be born into this time and space. The little ones choose their parents as well as the time of their conception. Their birthing is also marked by their influences," the large raven said as it hopped to a nearby empty rabbit hole to investigate.

"Mmm. Strange are the ways of the Great Universe. What does the

Man-boy fear in the birthing of this child from his seed?" I asked as I lifted my trunk and sought the air for signs of any nearby danger. "Does this child pose a threat to the Man-boy?"

"We will see. I do sense that this girl-child has much to teach the Man-boy about life. The girl-child is already the sparkle of his life," Thought answered now as a deep purple butterfly that fluttered around my huge, flapping ears. "The demons that torment the Man-boy were evoked by her birthing."

"The fears he feels are not his. They belong to some forgotten time in his past. He fears the demons that were of his sire," the fluttering wings of the butterfly told me. "He fears the destructive berserker that haunts his dreams and visions. I believe the Man-boy once said, 'I am my father's son. And the apple does not fall from the tree.'"

As I shifted my ponderous weight from one foot to the other, I spoke to a passing rain cloud. "His fear begets more fears. The Man-boy binds the demon he wishes to dispose of by very act of thinking of the demon. He attracts fear from the fear he holds onto."

"The Man-boy soothes his pain with the separation from his 'self.' This strategy could prove to be his bane," Thought crackled as a distant black thunderclap.

Part 6:
In the Land of the Mountain Lion

34. The Catskill Mountains

The dire trials and tribulations in one's life are placed there for a specific reason. There is no random this-or-that in the Great Universe. In the many lives I have been reborn to I have learned this phenomenon to be true. One would call these dire trials and tribulations, "lessons to be learned." Yes, they are that and more. Blaming this person or that person, or feeling one is damned and cursed is simply rubbish! I believe the saying is, "You make the bed you sleep in"—no doubt said by an enlightened one, or a sorry fool about to jump from the high treacherous cliffs, resigned to start the karmic life cycle all over again from scratch.

—The Queries of Woolly Mammoth Boy

The Catskill Mountains appeared blue in the distance. In the deep ravines and gorges fresh water tumbled down toward the wide Hudson River below, and eventually to the vast, cold, and grey Atlantic Ocean. Wild animals haunted these mountains. The elusive cougar had been spotted in these parts, though the great predator was supposed to have been hunted to extinction decades earlier—but there were other things as well. When the ever-belligerent and arrogant White Man entered the Woodstock Valley there lived the Red Man. The Native Americans used these lands as energy zones to charge, rest, and then move on. The Woodstock Valley was never meant to be settled, occupied, or labeled as "owned," but the White Man, in his usual self-centered wisdom and childlike desire, kicked the Red Man out and settled this sacred land. The legend goes something like this: the departing Red Man said to the White Man, "You can take what is not yours, but your lives here will be cursed, and those of your future generations." The White Man responded, "Yeah, yeah, yeah...don't let the door hit you in the ass on your way out!" It was no wonder that one found in the hamlet of Woodstock a healthy population of single mothers, and their carpenter/artist ex-boyfriends or husbands. (I also knew of many strong relationships in my almost twenty years in the Woodstock Valley area.)

Andrea, Josie, and I moved into the Woodstock Valley in the summer of 1989. The place was beautiful and the hot and humid Northeast summer was well received. Andrea had found a place a mile out of town at the dead-end of an old quarry road. The hamlet of Woodstock reminded me of Soho in Manhattan—filled with shops for tourists. I got to know many shop owners and became good friends. As I started to teach in Woodstock I grew to know many parents and children-turned-teens as the years went by. It was pleasant and "a Woodstock-state-of-mind." Wealthy New Yorkers had their summer homes here. The tourists packed the small hamlet every weekend during the busy months of the year. The valley was sweet with grand views and good air.

I went down to the local lumberyard and introduced myself to the owner, Andre. An excellent soul with a handlebar moustache, he took a liking to me immediately. He offered some leads for work, and I was deeply touched by his friendship and trust. His son and wife worked there as well. There was a strong building scene, and many of the fixer-upper summer homes were in need of renovations and constant maintenance. It seemed the place was busy for a little hamlet. In this land anything made by man took a severe beating from harsh winters and moldy, hot summers. There was work for the right carpenter.

I started to look into places to teach dance. There was a small dance community, but no male danseurs for teaching or performing—I was a big fish in a little pond. My reputation started to move through the community. There was also a splendid little aikido dojo run by my teacher, Harvey Konigsberg, from the New York Aikikai in Manhattan. The dojo was in a small barn with no insulation or proper floor. During the winter it felt like a walk-in freezer. The dressing rooms were behind farm tractors and old horse stalls. I was welcomed by Sensei, and felt I had come home.

Andrea and Josie had made new friends in Woodstock while I was still in San Francisco. Having come out to New York two months before me, they had a nice routine of biking into town for shopping, and playing at the new playground at Woodstock Elementary. I was happy and troubled at the same time. I felt the pressure to make ends meet, and everything felt new and unknown. There were not many people of color in town except one or two Native Americans; I felt really out-there and exposed.

The anxiety and stress came from my own making, and the reality of being in a new a place. Being back with Andrea and my growing Josie-girl brought up more parenting conflicts. Andrea and I began to argue and fight on how to teach and discipline Josie as she entered her "terrible twos"—bickering over the smallest things. What caused the trouble was my inability to "hear" Andreas's opinion and wisdom. I knew an old pattern was developing again—my rigidity to another person's point of view (including Andrea's). It seemed the more I wanted to open up, the more I grew stuck in my thinking and tunnel-vision. Why? Why could I not adjust and shift? I must keep trying. Our arguments became more frequent and charged. Issues that would normally be a point for discussion would end in screaming, which was the only way I knew how to express myself when I was tense and overwhelmed emotionally.

The aikido dojo was a place I went to train and settle down. I met a couple of men there my age. One was an Englishman, Steve Johnson, and the other an Argentine, Carlos. We swore a brotherhood to each other. Both of my new brothers were bachelors, and I started to invite them to my home and share my family with them. Andrea and Josie liked them both, and I was happy. It felt good to have some male friends in my life. I thought having some "brothers" around would balance my life at home as a father and husband. It was nice; I was really starting to make some friends.

By September, I was working in carpentry and teaching dance classes. I had found in the community center a place I could use; a space to teach jazz dance classes and my BodyKi Mind–Body fitness classes. It was wonderful to teach dance and be moving again. The fall season was settling into place and the Woodstock Valley was beautiful and vibrant with reds, yellows, and oranges. The air was getting cooler and the night brisker.

Andrea and I were not doing well. She could not take any more of my behavior, and I felt trapped not knowing how to make things better. Feeling the stress of working and trying to understand how to be a father and good husband wore on me. I just did not know what to do. My social skills in a intimate relationship sucked, and the pain I was causing Andrea only intensified the guilt and shame that arose from feeling that I was hurting the woman I loved. My anger blow-ups were frequent and destroyed the harmony of our home. I confided in my brothers Steve and Carlos. They were supportive, but had no advice. One day Steve came in with a black eye.

"What the hell happened to you Steve?" I asked

"A guy thought I was messing with his girlfriend," he said in his English accent. "I was not, of course, but he hit me anyway."

"Damn, brother! That is a real shiner you have!" He seemed like a great guy and I could not see how anyone could be pissed at him. I was inviting him over to my home for dinners and to hang out. One evening I wanted Andrea to get out of the house; I would watch Josie so she could get out and have some fun. I suggested she go into town with Steve and listen to some music. I would be with Josie and all would be fine. She and Steve went out. Within a couple of weeks, Andrea said it was over between us. She wanted me out of the house and said Josie was going to stay with her. My heart was shattered. I knew things weren't great, but I thought we could work things out because we had Josie.

"Ron, we can't just stay together because of Josie. It would not be fair to her or you and me," she said to me over a quiet dinner.

"Listen, Andrea, give me some time to get it together. I am so sorry for having made your life so hard. I love you and Josie so much. I want you to be happy and I understand, but I do not know where to go and I do not have enough money for rent."

"Ron, you have to get out of the house. You can see Josie on the weekends and we will get it sorted out."

Before I knew it, I was out. Sensei said I could stay at his house since he was down in the city during the week and his Woodstock house was open. I took him up on the offer. My life seemed to be crumbling around my head, and I was giving money to Andrea to help her with rent for Josie and her.

Then a real shocker occurred. I went up to the house to pick up Josie, and Steve's car was in the driveway. Andrea heard my truck and met me out front.

"Ron, I will bring Josie out. Steve is here..."

My heart turned cold and anger flowed like crazy through my veins. Steve was supposed to be my brother. He was supposed to be there for *me*. That bastard was with my wife and my kid, and I had barely left the house. I saw blood and retribution. I saw murder and destruction. I waited for Josie to appear and I took her away, masking my anger. Josie and I shared a small alcove bed in my sensei's home. Josie had only just turned two years old. Her breath kept me awake as she slept. I had to do the right thing and make her life the best I could make it. Andrea had already moved on, and she said Steve and she were taking their time not to rush things...but screw them. *Thank you for your consideration.* It wasn't that they wanted to be with each other that angered me, it was the fact my "brother" Steve couldn't wait a couple of months until Andrea and I found a mutual and safe departure from each other. I was devastated and confused; I couldn't communicate my sense of betrayal and pain.

Betrayal. Deception. Heartbreak. Apparently there was some good reasoning behind the black eye Steve had received from a jealous friend. Steve was a parasite and an opportunist. I had no idea what to do. I could not do him bodily harm even though I wanted to kill him—I could not afford to go to jail because of Josie. I wanted to report him to immigration because he was an illegal alien, but a friend said that would be really bad karma so I let him live, and I sat with a cold, black, broken heart. I was destroyed by losing my wife to a person who was supposed to be my brother. How naïve I was! How childish and blind I was. I had invited him into my home, and he took it for what it was worth.

By December I was utterly confused and lost. I moved through the days and nights with unspeakable pain and sadness. Death songs played loud in my ears and death poems fell from my lips, but Josie liked Steve. I saw pictures of all three of them together—Andrea, Josie, and Steve. I was a loser and worthless in the matters of love. I saw no hope or way out. I was alone once again, and it was entirely my fault. Who would want a beast like me? The "Rubio curse" had struck again. It started to snow. The winter came with a furious and bitter cold. It made my loneliness all the more dark and deathly. My truck was diesel and hard to start in the winter. The diesel turned to thick molasses in the engine; only when it warmed up enough would the diesel fuel have the right viscosity to move through the engine. My blood felt the same. Sluggish in my veins, dulling my mind, barely making my heart beat with life, my life's blood was as black and thick as the blood of a dead person.

Death called me again. Like the many callings of my past, the sirens of death offered a release from my searing pain and deep anguish. I was my mother's son, and her numerous suicide attempts during my childhood began to make sense. Why try to deal with the pain when I could escape into oblivion and silence? To hell with karma! Screw it all! I was alone. Josie was safe with her mom. I saw no way out. I was blind from the pain.

On New Year's Eve, in a blinding snowstorm, I drove up Ohayo Mountain. The mountain overlooked the village of Woodstock, and held court over the vast Hudson Valley below. My VW truck barely made it up the long, steep, and winding road. I parked the truck and started the uphill trail to the summit. The snow was falling heavily and the trail was already covered with thick whiteness. The air was biting cold, but I felt nothing could deter me. I walked for what seemed like a long time, slipping and sliding on the newly fallen snow. The trail was long past obliterated. There appeared on my left a break on the tree-lined path. I abruptly veered into the dark, silent woods. Finding a clearing in the trees, I made out what seemed to be a large boulder. Standing next to the boulder I began to cry profusely. The snow fell in thick blankets and the temperature seemed to be dropping. It was close to midnight, and the new decade of the 1990s was at hand. I realized I wanted to end my life there in the cold of winter. If I could knock myself unconscious, then I would sleep until frozen and dead. I began to hit my head upon the boulder. The pain seared into me with each bashing. I was out.

Images of my childhood flashed—a silent little boy all too quirky to be loved. Screamed at, beaten, and abused, the little boy struggled to breathe. The little boy wanted his mother, who, when tired of her life, attempted to abandon her children though death, but failed. The images jumped to the loneliness of a lost adolescence. Work and more work. Pushed and pushed. Disowned and laughed at by those the young teenager trusted, he threw himself into the world to die or survive, and survive he did...alone. Images came faster to me. Images of dancing in New York City, images of flesh and desire, images of a dead boy in an elevator, images of being conquered and of conquering others. Wetness and bitter cold seeped into consciousness. Bone-hard frozen death. Then an image of a little girl smiling at me appeared. It was Josie! She was smiling because I was reading *The Wizard of Oz* to her for the billionth time with the gusto of every character. She laughed and called to me, "Papa! Papa! Again, read it again!" She took my hand and shook me in a playful way urging insistently, "Papa! Papa! Please again!" I startled myself awake.

My head hurt. There was a lump. I was shaking; my teeth were chattering and I was covered in a blanket of snow. Above me filtering through the trees more snow fell. I got up slowly from where I lay. I did not know how long I had been lying in the snow. All I knew was I was freezing my ass off, and my little girl had called for me. Stumbling back through the high snow toward my truck, I took a hair-raising, slippery ride down the mountain to my sensei's house. I realized I had to stay around for my daughter, and if I was too much of a coward to live for myself then I would be man enough and a father enough for my daughter.

Happy New Year 1990!

The New Year offered paying work and a place to practice aikido, but I had to find another place for Josie and me to live. Sensei needed the space, and I wanted more privacy for Josie and me. My old bandmate from New York had moved up to Woodstock, and offered her house during the weekends. My sensei's house was available during the week. *I will survive the heartache and move on!* Andrea, Josie, and Steve were doing their thing and they seemed happy together. I saw Josie on the weekends.

I met a woman from aikido and we started to date. She was a fine woman, and a caretaker of a great property I could stay at to get away from Woodstock. She shared her life with Josie and me. We decided to try living together, but the relationship was short-lived and I took over the place we found. I broke up with her because I felt that I was being torn between her and Josie. I also realized that I was not ready to start up with someone yet. There needed to be more space for me to "clean the slate" so I could move forward once again. At the time, Andrea wanted Josie to go to a groovy alternative school we couldn't pay for, so I traded my portion of Josie's tuition by cleaning all the classrooms and bathrooms before the schooled opened. It was hard but for a clear purpose. Josie went to preschool there and thrived, but Andrea and I were barley speaking. The Steve element made it almost impossible for me to pick up Josie at her mom's house—our old house—so a neutral place was chosen and that was helpful.

"Sensei, I can't train with Steve," I said one day after aikido practice. "I am too angry at him."

"I understand, Ron. You do not have to. Keep coming in and keep working out; you need this," Sensei said.

"Thank you, Sensei, I will. I am sorry for any disturbance in the dojo because of what is happening between Andrea and me."

"Let it be. It will all pass," Sensei said, and that was that.

I knew that I had to keep busy and I needed to make some serious money to start my life back up. As I continued to slowly recover, I hooked up with a friend I had met, Kemp Loeke, in New Paltz. He was a fine carpenter and tile man I could join forces with. I had work in the hamlet of Shady that started off as a simple job hanging kitchen cabinets, but the place was an old glassblower's shed from the turn of the century—it was just a crooked little shack. I told the owner the whole place was off because one corner of the building, where the kitchen was located, was sitting on dirt and the foundation was totally gone. He asked me to fix it. He paid me in cash and the project ended up being a total renovation of the entire house. The owner got custom handmade doors, a new staircase with inlaid original designs, new wood flooring, and a new foundation (we had to jack up the house to put it in). A carpenter friend told me I had made a purse out of a sow's ear. Kemp and I were set for money for nine months. It was a great blessing.

During this time I was also meeting some important mentors. Lowell Miller, who was one of my aikido teachers at Woodstock, provided work and supportive guidance. I said when I was his age I hoped to have my act together like him. He was into finance, and was moving through the world with ease. Anthony Rullo was a bio-energetic therapist in Woodstock who helped me along by teaching me to heal myself, and understanding how to charge and discharge energy based on the work of Wilhelm Reich and his protégé, Alexander Lowen. Richard Zarro, the incredibly charismatic healer-teacher, introduced me to his Holographic Hypnotherapy. He admired me tremendously as a martial artist. He sold me my first Apple computer, a small 9MB Mac Plus. Richard drew me into his world and I went there. He trained me in holographic hypnotherapy techniques and business. He once said to me, "Ron, you are a Warrior of Light like me. Remember we fight the good fight for others. Not everyone can be a warrior. You, Ron, are special. When the battle commences between the forces of Light and Darkness, you will be a leader of the Warriors of Light. Don't despair, for others will depend on you."

Another important mentor during this time was the handsome

southerner, Charles Revty. He was older than me, as the other men were, and a caretaker of numerous properties in the area. He was a former college swimmer and a great guy. We came to know each other well and became close friends. He reminded me of the importance of the here-and-now. When Charles became engaged to a beautiful woman, I rightly predicted the birth of his first daughter. We were very comfortable in each other's presence and sought each other out as much as possible. The mentor-shaman Christina Stack played an important part in my understanding of the powers and spirits that run so strongly in my life. She told me I was destined to be a powerful healer and teacher, and the world would be best served if I stayed true to my calling as a warrior of service to others.

But the person who influenced my life the most was Robert Stuart Allen. A Vietnam Marine veteran, Stuart was the only other person of color I knew in the Woodstock area. A tall black warrior who trained me in the martial ways, Stuart kept me focused from the distractions of my petty ego and those around me. He had a daughter from a previous marriage as well, so we had much to share. Robert became not only my *sempai*, a senior warrior to me, but also someone who balanced my overzealous energy to right all the wrongs.

I was truly blessed to have these mentors in my life. They provided me with a foundation for my own work. I started to write the first draft of my mind–body training book on the computer I had bought from Richard Zarro. All the teachings of my mentors made sense of the ideas of health, well-being, spirituality, and warriorship that became the focal points of my teachings in a world I knew I was meant to serve. Richard Zarro was indeed right: I was a Warrior of Light.

Feeling the time was right, I started teaching again. I was teaching kids creative movement classes and adult jazz dance classes. I was getting a lot of exposure in the local newspaper, the *Woodstock Times*. I also began a private practice of BodyKi out of my home. My clients ranged from bodybuilders and those coming back from major surgery, to a woman who wanted to hike up Ohayo Mountain but who saw it was her own fears she was really facing up to. My private practice developed into a therapy of the whole person, and not just the body. I knew there was more to my teachings than just healing the body. I had no fear or hesitation about suggesting new avenues to my clients to encourage the healing of the spirit and clearing the mind of their old fears and pain.

Despite my emotional challenges, life was rich for me in so many ways. I was basking in the light of validation from my work with grateful clients. I had name recognition and my work was moving through the community. One evening I was teaching a jazz class at the Woodstock Town Hall space. It was a cold November night and attendance was small. I was going to cancel class because only two people showed, but then in walked a fuzzy-haired woman. She wore a long winter coat, and upon her face was an incredibly bright smile for such a dreary evening. I introduced myself, and decided to hold the class with only three people.

After class the woman came up and introduced herself. I could not get over her abundance of hair, and her smile. "Hi," she said, "My name is Irene Brody."

The late spring air was tinged with the electricity of an upcoming storm. Being out in the open, the herd was seeking protection from the sometimes-deadly lighting-laced storms. Woolly Mammoth Boy saw the new calves scurry amongst cows, seeking the safety of their mothers. He saw his own calf, born only a moon ago, near the cow who had chosen him to mate with.

I wondered why the Man-boy I was connected to was still in such turmoil over the birth of his own offspring. I understood that the fear the Man-boy faced came from his past as a young manling, as Thought had explained to me. "Why does Man-boy continue this path of sorrow and pain? Why doesn't the Man-boy just change?" I thought, as I experienced calmness and strength from fathering a healthy calf that would someday contribute to this herd.

"Because he has yet to mature in his perceptions of his life. The Man-boy knows of his follies and pains that he inflicts upon the ones he cares for," Thought answered my quiet questioning as a hummingbird. "He migrates now to start anew."

"Migrating does him no good...he carries his self-doubts and pains wherever he goes, like the giant land turtle carries its shell upon its back," I said to the hovering hummingbird in front of my head. "How will the Man-boy learn these lessons?"

"He must first come to the realization that he cannot catch his own shadow. Secondly, it would be to his great benefit to accept the true nature of his mind, and release all that he conjures in his maddening quest to flee his pain. He is loved and he denies himself this gift from others," the wings of Thought-hummingbird sang to me. "He goes now to the place where he *will be rendered to substances that will feed his open wounds that never healed."*

I sighed at the idea of my ward in such pain and desperation.

My attention turned to the gathered calves now under the protective umbrella of their mothers' massive frames. I wanted for the Man-boy the peace I had felt since fathering my calf. I moved toward the herd, toward my family.

35. The House of Yin

"When you seek, you are blinded. When you speak, you are deafened. Observe and keep your mouth shut," my mentor instructed as we grazed the great plain before the massive blue-white glacier.

"Then what of our own thoughts and opinions?" I asked.

He rapped me with his trunk and jabbed me with his curved tusks. "What of them? You are not listening, are you! There will be a time for that. For now observe and learn."

—The Queries of Woolly Mammoth Boy

IRENE WAS UNLIKE ANY WOMAN I had ever known. Older by only four months, she was the "older woman" in my life. She had come in for the dance class I was teaching, which she had learned about from reading an article about me in the *Woodstock Times*. The article featured a photo of me holding Josie on the front page. We met a second time and had a sandwich together. Irene hadn't been in my dance class for a couple of weeks, and I thought it would be pleasant for us to catch up with each other. It was then I found out she was a recent widow of ten months with two young daughters. On most weekends, she drove up from Manhattan with her daughters to the country home her late husband and she had bought. It was an old Victorian farmhouse on three acres in the hamlet of Shokan, about twenty minutes from Woodstock.

I remembered being struck by her incredible moon-face, rich with big, gleaming blue eyes and a generous smile, topped with an abundance of curly golden brown hair. Irene's beauty was captivating. She exuded a confident sensuality that could not be denied. Irene was independent in her strength and it showed. She seemed connected to a wisdom that spoke of being an age much older than she was.

Irene's eldest daughter Annie was six and a half years old, and her youngest, Zoë, was a little over a year old when I met them the first time. I was intrigued by Irene's life story. Her husband, her teenage sweetheart, had died of cancer the year before at the young age of thirty-two. I was stunned. I had never met a widow before. Her fragility was balanced with the power of someone surviving a catastrophic personal event of immeasurable pain and loss. There was energy, and a feeling of familiarity with her I could not place. Was it the tragic loss of her husband, the loss of someone so very dear? Was it that we felt very much at ease and safe in each other's presence? Was it a naïveté of life we both shared in a simple way? Irene was not a simple woman in the sense of intelligence; like her father before her, she was working on her PhD in Clinical Psychology. No, Irene was special and I wanted to find out why. I was in Manhattan to take aikido classes, and to celebrate my birthday and stay with my *sempai* on the Upper West Side. I had never dated a student before; it was just against protocol, though teachers still did it. Irene had given me her home phone number in the city, and since she was not technically a student any more, I called her.

"Hello," a rich, sultry voice answered my call.

"Hi, this is Ron Rubio. I am calling for Irene Brody."

"Hi, this is Irene. What a surprise, Ron Rubio."

"Hi, Irene. I am in the city to celebrate my birthday and wanted to know if you would like to meet for coffee or grab a bite to eat?"

"Sure. Where are you?" Irene said she was on West 110th and Broadway, which was about twenty blocks uptown from me.

"I can meet you up where you live, Irene. Just let me know."

"How about in an hour? There is a place I go to on West 107th and Broadway, on the west side of the street."

"Great! I will see you in an hour. Thank you, Irene." I got off the phone jumping up and down like a teenager. What a nice birthday I would have!

I got there early—that was my way—and found the restaurant. I scanned uptown in the direction she would be approaching. I noticed her hair before I saw her face. From a block away I saw this woman with a halo of hair blowing freely in a brisk pre-Spring breeze. I watched and confirmed it was her crossing the street. Even with a long coat on, her smooth "island" hip-sway was prominent. As a dancer I recognized the flow of her walk, and her relaxed hip movement displayed her confidence and command. She was a goddess on earth! That was it! I realized I was in the presence of a woman who, though processing the recent death of her husband, was in her power. Irene was present to this moment in her life. She was aware of her power, and it was this vibrancy I felt so familiar with.

I watched her cross the street and our eyes met. She smiled a smile that could melt glaciers.

"Hi, Irene!" I was beaming. I did not care if I was going overboard or not. My extreme exuberance was part of my blood—as was my extreme rage.

"Hi, Ron." We shook hands and she led me to the restaurant. I opened the door for her and followed her to our chosen table near the window.

We talked for hours, laughing and questioning. We shared the same music tastes and grew up experiencing the same crazy period in American history—of civil rights, Vietnam, bell-bottoms, and revolution. She spoke of her growing-up teenager years as quirky and herself as being so eccentric that she left her classmates in a haze of questions of "who is this girl?" Irene told me stories of being a loner and on the fringe of the social world of Scarsdale, NY. The more we talked, the more I realized she was the girl I would have gone after in high school.

Our time together ended too soon. I walked her to the co-op apartment building on West 110th Street where she lived with her two daughters. I was going to offer a simple kiss on the cheek, but she avoided me and we shook hands instead. Thinking nothing of it, I turned and walked away. Once I was out of her sight I started skipping down the sidewalk to Broadway. I was extremely happy. I saw her again the next weekend when she came up with Annie and Zoë. I met her at her house in Shokan. She had hired a nanny from the Philippines who helped take care of the kids when her husband died. After putting her kids down we hung out. As I was preparing to depart we had our first kiss. Irene revealed by her kiss she truly was a goddess on earth. We realized we were very much on the same wavelength. I left her home and whistled all the way back to mine. I had just turned thirty-five years old and my world was looking up again.

I suggested to Irene that on her next trip up from the city, our girls should meet. Josie was excited to meet Annie and Zoë. Josie and I went to Houst's hardware store in Woodstock and bought some balloons as a gift to the girls. Josie and I arrived at Irene's home, and the three girls met. Later, Josie remembered looking under the dining room table as we all ate dinner and seeing Irene and me holding hands. The first meeting went really well, and Josie asked me on the ride home about Irene. Yes, I liked her. Yes, I would like to see Irene again. Yes, I liked Annie and Zoë very much too.

In time Irene and I became more intimate with each other, and it was a beautiful time of passion and exuberance. It was like dipping my head and heart under a cold mountain waterfall. She awoke me and I awoke her. The day I picked her up in my VW truck for the first time she said, "You know Ron, I saw your truck in a dream. I saw me riding in this truck." She caressed the hawk feather I had hanging off the rearview mirror. "I saw this feather." I listened to her and felt at ease. On another occasion she said to me, "I dreamed of you, Ron, before I saw your picture on the cover of the *Woodstock Times*. I prayed for you to come into my life." I held my breath as she spoke. "After Ricky died, I did not want to live. I was barely able to take care of Zoë who was just a little baby. I was wasting away, and yet I knew I had to be there for my daughters. I started wanting to live with vibrancy and strength. It was then I began to ask for you. I wanted an artistic man who was into his body and health. I wanted a strong man who loved children. When I saw your picture in the *Woodstock Times* I knew it was you." She kissed me and I felt I had come home in my soul.

Irene opened her heart, home, and life to me. I was humbled. I had always taken care of myself and provided for those I was with, and Irene wanted to share her life with me unconditionally. I felt totally out of place with her family, and especially her late husband Ricky's family—with whom Irene was still very close. Irene's and Ricky's families were both Jewish and well-to-do. I felt like a pauper compared to them. They were well educated, and would correct and smirk at my English fumbling, especially her brother and brother-in-law. I guess they all feared I was a gold-digger digging for a rich widow. I could almost hear them thinking, "Who is this guy dating Irene? What is he after?" I always felt I had to defend myself. I was confused and belittled by it all. I was falling in love with Irene, and she came with a history that was enormous and challenging for me—actually, it was my worst nightmare. All my past experiences with racism and being stereotyped reared their ugly heads. I told Irene and she understood. Ricky's parents were supportive, and were so gracious to Josie and me. Irene's family was cautious around me except for her father, Hal. He was a fellow Piscean and we hit it off. He offered me validation and respect. I was humbled by his generosity. I always tried to be my best with them, but it was tough. Though everyone was cordial to me, I felt I was walking on thin ice. I was constantly aware of how I spoke and acted. Her family also seemed so unemotional to each other that I did not know if I was too exuberant to them. I was just one confused puppy.

I felt clear in my heart with Irene and her daughters. I knew I was not there to take the place of Zoë and Anna's father, but I vowed I would be their protector and be there for them in any way I could. I would lay my life on the line for them, anytime and anywhere. If Irene and I were to someday join families, Annie and Zoë would be like daughters to me. I would do my best to treat them as my own. When the time was right I would tell them so. I felt so sincerely for the loss of their father, and I wanted to do my very best to be the best for them as long as I was in their lives.

With Irene I felt how tough it was to fill the shoes of such a beautiful man as Ricky. It was one thing going out with a woman who had broken up with her boyfriend or husband, but I had never been with a widow before. I knew she still grieved for Ricky, and rightly so. I did not want to be jealous of a person who had passed on and was not even on the planet physically, but Ricky was very much there. I remembered speaking to him often, and letting him know I would do my very best for his daughters, but I also felt I had many faults and challenges. I knew I was joyful and loving and loud, yet I was also hyper-boisterous, overly sensitive to criticism, and a rigid thinker about the behaviors I was safe with that were always in-line with others. The girls were, well, little girls, and they were not into being neat and tidy, or aware of saying "please" and "thank you" upon receiving things from others. They were not great time-managers—and I, being a stickler for being on time, pushed others to conform, like my father did to me. The situation was all so new, strange, and unprecedented in my life.

Soon after meeting Irene and accepting the invitation to be in her life, I decided to go back to school and try college. My dance career had been great and now I wanted a college degree, so I went to the local junior college and signed up for classes. I chose a program that offered a double degree and certification in Environmental Water Quality Control. I felt water was an element that resonated with me, and it would be a very precious commodity in the future so anything related to water would provide a job. The challenge was that the program requirements included college-level chemistry, biology, and higher levels of math—up to calculus. Well, I was a strong C+ student in high school, and I had been out of school for almost twenty years. I had been working the right side of my brain all this time, and now I would be asked to use the left side of my brain. It was going to be a battle, but it was a battle I wanted. All this college work was going to balance my mind, and I was going to use both halves of it to succeed.

I started by attending classes in the late afternoons and at night. I would see clients and teach dance during the day. Irene said I could stay in her home in Shokan during the week, and we would be together on the weekends. Her home was the perfect place to study and focus; it was empty, quiet, and secluded, but that first winter term was still a real brain-buster. I knew I wanted to achieve this, unlike when I was a teenager, hated school, and was too distracted to get any studying done. At the end of the first semester in college I made the Dean's list, and I would stay on the Dean's list for three semesters in a row with a 3.5 grade-point average. I showed myself I could hunker down and do this. But then one foul, week-long blizzard closed the college and knocked me out of my highly disciplined and rigid study habits. I did not recover, and failed a few classes. My advisor sought to salvage the remainder of my last semester and suggested switching majors so I could graduate on time. The college would give me tons of life-experience college credit for my documented dance and teaching career, to make up for the classes I failed. I graduated with an associate's degree in Independent Studies and an emphasis on Science. Not bad. Years later, I received my BA in Dance, when I was well into my forties.

That first winter in school was a smash-in-the-mouth time of Nor'easter winds and an abundance of snow—I mean, over-your-head eight-foot-tall snowbanks! I loved it. Irene and I called each other often and were very much in love. Passionate from the very beginning, Irene and I could not wait to be with each other. When she came up to the Shokan house on the weekend from the city with the girls, our time was packed with fun, passion, and joy. Irene and I enjoyed the adventure of life. Her journey as a widow was moving forward, and my journey along the trails of recovery from early trauma and shame made us understand what we wanted from our relationship. It was like we were teenagers all over again, and we would often say that to each other. We were young, hippie revolutionaries in love and going to change the world.

That spring she moved out of Manhattan to join me in Shokan. We became a "Brady Bunch" family, and Josie fit right in the middle of the older Annie and younger Zoë. I had wanted Josie to have siblings and this was a dream come true. Irene accepted Josie in the house and we became five. I loved our combined family. I saw Annie and Zoë as my own. Annie was seven now, Josie was turning five, and Zoë was going on two. Josie had a hard time with Zoë; she did not want Zoë calling me "Dad," or anything like that. As much as I tried to mellow her out, Josie would not have it any other way. I told Zoë she could call me anything she wanted. I loved Zoë and that was that. Annie had a hard time with Josie following her around. Josie wanted to be like Annie. Zoë just wanted to be included in the games her two older siblings played. They started to call themselves "The Three Lost Sisters." It was very cute.

Irene and I started to sort out the child-rearing duties. She was often busy working on her dissertation. I was in college but had more time, so we split some duties while I took on most of them. She was raised Jewish and I a strict Filipino; clash-time started up. She was the classic "Jewish mother" who tended our children with an ever-giving and accommodating style that clashed with my very disciplined and strict Filipino/Spanish family-rearing knowledge. Irene would always say to me it was not what I wanted to teach the children that was the problem, but rather my presentation. Try as I would, I was locked into the rigidity of having the children do what I said, and with no questions asked. Annie and Zoë hardly said "thank you" to their grandparents upon receiving gifts, or "please" when wanting something. I guess I did not understand Jewish grandparents, but manners were manners and I felt they had to be learned. I expected my children to be grateful and show respectful manners with their elders; Josie knew this from my parenting. Irene's daughters were not being corrected in their manners by their grandparents or Irene. I saw their behavior as spoiled. There was also an abundance of plastic toys and a flood of material junk around the holidays that seemed so wasteful. Coming from a childhood where we didn't have much, this abundance of material things was really overwhelming to me. I grew up with working for all I received. I saw their privilege and I was not used to such privilege—to have access to real nice and current toys and material fads. I felt this pattern of not showing grateful behavior and etiquette to others was too much, and I thought the children needed to be taught the difference between having and not having. Did we really need all those plastic toys?

It was a cultural clash. I prayed I would see the light behind all of this. I loved Irene so much, and she loved me so much. We both realized the pain of our separate childhoods. Her father was stern and uncompromising; she had to fight for time to have her voice heard. Being the eldest of three children, Irene was the icebreaker. She had been a quiet girl who was often shy and easily bullied. We shared many pains: the pain of overbearing parents, of loneliness and lost childhoods, and quirky teenage lives. She met Ricky in high school, but I had met no one. Our passion for love and expressing love was the glue of our relationship. We also loved adventure; I was the instigator and she would put things together logistically. We mostly clashed on how to raise the children. Though Annie and Zoë were her daughters, I promised Ricky's spirit I would do my best to help them. I was doing my best and Irene was very patient, but I knew her patience would not last too long. My frustration grew into anger and rage. Old patterns reappeared and I was caught in the swirling, spinning waters of guilt, shame, and depression. I loved our daughters so much, but I was too strict in Irene's eyes. From my perspective I was providing structure, and teaching values of worth.

Zoë became the lighting rod between Irene and me. To me it seemed everyone was covering for her, for Zoë was the youngest. She was just not getting it. Irene and I argued about Zoë, and I saw so much of myself in her. Though it was hard for others to see, I loved Zoë the most. I saw the little boy of myself in Zoë so clearly that I wanted to train her to be tougher and more independent to keep up with her sisters. I wanted to push her to see her strengths and take on her own life, but the more I did that the more Irene protected her. The more the kids saw how strict I was with Zoë the more I could not explain myself. I just could not communicate with the girls. I tried to tell Irene. She understood, but this was her youngest daughter and she was going to protect her. I was caught between a rock and a hard place, and so was Irene. I thought we as parents should always put on a united front, but Irene did not see it this way. I would say "no" and she would say "yes." It was tough trying to do the "parenting thing," so we started to attend couples therapy. All the while Irene was focusing on her college studies and I was driving the kids to art and piano classes, keeping the house clean, and cooking dinners. The girls got used to my steamed kale, tofu, and rice dinner every night. They loved it when Mom cooked.

Soon a female puppy entered our lives. I named her Star. A few months later two female kittens, Willow and Lilly, joined our family. Before I knew it I was surrounded by all females—three daughters, two female kittens, one female puppy, and Irene—I was in a house of Yin. I built a little eight-by-eight-foot hut in our woods. I called it my Jack London hut. It was my escape, but stress led me to smoking pot more often for my nerves. I also became obsessed with computer gaming. After cleaning up after dinner, I would play for hours and hours. Losing was not in my blood and I became so obsessed with winning. I was often driven to raging at the screen. I was turning into a madman. The kids and Irene would be in one room, and I was in the other room fuming and yelling at a computer. How I wasted my time and my life! I was losing my mind. I was losing my family. I was losing Irene.

Irene and I worked hard for our love. She thought I was bipolar, should be on medication, and believed I had autistic behaviors as well. For me, the anger, sadness, and fear I was creating in my family grew into a dark depression, and more self-directed rage from feeling so out of control. There was often joy and happiness in the home, but not enough. Annie, the oldest, was dark and depressed. She remembered losing her father. When I could get out of my own way I tried to focus on her. When we had first met, I wanted to show Annie that I would support each and every dream she aspired to. I tried to share with Annie my own depression and darkness from my childhood. This was not what Annie needed, though—she just need a good ear to listen to her, and that is where Irene excelled as a parent. The girls knew how much I loved and cared for them. They would say how safe they felt at night and everywhere else because I would always protect them. They knew I loved Irene and they knew Irene loved me, but they heard all the arguing and it made them edgy and uncomfortable. The girls wondered why Irene and I stayed together. We all stuck together in spite of everything. Love was the glue.

Then a tragedy occurred. It was Columbus Day and Irene, Annie, and Zoë were home from school on break. Josie was with her mother in Woodstock. It was a beautiful fall day. I was cleaning the kitchen and Irene was in the office I had built for her. Annie and Zoë were outside playing. I had asked the girls to watch the kittens and Star, our two-year-old dog, while I finished outside. Star and I were starting to have a great relationship. The night before we had laid together in our field, and I was at peace with her. Star was attentive to me and I was enjoying having her around. That morning as I was cleaning in the kitchen there was a knock on the back door. I dried my hands and answered the door to find the driver of a gas delivery truck.

"Sir, do you have a black and brown dog?" he asked.

"Yes."

"I hit the dog with my truck...I am so, so sorry. She ran into the street in front of two kittens..." he could only stare at me.

I ran out the door to the front of the house. There was Star on the street, dying. Her side was ripped open, and her guts spewed onto the asphalt. The girls came to see the commotion and began to scream. I rushed them away from the scene. Irene came running from the office and took the girls. I ran inside to retrieve something to cover and gather Star. I found white sheets. I ran to the garden shed and grabbed the wheelbarrow. The girls were screaming and crying loudly. I was leaving my body, and moving with the speed of a shooting comet. I was moving without thinking. Everything seemed like a dream. Annie and Zoë screamed and screamed. I came to Star's side as she lay on the warm pavement. Her eyes were open and wet. I hugged her dearly and tightly, and whispered in her ears how much I loved her. Her blood was all over me. She died. I gathered her up and carried her to the wheelbarrow and off the street.

I focused on the girls as Irene gathered them close. They turned toward me and screamed. I was covered in Star's blood. I ran in to change my shirt. Then I called Andrea to tell Josie about Star. Andrea drove Josie to our house to be with her sisters. We decided to bury Star on our property, and found a nice blanket to wrap her in. As the girls and Irene gathered around I found a nice place and started to dig. I quickly found rock-hard Catskill ground. I chipped rock and stones trying to dig a large enough hole to place Star in. I broke down and finally howled in animal pain. The girls and Irene stared at my pain and cried. I wept as I placed Star's body in the hole I was finally able to dig. The girls placed Star's collar and playthings into the hole, and everyone said something sweet to her. Laying large stones on top of her, I filled her grave, and then she was gone. The day ended and so it was.

We realized later that Star had saved the kittens' lives. Seeing the kittens running into the street, she ran ahead of them to herd them back onto the property when she was hit by the truck. She had died a very young girl; she was just becoming her self. She did what came natural to her—herding and protecting. Thank you, Star. I felt empty. I felt like a living being that gave me strength and joy to face all I was facing was suddenly gone, and that was how it was.

The house tried to settle back into some sense of normalcy. The girls,

Irene, and I were shocked for days and weeks, but life moved on. Irene focused on her dissertation and classes. The girls went back to their school lives. I focused on writing the first draft of my BodyKi manual. Months later we went to the SPCA and tried looking at dogs, but I wanted no part of it. I did not want a replacement for Star. I only went because the girls wanted to. Most of the dogs the SPCA had were older; there were only a few puppies. I stared into each cage and noted one little, golden, sickly puppy. I told Irene there was only one puppy that looked decent. The girls were drawn to the cage with Irene in the lead. The puppy was four months old. The worker took the puppy out, and it clambered all over the girls and they squealed with joy and happiness. Puppies do that to kids. I said, "Let's get out of here." One week later, the puppy was in our home. I named her Phoenix—"one who rises out of the ashes." She had kennel cough and other things wrong with her. The first night in our home, I took pity on Phoenix and slept with her on the kitchen floor. She was now part of the family. I insisted on an electric dog fence around the whole property; there would be no more dog deaths.

Living in rural New York State was a time of detaching from the hustle and bustle of urban life. I went down on the bus to Manhattan to take aikido classes at New York Aikikai, and I continued my enrollment with Woodstock Aikido. Other than that, my life was in a small hamlet two-and-a-half hours north of the Big Apple. Our 1906 Victorian farmhouse home was on three acres of trees with separate lawns, and one sprawling pasture I mowed with a walk-behind 36" mower. My neighbors thought I should get a ride-on mower for such a large job, but I figured I was young and fit, and the days of sitting on my ass were far in the future. It took two hours to mow the lawns. It was very Zen and meditative to walk and mow straight baseball-field-like lines. The place was well kept by me. The property was ours, and I was trained to maintain order and security. I was obsessed with privacy and insisted on fences and planting trees to block out the neighbors' views of the property. Since there were no streetlights, the nights were dark and the night sky was filled with stars. We loved it tremendously. Living in a small hamlet you knew your neighbors, and being one of a few persons of color for miles around and also having a long black braid, I was known in the area as the "martial arts Indian." Because of that recognition I received no racial harassment—just a bunch of the usual stares and attitudes found in a small isolated community.

The girls grew tight together, but had the usual sibling battles. Irene and I had our good times and our fights. Therapy was a weekend chore. In sessions I was told about my anger issues and overbearing manner of parenting. I was praised for being protective of my family and being active in my children's life. I was praised for what I wanted my daughters to learn, and hosed down for my rigid, archaic presentation skills. Damn, I was trying hard and sticking with trying to be better. I also wanted to run away and just screw all the trouble. My love for my family and Irene was strong, but, again, I was being a very rough and rigid thinker. I was too impatient to listen to Irene or the girls' opinions or their side of the story. With Irene I felt I knew better than she, and therefore I should have the last word. I was so out of touch with the basic social skills of being a good listener. I would cut Irene off in mid-sentence or yell at her to silence. I just had a hard time understanding why something so obvious to me was so hard for my family to understand. I saw my father's impatience coming out in me all the time, and his intolerance of stupidity and slow acting. I was my father's son. I hated myself for it, and hated how hard I was on my family. I just could not leave them alone. Our family vacations were marked with at least one incident of me blowing up. An anger meltdown could develop from their slow ordering of food off a menu, from forgetting something in their hotel room and having to turn around, or just because I had low blood sugar and was plain-ass irritable.

During this time I felt I was being misunderstood in the aikido dojo I belonged to in Woodstock; I felt I was being left out of due process and recognition for time put in and effort put out. My fault was letting everything go to my ego, and I felt my ego was getting bashed. My sense of myself was being beaten on all fronts. I kept thinking I was doing the right thing, only to find out I was completely wrong in how I was reading the situation. It was so frustrating. I thought, as a company man, "do right for the company and the company will do right for you." I put in my hours and just wanted the validation of that in being able to move to the next rank. I did not read that there were other social innuendos present, like favoritism and jealousy from others. I had failed to recognize that the dojo was a smaller version of the big world around me. Petty competition and feelings of unfairness abounded in any dojo, in any social grouping like a workplace or organized competition.

These two important places in my life—home and dojo—were confusing me, and kept me askew from the stability and safety I so vainly sought. I felt damned and cursed to never find happiness. I just wanted to love, share love, and receive love. It was like groping in the dark. I was totally confused. I just kept putting one foot in front of the other, though I wanted to be in a dark, cool cave alone and not hurting anyone.

In time Irene graduated and received her PhD in Clinical Psychology like her father and younger sister. We worked at establishing a home office for her so she could work out of our property. I built the office, bathroom, and waiting room in a separate carriage house we had. Irene was set. Though she had a general practice, her expertise was working with people, young or old, with autism. Autism was slowly being recognized. ADD (attention deficit disorder) and AD/HD (attention deficit/hyperactivity disorder) were the big diagnoses for the "troubled kids" in school in the 1980s. By the 1990s, Asperger syndrome—a high-functioning autism—was taking over the scene. Irene was the local expert in this field, and people traveled for hours to see her and have their kids or themselves tested, assessed, and supported. She was great. Irene was a true loving angel healer.

I was teaching BodyKi classes, dance/movement classes for adults and teens as well as children, and had a private practice in mind–body training with an office in Woodstock. Once a parent asked me to help her nine-year-old son, who had been diagnosed with ADD, then AD/HD, and then, finally, was confirmed to have Asperger syndrome. I saw a lot of myself in this young boy. As a child I was like him: socially awkward, physically clumsy, a rigid thinker, prone to anger meltdowns, challenged with transitions, lousy with writing and penmanship, particular with eating habits, speaking in a "funny" way, obsessed with certain things, drawn to the world of fantasy, and other quirky behaviors, cravings, and obsessions.

Was I autistic? Did I have Asperger syndrome? I did not have the time or desire to be tested. Irene thought I was out there, and that I might be on the autism spectrum. She also thought I was bipolar and from hearing about my childhood from hell—filled with beatings, head injuries, emotional abuse, and humiliation—and believed I suffered from PTSD (post-traumatic stress disorder) and TBI (traumatic brain injury). She felt medication would help. I was self-medicating with marijuana; no alcohol, just pot. I did not want to be on any pharmaceuticals. Pot was organic and not made in some lab (at least that was my belief). I had lived and survived this long, but I was still a social wrecking ball in a glass house.

My working with this Aspie boy through my Mind–Body techniques was really helping him succeed. I soon found myself teaching life skills—mostly how to negotiate the world of distraction, depression, and anger—to young people. I was using what I had learned from growing up on my own. Word started to get out in the community. I was already an established martial arts and dance teacher, wonderful with reaching troubled young people, and now I was being very successful with those on the autism spectrum. Irene was funneling young clients to me, and I was soon packed with a private practice I enjoyed. I became known as a mentor *par excellence*. Local schools wanted me to work with their "challenged" students. I developed adaptive PE classes. I ran afterschool programs that took normally high-maintenance and unmanageable kids and transformed them into disciplined, focused, and aware beings. Parents and teachers would sit stunned and crying in their seats at the end of the program demonstrations, watching their sons and daughters who were once family liabilities and hell-raising chaotic tornados performing highly disciplined martial weapons movements, and sitting on stage very attentively while awaiting their turn to perform. The word went out: Ron Rubio was the real deal.

Ironically, I was struggling to maintain my own life. Though highly disciplined, I was very rigid in my personal life at home. I was exhibiting all the detrimental behaviors that I was mentoring the young people I was working with to resolve and evolve from. It was like I was my own worst enemy. Damn it! I needed a mentor to help me! The paradox was killing me. I questioned my sanity—was I a farce, a charlatan? How could I be such a positive force in people's lives and still wreak havoc and sadness on those I loved the most? *Questions...*

The 1990s flew by. The girls got bigger. Irene was really busy in her practice as I was in mine. Irene's practice was filled with clients, and her nights were packed with endless paperwork for insurance reimbursements, school reports on children, and typing consulting reports for schools. Our time together was absorbed by our work, and by our parenting differences. The time we did focus on each other was great, but those times were growing too few and far between. We were drifting apart. I was desiring Irene and getting annoyed and frustrated by the little time we spent together, and Irene was fed up with my angry, rigid behavior. Irene had told me in the beginning of our relationship that she did not often express her feelings, and this trait ran true in her father and mother. Irene's childhood was similar to mine in this respect. Since I was so emotional and sensitive to all around me, maybe too much, I felt left out of Irene's world. I had received very little emotional and physical validation in my childhood from my parents and siblings, and this made me very needy. The neediness showed up in all my relationships and past marriages. I hated this about me. In order to not feel the pain, I became harder on myself and separated myself from the source of the pain—me. I felt that I really did not need anyone close to me. I was a liability and a curse to anyone close to me. I started to withdraw into a world of self-martyring and self-pity, and detaching myself from loving myself. In so doing I was also separating myself from Irene. It was a life cycle that seemed spawned in hell. It was oh so confusing to me.

Unhappy with my local martial arts training in Woodstock, I became a traveling *ronin*, a masterless samurai, going to many distant places for intense martial study. Training in aikido, close combat martial arts, Filipino martial arts, Chinese martial arts, boxing, and others, I was seeking. My ronin training took me out of the martial organization I was affiliated with, and most of my training became covert. I did not speak about it at my aikido dojo to avoid rankling my teachers. One teacher I met on my travels was an aikido sensei from Milwaukee, Mike Mamura. By the time I met Mamura Sensei, he was in his late seventies. When I first saw him at a seminar in Washington, DC, he was a frail-looking man of Japanese descent. Supported on either arm by his daughter and a top student from his dojo, he was helped onto the mat to teach the first class. Upon reaching the middle of the expansive mat space filled with hundreds of aikido practitioners, he was released by his two assistants. Standing alone he seemed infused with an unseen energy force. During his first exercise, he asked two burly men to grab him, one on each arm. It looked like they were going to rip him apart. Suddenly, Mamura Sensei issued a *kiai* (a focused audible sound that accompanies an exertion of energy from a martial practitioner, as when he is finishing a punch or kick or completing a sword cut). His voice rattled the rafters, and the two men were flung from him. To establish that this was not hocus-pocus, Mamura Sensei did it again. And again, the same results occurred: both burly men flung away. I was hooked. This old man knew something; he had discovered something very special. During his class, he came to watch my training partner and me. After watching us for a long minute, he beckoned me to stand close him. I looked into his bright, gleaming eyes as he said to me quietly, "You seem to be the only one in this whole place who is actually doing what I showed." I recognized this sensei to be something special. I recognized him to be a teacher to follow and learn from. He lived in Milwaukee and I was in New York. I approached him for a photo after his class. As I neared his presence, he was immediately surrounded by his top students; they were wary of me because this was their teacher who was so fragile, and needed all of his visitors screened so he would not be overwhelmed and fatigued. Mamura Sensei smiled at me through his students, shooed them away, and granted me a photo taken by one of his students. He said he would mail it to me. Giving his daughter my address, I gratefully left.

A week later I received the photo of him and me. He also attached a short note. It read, "I had a great time at the seminar. '*Shugyo*' means 'constant practice.' I know you know the meaning of this word. Sincerely, Mike Mamura." I ended up flying to his dojo in Milwaukee one weekend every month for the next two years until his death. The first time I came to his dojo, his students asked, *"Why?"* They told me I came from the best aikido school around, the New York Aikikai. I replied that they did not know what they had under their own roof. All they knew was some highly proficient aikidoist was traveling to Milwaukee from New York, at his own expense, to study with their "old man" sensei. I was a mystery to them. But I did not care what they thought. Mamura Sensei and I had a great relationship going. The time alone in my travels made me tougher and tougher. I missed Irene and the kids a lot when I was away in my training. I was seeking and seeking, and questioning the "why" of everything I encountered.

All three girls went to the same local elementary school. Upon graduation they started to part from home. Annie opted to go to a private school at thirteen years old. There was money from her late father for this purpose. It was a private sleep-away school in Massachusetts; she hated public middle school. Josie wanted to go live with her mom after graduating, and Zoë was left on her own when her sisters left. True or not, I felt that I had driven my daughters out of the home with my abrasive behavior. They did not doubt my love for them, but they hated my yelling and scary, disciplined behavior. I felt like shit.

I focused on what I knew was the core of my life—my love for Irene and my girls—but it was beating me up. Being in a house full of females for years had worn me down, and left me impotent in my power. I recognized that my mentoring practice was rocking, and my martial arts training was meaningful. I saw clearly I was most happy and powerful in my public life, and powerless and confused in private life. I had very few male friends of quality, and lots of acquaintances. I saw my mentors when I could but that was hard, so I kept to myself. The paradox of my life continued. I had been a paradox since birth, so what else was new?

As the twenty-first century approached, I moved down to New York City for one year to prepare for my aikido *sandan* test, my third-degree black belt test. I visited my family on the weekends and they were happy to see me. Having time away from me allowed my family to enjoy some peace and quiet. I found a small place a few blocks from the dojo. I took every class and trained every day. I was able to see some clients in my city apartment, but the main focus was to train and test in front of my teacher, Yamada Sensei, and my aikido family from the New York Aikikai. Mine would be the last black belt test at the New York Aikikai in the twentieth century.

My hopes and dreams of being a good father and husband seemed like they might not be. The year 2000 came in with new hopes, visions, and inspirations. As the new year began, I received the startling news from the West Coast that Dad died on January 5. The news hit me like a kick in my heart and stomach.

Dad and I had not spoken to each other in the last four years. He had disowned me again. Four years earlier, I had made a trip to the West Coast to speak on behalf of my younger sister and older brother. From speaking with my siblings I learned that Dad paid little attention to his grandkids. I told my brother and sister I would talk to Dad about this; they said that would be okay. After setting up a time with him, I spoke to Dad about how the family needed his guidance and strength—that his grandchildren needed his love. The fact that he paid little attention to his first grandchild, my daughter, hurt me, but I said nothing about this. I was speaking for my brother and my sister. I spoke about his health, how everything was powerful in the present moment, and that anything can change for the better. He was thankful for the time I spent with him, and sent me off with great feelings. His last words to me were, "Ron, I am!" Smiling, I yelled back at him, "That's right, Dad!" I had shared with Dad a powerful affirmation that I taught my clients: only in the present moment are we able to create and live the positive changes we want in our lives, not changing in some future date but right "now!" "I am!" is a declaration that one is aware in the present moment and doing something right here and now. For my dad to say this to me was very touching and important to me. I felt we had made a real connection. I called Irene back in New York to tell her about the successful time with Dad. My sister and brother were grateful for my efforts, but upon coming home to New York I received a call from my sister that Dad had mailed a letter to all our family members saying I was instigating negative feelings in the family. Dad killed the messenger. He killed me again. I thought my dad and I had a great time together, but it was an illusion. For the next four years he would not call or acknowledge me. I was saddened by this and tried to forget about him. That was impossible though, and now he was dead.

 My family waited for me to fly to San Francisco from New York to view his body before cremating him. Irene stayed home with the girls, for the call came of his death on a Wednesday and I quickly left on a Friday. I knew it would be a highly charged atmosphere and Irene did not need to be around it. I was driven to the hospital morgue by my stepmother. I was led to the basement floor of the hospital and brought to a viewing room. Alone, I waited to view Dad's body. Wheeled in by a nurse orderly, his body bag was zipped down to his waist. Dad was naked with a long incision down the middle of his chest. He had died of a stroke or something and fell, smashing his head. He died alone. I told the orderly to leave the room. In the silence I stared at the body of the man who had placed so much fear into my heart, who had beaten me, humiliated me, and taught me much at the end of a scathing voice and hard hand. Here he was naked like a baby, a large cut above his left eye, and his right eye partially open. I expected him to sit up on the gurney and say something to me. In silence, I viewed the man I loved so much, and wanted so much to be loved by. And now the bastard was dead. We hadn't talked in four years and now his voice was forever silent. I moved closer to his body. I leaned over him to look directly into his face. A shell. I was viewing the shell that once housed a man with youthful hopes and dreams, a man who wanted so much and was so frustrated by a world of racism and hypocrisy. I looked deeply into his face. There were short whiskers. I remember watching him shave with a razor as a little boy, looking up at him, so tall, so powerful, and wondering how he did not cut his face to ribbons.

I was his son. I had his temper, anger, and intolerance. I had his creative mind and his perseverance to conquer the whole damn world. I had started smoking cigarettes as a teen to be like him. I stared at his silent, dead face. I allowed my eyes to study his naked body. He was gone. I said to him, "You know Dad, we are going to have to do this all over again. You and I have unfinished business to take care of. So while I live my life out here on this planet, to whatever amount of time measured out to me, stick around and kick my butt once in a while. Continue to teach me. I will miss you. You know I always loved you even though you found me so weak and worthless. Until we meet again. Later, Dad."

I left the room and never looked back. I attended his funeral, but did not stay. I left as soon as my brother began to speak. I waited outside. When it was over I went out to dinner with my stepfather, mother, and my siblings with their spouses; Irene was back in New York. Over dinner my stepfather said something that floored me, "Ron, it wasn't that bad with your dad. Your dad was not such a mean guy." I looked at him like he had two heads. I yelled something, freezing all conversation in the restaurant. I was crushed, and stormed out. Was this how it was going to be—lies and illusions to cover the past? My sister and her man met me outside. They told my stepfather to stay inside. I returned to New York the next day. There was life to live, and the world was not going to stop for one mixed-up Filipino!

Back in Shokan an opportunity emerged for me to open my own dojo and center near my home. After conferring with my Woodstock sensei, the highest ranked teacher in my area, for permission to open my own place, I proceeded to build a dojo and mind–body center. Irene was very supportive, and I was excited to be close to home and part of my local community. Being on the other side of the mountain that separated the area of Shokan from Woodstock, I was going to serve a whole different population of locals. I wanted to share all this with Irene. I dreamed that Irene and I would teach together and join forces. It was a dream I had had with all my lovers and previous wives, but Irene did not share the same dream. Her unwillingness to move together on the center flattened me. I moved on with the center as my own.

As life continued at home, Zoë, Irene, and I danced the dance. Annie was away and Josie lived with her mom. I wanted to strengthen Zoë, so I trained her in aikido. Zoë was twelve or thirteen years old and had trained for a year and a half, and had mastered everything I taught her. She was great. In time Zoë was good enough to teach in my absence. I felt this was my way of showing Zoë I loved her, and validated her strength and voice. Though the aikido teaching responsibilities helped, my rigid behavior at home was not healthy for her. I felt for her, and yet I was too rigid in my ways to let things slide. I loved her so much, but I kept stumbling. I was not a good listener to Zoë and would cut her off, offering my inflated sense of righteous advice. I was undermining the very thing I wanted for her, a strong, independent voice and presence. Sincerely apologetic every time I put my foot into my mouth by saying something belittling or insensitive, or becoming overbearing and not respecting Zoë's boundaries, I continued to stumble and fumble away at our relationship that I wanted to support so badly. *"I am so sorry, Babe."*

That July my mentor, Mike Mamura, passed away. He finally moved on at eighty-one years old. I went back to Milwaukee for his funeral. I was recognized for the friendship he and I shared. He was gone. I felt his void in my life, and also was very grateful for the special times together he had offered me. I was at peace with his passing.

In October, Irene's late husband's father passed away. Len Dutka was an incredible man and very generous to me. Proving that I was a good man for Irene was important to me. This was his late son's wife, and she was like a daughter him. At his funeral I thanked him for all he gave me. In all those years he was alive, his family had been so loving to Josie and me. He was a good man of integrity and quiet intelligence; now he was gone too.

One day when the girls were all home—Annie from boarding school, and Josie visiting from her mom—Irene and the girls walked into our home with a kitten, a male kitten. I looked at this kitten as another responsibility to look after. I took care of the animals, or had to fight with the girls over the years to take care of their animals. And now here was another toy for the girls to play with, which I would have to look after. I named him "Cosmo."

I have to admit it was nice to have another male energy in the house, and for the first time. We had picked up another female dog to keep Phoenix company the year before; I named her "Sade." The dogs sniffed Cosmo's ass, and he was accepted. The two older female cats saw Cosmo as a nuisance and would have no part of him. I waited, watched, and wondered about him. Cosmo only related to me and we bonded, man to man. So let us see how this would work out. Another winter was coming; I prepared the house and property once again, and made sure all would be cozy through the long cold season. Life continued and the world was not going to stop revolving for nothing.

Though it was late afternoon, the sun's heat was undiminished in its intensity. On the wide glade before Woolly Mammoth Boy, the mammoth herd had sought out every available shade and shelter. Already the relentless sun had taken the lives of the weaker ones. Woolly Mammoth Boy stood unmoving to conserve energy, though his very mass consumed much.

He stood contemplating the Matriarch. Next to him stood a juvenile male mammoth badgering him with questions. "Why do the males of the herd follow the Matriarch?" the youngster asked again. "Are we not stronger and wiser than the females?" Woolly Mammoth Boy shifted his weight to stare down at the young male mammoth. "Listen and learn!" he said with command.

I once witnessed the Matriarch take a raging bull mammoth brother down with one swipe of her head, sending the bull crashing to the ground unconscious. I also remember clearly watching a Matriarch of our herd sacrifice her life after foiling an ambush, and then turning rather than fleeing, she attacked the hunters who followed and sought all our lives.

A Matriarch leads the herd, not a bull mammoth. All males of the herd grow to be mighty bull warriors, and we follow the law of the Matriarch unconditionally. She, who leads, remembers all the ancient tales and sacred rituals that bind our lives to the very fabric of our existence. Without her silent authority we would fall prey to saber-toothed and clawed predators with the naïve blunderings of a newborn calf. She renders fear into a strength that could withstand the fury of a lighting-charged summer storm. Her wisdom is uncontested, as her strength is undeniable.

I have witnessed the Matriarch facing down and soothing the berserker-spirit of my fellow brothers after returning from battle. She has led us through the high, dangerous, craggy mountain passes, and helped us transverse the great wasteland safely and confidently.

Though my brothers and I can boast all we want—bellowing and trumpeting our challenges to the known world around us—we would easily be a buzzard's feed without the guidance and wisdom of the Matriarch.

She now calls us to gather. I hear and heed.

I will listen and learn from her teachings.

36. Mind–Body and the Ground

In a perfect world all your dreams come true. In a perfect world your skin is unblemished, your car starts every morning, your house keys are never lost, and your checkbook always balances out. Naw! This is not a perfect world, and you should thank your lucky stars for it. The stresses that all creatures on this planet face are necessary for individual growth, creating stamina, and building strength. Though at times these stress factors—that all living beings are faced with in their lives—are capable of producing extreme anguish and despair, to persevere and survive them will ultimately reap great benefits, and the continued survival and evolution of the being is guaranteed.

—The Observations of Woolly Mammoth Boy

THE DESTRUCTION OF THE WORLD Trade Center occurred on September 11, 2001. It was a bright, clear, and perfect fall morning. I was teaching a BodyKi class at my new training center when word came of a plane crashing into one of the towers. News of other jets crashing with all lives lost filled the airwaves. The nation was stunned, but nowhere more so than in Manhattan and surrounding areas. Our rural upstate community was locked down because of the nearby reservoir that was a source for Manhattan's water supply. An energy of fear and doubt permeated the entire area. I focused on my students to keep them together. I would do my job to take care of those I was responsible for—my family, my clients, and my students.

Irene and I were married in October 2001 after being together since 1992. We had always felt, even in the worst of times, that it would be impossible to live without each other. We knew that our love was so strong that we could persevere through the ugliest and most unpleasant of circumstances. We decided to hold the ceremony on our property. In our many years as a couple we had stuck together through the joys and battles of our developing relationship. Marriage was a significant step for us, and we were supported by many people in our community, but others doubted the wisdom of us being together. Our relationship had held tightly for years by our intense love for each other, but it was also threatened by the tearing and fraying that came from our slugfest battles over parenting. From the perspective of our friends we matched and balanced each other. From our daughters' and families' perspective, our love for each other was undeniable but our differences made our relationship seem crazy. Irene and I wanted to see our relationship through the entire spectrum of emotions, joys, and challenges that our unique bond offered us. Irene and I balanced each other's weaknesses and strengths. I taught her much and she did the same for me. We did not care what others thought, because we knew at the end of the day I would be in her arms and she in mine.

Irene and I were right, but our families were not wrong either. Two years before, despite our trust, one incident had caused me to lose faith in Irene. My Asian-Filipino background made me old-fashioned in my views on relationships, and I saw the commitment between two people to be a pact of covering each other's backs. For example, I had told Irene of my experiences with racism and white police. Living in rural New York State, a brown man like myself stood out. One day I was stopped for a traffic violation—later thrown out in court—and was taken to the state police barracks which happened to be in my small town. After finishing a battery of tests I was released. I called Irene to please pick me up from the barracks because I had no other way home. Though I was only minutes away from our house, Irene said she could not pick me up because she was in session with a client. I mentioned to her that this client was well acquainted with us and would understand if she disappeared for five minutes. Irene said no. The trooper said he could drive me home, but the thought of being dropped off at my house by a law enforcement officer did not sit well with me at all. It was matter of saving face (an Asian perspective I had absorbed from my parents). I had no choice but to accept the ride. I was embarrassed. That evening I expressed the humiliation I felt to Irene. I was traumatized by the experience. I had needed Irene so much, but she had let me down. I told her if the situation were reversed there would be nothing in the world to stop me from being at her side in a time of need. She understood my position and showed great remorse, compassion, and empathy for me. She understood my history with racism and law enforcement, but the pain, shame, and embarrassment stayed with me for a while. My sense of trust in her had taken a major hit.

Why did this incident affect me so deeply? I found it hard to admit the fact that I had history and trauma with injustice, racism, shame, loss of face, and betrayal. I could not separate the past from the present. These events had shaped my perspective about living my life in the social world. I found it hard to release the feeling of betrayal I felt with Irene. I could not put the broken pieces of trust back together. How can someone say one thing and do another? I was confused because my love for Irene was so strong, and yet a fundamentally essential component for me to feel safe with her was not there. That component was the feeling of trust.

Irene apologized to me and I to her, but something had been carved out of my heart and body. A trust and bond between Irene and me had been severed. My love was there, but trust wasn't. Irene felt the void and we were both saddened by what happened. Though we made efforts to move on, I struggled to be engaged in our relationship. During this time Irene was extremely busy with her private practice. She worked late into the night. I saw she was leading an unbalanced life, and offered to help relieve her. I felt she was working herself into a place dangerous to her spiritual and physical health, but Irene continued her lifestyle because of her devotion to her clients. She was a healer. She was driven to do all she could for her clients. We were drifting apart at a slow, excruciating pace, but our love held us together. I felt strongly there had to be more reasons for being in a relationship than love alone, though. Slowly, I forgave Irene, but I did not forget that she had undermined my efforts to be a stepfather and parent to Zoë.

Despite our troubles we continued our work together. After this incident with the cops, a good friend of Irene's, Dr. Valerie Paradiz, invited Irene to participate in the opening of the first high school in the USA that focused on individuals on the autism spectrum. It was called the ASPIE School. I was invited to develop and lead the adaptive PE class, basically a BodyKi class, and be a mentor to fifteen students. Most of the students were male, twelve to sixteen years of age. Irene and I were great assets to the ASPIE School, along with an excellent staff of specialized teachers and therapists. The school focused on building academic and social strengths needed by students in order to be partially mainstreamed into the high school next door and, in the bigger picture, to learn skills for a successful life in the future. The ASPIE School showed parents and teachers what was possible when we thought out-of-the-box and pulled together to make new ideas work. Irene's professional wisdom and compassionate spirit helped the ASPIE program through the rough bumps and scrapes of a developing and innovative program directed to support the autism population.

Work with the ASPIE students inspired me to develop and finish a book based on the successful development of my mentoring concepts and techniques. The book was titled *Mind/Body Techniques for Asperger's Syndrome—Way of the Pathfinder* (Jessica Kingsley, 2008). "Pathfinder" came from the name of my mentoring practice, Pathfinder Mentoring. With all I had experienced in life, Pathfinder Mentoring was innovative and on the cutting edge of work with those on the autism spectrum. Though I focused on the autism population, what I truly saw, and what others around me recognized, was that Pathfinder Mentoring was applicable to all walks of life. In its essence, Pathfinder Mentoring was based on my BodyKi Mind–

Body training. For years I had applied BodyKi to clients who faced life's challenges—severe injury rehabilitation, PTSD, teens in crises, major surgery recovery, or people preparing for intense treatments for cancer and other life-threatening aliments.

As my friend Dr. Steven Edelson, director of the Autism Research Institute, had said to me, "Your work is about five years ahead of its time. I see your work as an essential component in supporting those on the autism spectrum. Now, being ahead of your time is a two-edged sword. First, it might be challenging for others to accept your work. You have no statistical data to back it up, though you have real-life examples of the success of your work spanning twenty years. The other side is that once Mind–Body awareness is accepted, you will be at its foundations. You will be the expert in the field."

For now I was riding the wave. I was ahead of my time. As my publisher would say to me when researching the title of my 2007 book, "Mr. Rubio, you are the only author with 'Mind/Body' in any title that pertains to autism or personal health globally." I was ahead of my time, and I knew it.

As I focused on the ASPIE School, my own center, the High Point Mountain Aikikai and BodyKi Center, was developing. Irene knew the center was growing, but we could not use our own resources to support it financially. I knew that all businesses took time to kick in. I understood her thinking so I decided to leave the space I was leasing and re-open the dojo in a less expensive location. At the time I was told by my New York Aikikai sensei to "clean up my relationship" with my local sensei in Woodstock. I told my sensei I did not know what he was talking about, so I approached my Woodstock sensei and asked him what needed to be cleared up. It seemed that members of the dojo felt I was insulting their sensei by opening a dojo so close to his. In speaking to him I found out this was the case. I was stunned. I asked for a "pow-wow" to clear all this up. Present at the meeting was my Woodstock sensei, his second-in-command, a senior student (my *sempai*), and me.

"Sensei, I do not know what I need to clear up. Yamada Sensei wanted me to clear things up with you. What did I do?"

"I never gave you permission to open your dojo," he said to me. I was floored. My dojo had been up and running for three years, and this was the first I was hearing of his complaint.

"Sensei, I cannot believe this. You are telling me for three years you have had bad feelings toward me and my dojo but you never said anything? I have been a member of Woodstock dojo for twelve years. You have been my teacher since day one at the New York Aikikai. You are saying I opened my dojo without your permission? This is totally catching me from left field."

Sensei looked at his lieutenant and asked, "Didn't Ron say he was opening his dojo, and the contract for leasing the space was signed already?"

"Yes, he did," his lieutenant answered. *What the hell!* I was floored.

"I am stunned this is happening, Sensei. I am surprised you think I would be so disrespectful. When I approached you three years ago to open my dojo, I repeated to you both that I had found a place and it was far enough from Woodstock, and served an entirely different population that never comes to Woodstock. I said repeatedly, 'I do not have to open a dojo if you do not approve.' I clearly said I did not sign yet. I asked you twice in front of both of you. And at the time you gave me the go-ahead."

I was stunned and brokenhearted! There was silence. I was out of my body. I felt betrayed by my teachers of a martial art that meant so much to me. It became clear to me why people I had known for at least twelve years had become distant. I was perceived as insulting a favorite teacher and sensei.

"Sensei, I am sorry you took it this way. I would have never have invested so much money and effort to open a dojo if you did not want me to. I am stunned that the both of you see me as such a disrespectful person. You both mean much to me, and both of you have been my mentors for many years. I am speechless."

"Well, this is what you said to me three years ago: You did not ask me if you could open a dojo. You said you signed the lease and were going to open it," Sensei said to me.

"Right?" he asked, as he turned to ask his senior student to confirm.

"That is right, Sensei."

The meeting ended with me being able to continue to teach. It was chalked up as one big misunderstanding. I felt my teachers had let me down, and that they could have stopped me at any time. Damn, I was their student. I was not above them. Was I that intimidating to them? They had allowed the aikido community to shun me and create hard feelings toward me, and I knew nothing of it for almost three years! I felt lost and gutted. It would take a while for our resolution to clear through the aikido community. To me, though, I felt like quitting all of it.

I looked at my life at the time and I saw it all coming apart. My relationship with Irene was drifting. My daughters were not relating to me. Aikido, the one practice that meant so much to me, was all lies and illusions. Sure, my professional life was good: I had been accepted by the publishing company I sought to publish my book, and my clientele was strong, but it meant nothing to me. It all panned out to be so superficial compared to the

Hawaiian war deity Kuka'ilimoku.

soul-and-heart world that meant so much more to me. I felt adrift.

This is when my friend, mentor, and shaman Christina Stack guided me on my journey to the Lower World, where I met my Woolly Mammoth Boy spirit guide for the first time. As I related in the Author's Note, it was a profound and life-changing experience for me. Weeks later, Christina suggested I go to the Upper World to meet my teachers and asked if I wanted to meet and speak with my departed dad. It didn't feel like the right time to see Dad, but I made an appointment with Christina to do a journey to the Upper World to meet my teachers.

I realized I could use all the help I could get at this time in my life. I remembered my session with the famous psychic in Manhattan that a friend had treated me to back in the early '80s. The psychic told me the Greek goddess Athena was my teacher during that period in my life, and with typical zealous obsession I studied all I could find about Athena. I shared this information with Christina, and she said "Let's see who you meet in the Upper World this time."

As before, I was recorded, my eyes covered to shut out all light, and I was to speak out loud of all I saw and experienced. My journey to the Upper World began...

"See a path, an upward path leading to the Upper World," Christina directed me.

I saw myself climbing a mountain, a very tall mountain. I reached the summit and jumped upward into a layer of clouds. The clouds supported my body, and I was safe.

"Continue upward."

I walked around on the clouds and saw a ladder to another layer of clouds, a much higher layer.

"Please, continue to ascend."

I climbed upward to reach the upper layer. The sun was bright and clear. The clouds were firm under my feet. They stretched out all around me.

"Walk around here."

This place was so beautiful! I was walking now and...there is Athena! I am walking toward her and she is staring at me. Wait...she is turning to leave me...

"Continue to walk around."

I was walking again. This place was so beautiful and peaceful. I wanted to stay. The sun was so bright and comforting. I saw a figure walking toward me. The figure was dressed like a Hawaiian warrior with a helmet made of flowers and a long cape made of feathers. His skin was a rich brown; he was mighty in stature. He held a shark tooth-tipped spear. He stood before me now, me looking into his eyes. He plunged his spear into my chest piercing my heart! I was bleeding. I felt no pain. I had no fear. My deep, red blood poured from my heart pooling at my feet. He just stared at me. I looked deeply into his brown eyes. He withdrew his spear and stepped back from me. I looked at my chest but there was no wound. I was no longer bleeding. He turned and began to walk away. I was alone.

"You must return now...please retrace your path."

I wanted to stay. I began my path back down.

"You are back. Slowly take breaths and open your eyes, slowly. The journey has ended."

At first I did not know who this Hawaiian warrior was. In researching I found out his name is Kukaʻilimoku. He is the Hawaiian God of War.

Christina shared with me that Kukaʻilimoku, by piercing my heart with his shark-tooth spear, had bled my heart of old energies, the "toxic blood" of my past. Meeting with Kukaʻilimoku made sense for where I was in my life at the time. Now, with the revelations that my animal ally is the woolly mammoth, and that one of my teachers is Kukaʻilimoku, I understood what I must continue to do. My path was clear. I was asked to continue to walk the warrior's path of truth and awareness. I was being asked to remember my strength and joys with compassion for those around me.

The next day I began incorporating into my life what I had learned. I touched my heart where Kukaʻilimoku's shark-tooth spear had pierced me. My heart felt lighter. My world was still filled with challenges of the social relationships I was engaged with—my sensei in Woodstock, my wife Irene, and my daughters. I knew I had to persevere. I was not just going to give up. I questioned myself. I asked questions of Irene for feedback. "How was I communicating with the girls?" "How can I better communicate with them?" "Was I aware when I was in pre-meltdown stage, and what do I need to do to decompress the situation?" I wanted to be better for my family and myself. I still had my desires and self-imposed obligation to serve others. I worked on balancing out my life so that I spent more time listening and less time yapping my jaw and pushing my ways onto the ones I loved. I also realized I was who I was; I was still my father's son. My anger and years of unexpressed grief seemed so close to the surface of my sensitive emotions.

I looked at the relationships I had with other men. The male mentors and brothers I had in my life were few. It seemed I could not hold on to the people dear to me. I thought it might be a lack of trust on my part. My dear friend Charles Revty, who I had known since entering the Woodstock Valley, was no longer talking to me. He shut me out of his life over something very small. One day I was sick and could not see him as we had planned, and when we talked on the phone I felt he was forcing an issue I was not prepared to face. He called me "insensitive and self-centered." I said, "I am sick and cannot get out of bed." He dropped me. Later, I began to think he was mixing his meds with alcohol. I found out about Charles's passing from the obituaries by accident. I was stunned and saddened. Another mentor, Richard Zarro, drifted away. He spiraled into a self-destructive world of addictions, blowing his brains out with a shotgun. Again, I only found out by stumbling on the obituary. His death made me angry. He always told me we were Warriors of Light, and we needed to be here for others. He recognized my power and light and always pushed me to succeed. In the end I had to take space from him because he was losing it with drinking and pharmaceuticals. I would go to his house in the middle of the night on a frantic call from him. Arriving at his house I would find him with a loaded .44 Magnum pistol. Once I talked him down, he would mellow out and then sleep it off. Soon after Richard's death I heard of a gathering of his friends for an opportunity to talk about him. There I had a chance to talk to a mutual close friend of ours.

"So why did he do it?" I asked Peter.

"He wanted it this way. He was estranged from his true love, his daughter, and his health was going quickly."

"That pisses me off, Peter. He always told me we were Warriors of Light and we had to be around to help others. I am angry!"

"Ron, you know he blew his brains out with a shotgun, right?"

"Yes, I heard."

"He did not want to make a mistake and be a burden to anyone. Now that takes guts," Peter said to me.

"I got to go, Peter." We hugged and I left.

I went to Richard's dark house. I broke in, and no one was there. I knew his place. I had to see Richard one last time. I broke the police tape and went into the bedroom where he shot himself. The bed had been removed from the room. The wall behind where the headboard should be was dark with blood splatter and strewn with strands of hair and bits of white bone. I stared at the wall.

"Well damn, Richard, you were not kidding!" I sat on the bedroom floor and stared at the wall. "I will continue to be a Warrior of Light. I will continue to be here for others. Thank you, Richard. Good-bye brother." I left, never to return.

Months passed and my life continued. After closing my first center I looked for other spaces to open another one. I took a while to find a space because the first place I found became mired in major headaches with the owner. It took time to find the right place. Deals came and went and I was left without a place to teach, but my private practice continued to flourish. The ASPIE School closed after a number of years of great service. Though a huge success, the school fell victim to the financial fears and narrow minds of the public school system. It was a drag. Irene was busy with her work; her good friend, a shaman healer, said to Irene that she was working herself to death, and she was forgetting about the relationships closest to her. Irene tried to change, but she was so good for the local autism population, and her personal calling to help others was so strong that she kept up her schedule. I drifted from my aikido training. I delved into other martial arts, but I was restless and lacked peace with my life no matter how I stayed the course. I sought support in meditation from my animal allies, ancestors, and teachers. Soothing as it may have been, I found it challenging to distinguish the illusions of my chattering-monkey fears from what was real. I went into depression.

I helped those who sought my mentoring. I was the best. But when my day was done, I was alone. Irene was always busy in her office. Zoë, our youngest daughter, left home and went to the same private school her older sister Annie had gone to. Our home was empty. Irene and I had been married for a year and a half, though we had been together for almost thirteen years by that time. It was just Irene and me. It was very lonely at times. I knew Irene loved me, and I loved her with all my heart, but I started to think we should part. She was so into her work that she would come in from her home office late and tired. I started to feel that maybe she would be happier with someone else. Maybe I would be happier with some else? We still had good times, yet the fire was burning low. As much as I thought this might be the answer, I threw that idea out the window. Irene was my friend and mate, and I was hers. *Until death do you part.* I felt I was withering, becoming a Ringwraith like in *The Lord of the Rings*, and ready to fade away.

News came one day that Hal, Irene's dad, was not doing well and had to go into the hospital. A year before he had gone in for a minor illness and the hospital screwed up. He had a stroke and the nurses did not catch it. Once a vibrant, independent man—and the most senior of ALL psychologists in New York City—Hal was left with partial speech and loss of motor skills. Hal was a man who woke every morning to play his piano at 4:00 a.m., he was an accomplished jazz musician before and after World War II, and drove to work at his Manhattan office for forty years. Hal was a different man after the stroke, and his body just began to let go. Hal was a fellow Piscean. Irene and I, along with her brother and sister, helped their mother Helen take care of Hal during his final days. I remember playing "Somewhere Over the Rainbow" on my kalimba (an African thumb piano) for Hal as he lay sleeping. He died in his sleep at the age of eighty-nine years old. He was a very, very special human. The night after he died, a large old tree crashed into the house, over where his home office was. Hal was saying goodbye.

The inevitable circle of life and death continued as it does for all beings on this planet. I had grown older since returning to the East Coast. I came as a young man, and now I was in my middle years, though people would always mistake me for being much younger than I was. I never saw myself aging in my mind. I had work to do. I was a warrior serving others. I was on my third marriage, and had lived a life of incredible trials and adventures. I had become a father, and a husband (three times). I was a dancer, musician, carpenter, chef, teacher, martial artist, oil painter, poet, and warrior. I created a practice, BodyKi, to help others, and was going to have a book published. I had destroyed harmony in my home, and provided love and security to those I loved. I was a living paradox like the astrological sign I was born under—Pisces, the two fish swimming in opposite directions, one below and one above. I suffered from post-traumatic stress disorder and traumatic brain injury from childhood beatings and abuse. I was a loved teacher and inspired others to shine and shine. Who was I?

A phone call came from a friend that Christina Stack was found dead in her bathroom, possibly from a mixture of alcohol and pharmaceuticals. My shaman mentor had dealt with her own demons all her life, and now she suffered no more. I went to her funeral. It was packed. Strange, so very strange—the healers need healers. Her death kindled my fire to be strong for those I served and who called upon me for help. Christina would be one of my teachers in the Upper World.

I went to Manhattan for aikido at my aikido home, New York Aikikai. I had been making this weekly trip religiously for years. During one trip I went to the Upper West Side to check out my old neighborhood. Like most of New York, the whole area had changed. It was all gentrified. The great spice of old ethnic neighborhoods was now gone, transformed into white bread and Starbucks coffee city blocks. I was walking in front of a new Barnes and Noble bookstore when I saw a frizzy-haired, old black man begging for money. Our eyes met.

"Filipino young blood!" The tattered grimy street man said to me.

"Mel? Brother!" I reached out to him. People stopped and stared. I hugged him. He smelled fiercely bad. I held on. "Brother?"

"Filipino..." Mel said to me sadly.

"Brother, what the..." I stood looking at him. When we met in 1979 he was my neighbor—a strong, fit, and strapping Caribbean island man working as a bike messenger and teaching me how to be NYC streetwise. It was now 2007, and Mel was a street person. He was skin and bones.

"Brother..."

"Filipino, how is Andrea? That beautiful girlfriend of yours?"

"Damn, Mel, Andrea and I got married, had a beautiful daughter, Josie, and got divorced. She lives in Woodstock. I am married again. Number three."

"You look great, Filipino young blood."

"Mel, what happened?" I asked in a whisper.

"Crack cocaine. Filipino, that shit is bad. I lost everything. I live on the streets up in Harlem. I come down here where I can get money."

We stared at each other. Mel had taught me professional Frisbee throwing in Sheep's Meadow. We had partied together; we were neighbors a million years ago in a time lost to a bright, sunny day in Manhattan.

"Filipino..." Mel started to speak.

"Here is a twenty-spot, Mel." I handed him a crisp twenty out of my wallet. "Look brother Mel, be well, take care of yourself." We clasped in a Roman handshake.

"Filipino, you do the same."

I turned on my heels and headed downtown. I turned one last time. He was looking at me, and then he turned to the opening doors of the Barnes and Noble bookstore and put out his hand for a spare buck. We never saw each other ever again. I was saddened by what had happened to Mel. Once a statue of vibrancy and health, Mel had been reduced to something less than

340 | Mind–Body and the Ground

human by his addiction to crack cocaine. I did not want to remember Mel this way. He would always be my Apollonian frisbee mentor of old...forever.

In December of 2007, I planned a trip to the Philippines. I had last visited there in 1979. My sensei, Yamada Sensei of the New York Aikikai, was making his first trip to Manila. I was the highest-ranking Filipino in the dojo, and I thought it would be a great opportunity to be there for my Filipino countrymen and fellow aikidoists. I also decided to honor my maternal grandfather, Vicente G. Ponciano, a survivor of the Bataan Death March and the first Filipino officer in the United States Navy. I would go to Bataan and go to Kilometer One, where the march started in April 1942.

The journey across the ocean by plane was long and arduous. Once there it was a great trip. I met many great Filipinos who took to me like lost cousins. I was invited to teach aikido on the island of Cebu, where the Spanish bully Magellan lost his head in 1521. It was on my personal journey to honor my grandfather that the whole trip came together. I saw in my mind the thousands of Allied prisoners—Americans and Filipinos—herded sixty-odd miles during the hottest time of year with very little food or water. The Japanese killed many out of cruelty. My grandfather survived. It was his personal story that inspired me as a child sitting on his lap.

I returned to my home in New York, and to Irene, with purpose and

Me at the marker for Kilometer 1 of the Bataan Death March. Author's photo, 2007.

vision. I was reconnected to my Filipino roots. I saw my past and future blend. I was living it all in the moment of each breath I took. In 2008 my book was published. Though it represented only the fundamentals of my work, it was now out in the world. Irene was very instrumental in putting it all together. The publishing company was already known in the field of autism, so it was a great opportunity for me.

September 2008 was like any other September for me, and it meant the NFL season was here again! Having played football in high school, it was the only sport I would watch on TV. I was going to see a new client for his second session on a Sunday, which was something I rarely did, but I could not refuse him. He was a handsome young man who had just turned eighteen years old. His name was Derrick Stroh. He was challenged with learning disabilities, tall, overweight, and had an incredibly beautiful smile. His parents had heard of my mentoring work and after the initial intake session they wanted me to work with their son. Derrick's parents knew about all his challenges, and of the limited future he was facing. I saw a young man who expressed to me that he wanted to change his life, and to me that meant there was no limit to what was possible—as long as he wanted it. I would be there for him. I told the parents Derrick would someday drive a car. They looked at me as if I had two heads. I was very serious. After his first session with me, Derrick was sold. His parents said he came home beaming. He was different in some subtle way, and they noticed a shift in him.

Four days after Derrick's initial session, on NFL Sunday, his mother dropped him off for his second session. He was in poor physical shape and had very little body coordination. His mother said Derrick was medically cleared to see me. The day was warm and humid, so I took it real easy with him. He jumped on the trampoline, which was in the shade. I wanted him to feel his legs underneath him. He was buoyant and giggling. Next he had some water, and then I had him lift two-pound weights so he could begin to organize and coordinate his breathing with his physical actions. I brought him inside to the cool house and continued to do some simple exercises. The session was half-way through. In my living room we did a simple ball workout that he had done in his first session with me. He stood about ten paces from me, and I bounced a small rubber ball to him. He was first to catch the ball with two hands, and eventually, as his confidence grew stronger, he would catch with one hand, alternating left hand and right hand.

I bounced the ball to him and he caught it. He smiled hugely at me as I praised his accomplishment and I smiled back. His smile was infectious. He bounced the ball back to me. I bounced the ball back to him again, but he dropped it this time. He reached down to pick up the ball as I moved toward him to demonstrate how to close his hands strongly and use his hand-eye coordination. As I drew near him he stood up, smiled at me with that big smile of his, and then collapsed.

He fainted. What? This had never happened to me.

I caught him as he fell. He was dead weight and heavy as a mountain. I fell with him trying to lower him and cushion his fall. Derrick was out. I slapped his face a little and called his name. Then I noticed he was having trouble breathing.

Was this really happening?

I immediately laid him flat and cleared his throat. I started CPR.

Was this really happening? This is football Sunday for god's sake! His mom is coming to pick him up in ten minutes!

I got him breathing and he opened his eyes.

"Derrick! Derrick!" Then his eyes closed. He was out again. I did not want to leave him, but I had to run to the kitchen for the phone. I called 911. I was alone in the house.

"What is the emergency?" the operator said.

"My client just collapsed on my living room floor. He is a young man, eighteen years old."

"Is he breathing?"

"I have started CPR. Please send someone!" I tried not to scream.

"Please start CPR..."

"I did! Please send someone!"

"EMTs are on the way. I will talk you through the CPR."

"Okay..."

The voice on the end of the phone I had up to my ear was telling me what I was already doing. I closed his nasal passages and breathed into his mouth. I saw his lungs rise and fall. Just then his mother knocked at the back door. I called her into the house.

Upon seeing her son on the floor of my living room she began to scream.

"HE IS DEAD! DERRICK IS DEAD!!!" She ran out of the living room into the kitchen screaming and crying.

This is really happening! I have to keep going. Do not stop. Keep going!

I began to taste vomit in my mouth, Derrick's vomit. I turned him on his side and cleared his throat and laid him flat and continued CPR. My neighbor was a retired fire captain. He came in the door the same time the EMTs arrived. I was drenched in sweat and continued to do CPR. They checked his pulse and then stood back. They did not even open their bags. Derrick's mom came back in and continued to scream. I looked at my neighbor.

"I have to keep going for her," I said. He nodded. They all watched as I continued to do CPR long after Derrick had died.

His lips were soft upon mine. Like a little baby's lips.

The vomit and fluids were on my lips. Finally, a gurney was brought in. His mom was still screaming in the kitchen, her dead son lying on my living room floor. There were people all around me. I had left my body long ago. Someone came and picked up his mother. They loaded Derrick on the gurney; it took four big Shokan men to do the honor.

When they left, the New York State Police came. They had to investigate. Someone had died. They took pictures of the trampoline. They took pictures of the two-pound weights. They took pictures of the rubber ball. They took pictures where Derrick collapsed and died. Questions and questions. I opened my mouth and answered. They left and I was alone in the house. Irene would come home soon. It did not matter; I was floating in the heavens and pulling tall ripe grass with my woolly mammoth trunk.

On September 21, 2008, Derrick died in my arms. I never got to watch the NFL games that day. I was lost for days afterward. I had asked some brothers from Woodstock to show up to Derrick's funeral as a kind of honor guard. His funeral was packed. The community was stunned by his death and I was told numerous times it was a blessing he had died with me. His mother blamed me. His father told me he was so grateful that Derrick had died on such a beautiful day, and on a beautiful property with a person who loved him and cared for him.

As I stood before the gathered community at the funeral home, I told them all of Derrick's final moments, how Derrick died like a warrior, with bravery in his heart and determination in his veins. He had died doing what he wanted to do—changing his life.

His grandparents came up to me and said the day before he died they saw him and said I had given their grandson Derrick something he had always wanted, and that was validation and having the faith in him that he could succeed. They thanked me. I felt humbled and empty.

I floated for days and weeks. I continued on my path. Derrick was now my teacher in the Upper World. In time I knew I would come to understand why I was there for Derrick. For the time being though, I floated.

Irene and I started to pull our relationship together. We came to terms with our differences and realized we still wanted to be together no matter what. I believe that Derrick's death also awoke in us an understanding of how living life is so fragile and fleeting. We decided to live the rest of our lives together. The girls were all grown up, and we had a life ahead of us. We wanted to continue to work in the field we were in: helping the population with autism was our path and that was fine for us. The summer of 2008 and into 2009 I started to go to Eugene, Oregon with plans to develop my mentoring practice there. Oregon had always stayed in my heart after I had moved away in 1978. I loved the people and the peacefulness of the land. I wanted Irene and me to settle there. She liked Oregon as well. I flew to Eugene once a week and saw clients twice during that time. Within four months of traveling back and forth from New York to Oregon I had built a clientele, and I was making many new connections. I told Irene I wanted to work like crazy so she could stop working. I told Irene I wanted her to take a break, and garden or do whatever she wanted to do. I wanted to build a house for the two of us, and for her to enjoy the rest of her life. The plan was to sell our Shokan home, downsize, and enjoy a stress-free life in Oregon. I was doing fine financially and envisioned writing the BodyKi manual and doing more speaking. Through the years, with Irene's help, I had cleared all my debts and was doing great. Now I wanted to give back to her. I wanted the best for my woman. I had come to the conclusion that Irene and I were two different people who were madly in love with each other. We had fought over raising kids and now our daughters were off on their own. For good or bad we had done our best. There was nothing we could have done differently. It was our karma to be together and that was that.

    I was a carpenter and she was a gardener. We would build and plant a wonderful life for our grandchildren. There may have been other beautiful women for me and other beautiful men for her, but when push came to shove Irene was the woman for me and I was the man for her. We still had our ups and downs. We cried, yelled, and loved. We knew that no matter what had happened in our past, and what would happen in our future, we were very much in love with each other in the present. I had come to terms with the fact that I would choose to relinquish all my rigid thinking mayhem to be a more receptive and loving husband. All my old baggage was just not worth a pot of beans to me; I did not want to go to my grave a bitter man because I drove all those who loved me away because of my ego and past selfishness. I wanted to be Irene's man for the long haul, and this looked like a beautiful future for me and for us. And that was that.

The old one-eyed warrior bull mammoth told Woolly Mammoth Boy a tale as they both trod together behind the slow moving mammoth herd before them.

    "As a young bull like you are now, I once found myself surrounded by a pack of wild hyenas hunting for any stragglers of our migrating herd while we crossed the vast open plain. I had been chosen by the Matriarch to guard the rear of the herd, to check on any mammoth that might be lagging behind and separated from the herd. It was then that I was ambushed in a

Mind–Body and the Ground | 345

deep depression of a dry riverbed."

Woolly Mammoth Boy could imagine, in his mind, this ancient bull mammoth speaking before him trapped in an ambush. He knew this old one-eyed bull was lucky to survive, for a pack of hyenas could easily bring down a mature fighting mammoth by working in concert with each other as a team. Woolly Mammoth Boy listened intently to the tale being told. It was a tale of survival. The law of the herd was that any straggler confronted by predators was to decide whether to place the entire herd at risk for slowing down to stay together, or surrender to the inevitable death and perish so that the herd could survive. The old warrior bull mammoth had been in a similar situation. How did he survive?

"As the pack of these filthy yet highly efficient hunters closed in, I knew my time had come," the old bull mammoth said as he continued his tale. "I knew I would receive no help from the herd because I was acting as rear guard, and all knew I was going to go it alone and not put at risk any other of the herd.

"The sheer mass and weight of this pack of hyenas spelled my doom. Yet I knew that I would not perish, though I knew I might the suffer the consequences."

At this, Woolly Mammoth Boy now knew the answers to how the old warrior bull's vacant eye socket, ripped torn ears, and deep scars that laced his head and chest were inflicted.

"As I quietly and quickly gave thanks to the herd and the Matriarch for my life, the hyenas attacked me. I was bitten and torn by many fangs. I lost my eye to a leaping slashing hyena that I then crushed underfoot. I was almost disemboweled by three that attacked from the rear.

"Woolly Mammoth Boy, I lived to tell this tale to you by my sheer will to survive, and never once did I see my death. I saw in my mind as their attack began that I was invincible! Be not be fooled, young bull, I was most certainly visited by Fear and Doubt.

"Yet I marshaled my mind and willed by body to fight the great odds against me. I became immune to the pains of the serious injuries the hyenas inflicted upon my flesh and hide. I killed many of their number, and the rest finally scattered—I was too high of a price to pay to fill their bellies." At this, the old one-eyed mammoth roared and trumpeted a call of victory.

"Woolly Mammoth Boy, heed me! Never give up—never give in! Your mind is stronger than your body, and your body obeys your mind. So, young one, keep clear your mindful intentions, and then your actions will reflect the pure thought of fearlessness!"

37. In the Land of the Woolly Mammoths

Old Turtle looked up at the massive woolly mammoth grazing next to her and asked, "Brother, what is the view like from up where you stand?"

The woolly mammoth looked down at the aged Old Turtle and said, "Fine, I can see for a long distance. And what is the view from down there little sister?"

Old Turtle slowly answered, "All I see is in great detail from where I stand. I can see Brother and Sister ants working feverishly near my feet. From where I stand I can see that each petal of the flowers next to me is most delicate and oh so intricate."

The woolly mammoth listened to Old Turtle as he tore at some sweet grass from the ground and ate. In between bites the woolly mammoth offered, "If you wish, my sister Old Turtle, I can place you upon my broad back and carry you along much faster than you can travel on your short legs and you could then see for great distances."

The Old Turtle considered the invitation, and then slowly replied with a smile, "I thank thee my massive brother. I like going at my pace down here. I am closer to earth."

–Story retold by Woolly Mammoth Boy

We got back to Shokan, NY, from Oregon at the end of August 2009. Irene and I had spent some time visiting my younger brother Shawn, sister-in-law Karen, and their baby twins, Madison and Tyler, who would turn one year old that September. Shawn had always been in touch through the years and we had kept a good relationship, though I was 11 years older than he. I remembered the night I held my newly born nephew Tyler in my arms soon after his birth the year before; it was two days after Derrick's funeral in New York. Derrick had died in my arms at only 18 years old. I remember Irene looking at me as she offered Tyler for me to hold at the hospital. I was scared. I was so afraid Tyler might die in my arms. Irene soothed me with her spirit and I took Tyler into my arms. I held Tyler tightly; I was not going to let go for anything.

After seeing the family in Creswell, Irene and I drove to the Three Sisters mountains in eastern Oregon. We camped, loved, bickered, and laughed together. We told each other we were in it for the long haul. We just could

Uncle Ron and Tyler. Photo by Irene Brody, 2008.

not see a life without each other—as hard as life together was at times. I knew in my deepest of hearts that I wanted to grow old with Irene and forever be with her. Our time in Oregon was splendid. We planned to go back to New York, sell our Shokan home, and move to Oregon the following year, 2010. I would build a nice little home for us, and we would garden and enjoy the wondrous nature of Oregon. I would support us both as a mentor and author. Irene was going to take a big break, and take her time figuring out what she wanted to do in the next phase of her life. We were so excited and we were so much in love with each other.

September was turning into another beautiful Fall. Irene had a scratchy cough and felt a bit congested in her lungs. She had gone to our family doctor twice before asking for an x-ray. The doctor sent Irene home with an inhaler and said an x-ray was not necessary. Being an asthmatic most of my life I told Irene the inhaler was crap, and we could use nettle teas to keep her clear. She was having so much trouble breathing that she went back to our doctor and said she was going into the hospital for an x-ray that very night. I thought it might be asthmatic pneumonia. I had a client that evening, and so I asked her friend to go in with her. I got a call around 8:00 p.m. on September 23 from the hospital.

"Baby, are you still at the hospital?" I asked after picking up the phone.

"Yes, I am. They took an x-ray. They found something. I am with a lung specialist." Irene paused on the phone. "Ron, she does not think it's a pneumonia."

"Irene, what could it be if it is not pneumonia?"

"Ron, the specialist thinks it is cancer."

Silence.

"Ron? The doctor thinks it is lung cancer."

"Baby, I am coming down to the hospital right now." I could barely breathe.

"Ron, I am with Lainey. I will be home soon." Irene sounded so far away.

"Irene, come home. Come home right now Irene...I love you."

I sat in the darkened living room for an eternity until I heard a car pull up in the driveway. I ran to the back door. Irene was there waiting.

I opened the door, grabbed her, and held her tightly.

"Baby..." We walked inside and sat in silence in the living room. We held each other. I thought this was some huge mistake. Cancer? Irene, who had never smoked and was so healthy? Finally, I spoke.

"Irene, they do not know for certain."

"Ron, there is a mass in my right lung. Just where I have been feeling tight all this time for the last few years. Ron, remember when I remarked I felt pregnant this summer in Oregon?"

"Yes."

"I think the cancer had started already."

I wanted to scream and get angry at the whole f*cking world! I wanted to lash out and protect Irene. How could this be happening to Irene? How could we tell our girls?

"Ron, more tests will be done," Irene said quietly.

"Irene, I am with you no matter what. I will cancel all my clients and go with you."

Silence.

That night we lay in bed holding each other, snuggling warmly like we had always been able to do for years; we were one.

"Baby, no matter what anyone says, no matter what you face, you are coming out of this. We will do whatever it takes. I am with you forever."

The tests confirmed our worst fears. Irene had Stage IV lung cancer in her right lung. The prognosis was one year to live at most. She was not a smoker, and had eaten healthfully most of her life. How could this be?

Hold on Ron! This is what you have trained your whole life for. You have trained to protect and preserve life. Irene will live on and she will make it. Have no fear. Vision. Affirm. Do your healing work that you know you are capable of doing. NO FEAR!

"Baby, you are going to survive this cancer. I know you can do this. No matter what you are faced with, you will survive! I am going to be with you. We will do this together."

"I hear you, Ron. I will kick this!" Irene was strong, young, and vibrant.

"We are going to beat this with love and positive energy, light and heat."

"Ron, help me keep this together. Help me to devise a program."

"Baby, I am on it!" I was bright and determined. This was my wife, and that was that!

"Baby, this cancer picked the wrong person to f*ck with!" I declared. "We are going to kick some serious ass on this cancer!"

"Ron, we have to call the girls," Irene said. Annie was in living in Massachusetts. Josie was living in Manhattan. Zoë was in Venezuela. All the girls were out of college except for Zoë. I made the calls. Josie came the next day. Annie came soon after. Zoë came a bit later. It was great to have our daughters home with us. Irene needed them. I needed them.

Two nights after finding out Irene had cancer, I made a decision. I decided then and there I would do what needed to be done. I began to do deep energy work on her as she slept. I began the process of drawing out the cancer from her lung and taking it on for myself. This is what I had trained for all my life. All my healers told me I had special energy to heal others. I wanted the cancer. I had no doubt I would be successful in taking this cancer from Irene and fighting it from within my body. Should this cancer run amok, I felt our daughters would be better off having Irene around than me—should one of us have to go. The girls would have their mother. Josie would understand. I believed Irene was far more precious than me. Letting my hands hover over Irene's right lung, I worked quietly in the dark hours of the night. I wanted this cancer. This cancer was mine. Irene would not be threatened.

Irene awakened the following morning feeling comfortable and rested. She felt new energy. I was overjoyed by her smile. I was doing my job. I was doing my service. Then, one night, three nights after I had started, I stopped. This was not right! This was Irene's life. This was her path, her karma. What right did I have taking control of her life? What right did I have to take away Irene's power to heal herself? I released myself from the task. I decided I would do whatever Irene wanted to do, and go wherever she wanted to go. I did not tell her what I had been doing.

At one appointment Irene's oncologist was clear and let us know the odds were against her. However, being young and strong made her a great candidate for traditional cancer treatments. Irene said no to this path. Her first husband had died of melanoma, she had seen the effects of the cancer treatments he had gone though.

"Ron, I am not going to do radiation and the treatments Ricky went through. I am not going to lose my hair, and be sick and throwing up blood. I would rather live one year doing this my way."

"Irene, I am with you in whatever you want to do. I am with you, no questions asked. What you want, you will get."

All my life I had gone against the odds. I had gone against what people said I could not do. Irene shared this fire. We were both rebels and we were going to fight. I knew I had to be strong for her and the girls. I had to be fearless and brave. To describe my belief that Irene would recover from Stage IV lung cancer as "denial" just did not hold water for me. I believed in the mysteries of the Great Universe, and had seen miracles up close. It had been just one year since Derrick died in my arms. I believed his death prepared me for this life-and-death battle for Irene's life. To say I was blind to the enormity of what my beautiful Irene faced was not true. I was scared and doubting, but I threw those thoughts out the window quickly. We were in battle. There could be no place for fear—*phobia*—to be in my consciousness, in my breath, mind, or body. I had trained my mind and body for this moment. I had trained people, young and old, for the last twenty-five years in preparing to face their individual battles with darkness. I was a Warrior of Light. Irene was going to beat this cancer, and we would grow old and be grandparents with grandkids playing at our feet.

The next two months were filled with tests and health programs to slow the cancer down. Driving and doctor's appointments packed our time. I could not work; in fact, I did not want to work and canceled my clients. I wanted to be by Irene's side at all times. This was what a husband was supposed to do. I did not give a shit what other people said I should be doing for myself. Irene's life was at stake, and I was going to be by her side. Irene's leg and her back started to hurt. It was hard for me to be close to her. I could not even snuggle up at nighttime to comfort her. She was in too much pain.

Her right lung needed to be drained of fluid build-up. My baby was very uncomfortable, but hardly complained. The girls and I admired her strength and spirit. We fed off it. And when the night came and the girls huddled amongst themselves, I was alone with Irene. I hardly slept and lay awake just listening to her breathe. *Be strong. Release fear and doubt.*

I set a routine for Irene to follow. It included all her times to eat, rest, meditate, and her many appointments. Annie and Josie did tons of cancer treatment research. When Zoë finally arrived, she jumped right on in. The extended family gave moral support and more research. Irene's fifty-fourth birthday came around on November 21. All her friends showed up. Irene looked beautiful and strong. There was great light and energy surrounding her. I breathed and relaxed; there were others to hold her up and give her strength.

"Irene, you are not staying here for the winter. You are going to move out west. There is no way you are staying during the snow and cold," I said to her after her birthday. Soon I began researching a move to San Diego, California. Annie and Irene's sister-in-law out in LA found a rental in La Jolla. The place was bright and beautiful. Annie and I would move Irene out there and set-up house. Zoë would follow. I would go back to New York, check on our Shokan home, and try to see my clients. I would also try returning to Oregon. The girls were going to be with Irene, and I had to close up relationships with my clients correctly.

New Year's 2010 was quiet and subtle. Irene loved La Jolla and the bright sun of Southern California. "This is where I want to live," she said. When I came to visit, I saw my old controlling self raise up from of the depths. I wanted to control a very uncontrollable and fearful situation: my wife had 4th stage lung cancer. I felt helpless and so I wanted to clamp down. Thank the Great Spirit for our daughters, who stepped up and helped relieve the stress that was killing me. I felt that through discipline and focus Irene could kick ass on her cancer. I realized it was too much for me to go to New York, and then Oregon, and then to La Jolla. Irene said it was all right and that she could handle her routine. Annie had to go back to her life and Zoë needed to get back to hers.

I ended my travels and moved out to La Jolla to be with Irene full time. We found a smaller place to live, a place called Windansea Beach. It was a two-minute walk to the beach. It was perfect for her. We shipped Irene's car, a Mini Cooper, out to La Jolla. I drove her everywhere and tried to prepare all her morning meals and attend to her other needs. Trying all that I could, we still argued at times over tiny, meaningless crap. "Please do your exercises now!" "Drink your teas, now not later!"...on and on, I tried to make order for myself by controlling the situation. I felt like shit because I was causing her disharmony, but sometimes I was just too overwhelmed. Because of Irene's discomfort, we were not intimate. Irene's routine in La Jolla was filled with appointments and ongoing tests. Her traditional oncologist and doctors were narrow-minded. They were infuriating to deal with and I wanted to punch them out. I didn't realize I needed recharging and my own comfort. I started to do my own training.

I awoke every morning before dawn and went down to the beach. I had my morning coffee while I did my meditation reading facing the great Pacific Ocean. Then I would enter the pounding surf and stand where the waves broke, and do my breathing exercises. I finished in time to begin Irene's breakfast and her morning rituals. Irene had strength for her Qi Gong exercises. She had lost weight but still looked healthy. We spent my fifty-third birthday, in March 2010, at a favorite place of hers: Joshua Tree National Park. It was great for the most part. I caught myself when I was being rigid and thickheaded with Irene with my oh-so-caring but demanding suggestions.

To me Irene's journey was all too surreal and very real at the same time. We were together, and yet not together. Irene was fighting a deadly cancer and I was on the outside. I wanted so much for her to survive this cancer that I was going crazy. It was a place of dreams and magic, but this was a deadly dream where death lurked right behind the light.

By June 2010, Irene's health was showing small signs of stability and holding the line. Her cancer cell count was up and down. Her oncologist wanted to get serious with radiation treatments. Irene refused. Annie and others found a doctor in Germany whose methods for treating cancer relied on the patient's own immune system. It sounded perfect for Irene. Through long-distance phone calls spanning the many time zones from California to Germany, Dr. Lentz said he had space for Irene if she wanted to come. By the end of June, Irene's health became crucial enough to make the decision to go to Germany. The treatment would be costly and a logistically challenging endeavor. We would have to live in Germany.

"I have to go to Germany, Ron," Irene said to me one evening after getting back test results that showed her cancer cell count was up again.

"Baby, let's go! I do not care where we have to go and what we have to do. We are going to do what you want to do," I said to her with a smile.

"Ron, this could wipe out our savings."

"So what! Money is money. I am a worker and I will work. Money means nothing to me. You are the most important thing in my life and that is that!"

We hugged and held each other tight.

We worked out all we needed to work out about our belongings and our place in La Jolla. Annie would fly with her mom and me to Germany. The *Klinik* in Germany found us a place to live long-term, and we secured a car.

By July 26, 2010, we were in Prien, Germany. Prien, the town where the Klinik was located, is in the southern Bavarian Alps and borders Austria and Italy. The town we lived in was called Bad Endorf.

One of the local attractions in the deep valleys of the southern Bavarian Alps was that, in prehistoric times, this land was home to the woolly mammoths! Irene and I would do just fine here! Irene was going to do just fine here! This was an area of ancient power and strength. I felt relieved. I was home—I was in the land of the woolly mammoths!

With the Matriarch leading her woolly mammoth herd, they entered the wide lush valley. The journey that coursed through the deep ravines and canyons were the hunting grounds of the feared saber-toothed tigers and ferocious mountain cave bears took many of her herd. Yet the Matriarch protected the survivors, with her bull mammoths battling the whole way. As she broke through the last remaining ambush sites, the Matriarch initiated a stampede to freedom.

They had reached the promised land of old.

Before them now lay the home grounds of the woolly mammoths. Ample feed and fresh water was abundant. It was here that all mammoth herds, led by their Matriarchs, met for their annual mass gathering. It was a time to share tales and valuable information of lands discovered on their separate sojourns across the wild earth. The Matriarchs held their own counsel to initiate and accept the new Matriarchs that had taken the places of ones who had died while on their separate journeys.

The valley (which in the distant future would become the rich pasturelands of the Bavarian Alps in southern Germany) was steeped in healing and rest. It was here that prehistoric mammals of proto-Western Europe gathered, rejuvenated kinship bonds, and grew strong.

The woolly mammoth herds were just one speck of the multitudes of life

The Matriarch leads the way.

forms that flourished during this ancient time in Earth's history. It was the promise of precious life that drew them all, It was the promise of vitality and deep healing that for hundreds of years drew them all, guided by the sacred routes embedded in their cellular ancestral memory. They had just to survive the arduous journey to get here.

I trumpeted a call of victory that spurred the whole mass of gathered woolly mammoths to join in. Hundreds upon hundreds of individual calls reverberated and shook the very earth, startling the little ones and sending to flight all the feathered ones.

"*We made it! We will continue to survive!*"

Part 7:
The Fury of Fire and Ice

38. The Journey of Irene Bell Blue Pele Old Turtle

Great tales are told by the light of the fire so as to remember all that was of the grandeur and bravery, of the darkness and fierce storms. Yet, be not mistaken—the strength in the tale lives in the listener, so as to pass on to others.

—Woolly Mammoth Boy Speaks

THE FOLLOWING ARE EXCERPTS FROM e-mails I sent back to family and friends in the USA during Irene's and my time in Prien, where Irene began cancer treatment[1] under Dr. M. Rigdon Lentz. I don't have the words, or the emotional distance, to summarize or write about this time in a new way. Not yet. For now, these email messages I wrote from Germany to the team of family, friends, and loved ones who were praying for Irene across the world will tell this story for me.

2010 JULY 26

Bad Endorf, Germany

Hello from Deutschland,

The Germans, what can you say about them? Very orderly, very hearty, very friendly (even when they are scowling at me), and oh so…German! The countryside is very beautiful with that fairytale quality of a scene from Hansel and Gretel. Our place we call "home" is a 10-minute drive from the clinic in the town of Bad Endorf. We have a room with a breathtaking view of the Bavarian Alps and Lake Simssee.

Our guest room for visitors is down the hall. We have a kitchen with a hotplate stove, and mini-refrig and bathroom with a great shower with really hot water and very cold water. Most Germans are mostly friendly, except some women and men who look at me as if I am on the wrong side of the tracks and should get back where I came from…I am the only person of color I have seen. The German kids and some real old folks look me at as a real novelty piece—like a dark gypsy crossing the border and passing through the area with the traveling circus.

---

1. After Irene was diagnosed with Stage IV lung cancer on September 24, 2009, we sought alternative therapies to combat her illness. The family found a cancer treatment in Prien, Germany. By June 2010, her cancer had become so aggressive it was decided immediately to go to Germany and begin treatments.

Bad Endorf, Germany

Today is Tuesday and the treatment is starting. Due to a money logjam we could not begin yesterday—frustrating!!!! Yet all is cool and under control here in the Fatherland. Rain is the weather and that is okay with us. We are here at the clinic and Irene is getting hooked up for the first cancer ass-kicking session...YAAAAAAYYY!!!!!! Those cancer assholes will not know what hit them! It has been an up-and-down emotional ride for me, and I am so happy this day is finally here. Irene's immune system is so strong and her spirit is so in line to do what needs to be done.

Annie is rockin' the house with learning German, and her native dress except her boots. She has taken many pictures of cows—they love her—they moo to her in her dreams! Irene has been doing well, eating what she wants and getting rest.

It seems after the first session her immune system will be rockin' quite severely on those asshole cancer cells. As they die and her system works on disposing them, she will have a very high fever—a good sign, but it can be uncomfortable for her. I plan to make some chicken broth and veggie soup.

Organic foods here are called "bio" foods. Sounds kinda futuristic! Oh... one day at a time. Breath and light. I am constantly staying grounded by focusing my mind and clearing all fearful and limiting thoughts...this can be challenging to me at times.

I prevail.

Bad Endorf, Germany

Dear family: The fourth day started early as usual @ 0900. The Bavarian Alps are a spectacular view to see every day as we come into the clinic. Irene's brother Jon is here from the States. Irene's treatments are going forward with results that are okay for the first third of our 1st round of treatments. Irene is having treatments every day rather than every other day. She is strong like a Bavarian cow! (She is a helluva lot better looking of course than one of those four-legged mammals! Annie loves cows and they love her!)

The usual high fever that indicates one's immune system is kicking in as the cancer blockers have been filtered out of her blood has not been present except for the first day of treatments. Needless to say this news made Irene and me concerned, but the staff and current and former patients tell us that each person is different and the first days of treatment results do vary. With this in mind they are going to up the amount of blood to be filtered.

The strategy to the treatment is that the amount of blood filtered by cancer blockers will start the destruction phase of the elimination of the cancer by the immune system response. This phase would be best matched by the body's ability to heal and fill the voided spaces where the cancer was with new healthy tissue, as well as the body's ability to expel the waste matter of dead cancer cells and tumor tissue. (There you go as reported by Dr. Ron Rubio—I am not really a doctor, but would like to be when I grow up!)

At the Klinik, Prien, Germany

Day 5—2nd week of treatments, August 2nd—Dear family, friends, and fellow Germans (Oops! Got carried away), Irene started the second week of treatments and her 5th treatment total. Irene is tough as nails and strong like the Alps! Her 1st weekend after a week of treatments was marked with a high fever...mellowing out by Sunday...just what the doctor ordered! The first three treatments did not wake the immune monster inside of her, and we were wondering when it would.

This week marks the two-thirds point in a three-week cycle. They were planning for her to finish with a 15th treatment in three weeks if her body responds in a way which allows for the healing as well as the destruction of the cancer to occur at the same time. So every-day treatments is great only if her body says so. Quality over quantity.

Friday July 30—4th treatment—the beast finally woke up and was really, really pissed off at the cancer big time! Irene ranged from intense, teeth-chattering, hot-water-bottles cold...followed by an excellent, cancer-killing, white-searing heat peaking at 103.7 for a couple of hours! Dr. Lentz called and checked in over the weekend. He is very cool, confident, and caring.... Irene and I feel that since her immune system was untouched by chemo and radiation treatments, her immune system just wanted to keep on kicking some serious ass until they ran out of juice. So Irene had a real hot weekend, and it was not with me! Brother Jon has been very helpful both as a German interpreter and cooking a very nice veggie soup Saturday night.

We miss Annie (who left on Thursday) a whole bunch, and I am so happy that she is back in the USA cooling out and re-charging. I hope her German doesn't get too rusty while she is away from the Fatherland! Josie is due here this Wednesday/Thursday Aug 5th.

So now there will be at least two black-haired people in southern Germany and *Nien!* We are not lost, and *Nien!* We are not opening an Asian restaurant in Prien soon!

12:36 p.m., at the Klinik, Prien, Germany

Just off the press! I just talked to Irene—she gets a 15-minute break if she is awake. Dr. Lentz believes the liquid is gone from her lung! He hears nothing, though the pleura is still inflamed. Her heart is back where it should be in her thoracic cavity instead of being displaced by the former liquid mass!

Though her fever has not come yet, her body is still working on kicking ass! Irene feels so much better and knew about the absence of the liquid before Dr. Lintz said anything to her. Like she has always said to all the doctors, "I know my body! Listen to me!"...

Some people have been kind enough to ask how I am doing with all this...well... I am butt-tired and I have been sleeping about 2-4 hours at night, feeling ready to really go to sleep about 15 minutes before I awaken by my internal clock at 0600. Isn't that the way it usually is though? Like trying to sleep before catching a flight! There is much to do before we leave our hotel for the clinic at 0830. I prepare, and set it up for Irene so she can just keep moving without having to deal with any logistical B.S. like cooking, cleaning-up, getting the meds up, etc. While Irene is washing up, though, I do go for a short walk and enjoy the Bavarian mountain air—ah, the smell of fresh cow dung—so sweet, so light. I train every day on the weapons systems I know: aikido sword and staff, and Filipino stick. I stretch, and in fact, I am able to do some very deep ballet plies and some very high kicks. I thought those days were over for my body! I use the balcony rail as a ballet barre and give the folks a real show.

Yesterday, I took my first nice, long stroll in the very hot Bavarian sun as Irene rested at home. I found a very beautiful and fast-moving stream where I sat and watched the long, green streambed reeds sway with the gentle flow of the stream's current. Very calming.

Letting go because life is always in motion—if I like it or not. The water was very clear and cool. These short moments alone allow me to cry and shout and just let go. In the deepest place in my heart I have great faith in Irene being able to heal herself and kick ass on this cancer with a little help from the treatments. Yet naturally, phobia rears its head and challenges me constantly...the chattering and blah, blah, blah of darkness and sadness. I breathe deeply and give phobia a great big kick in the face and *Ciao Bella* baby! There will be the day we will all look back at these crazy unpredictable days and wonder...how in the hell did it all start...the whys...the maybes and the great ifs! And we will all say how it is so amazing how she kicked ass on the friggin' odds that were stacked up against her last September 2009. And some day I will rest...but not now! It is an amazing tale to tell. Peace to my friends and family.

Miss you all.

At the Klinik, Prien, Germany

Treatment Day #6—Well, well, well! Dr. Lintz wanted Irene to have a day off for her body to catch up with destroying the cancer to allow the healing of her body and filling the spaces voided by the cancer with new healthy cells! Oh, yeah Baby! That is what the doctor ordered! Irene feels great and had a wonderful STEAK dinner last night. I was amazed at this feast. This is the first red meat she has eaten in over year and a half. I have been on protein shakes and smoked fish and herring and...Boy, it is great to eat red-blood meat once in a while. We all had great energy after our meals. Josiegirl arrives tomorrow! Jon leaves tomorrow...sigh! It has been a real joy having Jon here. He is funny, and oh-so-German! So today is another strong workday for Irene. I am so proud of her and she deals with all the shit she has to put up with, with great elegance, beauty, and strength. Daughters, take heed of your Mother's great example of perseverance and fighting, kick-ass spirit!

Our German is still very minimal, at least mine is. Irene studies while she is having her treatments through her language tapes. I want to learn how to say something special to the German folks who find it all right to just stare at me as if I am a zoo animal on the loose amongst them. From kids to older folks, they just stare at what they perceive as an American Indian in their presence. On the Hawaiian Islands we have a saying when someone is staring at you in a way that is rude or inappropriate: "What? Do I owe you money or something?" Perfect!

I think the German translation of this would be a bit too much and they would not get the sarcasm of it. I tried to dress more conservatively, but my long black hair and dark brown skin is a dead giveaway. So I really do not care and wear my tank top shirts and dress for a Hawaiian summer and be as comfortable as possible.

I have much more important things on my plate.

At the Klinik, Prien, Germany

Day 7–Day 8. The days here started with cool grey skies. It seems we get a couple of days of sun and then a couple of days rain. Wednesday was a plasma-replacement day only. Amazing to see the amber-colored plasma go out, replaced by this very clear plasma. Simply amazing technology! Yesterday, she had a "shake and bake" filtration session—this is to say you experience extreme chills and then a ravaging fever. The weekend is a time to sleep in, and that means around 7:00 or 8:00 a.m. Irene seems to be changing in her energy field. To me it seems that her mind/body is more in control, and more awake to what is going on inside and the battle it must continue to wage. She is eating a little bit more substantially, and she is getting rid of her toxins more on her own. Her body is really awake now!

For me, certain store staff where I buy our supplies are beginning to recognize me and are so gracious in allowing me to fumble and stumble in my German communication with them. It is still a "point at and mime" kinda communication with a total butchering of their language.

We hope all is well back home.

Bad Endorf, Germany

Today is the first day of Irene's week off from treatments. Her first round of treatments was for a total of 12 sessions in all. She will begin her second round on August 23rd. One of the other ladies, a client who is a dancer from NYC with an irreversible cancer—so her oncologist had told her—brags how she is on her 19th session and rocking the house! We all share in her joy and cheer her on as we all cheer each other on. It is very touching and makes me want to cry at times for all the hope and faith we have for each other and ourselves. The cancer patients, we the caregivers, and the staff are all in this incredible environment of healing. Irene and I awoke late—0830—this morning and I tell ya, I could have slept for another 24 hours, though I know that would be completely impossible for me because it is in my blood and bones to pop up awake at 0600 all the time.

Josiegirl left Sunday at 0530 and went back to her job in NYC this morning crisp and sharp...way to kick it Josie! Josie's visit was a real pleasant energy to have and was a big help like Annie girl and Jon were. On Saturday we all (including Irene!) visited Salzburg, Austria. I scooted up *zee* Autobahn at a measly 140 kilometers/hour. There were quite a few Audis, BMWs, and Porches zippin' past me...show offs! I was driving an Opal, a family car, or I would have challenged them to a race. I was pushin' it though...pedal to the metal! The damn steering wheel was shakin' in my hands! I thought I would lose some screws or something! FUN!

Austria is the homeland of my stepfather, Horst Herman Victor Hittenberger. He told me that where we are in Prien, Germany, and the Chiemsee area, is about 50 kilometers from where he grew up. I was very happy to be so close to where he grew up.

The days have been long and the nights seem longer for me. Irene has been sleeping better and has been waking less. Yet I will be checking in on her as she sleeps—listening to her breath and waking if she coughs—then I am awake. I am in warrior mode and caregiving mode, and it is a hard mode to get out of and let my guard down. It has been like this for a while. I am happy to report that Irene is eating quite well and gaining a little weight...a little. We love everyone so much and I thank you for all your continued prayers and positive thoughts for Irene's continued success in her health journey.

At the Klinik, Prien, Germany

Today finishes Irene's one week off from treatments.... Irene's right hip started to hurt. Thursday Irene was not able to stand at all for one complete day and was in terrible pain in bed. The x-ray revealed that she was negative on the hip fracture; the x-ray showed the cancer cells in her right hip, left hip, and lower back...we knew this already. Bottom line was that Irene and I overdid her rehab training, and she had severe tendon strain in her right hip. Heavy Ibuprofen and she was comfortable for the evening. Whew!!! Going to the hospital emergency retraumatized me and I was drained from the whole experience...nothing a little Indian food could not help out with afterward.

New clients from the USA showed up Friday. It is truly amazing to see everyone getting better from the various cancers they are challenged with. We caregivers—spouses—are steadfast and we support each other with banter of our terrible experiences back in the States due to the tunnel-vision oncologists we had to deal with. The oncologists in the USA are truly lost, and to a person here at the Klinik our individual experiences are identical.

At the Klinik, Prien, Germany

The summer days are here in the Bavarian Alps...warm, slightly muggy, and chances of summer rain. I was out doing my usual Monday: dropping off laundry, shopping, cleaning the apt, and for the first time since getting here in July, I took a one-hour nap from 1200-1300! I was very refreshed and ready for the rest of the day. The whole weekend Irene was very uncomfortable and unable to leave the apt for four days. She walks around the apt with a hiking staff I found...she looks like Moses coming out of the desert!

Her cancer cell count was at 210 when we arrived here in Germany with her other body signs looking very bad. As of last week her cancer cell count was down to 143! If Irene continues at the current pace of her strong immune system we might be looking at another 60-point drop in her cancer cell count to 80 or less by September 10th.

It will be the one-year mark since Irene first being diagnosed with Stage 4 lung cancer on September 24, 2009! Amazing healing.

As I write this it is 2126 on Monday night. She sleeps after a good "shake and bake" session today at the Klinik. I made a nice meat pasta dish and put her to bed. Her fever is down and she sleeps comfortably. I will join her. It was another good day of healing and kicking serious booty on cancer!

At the Klinik, Prien, Germany

Dear Annie, Josie, Jon, and Eve, I am hoping I can get a break and come back to Shokan, NY and start major work closing up the Shokan home for the winter. I have been here since July and could use a break....

Speaking quite frankly with all of you...my business in the USA is completely gone. I have no work. I have no real inspiration to start up anything or get back to anything. I am quite honored to be part of Irene's healing journey, and I am quite drained as well by it. I am prepared, though, to stay with Irene as long as Irene is in this process of healing here in Germany. ...Everything pales to what is happening here. So please confer with each other and see what can be done about someone coming to stay with her for a while.

At the Klinik, Prien, Germany

This finishes the third day of the second round of treatments, and Irene has had fevers for all three days in a row after coming home from the Klinik. This is a great sign! It seems that Irene's immune system is really understanding its job now. Ralph Moss has recently put out his most recent report on Dr. Lentz's work here in Germany. Please google "Moss Reports" and download the following PDF file: "Unleashing the Immune System: New Insights Into Cancer."[2] This report explains how the procedure works, and is a great resource for anyone you may know that is getting the oncologist's runaround in the USA and needs serious help.

Here in the Klinik every cancer patient and their spouse/caregiver tell of their sad and depressing experience in the USA. They come here after reading about it and tell their doctors to jump off a short pier.

---

2. See the Defeat Osteosarcoma blog: http://defeatosteosarcoma.org/2010/08/unleashing-the-immune-system-new-insights-into-cancer/.

People are healing here. *Really healing.*

Irene has been using crutches here because of the right hip challenges. As the cancer in her bones is dying and exploding, this process puts pressure on the bones and this must hurt like crazy. She is getting around better and slowly the pain is decreasing.

A letter from Irene to family planning to visit

Dear Eve, Annie, Josie, Jon and Zoë,

Glad to hear you are thinking of coming out. Let me explain what is involved and perhaps this will help with the decision-making, or scare you away! I am currently having difficulty entering and leaving cars, thus I ride in the front (just thinking of Mom). While I am in treatment, someone else usually runs chores such as buying food and dropping off laundry, once a week.

Usually, Ron makes my coffee enema and oatmeal breakfast, my dinners, and does all the dishes as I am pressed for time and also low on energy during treatment. The kitchenette is 2 burners, a small fridge and sink—tiny, closet-sized but serviceable. I can sometimes go out to eat—especially on Saturday and Sunday night—but the rest of the time I may be too tired and have a fever. I am pretty flexible with what I eat, though I am no longer sticking to the meat-free, gluten-free challenge. In the apartment, I am usually okay on my own, but if my fever is high it is wonderful to have company and some extra attention (getting some tea or whatever). Ron washes my hair once a week and cleans the apt and changes all sheets twice a week.

We leave the hotel at 8:40 a.m. and usually get back around 5:00 p.m., but you are free in between. The hotel does not have internet service so we use the service at the clinic, although rumor has it that there is an internet café somewhere.

Five nights a week Ron gives me an injection of Leukine—just under the skin, like a diabetes shot, but I haven't yet mustered the courage to shoot myself up! Not for the faint of heart, or faint of needles.

The room we are in could sleep 4. There are two twins and a firm comfortable couch bed—not a pull out, but it is free-standing. However, there's one bathroom and I use it for 1 hour in the morning before I leave weekday mornings. Still doing that coffee thing, which I find helpful. Right now Ron just showers and does all the morning routines before I get into the bathroom which is around 7:15 a.m. With more than 2 people it might be hard, unless only one person gets up to help me and take me to the clinic, and then it would work.

On the plus side, I am able to go on excursions on weekends. The immediate area has trails for hiking and a hot mineral bath, and lots of things to do and see, very picturesque villages and scenery, great beer, and potatoes with every meal.

Love, Irene

At the Klinik, Prien, Germany

Today is the second day of the second round of treatments for Irene. She has recovered from her inflamed right hip and now she can walk more comfortably. The Klinik is packed with a full house of nine clients. They all have very different cancers that have metastasized into their lungs, unlike Irene whose cancer started in her lungs.

The weather this weekend turned into an early Fall-like coolness with blustery winds and gales. The distant Alps seemed to be the playground of the thunder gods and the wind spirits for they were wrapped in dark grey clouds swirling and hanging onto the high peaks.

By Sunday Irene and I were able to take a road trip that took us in a very wide circle deep into the Alps bordering Austria. It is so hard on her, and hard on me watching all of her pain and being helpless to relieve her being so uncomfortable. In my heart I know she is kicking ass on the cancer, and that is the redeeming factor.

At the Klinik, Prien, Germany

Irene's sister, Eve, her son Henry little-man, and our youngest daughter Zoë will be coming here for Irene's off week before she starts her third round of treatments on September 20th. I will be coming back to the States and Shokan, NY for a week off and then back to Germany for the last round. I am looking forward to the week off—the first one since May.

At the Klinik, Prien, Germany

THE GOOD NEWS IS OUT! A lung drain was performed last week and a sample was obtained of the fluid in her pleura of her right lung.

Results: There were NO CANCER CELLS FOUND IN THE SAMPLE!!!! Doctor Lentz indicated that there was a lot of debris in the sample: dead tumor and cancer cells were found but that was about it! I am so proud of her and so damn happy for her. There is still more work to do—to build back her weight, strength, and stamina, but she has kicked the cancer out of her lung!

6:19 a.m., Bad Endorf, Germany

Irene burned through the night. Her spirit and body did not give those little cancer cell creeps and tumors a place to hide or an inkling of mercy! Burn the disco down!

She ate quite heartily, and was ready for her last day of the second round! Incredible!

Bad Endorf, Germany

I spent the early morning today at the Klinik as Irene slept in and had a chance to talk to Dr. Lentz. He said the following: "Ron, you know that Irene's response to the treatment is not what I expected. With Irene's cancer, which is a very aggressive cancer, there is only a 4% chance of survival 4-5 months after the initial diagnosis. She is going on one year this month, way past anyone's expectation or any known data on small cell lung cancer that had also seriously metastasized to other parts of the body. Her unusual bouts of temperature [like today I was thinking] her inflammations at known tumor sites, her recent fluid sample showing the presence of dead cancer cells from her pleura, her steady decline in her CEA numbers (cancer cell count in her blood)—Ron, these are significant indicators. Her body should be completely saturated with cancer cells and these tumors would be only getting larger and her body's systems being compromised significantly according to the information that I am currently getting. Irene's progress is really off the charts. Ron, there is more here at work than we know. Irene is doing very well."

Munich Airport

As I await my flight back to Newark airport, NJ, I can actually take a breath from the hectic weeks I have experienced since May and arriving here in Germany in July. Irene continued through the night with a fever; she sweated, tossed, turned, and was generally very uncomfortable. I did not sleep much and was bummed out she was so uncomfortable and had to go through what she did, but the more she fevered the more she was killing cancer cells and tumors.

The lobby is filled with Americans all speaking English—weird! The energy is already starting to become edgy and frantic, very different than the low-key, take-it-slow Bavarian pace I have been living. The eight-hour nonstop flight back to the US is going to be my time to do my Zen training in breath, body calmness, and pretending I am the only passenger on the plane out of 300+. Josie girl will meet me at the airport and then take the two-hour drive up to Shokan. What a real mind/body trip. One moment Bavaria, next moment—same day—Catskill Mountains!

At the Klinik, Prien, Germany

I just got back to Germany after a week of rest in Shokan, NY. My beautiful sister Valerie and her man Mark surprised me at the airport. They came in from San Francisco to pick me up at Newark airport and took care of me for the first two days—very, very sweet and a great surprise! After that, I hardly left our Shokan property the whole time. Those friends who came out to visit were few. I rested, played a lot of billiards, and basically did nothing. I saw my beautiful daughters, Annie and Josie, briefly.

I could not think very much while I was in Shokan. I was very pooped out and way over stimulated from the Newark airport, an 8-hour flight, and being around overweight, out-of-shape Americans. (It is amazing and very refreshing to see 60-75 year old Germans riding bikes and moving around quite briskly back in Germany!) The last thing I wanted to do was chores.

Irene is strong and ready for this last three and a half weeks of sessions. She is still coughing and a little tight with her breathing when the air is cool. She had a great time with her sister, Eve, nephew Henry, and our youngest daughter Zoë during her time off.

Thank you Eve, Henry, and Zoë for being such a bright light in Irene's life. Coming back to the USA for me was really a shocker. I could only imagine how it will be for Irene to come to the USA after being here since July.

At the Klinik, Prien, Germany

This is a blessed day! Get up and Dance and sing and smile and laugh a good laugh! Today last year, Irene went to the hospital thinking she had walking pneumonia and was told she had Stage 4 lung cancer and it was very aggressive and it had gone to other places in her body. With the prognosis of months to live, she and the family took the cancer bull by the horns and battled it with determination and grit, and today the results show she is living, quite well if I may say so, and is kicking the bull in the face with gusto!

The day here in Bavaria is beautiful and sunny and warm! I was moved to such tears this morning realizing where we were one year ago and where we are today in this moment.

Irene is blessed with such great family and dear friends. Thank you so very much for all your thoughts and prayers and love. We bought plane tickets for the States and are planning to arrive in New York on the 10th of October! It is a relief to have the strength in her prognosis to actually be able to plan for a future date. It seems like such a long time since we have been able to plan for something simple like this. Day-to-day. Moment-to-moment!

For me, it will be grand to have a good chunk of time to settle with my family and friends in New York and Oregon. It is still a shock to me that my private practice that took years to develop is quite cleared and still. I was so busy and planning and...it all means little in the big scope of life and dims in the light of true healing. I know all will be fine and all will be provided for. Today is beautiful. I hope your day today is filled with joy and love and laughter.

At the Klinik, Prien, Germany

We all took a sad blow to the heart here with the passing of one of the clients yesterday (Monday). I had been visiting Sara at the hospital for the last few days. She was having trouble breathing due to treatments. She came here to Germany from the States, where she had been beaten up so badly from radiation and chemo that when she started treatments her body responded brilliantly at first. It was just that there was too much waste of dead cancer cells and tumor cells flooding her body, and she was just too weak to get rid of it.

Everyone here is very tight group, because we are all fighting, as patients or caregivers, against some impossible odds. It is a grey, cold day and Sara is missed. She was doing well and we thought she would get out of the hospital and back to treatments. She goes home to Mississippi Thursday, accompanied by her two remaining family members: her brothers.

Two other clients are being challenged big-time and we are all putting out the good energy and prayers for them. Living a peaceful life is not guaranteed...not one bit. Life is so damn precious and that is that. We make our own beds and sleep in them (sigh).

Irene is doing well and fighting hard herself. We are coming back in October for a short rest, and then back to Germany in November for more treatments.

I am tired and worn out from the last few days. I am finished writing for now and I will get back to Irene and see her through this night.

At the Klinik, Prien, Germany

Happy Indian Summer or Fall season!

Earlier this week, starting on Sunday night through Tuesday night, Irene was in extreme pain. She had been feeling tight in her right lung/rib cage area for a while. Monday's treatment and the pain meds given to her made her sicker than a dog, and she had some pretty violent vomiting spells that night. She did not even go in for treatment on Tuesday. It was very difficult for her to feel comfortable, and at some points the pain she felt was so bad she wanted to scream and tear our poor apartment to pieces. I felt so helpless I was going insane from the frustration. No sleep for both of us, and our nerves were worn thin worrying and fearing the worst. We just could not figure this one out.

Yesterday, Wednesday, when we were able to get back to the Klinik, the doc was able to look Irene over and discovered the cause. Get this: Irene had a broken rib! She has had a broken rib for at least two weeks, and it was in fact in the healing process! Her coughing spells and her violent throwing up re-aggravated the break and thus, the intense pain. Poor Baby!

The broken rib was located on her right side, the same side as her lung cancer, and so that is why Irene and I were fearing the worst not knowing it was a broken rib...big release of tension.

The doc numbed out the area, immobilized the injured right rib cage, and we were back in business! The rib will continue to heal in this fashion. Finally, Irene was able to sleep comfortably and through the night, last night. The week is drawing to a close. That means only three more treatments next week and we fly home! Amazing!

At the Klinik, Prien, Germany

Where do I begin? It has been a long week. Heavy heart stuff for me, and challenges for Irene. Irene's broken rib flared up over the weekend and it was a real drag. It was a tremendous amount of pain for her to go through and resulted in sleepless nights for both of us. This happened on Saturday (Oct. 2), after a joyous day of shopping for Irene. It was a real pleasure for her to buy some very beautiful clothing and feel beautiful. She looks great and is very beautiful considering the incredible journey she is going through. On Monday the doc took care of her pain and she slept great once again. Blessings! For me, sleep is like catnaps—never enough.

Today is the second-to-last-treatment day for her and we fly back this Friday!

We arrived on 15 July and watched two seasons, summer and fall, here in the Bavarian Alps. She has missed her beautiful cottage by the ocean and beach in La Jolla and all her family. Many things were lost and many things have been gained. In all, she has been blessed and her life force is strong.

The day here is grey and cool and drippy with rain—argh! Tomorrow is the last treatment and then she will have her catheter removed and she will have 24 hours to get her mind and body ready for a 12-hour journey home, including wait time and driving to Munich.

I am putting our lives back into suitcases and organizing for leaving. This place has been an amazing area to heal with all its natural beauty and people. The folks here are very accommodating to me now and offer me friendship and help when asked. I have mixed feelings leaving, only because I know Irene's path to full recovery is a long one, and this Klinik, the staff, and Dr. Lentz are all like a security blanket I am not ready to let go of. Soon Irene will be done with today's treatment and I must be ready to go and pick up laundry and buy ingredients for her dinner. So be well for now and soon we will be home.

Summary

During October we first flew back to La Jolla, California, and then to New York. Irene celebrated her 55th birthday and we celebrated Thanksgiving at Irene's sister Eve's house. We flew back to Germany on November 27, 2010.

Bad Endorf, Germany

The winter now holds the land and all is still and quiet. The Bavarian Alps in the distance appear like old slate-grey warriors standing shoulder-to-shoulder, cold and silent, their crowns hidden in ghostly clouds and swirling soupy mist. All the ground is covered with snow and is brittle underfoot.

It seems like a dream that Irene and I were here for almost three months in the high summer days of bright yellow corn fields with blue skies filled with black ravens dodging and playing in the hot mountain air. I wonder where the feral cat I made friends with, that hid in those yellow cornfields, finds haven from the bitter white cold. I hope it is safe and cozy somewhere.

Irene starts her short treatments this morning at 9:00 a.m. at the Klinik. For the last month-and-a-half, life for her and me in the States had been one of frustrating pain and non-movement. The experience of getting back into the world of American oncology—a billion-dollar-a-year business—was numbing and nauseating for me. I spoke little at Irene's oncologist meetings, if at all.

When asked to look at her broken rib, the RN did not examine her at all. The only thing the nurse touched was her damn silver pen in her white medical pocket to write Irene a pain prescription. The RN will get her bonus at Christmas time. Drugs and more drugs!

Irene's CAT scan on the 8th of November showed no new spread of cancer. Her broken rib had turned Irene's quality of life to a place of smoldering frustration. She is unable to move, stretch, or strengthen her bones with walking. She can't do jack sh*t. I stay beside her in my own silent frustration in anger of the situation that exists. Thank the Great Spirit for family and friends.

Thanksgiving was a wonderful time of food, laughter, and support. All of Irene's daughters were together and in one place. Two days later we were on a flight out of Newark and now here. I will start my Germany routine of food shopping, laundry, cleaning, cooking, and seeing to Irene's needs before and after treatments. The five German words I know will be well used. I hope to learn a couple more words to dazzle my German host. "The dark Muslim man is trying hard, we got to give him that," the Germans will note.

1:55 a.m., Bad Endorf, Germany

My sleep comes in catnap timing. I collapsed onto the couch at the Klinik once I handed Irene over to the staff for the afternoon surgical procedure of placing her catheter back in. I fell into deep slumber only to be awakened within 10 minutes by the arrival of the current batch of new caregivers coming into the lounge area to pick up their husbands, wives, and sisters. I awoke bushy-tailed and ready to rock and roll. Amazing. Not healthy, but amazing.

Irene was knocked out peacefully for surgery and that was my savior. I went to go grocery shopping in Prien. All the shopkeepers and store folk immediately recognized me, and greeted me sincerely without getting out of their German character too much. I was touched by their acceptance of me, though I have not seen them in almost a month and a half. And the food is clean and fresh and gives the aura of health and earth.

Once fed, Irene crashed and so did I around 2030 hours (8:30 p.m. for those who are trying to figure out 24-hour time). I woke alertly 5 hours later in the darkness of our room keenly registering Irene's steady breathing:

relaxed without all the pain, moaning, sighing, and anxiety.

So I am now awake. Truly these are cat hours I am sleeping. I feel I should put my clothes on and do some night hunting of some field mice or something. Yummy! Crunchy little feet! I will try to get back to sleep. This morning will bring Irene's first treatment of immune system awakening and the killing of what cancer that is left in her. The battle will commence in 7 hours.

"Good night moon. Good night cow jumping over the moon...." –from a children's story.

6:15 a.m., at the Klinik, Prien, Germany

I hope all is well and this letter finds everyone in good health and spirits. With Christmas and all the other winter seasonal times of Peace at hand, please take a moment to share compassion and harmony with all those around you. Color, creed, religion, and tribalism are thrown out the window and just share peace and sincerity.

Irene has been in severe distress and experiencing intense pain these last eight days and nights. Needless to say, I wander in a place of helplessness, frustration, and anger from being unable to relieve her of so much pain. She spends each day and night in such pain that all of us would choose to jump off a bridge. She questions her quality of living, and that is hard for me to bear. My warriorship is tested each second, each moment. How can I serve comfort to a situation so out of my hands? Pain and anguish and depression fill Irene's complete being. She paces at night wanting to scream and gouge an enemy she cannot reach.

Eating is challenging for her, and therefore being able to "fuel up" for any battle is compromised. She awoke in such pain and despair that we fled to the emergency room of the hospital in Prien 10 minutes away. The silent, bitter, cold, black night was empty of everyone except our lone car driving down empty streets.

The pain came from an extremely packed large intestine filled with the waste matter of four days and a trapped large gas pocket. And the twist: the constipation was at a crucial and dangerous point. If she could not pass her waste on her own with the help of meds from the hospital, surgery would have to be performed. An incision would be made and a hole created in the large intestine to relieve the gas and provide an exit for the waste. The extreme danger was that there would be an exposed opening to her internal organ where infection could set. The doctor, all in broken English, explained this.

The doctor hoped that Irene would not have to go through this procedure and expose herself to a very dangerous situation that could easily spiral out of control. The meds worked and Irene was able to pass the waste. The pain meds given to her were more powerful than what she was currently on. It knocked her out mercifully. We stayed the night at the hospital and left yesterday morning.

A new finding was discovered by the x-ray: Irene may have broken an additional two more ribs. No wonder she was helpless to relieve the pain with the morphine given to her 8 days prior. When and how she broke two more ribs is irrelevant. The damage was done. Last night was okay and then the cycle of pain began to pick up again.

Today is a bitter cold morning and we are preparing for Irene to finish her last two treatments to finalize a six-treatment maintenance cycle. We are suppose to leave this Friday, December 10th, for the States. I plan only for the immediate hours before me, and no more than that. Friday is light years away.

My mood is fierce and unmerciful to the darkness of the soul from lack of sleep, food, and warmth. I will see what this day brings.

At the Klinik, Prien, Germany

The day was long and the sun shone brightly. After a battle yesterday at the Klinik stabilizing Irene's pain and morale, she is safe. I am too tired to write at any length, only to say Irene and I will make that 0930 Friday morning flight home.

She will get her catheter out tomorrow and have 24 hours to prepare for the eight-hour flight back to New York. I am looking forward, as she is, to coming home for the holidays.

Larchmont, New York

Well, my dear friends, family, sacred Warriors in the cancer battle and you glorious caregivers, have a seat and enjoy the story of Irene's journey back home from Prien, Germany. It is a real humdinger!

After taking her catheter out on Thursday Dec. 8, we were ready to fly home on Friday December 10th. We were to be picked up at 0530 in the morning for the normal hour-and-a-half ride to Munich airport.

Thursday was challenging for Irene with her mind-numbing pain, being short of breath, and her digestive system plugged and hurting. The deteriorating weather in the Bavarian Alps was changing from crappy to really crappy with icy snow, high gale winds, and bitter cold temperatures.

I had to release all my fear of the weather and pack all our stuff that would stay in Germany for our return in February. Preparing Irene for an arduous eight-hour-plus flight home to Newark airport meant staying mindful of every movement she made and controlling every phobia that came up in her chattering-monkey mind. Not an easy task for anyone dealing with intense pain and severe shortness of breath.

After seeing off all our friends and dear comrades at the Klinik who were staying on for treatments, we made it back to our hotel room and lights were out by 2100 hours (9 p.m.). Damn, if I did not wake before the alarm at 0300 hours. Looking out our window I saw the howling gale blowing icy snow in great swirls, pushed by the wind demons in the dark morning. Ummm...A great sign for a long day of beauty in motion. (Sarcasm. Yeah, yeah.)

Out we went into this early winter madness–after we had our coffee.

The 10-minute drive to our Prien pick-up point was slow, safe, and magic-like considering we were driving through the swirling mini-tornadoes of wind and icy snow. We got to the drop off place in one piece and waited for our ride—not knowing if it would even come in this severe weather with no way of contacting the driver. Great Spirit provided and the glow of car lights out of the icy gloom revealed our ride. The driver, whom we knew from previous rides, was steady and ready to rock-and-roll. She explained in her broken English that the Hwy 8 to Munich was a real hell-on-wheels, white-knuckle ride for the morning commuters.

Irene was doing major warrior focusing to keep her racing, short breath together, and to control her unpredictable, cancer-driven hot flashes and morphine nausea at bay. Damn, Lady is tough.

The ride to the Munich airport was a two-plus-hour ride through the Land of the Storm Giants on an icy, wind-swept autobahn. Upon arriving I moved through the airport weighed down with all our bags and roll-ons, as Irene was battling a severe shortness of breath. She moved as if the whole airport floor was a treacherous sheet of ice. Getting to the check-in counter we ask for a wheelchair and got immediate and gracious support.

Blessed.

Then Irene asked for oxygen for the plane ride. This started a flurry of emergency phone calls throughout the airport for portable oxygen, as the coinciding need to make our gate became imperative: our flight was still scheduled to leave on time. Her need for oxygen activated a series of flying protocols that questioned Irene's ability to fly at all. All this should have been taken care of weeks ahead of time, we were told. The clock was ticking away like the last seconds of a tight football game. I was losing my patience with this unreal and comical early-morning airport tension. I was contemplating taking on some German security officers for relief. A glorious battle was to ensue that would be sung about in the great halls of Teutonic warriors in times to come! But the German cops are saved by a Lufthansa airlines agent saying she would accompany us to the gate and get past all the security because our flight was calling urgently. Beads of cold sweat ran down the middle of my back. *Danke schoen!*

Just as we were going through the first security line, an airline official stopped us and said we couldn't get on the plane until Irene could convince the company and flight captain she is not a safety risk to herself. We had to retrieve all our stuff going through the x-ray machines and talk about this. Customers were looking at us. My skin was feeling hot. Damn! Minutes pass, and, so convinced, the agent allowed us to continue.

Our Lufthansa escort was great. She was so supportive because her favorite aunt had recently died of cancer, and she was determined to help Irene through this protocol mess and make our flight. We rushed through the security—as fast as one can rush through security in this day and age of phobia and threat—and made it to the gate. We boarded with great gratitude. The airport personnel were great in their help. All were relieved and happy for us. Until we meet again...

Next began the flight into the seemingly timeless oblivion for someone in great discomfort and pain. Eight thousand years passed and we arrived at Newark airport. Irene's sister Eve picked us up with her beau Lenny, and we arrived beaten and tired at Eve's house.

I finally ate and Irene slept on the couch. Irene really wants home oxygen to be comfortable. We began a search for options to make it happen. It boiled down to this: go to emergency, get tested, obtain her blood oxygen reading, and she could be set-up that evening with home oxygen tanks. Brilliant.

We went to Greenwich Hospital up the road in Greenwich, CT, not far from Eve's home in Larchmont, NY. We were taken in at Emergency and start the paper work. Irene and I had been up for at least 14 hours by this time. Basic tests were taken including an EKG. Now hold on folks this is where things get real wacky real fast!

The head doctor on the ER floor came in to our examination room calmly but very concerned, "It seems, according to the EKG tests, that Irene has had a heart attack. Maybe four."

"Uh..." I say.

Last time I heard something like this was when Irene was first diagnosed in September '09. We thought she had walking pneumonia. Nah, "I have fourth-stage lung cancer."

"Uh..."

The room became a whirlwind of activity. Flying tubes, lines attached, pubic hair shaved (uh...), beeping machines, people with worried looks but with professional action. Doctors talking to me and explaining the dire situation. I only saw lips moving. Irene was gasping but safe. I tried to explain she did not have any heart attack. I have been with her 24/7 for months and all is well. We are extremely tired and just flew in from Germany. That's all.

"We are going in to open her up and clear any obstructed arteries she may have."

"Uh..."

"Wait you guys...you don't get it. We want only to get some oxygen readings so we can get home oxygen tonight."

"NO, Irene has had a heart attack and we are doing this to save her."

"Uh..."

Specialists were called in. One doc wanted to go in and start cutting. An arriving cardiologist stopped everything. He wanted to do an ultrasound reading on Irene.

A Filipino nurse, Mark, knows me from aikido classes in NYC. There were four Filipino nurses working on Irene. I am Filipino; they recognized me, and were kicking down the door for Irene. The cardiologist started the ultrasound proceedings. Irene's heart appeared like a beating balloon in an ever-changing field of white and black pixels. Her heart beat...powerful... unrelenting...in your face, doc!

I could see her heart on the screen too. I have always known it to beat strongly. I could have told you this. The cardiologist concurred. All was well but the EKG reading was still berserk: it is reading that she was having a heart attack. Fluid around her heart was disrupting the reading. The fluid was from the cancer and the recent German treatments. Lights were turned on, and the docs talked amongst themselves. I left the room, ready to clobber anything.

It was now 17 hours of no sleep for me, and this whole wasted scenario was way too traumatic. It was bringing up a lot of pain from very recent life-and-death experiences of others that I have known and had yet to grieve for or address. My mind was red. My heart was breaking. Something had to break. Something will break. Mark told the other nurses and doctors I am a martial artist and was ready to crack. It was plain to see.

All personnel stayed a safe distance from me and peered at me through the protective glass of the nurse's station. I was a wild animal.

Hospital security was nearby, hovering and observant. A doctor tentatively approached me to offer support.

"Back off, Holmes!" my gaze to him communicated. He backed off soundlessly. Minutes passed. Another eight thousand years.

"Irene is safe. We will do a CAT scan and more test to make sure. She will stay the night."

You people are not listening at all!

Once the medical protocol starts up, there is no stopping the avalanche of tests and tubes flying, lights blinking and beeping, and paper filling. All is said and done. We were admitted overnight for observation. We got our room. We hade been up now for 25 hours. Irene was in her bed hooked to oxygen and resting. I slept on a fold-out chair. The next morning arrived and we were in one piece.

"You will go home by noon. A case manager will get the home oxygen set up and the doc will give you the final go-ahead to leave."

We languished past noon. It was now 1500 hours and we were still hooked up. Our daughter Annie arrived! The A-Team was here! Yay! I felt safe to change the guard.

"Mom should be released soon."

I left the hospital. I finally breathed the outside air. The world around me looked out of place. I was out of my body. I headed toward Eve's home. Irene and Annie finally arrived around 1945 hours—almost seven hours after the hospital said she was going to be released. She has portable oxygen, and home oxygen was finally being set up in the living room. She now rests in the living-room-turned-bedroom on the first floor of her sister's home. 48 hours have passed since we left Prien, Germany.

Welcome back to the USA!

Shokan, New York

Today is a bright day in Shokan, NY. It is beautiful in the bitter cold winter with the long lawns of our property swept clean of Fall leaves by the strong winter gales over the cold waters of the Ashokan Reservoir near by. I am here.

Irene is at her sister Eve's home in Larchmont, NY—about a 2-hour drive south, with our daughter Annie. The "A-Team" is giving the best care and support for her mom. Today, Irene is going in to receive localized radiation for the tumors in her spine. In a blow to Irene and us all, small spots were detected in Irene's brain on the recent CAT scan taken a week earlier during the emergency room saga. In conferring with Dr. Lentz, we learned that the best course of action is to radiate the spots in her brain at the same time as doing her tumors in her spine. Punch in the GUT!

We take deep breaths as Irene considers her options. Anything can happen when radiating the brain for tumors. Anything can happen if you leave the tumors be. Breathe. Pause and ground. Breathe.

In focusing on the energies I can control and manifest, I offer these visualizations and affirmations that I have incorporated in my supporting Irene. As I offered to you all when Irene was first diagnosed with her cancer in September of last year, I offer to you now again. I believe, as many do, in the power of the focused human energy toward a direction to achieve maximum empowerment. A goal, a place to reach, a battle to win. Irene is battling hard right now, as others with cancer are. This is how we can focus to help Irene. These are the battles at hand that Irene faces.

AFFIRMATIONS

"Irene vibrates at a very high frequency killing all the low frequency cancers and tumors and deposing of them with ease."

"Irene is safe and potent in her battle and healing."

December 25, 2010, Larchmont, New York

Today I share a poem I wrote for Irene.

Old Turtle and the Desert of Pain

I am in complete awe in her presence.
The tale is real.
She stands before me.
The journey had been made.
Desert of Pain had been crossed.
The toil of the passage shows clearly on her body.
Lean, non-sparing, she had prevailed.
She aches in a different way.
Her eyes are bright.
Her liver is strong.

Water…give me water.
She is attended to with vigilance and compassion.

I am here.

I see you all.
I am present in my whole Breath, Mind, and Body.
My backbone is strong.
I stand before you on my sturdy legs.
I crossed the darkest places where the searing whiteness of despair blinded me.
I was unreachable. Untouchable.
Alone.
Alone.
I walked the Path of my Clan.
I am of the Turtle Clan.
Long-lived and wise.
I Breathed in each hot Breath with the patience of eternity.
Pain.
Lonely Pain.
Pain of despair and depression.
One agonizing step after another I took, marking my passage by the songs of a solitaire Desert Bird.
The sands were sharp and stinging...I continued.
The despair was maddening with washes of pain, dull, sharp pain.
Pain.
Pain.
My thoughts were bleak and dark with despair.
I continued...

It is true, the Turtle Clan are long-lived and hardy folk.
Her story bears the truth.
I listened with water raining in my heart, drenching my soul.
Helplessness burns my blood and my skin inhibits me—my despair for her as witness.
Still...Turtle Clan are long-lived and hardy folk.
I was visited by many Spirits who kept me company on my lone trek.
Tricksters and devilish ones tripped me.
Some mean ones, some kind and simple ones.
Some Spirits were of Light.
Others of Dark.
There came my Teachers, comrades, and allies with wisdom and visions.
The Darkness came as well.

Dark desert thoughts of dried empty turtle shells crackling under a searing desert sky.
Dry, brittle—empty of all life—hot air moving through empty sockets—whistling of a time gone by.
I continued.
I persevered.
I continued on my Journey on my Path.
One Step.
One Breath.
One Step.
One Breath.
I stand before you now.
I declare my existence.
I declare my presence.
I am here.
My life song is and was stronger than the death songs of my cancer and tumors.
I live.
I bow my being in great thanks to her.
Old Turtle sings the song of the Desert.

Larchmont, New York

2010 DECEMBER 28

I am in a whirlwind of emotions. This is a very hard letter to write. My hands tremble. Since arriving from Germany on December 10th, Irene's condition has been very challenged by her breathing and pain. So challenged that she felt her quality of life was at a point where she was extremely unwilling to move forward. She said if she knew she was improving she would continue, but if not, she would like to depart this world while her body is a place of pain and death energy. We—Irene and I—feel that her body is continuing to battle her cancer. It is just so damn hard. The treatments in Germany did awaken her immune system, but she fights a deadly and aggressive cancer. The CAT scan taken on Dec. 10 showed her right lung packed: the cancer was prevalent throughout her spine, and the doctors feel the spots in her brain are also cancerous. Her liver is inflamed and there is water around her heart. I feel empty. No guts, no bowels. I float around her sister's house where she is bedridden. Irene has a morphine patch on, and last night she was hallucinating and speaking of things that had no connection. She tried to take off her oxygen many times.

Her friend and shaman, Valerie, flew in Saturday for what is supposed to be her last days.

I was in our home upstate on Sunday before the big storm when I got a call from Valerie to come down to Irene. Irene wanted to say good-bye to me. She was not sure she was going to make it through the day. Sunday's mighty storm outside our window raged like the battle in our four-walled room. All our daughters are here.

Hospice is supposed to arrive today. I am empty. I am not in the same frame of mind as most people are around me about Irene. I do not want Irene to suffer in any way. I am breaking at the seams of my being to see my wife and partner in a state of unhappiness and pain. She had been telling her daughters last week that she wants to go and to please let her go. She said this as she started radiation on her spine and brain. Our daughters understand and flow with their mom. It is so hard for them.

Am I being unrealistic to imagine Irene pulling out of this dire situation? No. I am not going to let Irene suffer, or to be living a life of unknown health and vitality of her spine, her breathing, her brain. She battles and it shows. I do not want Irene to be so morphined-out she no longer is connected to herself and those around her. My heart is breaking. I acknowledge the battle she faces. Her odds are not good according to the history of the cancer she fights. Screw the odds. That is who I am.

At this time, she is unable to travel to Germany, where she responded to the treatments. Her breath is short. She eats little and drinks little. Today we hope to set her up with an IV for liquids and get the proper oxygen to help her.

I am speechless only to say that even though this is the darkest of dark times I have ever experienced in my life, I continue to fight for her constantly. I feel guilty to have my doubts when I see her in a dazed slumber, short of breath, annoyed by constant hot flashes, and getting more drugged out. I am not ignorant of the telltale signs of the mind and body slowly diminishing until passing. I fight for her and will respect and carry out the decisions she makes about her life. All decisions are hers.

My tailbone is tucked between my legs and it trembles with fear of the unknown. I hate thinking of past good times with Irene—they make me lose my mind and they shatter my heart. I am not as brave as I thought. This is Irene whom I do not want to let go of. I will continue to fight and know that there is always a sliver of light somewhere. She lives right now. I do not know of the next day...she lives right now. I may not be able to write much or make connections these next days.

Larchmont, New York

Irene Bell Brody—Pele Old Turtle—has started herself on her final stage of her journey. She asked to be taken off her oxygen as of 1430 hours this afternoon. I ask that you hold her in your heart in these final hours and rejoice how she blessed your life and your dreams.

Irene Bell "Blue Pele Old Turtle" Brody-Rubio
Completed her journey here on Earth at
5:05 p.m., Wednesday, December 29, 2010

Irene Bell Blue Pele Old Turtle, 2008, Hawai'i, Big Island. Author's image.

After I sent the email announcing Irene's death, I felt empty of all that could possibly connect me to the physical earth—my flesh and bones, my body, my ability to process any sensory intake from anyone or anything. For me, an all-encompassing journey of love and triumph had ended in death, despite all my strongest efforts.

Upon awakening the morning of December 29, I washed Irene and dressed her in a pair of beautiful blue underwear and her favorite blue tank top she loved. The night before, Zoë and I had slept next to Irene's bed. With the Zoë's help, and sitting behind Irene to support her, I had Irene sit up in bed. Feeling her weight against me was a blessing. It was the first time in many months that I had felt her body next to mine. I cried quietly. I had missed this so much for so long. All too soon we laid her back down. Valerie wanted to talk to me upstairs, alone.

"Ron, I have to tell you of Irene's wishes," Val started off. The morning sun was bright and warm in the bedroom we were sitting in. "Ron, Irene called me here to help her with her passing. She wants to die today." Her words were like cold stabs of ice in my heart. "I know you have your duty as her husband. You have fought for her and have been by her side throughout this long battle. You strive for her to live. I will not stop you. I am here to see her through to the other side today."

"Val, I hear you. I was just about to send another letter out today for everyone to visualize healing..." I sputtered into silence. "Valerie, Irene and I made an agreement. I said to her that if she goes I will go with her. She knows this."

"Ron, I am a shaman. I will not judge your decision to follow her, but think of the girls." I could hear the girls downstairs in the kitchen below us. "They will need you."

"Val, they are all grown women. They are strong, and they have each other. They will have to understand. I will follow Irene when she goes today. Val, you must take care of the girls." Val nodded her head in agreement.

"Ron, there is something you should know. Irene told me that she was aware that you tried to take her cancer from her last year. She wanted you to know she wanted to give the cancer to you, but decided she could not do it. Irene wants you to know she was aware that you were willing to do that for her."

Silence. I was crying as I looked out the bedroom window.

"Ron, last night in my dreams I asked for help. My dream of Irene was dark and of death. My dream of you, Ron, was different. In the dream you were a much older man, and you were walking with a cane. You were holding hands with a young boy. This boy could be a grandson."

"Valerie, I do not care about a grandson! Valerie, I tell you now: When Irene goes today, I will go! You will take care of the girls and see it through. Do you understand?"

"Ron, I hear you. I cannot stop you. I will take care of the girls."

There was silence between us.

As I stood up to leave the room to go be with Irene, Valerie reached out and touched me on the chest above my heart.

"What did you do?" I asked her startled.

"Ron, I placed the little boy into your heart."

"WHAT!" I hissed at her. "I don't want that little boy in my heart! HOW DARE YOU DO THAT WITHOUT MY PERMISSION!"

Valerie looked at me and calmly said, "That little boy is in the Universe. That little boy is waiting for you."

"I did not want that little boy in my heart. You had no right to do that, Valerie. You had no right." I left the room and went downstairs to be with Irene.

Irene rested in her bed while I sat next to her, waiting in silence. Then I sat closer and whispered into her ear: "Love, Irene, would you be angry if you saw me on the other side?"

Irene shook her head, "No."

"Love, I want to be with you. Just like we talked about when we first found out you were sick. I go where you go."

Irene nodded her head in acknowledgement.

I kissed her forehead and stood up quietly to leave. As I passed the table that held all of Irene's medication, I scooped up all her morphine pills. She had a couple thousand mgs of the stuff. I was going to open them all up and make a "cocktail," and then lay next to my lover, hold her tightly, and go to sleep with her.

At 2:30 p.m. she asked for her oxygen tank to be turned off. I was devastated. My life turned into a surreal dream of death and destruction of my soul. My baby was dying and would be dead by sundown. I had no tears. I was numb to all life around me. The girls, Irene's mom, and her brother stayed in the kitchen, being close to each other. It seemed they had made peace with Irene's decision to die. I hadn't.

I went into the room around 4:00 p.m. and laid next to her. Irene was in a morphine dream-world. Her body was unresponsive to her mind. She was like a rag doll. I manually draped her legs over me as I snuggled up to her from behind as we had always enjoyed doing before going to sleep. I felt the bag of morphine pills in my pocket. My lover, my Irene, was breathing calmly and in short breaths. I laid there next to her realizing she was already three-quarters of the way to the "other" side of life. I said it was time for me to break open the capsules of morphine and make my drink that would allow me to join her. I thought of the girls. I thought of my family. I thought of all the people I had helped in thirty years of service.

Then a thought struck me: what happens if I drink my death potion and die with Irene, but we *do not* meet on the other side. What if our karmas are different? What if Irene meets Ricky on the other side instead? Or goes to another place altogether in the vast Universe, and that we are not together? What happens after we die? I realized that I might not see her on the other side. "Irene and Ron" would end when Irene died that evening. My heart was broken into small pieces of colored sea glass. The inevitable death of Irene could not be deterred. I would have to stay behind, alone in this world. I must stay and find meaning in a world without Irene.

I never gave in the whole time Irene was sick. I never thought she might actually die from her Stage 4 lung cancer. I never saw this moment coming. I did not understand when the hospice nurses came the day before. They were not there to give me a break from my caregiving duties. They were there to make Irene's passing as comfortable as possible for her. I had resigned to take care of her for the rest of my mortal days—to carry her on my back if she could not walk, and take care of her and love her until we both died. I never thought I would lose her. I slowly took her leg off my leg and got out of the bed. Valerie was in the room the whole time. As I left the room I reached in my pocket and took out the full bag of morphine pills.

"Here they are," I said as I threw the pills back on the med table.

"Thank you, Ron," whispered Valerie.

"Don't thank me, Valerie." I left to go upstairs.

I came back down around 4:45 p.m. Valerie and I were in the room when the setting sun beamed through the west-facing window. Irene was bathed in bright sunlight. Valerie and I stared in awe. There was magic power in the room. I knelt next to Irene and placed my hand on her sex. Valerie backed away.

"Irene you were my life. I will never see you again in this mortal world. I love you so much. Baby, I am going to go now and meet you in Shokan tonight."

I stood up. Her breathing became labored. The waiting minutes turned to long eternities. I went into the kitchen and told the girls I was going to go to Shokan and prepare the home for when Irene would visit me that night. No one questioned me. Zoë made me coffee. I went back into Irene's room. Valerie was alert and came to me.

"When you left the room, Irene became very agitated. She started to moan. I have never seen this before."

I quickly went to Irene's bedside. I spoke to my wife, my lover, my traveling companion, my Frisbee-throwing partner, my life...

"Love, Irene, my heart is breaking! I can't stay here..."

Irene started to moan louder.

My God! No! Don't do this, Irene! My heart was screaming and bleeding.

"I have never seen anyone come back to try to communicate. Irene..." Valerie whispered.

"Baby, I can't do this! I can't stay here and watch you die. I promise I will be there in Shokan waiting for you....Love, My heart is breaking...I can't watch you die," I begged Irene with my heart bleeding.

Irene moaned loudly. She was reaching out from the vast space between us, from the other side, to communicate with me. It was taking her mortal body great strength and effort. I stood up and looked down at her. I looked at my woman who I loved so very much.

"Okay Irene, I will stay here. If you are going to go, then be at peace and go...if you are going to do this, then do it. I will stay," I said in a clear voice pleading.

Irene took five or so more breaths and then she stopped. Her open eyes stared from the vast void. Irene died and ascended from this mortal plane. I knelt next to her shell and looked into her open eyes for the last time. I took Irene's wedding ring off her finger and put it on the pinkie of my right hand.

"Irene is dead, my god, Irene is dead!" Valerie cried. The girls, Helen, and Jon came in and sat around Irene. Suddenly, Helen screamed. Her daughter was dead. Her oldest child was dead. My daughters burst out crying. I stood up at the foot of the bed, and bore witness to all that was happening. I was still like a mountain and flying in the vast cosmos, lost. I quietly left Larchmont. I gave directions to Josie to close Irene's eyes. I drove up to Shokan in a major traffic jam to our home. I would go to Shokan to greet Irene should she want to visit me that night. My baby was dead. I was now alone.

The blue-white ice sheets crackled underfoot as Woolly Mammoth Boy moved through the frozen, dead, silent forest that spotted these high and foreboding mountain valleys. Suffocated by a white ash cover from an erupting volcano centuries before, these hollow, lifeless woods spread as far and wide as his eyes could see. White winter gripped this part of the earth in a stifling, lifeless embrace. Woolly Mammoth Boy lingered long enough to hear his pounding heart in his cavernous chest, remembering.

Earlier that day I had witnessed, with all the others of my herd, the passing of the Matriarch. She had finally succumbed to the many battle wounds of her long life. Laying herself down onto the frozen earth, the Matriarch was then surrounded by all her wards and disciples; she breathed her last breath, and was gone from the physical earth forever. In that moment of her death, I had paid attention to how the Matriarch had succumbed to the inevitable—without fight or resistance, she just stopped breathing and was still.

I had witnessed other, more terrifying deaths: some by saber-toothed tiger mauling, others by an enraged mountain bear sow's tearing and ripping, by stoning from sharp rocks, by slow drowning in black tar pits, or from being driven howling over the edge of high, ragged cliffs. Those deaths were all violent and anguished, with great despair.

I had watched with reverence how the Matriarch laid herself down, calmly waited for her moment, and died in the frozen land we were crossing by her lead. The Matriarch knew her time had come and followed its natural course to the end. I could still see in my mind the exact moment when the Matriarch's breath could not be seen in the frozen air, or the heaving of her ponderous chest in taking breath.

Leaving the circle, I had trod alone to gather and focus my thoughts. The herd must continue the journey and leave the high ice passes into the lower valleys. I had my responsibilities to the herd to be focused on. Dangers still abound here, so high in the snow-covered mountains. I thought of the new Matriarch who would lead the way now. I cleared my head and returned to the circle.

Here in the winter-swept wooded mountains, the body of the fallen Matriarch will lay to be shredded by ripping winds, devoured by the animals that haunt the high peaks, and eaten by time. Her scavenged cleaned bones will be retrieved in the spring thaw and brought to the hollow grounds of her ancestors.

I watched as the parade of mammoths moved on, filing past the body of the dead Matriarch and down the craggy path to the safe valley below. Then, before following, I took one last glance to honor her—the Matriarch—and then proceeded to dutifully assume my place as the rear guard of the journeying woolly mammoth herd. I walked on.

39. December 30, 2010: Shokan, New York

I drifted in the vast cosmos. Images of what was and what could have been flickered around me—all of them now meaningless and valueless. The cosmos is truly vast and empty. Somewhere out there Old Turtle walks the Great Desert. I floated in the quietness of a soul in numb darkness.

"Woolly Mammoth Boy! Woolly Mammoth Boy! Hey!" a voice cried out from the deep Void, "Hoy! Stand your ground! Your journey is not over yet!"

I drifted and drifted, weightless and unattached to the weight of the Universe. "Let me be, I am tired. I have been through too many lives already," I answered the bodiless voice.

"I do not think so. You still have work to do," I was answered.

I cried the deep pain and anguish of a million dark deaths, "No more."

–Woolly Mammoth Boy Remembers

The mortal man cried to the heavens, "Oh, Great Spirit—Great Universe, why is there such suffering and pain in this mortal world?"

"Little One, how can I explain to you? The nature of that which you experience is just the phenomenon of the illusionary world of the Mind. For how can you change the heavens? In the mortal world, to have and to have not are equal in both pain and suffering. You crave more of what pleases you, and you crave when you are without. Desire and craving, they are but illusions of the mind."

"Oh, Great Spirit—Great Universe, my soul aches, my life is but cold, white ash for I have lost that which is my life!"

"Little One, it is all an illusion…there is no difference between loss and gain."

With this the mortal man screamed toward the heavens, "Then be damned! For I am damned!"

–Story retold by Woolly Mammoth Boy

IRENE DID NOT VISIT ME that night. I slept alone in our bed in an empty house as the cold winter winds blew over the empty brittle fields of our New York State property. I had lit many candles, and floating in a bowl of water was her name written on a piece of paper, which I had placed in our living room for her.

I could not believe she was dead. Irene was dead.

Valerie Wolf's dream that night of December 29, 2010—*"Irene was standing next to a horse with a cat sitting on its back. She looked beautiful. Irene told me, 'I am fine.'"*

The first thing I did the next morning was to shave my head completely. The long black braid I grew during the 19-plus years of our relationship vanished. My head was shaven clean. I was in mourning.

Left: Twenty-year braid, 2007. Right: The morning after Irene passing, December 30, 2010. Author's photos.

The day after Irene's ascension from this mortal world, I experienced the following:

I witnessed two Bald Eagles flying over our property in the bright morning sky.
I witnessed two Hawks circling, and flying over our property.
I witnessed a flock of Turkeys running through our yard.
Irene's big blue exercise ball tucked tightly above our closet fell off by itself

and bounced away as I was thinking of Irene in the next room.
I witnessed a pair of Cardinals fly into our favorite apple tree.

I stayed in Shokan, alone and lost. I received a call from Larchmont from Josie.

"Papa, please come down. We need you. I need you." Josie was as broken as everyone else. Irene's body was still in the living room; the funeral home folks would come for her body later that morning.

"I will come down, Josie," I answered with a voice that did not come from my body.

"Please, Papa, come down here," Josie pleaded.

"I will baby. Tell your sisters I will be down tomorrow morning." I felt like vomiting while talking to her. I hung up.

Irene was no longer of the mortal world in which I had chosen to remain. She was no longer in pain, or in fear. She was amongst her ancestors, and with Ricky and all her loved ones. I was here on earth, and alone without her. My daughters, Annie and Zoë, were also still here, having lost their father years earlier, and now their mother. Josie had lost Irene. What a strange world. I looked upon the snow-covered fields of the property outside what was once "our" bedroom window where I sat in solitude in a different light. There once was a "we"—Irene and I. Now, there was just "I." Strange.

I knew I was not the first mortal to lose a partner. Hell, Irene had lost Ricky after their 16-year relationship, and I had met Irene when she was a widow. Now I was a widower. Irene was gone. What the hell happened? She was doing so well in Germany!

Questions upon questions. I roamed through the cold house that once was "our" family home. I walked outside and strolled around the winter-covered property, and I visited the empty, barren flower gardens that Irene had planted many years prior. I was not the gardener, she was. I was the carpenter. It was all so meaningless now. It all seemed like an eternity ago.

The next morning I drove down to Eve's house in Larchmont. It was the last day of 2010. Irene's body was gone. The living room was back to being a living room. All the tubes and oxygen tanks were gone. They saw my shaven head. That night I slept in the den, and the girls stayed together upstairs. It was New Year's Day 2011, and the next morning would be her funeral. I awoke and wrote a poem:

Pele's Sunrise

I awoke very early to a beautiful sunrise.
Irene Bell Blue Pele Old Turtle greeted me with a sign, a sliver of the moon and one bright star floating together in the morning sky before the break of dawn.

I am heavy with longing.

Today is her memorial.
Happy New Year's Day!
It is a day of light and song.

The memorial was surreal. Irene had been cremated and her ashes were there. Very strange. So very not normal. People came. People went. I left and drove back up to Shokan after seeing Irene's loved ones at Eve's house after the memorial. The day after the memorial, I wrote two poems, one before I left Larchmont and one after arriving in Shokan.

The Way of the Turtle Clan

Slow
Deliberate
Breathe
Breathe
Breathe
Step
Step
Step
–Pause–
Slow
The Way of the Turtle Clan

I am slow
I breathe
I pause

The Long Road

The road is long, long, long.
There is a place where my baby is free with her hair out flowing.
Her beautiful moon bright face of Irene Bell Blue Pele Old Turtle
    is smiling deliciously.
It is a long road through the hidden vales and shallow quiet
    brooks.
Water, the essence of all my tears...the searching currents in my
    blood...

Always flowing, the water is singing the midnight song of lovers
    and times gone by.
Pele, oh Pele.
I long for you as I travel and move through this mortal world
    without you.

    In a couple of days we had another memorial for all of Irene's friends up in Woodstock where we had lived together for 19 years. A hundred people showed up. I played congas for Irene. My daughters spoke to the gathered. People came and people left. I closed up the Shokan house for the long winter. I would not stay there alone during the dark months. Too many memories.
    A few days afterward, the girls and I flew separately to the West Coast. On the plane, I wrote this poem.

EWR to PDX - In flight to Oregon

The plane took off without my Pele by my side.
Her warm hand in mine as we would take flight is now invisible
    and unreachable.
The airport was filled with transients moving from place to place.
Side glances from others—coming and going.
Fleeting moments, fleeting interactions.
Pele is no longer on this planet for me to hold, to see, to touch,
    to listen, to smell, to converse.
My babe is gone.
This is going to be a long flight.
I ache in my whole chest with a longing for her that devours me.
The flight is 5-hours, 36-minutes into eternity.
Everyone tells me to take all the time to heal to rest.

Take care of yourself.
Rest.
Rest.
Rest.
Oh, by the way, how are you going to pay for rent at the end of this month?
Where are you going to live?
What are you going to do for work?
Oh, please take as long as you need to heal...take care of yourself.
Try not to stress.
Rest.
Rest.
Rest.

—January 9, 2011

We offered the last memorial for Irene's friends in La Jolla, California, at our beautiful cottage that Irene and I had shared at Windansea Beach. Irene loved this place so much. She wanted her ashes spread out over the Pacific Ocean. My good friends, who knew Irene and me in San Diego, had emptied the cottage of Irene's belongings and packed everything up. I had asked them to do this for me, for I could not touch Irene's belongings. I was to stay there for the next four months until the lease was up in May 2011. The day after we arrived, I wrote this poem.

She Plays the Blues

I am trying to stop smelling her clothing.
I grab her scarf, her bathrobe, and her 100% cotton shirts, to catch a slight fragrance...
A lingering of her.
The ocean is strong this morning.
The dawn has yet to break the eastern horizon.
Stars shine sharply in a bath of black ink.
A pulse bellows with each breaking of the waves.
Can I say her name?
Will it have the same power?
The Void is immense and deep.
Like hidden caves at the bottom of the sea.
Its gates ask for a token.
Pay the gatekeeper.

> Her fragrances come and go as she passes nearby.
> Her moon face beaming.
> Her eyes are the sun.
> She is playing a hármonica.
> She plays the blues.
>
> *—January 13, 2011*
> *Windansea Beach, CA*

This last memorial was again unreal. Many people came. Later, my brother and sister spoke to me privately and offered to help me financially. I signed an agreement for a loan from them. A friend from Woodstock gave me a large sum of money without question, and another friend in Oregon also did. I had not worked for almost a year and a half. I had spent all I had to look after my Baby. I was penniless. It was so weird and meaningless to me. Irene was dead.

Afterward, Annie, Josie, Zoë, Irene's brother Jon, and I took Irene's ashes to the shore to throw them out to the great Pacific Ocean. It was low tide, and I led them out to a rocky point—a point from which Irene and I would watch the waves crash on from the beach. Annie cradled a black plastic box that held a plastic bag, which contained Irene's ashes. I put my hand into the bag and grabbed a large handful of ashes and bone chips. This was what Irene had been rendered to: white ash and chips of bone.

The sun shone brilliantly as we all threw her ashes into the salty, blue-green water of the Pacific. Her bone chips drifted down into the water to be crunched on by little crabs. We watched in silence as her white-grey ashes briefly floated above the water's surface, and drifted inland slowly and gently. To me, her ashes appeared to take the shape of a figure, and then, slowly, they dispersed and vanished into nothingness. Irene was now one with the elements and the Great Ocean.

I told Annie to save some of Irene's ashes to spread them around our favorite tree—the old apple tree on our Shokan property—when she headed back east to her home in Massachusetts. I later spread some of Irene's ashes up in Torrey Pines Park, overlooking the vast ocean, in a place where the huge black crows gathered. Irene had resonated with crows a year before she had died. The crows had become Irene to me. As her ashes fell unto the ground I saw that little black ants were covered with white. Her ashes mingled easily with the soil of the Torrey Pines. Irene would have a nice view from here.

The next day, everyone left to go back where they came from, and finally I was alone in the cottage at Windansea Beach. Irene and I were last here together prior to leaving for Germany the year before in July. Now I was alone. Really alone. The crashing waves could be heard from the bedroom. I did not sleep. I could not sleep. I did not want to sleep. I saw Irene's big beautiful moon face smiling at me. My heart ached and shattered. Now my journey would begin without Irene in that cottage by the Great Ocean. Once, there was "we." Now, there was just "me."

The presence of the circling black mountain raven cast a dark shadow from high above Woolly Mammoth Boy's broad, hairy back. Foraging quietly away from the main herd, he found himself in a sun-bathed, open glade abundant in lush sweet grass to eat. He was not hungry—he was occupied in his heart, and eating while thinking soothed him.

I ate without relish. "The Man-boy suffers, and he is bewildered beyond living," Thought-mountain-raven cackled loudly, while swooping close to my head. "You, too, have suffered loss."

Stopping to chew, I whispered quietly, "Yes, but my loss is not the same as the Man-boy's loss. He lost his mate; I lost the Matriarch, a leader whose position is already passed to the new Matriarch. The Man-boy's lost mate will not be so easily replaced, if ever..."

The sun was hot on my back, making me uncomfortable. I left the sweet grass and made my way slowly to the large spring-fed pond nearby. As I started my first stride into the water, a coiled mountain rattlesnake near my front foot issued a warning with its rattle. Thought-rattlesnake venomously hissed at me, "His mate's death numbs his mind and heart; he has floated out of his physical body. He is in shock. He is alone."

As I slowly entered the water, I scanned the innocent surface of the pond. Shadows lay heavy on the other bank. I thought I spied large shapes at the base of the dark woods that bordered the water. I looked closer, and made out four large groundhogs resting. Though they were as large as small ponies, they were quite harmless.

Standing mid-calf in the cool pond water, I solemnly reflected on how I had heard the Man-boy's desperate cries in the dark of night these past weeks. I had felt the same creeping, suffocating feeling in my breathing that my Man-boy-self had been experiencing of late. I had felt as if I was drowning and unable to take breath as I saw the same flashes of the Man-boy's dead mate in my furry, woolly mammoth head—images that were fading away into the light of the unreachable distance between the Man-boy and his lost love.

"Is his grief taking his life-breath? Is the Man-boy dying?" I asked a large, brightly colored fish at my feet.

"We shall see. The Man-boy is lifeless, though his human shell endures life. We shall see," bubbled Thought-fish.

With that, a dashingly flamboyant red-and-yellow bird took flight from my broad back where it had been resting, shrilling a call, "Endure! Survive! We shall seeeee...!"

40. Poems by the Great Ocean

By the great ocean, in our cottage at Windansea Beach, I began the process of healing such a great loss. Though I lost almost twenty pounds and barely slept, I healed in very small increments. In deep solitude I sought the pain and darkness. The great Sun slowly brought heat back into my heart. The ocean accepted my tormented cries and despair in my darkest hours before the dawn. Salt and Sea. The life of the ocean beckoned healing. I did my best to be open to receiving the healing strength of Earth and Ocean.

While living at Windansea Beach I started to visit the San Diego rose gardens, where eventually I became a volunteer. Funny how life works out. The whole time in Shokan I rarely helped Irene in her gardens. I would mow the three acres of lawn, and do all the carpentry repairs on our property, but gardening—that was Irene's domain. Now here I was, a volunteer at a rose garden! Roses are my favorite flower, but I knew nothing about gardening. I was trained by some veterans of the rose garden in the basics, and then I was let loose.

I was at the gardens 7 days a week for almost 3-5 hours a day. It was so powerful for me. Earth, water, and living beings. The fragrances of certain roses made me cry and laugh. Others would make my energy slow down as I would be cut to pieces while working amongst them. I worked without gloves most of the time, which forced me to work slowly and with great care. During the last days of Irene's life she always asked us to move slowly around her

Irene's Point – Windansea Beach, California. Author's photo, 2011.

and with great care. Irene and the rose garden were one to me. By the time I left I had become quite knowledgeable about the rose garden.

After working in the rose gardens, I would walk down the street to the San Diego Zoo. There I visited the elephants and gorillas, and I spent many hours in the bird aviary. Being around the cool waterfall mist and the sounds of birds would lull me to restful meditation. I liked being around life and living things, but being around other humans was tough for me. I would become overly stimulated by people's energy too easily, and so I avoided others. My daughters did not communicate with me much. I understood and did not want to burden them. They did not need me and my grief. They had their own.

During these months, writing was my solace, my process, and my sanity. I filled many notebooks with poems and journal entries—here, I let them tell the story of my journey through darkness and back toward the light.

Greek Myth

She is not coming back. Ever.
She is not going to come out of the bathroom and join me in
    bed.
Going for walks on the beaches and singing off-key gloriously.
She is never coming back.
I brace for the final releasing.
Ashes will fly, melting into the salty ocean.
Dissolving back into the lifeblood of Terra.
She is not ever, ever, ever going to come back to me. Never.
"We" is now "Me."
She stands off my right shoulder.
I do not have to peer behind me to see if she is there.
She gleams and sparkles, yet I look before me.
Like the Greek myth: she is there as long as I do not turn and
    gaze upon her...
allowing her to be as she is, without my noise and clutter.
"The ash tree blooms late and leaves early. Don't worry, I tell you
    this every year."
She is not ever, ever, ever coming back.
Just keep walking forward, empty of fear.
Light blue is the early-morning sky as the
Stars sparkle, announcing the Sun's gentle dance of the new day.

—*January 14, 2011,*
Windansea Beach, CA

I Am the Ocean

The vast Ocean spreads before me.
Where the Ocean meets the rock...
Breath is slow.
Like a turtle I move slower.
One step.
One breath.
In a moment of a flashing wave...
I live and die.
One stroke of the Sword of Purification.
All is still.
All is quiet.
The water envelops the whole of me.
I am consumed.
I am the Ocean.

–January 14, 2011
Torrey Pines State Park, CA

Morning Pas de Deux

Her ashes were set free, adrift on an inland breeze, heading out
 to deeper water.
Whale signs on the open Ocean greet her arrival to the watery
 joy of their salty pas de deux.
The Torrey Pines coastal bluffs look out upon the vast Pacific
 Ocean...we are just zooplankton floating in the great currents
 to be eaten by whales.
The early dawn light rising in the east gently spreads warmth on
my cold shorn head.
She floats with mineral grace to the sandy soft earth.
Her bone chips mingle with piney needles.
Her ashes cover ants and little purple costal flower jewels.
She makes her way down into the roots of a pine.
She will have a nice view from up here,
where the huge black crows perch high above us mortals,
deep in her sweet smelling hair.
She faces the stiff breeze like Catherine did up on the
 Wuthering Heights.
Her soft gown flutters like sails pulled taut to gain speed on the
 open Ocean.

I find another spot where she wants to view for a while.
I sight a pod of dolphins heading north offshore, they validate her wish to me.
Ashes drift from my fingers out past the bluffs heading out toward the Great Ocean.
Irene soars on the thermal currents of the morning Sun.
Long beaches below me stretch out, melting with each pulse of the Ocean.
Crash.
Roar.
Sigh.
She sings in a different octave.
Her seagull shrills are right on tune.

                                      –*January 16, 2011 - Sunrise*
                                      Torrey Pines State Park, CA

January 17, Windansea Beach

Five grey pelicans drifted in a line.
Skimming the developing crest of each wave,
a fine mist coats their feathers.
The Sun sets.
Dawn on the other side of the Ocean...morning light.
Darkening orange sky.
Pele thoughts in my head.
A slick black seal greets me.
Over and beyond the horizon,
the Sun melts into the water.
One.

                                      –*January 18, 2011*
                                      Windansea Beach, CA

Irene Bell Blue Pele Old Turtle

A grand morning and day to ascend!
I thank you,
Irene Bell Blue Pele Old Turtle!
This gift is splendid and I treasure the beauty that is a delight!

Irene Bell Blue Pele Old Turtle!
Irene Bell Blue Pele Old Turtle!
Irene Bell Blue Pele Old Turtle!

You are a gift to me with each breath that I take.
My Pele!
My Love!
I thank you, my Love!
I thank you...
Irene Bell Blue Pele Old Turtle!

—January 31, 2011
Windansea Beach, CA

Morning Grub

I awake at 0336 hours almost all mornings.
Her name is in my mouth, upon my tongue.
Vibrating my teeth.
The darkness of the time before dawn and the night spirits' play
    comforts me in an odd way.
It is like wearing a shawl made of driftwood and sea glass.
I move like a night spirit: without gravity, without solidity,
    drifting here and there at the whim of my eternal jousting
    with the loss of her.
The Ocean song is loud, only a block away from my seagull's
    nest of twigs, shiny things and broken eggshells.
My stomach growls with emptiness.
I guess it time for seaweed and fish.
The time before dawn will shadow my approach to the Sea.
Only the Kraken will know I have arrived...
and She.

—January 31, 2011
Windansea Beach, CA

Adagio of the Heart

The sunset had faded to pastel oranges and blues—
He now rises gloriously upon Mt. Fuji.
Glass pockets of silver-blue played on the Ocean's surface.
—Could I walk on the water or would I sink to the deep, green,
   cold bottom?
The void between two worlds is as vast as the Great Ocean.
One inch from her could as well be as far as here to the Moon.
Moving slowly, for the adagio asks for the tempo of the heart.
One beat at a time.
One count at a time.
Honor the full note.
Give the full value of the moment.
A glistening black head of a seal appears from off shore,
to give audience to my solo performance.
Circles from a stable center.
Arm gestures that speak of the tenderness of the arrival of the
   evening stars.
Hands that speak of grace and elegance.
Gently.
Slowly.
"Please be slow."
Slow.
Slow.
Slow.
I will...

—February 11, 2011, 5:36 a.m.
Windansea Beach, CA

Daughter of Poseidon

Her seaweed fingers caressed my brown legs—massaging my webbed feet.
Irene Bell Blue Pele Old Turtle.
Daughter of the Great Ocean...she is a being of gills, light, and big fish-eyes.
Sometimes a black-headed seal.
Other times a lone seagull, whose predawn cries awake my consciousness to the beginning of a new day.
Another day without her.
The more I cried out her name, calling, the louder the waves crashed.
The more I cried out her name, moaning, the stronger the caresses became.
Her salt water mixed with my salty tears.
Deep, deep are the depths of the Great Ocean.
Ancient mariners ply the currents that passed through the thick, long strands of her sea hair.
The twinkling of the many-colored sea glass sparkles in the eyes of a deep-diving whale, whose ocean song vibrates my spine as I stand on the shore.
Connected by water.
Returned to the water...the source.
Her ash and bone chips drifted and sank lovingly to the bottom.
Accepted back by Poseidon.
Mixing with more sea glass, magic, and the Spirits of the dark storms that rage and frolic in the deep Ocean...she returns...transformed.
Irene Bell Blue Pele Old Turtle...daughter of Poseidon...
Daughter of the Breath of the Ocean.
Irene Bell Blue Pele Old Turtle...my love...
I walk my mortal life without you on my Terra-bound webbed feet.

–February 13, 2011, 5:14 a.m.
Windansea Beach, CA

At 0446 Hours

At 0446 hours the stars are still floating in a deep, black-blue morning sky.
In the distance I hear the Ocean outside my window,
which had continued its ceaseless cycle of ebb and flow: a wave building, curling and then crashing, to recede back to the Source,
to begin the cycle again.
Over and over and over again...
like a heartbeat.
And no matter how I sleep or dream, experience pain or joy, the devastation and the rising,
the Ocean continues her endless cycle,
like a heartbeat.
The temperaments of the Great Ocean are like the fury and passions in my heart.
From the intense heat that can turn flowers into grey ash,
to the wet, rich, red passion which is able to incite the manifestation of Heaven here on Terra...
I express the Great Spirit that is embodied in all life.
She had taught me much.
Of the peace and the gentleness of that of a spotted fawn, of her spring flowers—all cozy under an ice sheet ready to bloom in her unattended garden.
She taught me to look for the good in others...releasing the judgments that clouded and stagnated my life force... stopping my ability to express true compassion and empathy.
Her red-blooded heart has stopped beating here on Terra.
My babe walks in bright light, swimming in the Breath of the Great Universe.
Her summer dress is no longer needed.
Her gardening gloves are in the shed, folded and there waiting.
I remain here: a mortal standing on mortal sand,
watching and learning from her waves...
I am blessed...listening to her voice that ebbs and flows,
always singing to me even at 0446 hours.

—February 15, 2011
Windansea Beach, CA

To Search is to Surrender

There is a longing of something
worth the weight of a beating red heart.
To search is to surrender.
To seek is to go blind.
Kazumi, the mist and fog, covers the landscape of a vast desert
    whose night creatures seek solace amongst their own kind.
The crashing of scorpions...
a lone soul left dragging the remnants of itself.
Sighs in the dead of the night...
tears that evaporate all too soon to be validated.
My heart stumbles...
it requires a memory of a fragrance of beauty...
of a moment long gone.

                                   –February 15, 2011
                                   Windansea Beach, CA

The Void

The Void...
The damn Void!
So far away from my touch...so far away from my gaze...
the unspoken words that will never be uttered...the words that
    she hears me whisper when I am in my despair...
she cannot give me her piece of mind.
My heart flutters and stumbles like my thoughts of the Void that
    I cannot cross while in my mortal shell
"Courage. Courage. Courage."
I do not want to be brave and courageous.
I have strength...
I am so tired and weak...
I am breathing...
I want to stop it all...
I am. I live. I feel.
I process.
I persevere...
I stand on my own two feet.

                                   –February 16, 2011
                                 Windansea Beach, CA

Sea Fire* Dance

* sea fire, n. - light that is produced by marine organisms

As the full Moon coursed through my veins and bones, my
    teeth and eyes, my mouth, my fluttering stumbling heart...
I wandered to the Ocean.
Crashing and tumbling, the voice I could not hear was
magnified with each spray of salt water that misted my face.
I imagined the deep-sea creatures swimming and gliding in
    textures of sounds and semi-light.
Seeing me...
"He is one of us.
Release your troubles of flesh and bone: sell your old car.
You won't need it...your fins will get in the way.
When all is said and done, the essence of your heart is water."
Strength resides in Poseidon's trident, lancing the fears that only
    exist where aqua is absent.
Even Memba, a silver-back gorilla, whose domain is watched by
    many, dozes in the close proximity where water meets rock—
    where the salt air lingers on his long black eyelashes.
The Moon dances over the waves, touching each stub of hair
    upon my shorn head with the touch of a lover.
Always humming their watery lullabies, mermaids laugh at my
    brown feet that were once webbed, as they darn their dark
    green and blue shawls.
Sea glass and forgotten things cast aside adorned their tiaras,
    bringing to attention that all that glitters is not gold.
I have a wooden box filled with discarded things.
Heart things that no longer have moisture.
Bits of papers with love words that are empty as the space
    between stars in the sky.
Talismans of power depleted for the lack of attention.
The sea ladies wish for the wooden box.
They know where it is.
They will find it in the attic where the cats roam in the
    mountains and ice covers the land.
Have the wooden box.
Clear my slate.
A Moon clearance sale...just right for the Sea Fire Dance.

–February 17, 2011
Windansea Beach, CA

Looking at you Pele, my heart and body yearn for you. I miss you terribly without the despair. I thank you Pele for coming to my aid at night and helping me to breathe so I can rest. The mornings have been delicious and so uplifting.

I miss you and our comradeship...our love, our differences. The days are slowly changing in my heart and soul. I am ready to die and live. Pele, stay with me always. Give me the strength each day to live these days of my mortal life, without you by my side.

Irene Bell Blue Pele Old Turtle. You are in my blood, bones, and flesh. I await the day that you will call me to be by your side...and I will be there as I have always been in your mortal life. I continue to walk the Warrior's Path and serve this world...without you in your mortal flesh and blood woman. Pele, I love you.

–Windansea Beach, CA

Getting one hour of sleep was how I started today. Morning movement practice on the beach was brilliant and forgiving.

A deep sadness depression settled into me all day. A sense of bewilderment, shame, guilt, and remorse filled my voice and my soul. I know I can never take back what is done...I can only move forward and change. The limitless Great Universe guides me to expand when all I want to do is succumb to despair and death.

Irene Bell Blue Pele Old Turtle is always with me and I know that. I want the flesh-and-bone Irene, which I cannot have ever here in this mortal world I live in. I choose to continue.

At sunset, which was rich in hue and texture, I was sitting at my favorite rocky point. There, I repeated Irene's name over and over again:

Irene Bell Blue Pele Old Turtle
Irene Bell Blue Pele Old Turtle
Irene Bell Blue Pele Old Turtle

And then right before me in the surf, the black shiny head of Seal appeared. I ran to the shore and she connected with me and then was gone.

I counted myself blessed and went home. Thank you Pele.

–February 29, 2011
Windansea Beach, CA

This morning the waves were calm and fierce. Twice I had to brace myself... the waves pounded me to wakefulness.

Good day of planning and moving forward. Went to the zoo and walked very, very slowly the whole time...a ghost amongst the living.

Irene, I am at peace at times, and yet so broken-hearted. Today my heart fluttered and skipped. My guts felt vacant and absent in my body. There was a hesitation to think about you and to I see you in my mind. I want to be with you. I want to take you everywhere. Yet you are everywhere.

The moments are long and bitter. The moments are sweet and they ache. I rest at times in a place of restlessness of a soul wandering. The times with the mortal you are behind me and I can never have them back. The good thoughts of us are too painful to retrieve. The bad times with us rack me with guilt. I realized them with your help and support.

Last night I dreamed I was dancing a beautiful balletic sequence. It was a comforting vision. I am so longing for you...for us. It will never be. You are gone. You are never coming back to me. I am a mortal in my mortal life. You are a spirit of light and the universe.

—March 3, 2011
Windansea Beach, CA

I AWOKE NOT WANTING TO wake. The sun was slowly rising in the east and I was already in bed too long. I awoke feeling the call of the ocean...the call of the waves...the voice of Pele.

[at sunset] The cool stiff breeze from the west curls the pushes the waves. Water spreads before me as far as I can see...Unleashing the deep beauty of the rich green-blue aqua.

...There was no wrong or right. There was no right time for this or that. Life is what it is: sadness, loss, and heart pain. I miss your arms to hold me... to keep me safe. I miss holding you to keep you safe. The emptiness gnaws at my bones of marrow-less slumber. My skin has forgotten touch. My tongue has forgotten moisture.

How you must grin at me from your seat in the light!

"Your mortal feelings are anchored in Rock and the Sea.

Release me, my love.

I am here inside and around you always..."

I realize there is no forever. I realize that all stories do not have happy endings. The waves crisscross before me propelled by Poseidon's ceaseless thrashing. No rock or solid form can hold back the blending that will occur.

My path is simple: survive each day without you by my side. Get out of bed and linger not. The tide comes in. Soon the rocks will disappear beneath the waves.

—March 4, 2011
Windansea Beach, CA

I CLIMBED THIS MOUNTAIN FOR two people. I have been living for two people... maybe I should start thinking for one...I do think so. Irene Bell Blue Pele Old Turtle and I climb Iron Mountain.

Irene would have enjoyed this hike. I signed her name on the visitor's book. From the summit you can see afar. To the east: rock and dry terrain heading out to the desert. To the west: the lowlands before the Great Ocean. I am at peace with the silence here...with the vastness of my tender shattered heart.

My body yearns for her...for Irene. My senses seek her out everywhere I go...only to encounter emptiness and stillness. The "Someday it will be different..." The "Days will come when..." The "Time will heal..." ...they really do not make any sense to me.

The day was hot. Today I am fifty-four years old. Irene, my baby, passed away at fifty-four years and thirty days. There are times I wish I had joined her...

The Sunset was beautiful. I miss you Irene so much.

—March 10, 2011
Iron Mountain State Park, CA
elevation 2,696'

THE MORNING PRACTICE WAS IN *kasumi* (a Japanese aikido term meaning "fog" or "illusion"), to see through the fog and mist of the past and into the present moment of the Now. It is time to leave this home here in Wind and Sea for now. The sacredness and holiness of her spirit is strong and I will honor her and our home.

...In a certain way I am peace...though I ache so deeply for Irene with each breath I take.

The sunset was rich in orange. Pele, another day has ended without you by my side. To fill with nothing...To seek the emptiness... Where the ego is still and the call for service to others rings true.

In the great Universe there is a place where my Pele sings and rides a horse with her hair down and flowing! And Cosmo, our cat rides with her. The moment will arrive when I will see her again...yet not now. Someday there will be grandchildren to tell stories to.

—March 11, 2011
Windansea Beach, CA

THERE ONCE WAS: YOU, ME, and Us.
   Now it is: "You" are gone...you died...you are gone and never coming back in the flesh, blood and bones. "Us" is gone...only "Me" remains.
   I am alone with the "you" and "us" in me.

–March 17, 2011
Eugene, Oregon

Grains of Sand

Clear and bright, the ocean gleams with the vibrancy that is
    Earth power.
The vast open sky reflects the spirit that is potent.
Each wave sounds different from the one before: the silence
    between them swallows all thoughts.
In every moment is a pause.
In every heartbeat there is heat.
The blaze of Apollo's chariot makes brown my skin: the same
    hue of my eyes.
Wave upon wave pounds the shore...
endless circles within circles.
My beloved swirls in light soft fabrics that are caught in the
    white sea foam.
The space between waves.
The tempo of heartbeats.
She beams in that place.
I linger in another.
Separated by the deep green waters of *kai* [the sea],
my emptiness is immeasurable...like accounting for all the grains
    of sand on Terra.

–March 24, 2011
Windansea Beach

To Be Graced by a Rose

There are many types of roses...they all have thorns.
To move amongst them takes vigilance and great care...for the touch of a rose invites a drop of your blood.
The fragrance of a rose will vary...deep and rich like a dream you had, and awoke smiling.
Or as light as a morning drizzle that dangles like jewels on a spider's delicate web.
I was married once in a rose garden centuries ago...she beamed as the sun broke through the summer thunderclouds.
That was centuries ago...
The memory of a rose lingers long after its petals have fallen to decay...reminding us never to forget the glory and the majesty that is fleeting here on mortal Terra.
Throughout my travels in this world I sought the place where roses bloomed...always wary of the dangers that may line my path toward them.
As the centuries passed, so did the mortal lives of those who tended the roses.
I now ward and care for roses...in my feeble and humble manner.
Taught to prune and weed, I relish the task for it gives me great solace and breath.
I am there most days amongst the rose beds...picking up fallen petals and clipping dead canes...and taking time to smell all the roses to my heart's delight.
For it seems that is all I have... a lot of time.
There is no rushing in a rose garden. "...go slow...please go slow..."
My shattered heart, broken and empty...forgets its pain amongst the roses.
How appropriate it is to tend something so beautiful as a rose, after a lifetime of gazing upon the land through a warrior's vision..."She will survive..."
Truly it is heaven on Terra to be graced by a rose.

—March 30, 2011
Windansea Beach, CA

As much as I keep my beloved Irene close to me...up front in my Heart thoughts...she slowly moves to a quiet safe place in my Breath Mind. The days move slowly...as the seconds pass in solemn procession.

The Rose gardens have been a place to connect with the soil, roses and earth energy. I miss Irene painfully...the vacancy of her presence leaves me empty...as if I lack guts, internal organs and bony structure.

I miss you Irene. I miss holding hands and loving you, though at times in our past we were distant...I long for every cell of you. You are dead and gone...never to return. Your mortal flesh and bones were fired into white ash and bits of calcium...you were transformed back to the earthly elements.

Someday I will join you in the place of light and breath where you exist now. Living this mortal life without you crushes my breath and weakens my bones to mush. The coolness of the waterfall makes heavy my eyelids.

I hold a rose in my hand...a treat from my work in the rose gardens this morning. Its fragrance calms me and awakes a deep sadness for you. I will start walking or I will fall asleep on this bench. It seems at the times the bustle of the life around me stops when I sit and breathe.

—March 31, 2011
San Diego Zoo, CA

By the end of April 2011, it was time for me to go back to Shokan, New York. The lease on the Windansea Beach cottage was up, which was just as well since the cottage was too expensive for me to stay in on my own. Anyway, it was for Irene that we moved there in the first place. I saw in my visions that I would return to San Diego—and get back on track as a mentor—once I was ready to rejoin the living. Before leaving, I did make some connections with the autism community in the area. My friend, Dr. Steve Edelson of the Autism Research Institute of San Diego, was very helpful to me. But before I could begin mentoring I had to be ready to work and be around people again. I was too emotionally unstable and disabled to work. Breaking down in front of clients would be very uncool.

Some people understood my predicament. Others said I should just move on. Life was tough. I broke down crying in stores, banks, and on the street. I was not very good around people. Strangers at the checkout stand would wait patiently for me to compose myself after losing it hard in a crying moment. One minute I was fine, and in the next I was adrift in thoughts of despair over the loss of Irene. Nothing mattered much to me, but I knew that someday it would all be different.

During this period, all my living expenses were paid by credit card, and I had no savings. I could not keep up with life expenses, and the medical bills incurred by Irene's treatments had wiped out our financial holdings. I was going back to our Shokan home to prepare it for rent or sale. It would be hard living there, but I had to. I knew the house and I knew how to repair it. I also had to help my daughters with everything that had to be packed and stored.

I placed a home start-up kit in a rental storage unit for when I returned to San Diego. That was the plan: Into storage went kitchen essentials, basic clothing for the sunny San Diego weather, books, and the martial arts equipment I would need to start mentoring. I felt this place of Sun and Sea was calling me to return some day.

Around this time, an old buddy of mine offered me the opportunity to be part of a reality show he was developing back on Long Island, New York. He was a boat captain, and lived in a community of professional sailors and people accustomed to a life near, and on, the Atlantic Ocean. I said yes to his offer, made a plan to settle the Shokan home, and then met him down in Point Lookout, New York to work this new project.

After packing all my stuff into storage and securing my few relationships with people I had come to know in the San Diego area, I paid for a one-way flight to New York and headed back east. The flight from San Diego ended a cycle of coming to terms with Irene's death, and accepting the end of our relationship in the mortal world. My hair was growing back a little, but my heart was still as fragile as a broken vase that had been glued together. The world was big and wide, and I was stepping into my life alone. The unknown was before me, and old death songs and death poems lingered in my heart. Bravery and courage were being forged in the heat of my loss. I reminded myself I was a warrior. I was a wounded warrior.

41. Into the Haven of Pirates

In the end the Wanderer returned to the ancient land of his past. Seeking what once was, he found only the emptiness of times that were forgotten and lost in dust. In the ensuing days and nights he slept under the wings of crows and seagulls. Remnants of the ancient treading of the woolly mammoths were found on his path, and in the conclusion of his travels he was led once again to the Grey Ocean.

—Story retold by Woolly Mammoth Boy

SPRING WAS IN FULL BLOOM by the time I made it back to Shokan. The cold, wintry days that held fast to the land during Irene's passing were long gone. I entered the archway leading onto our property and discovered water lilies in the pond Irene and I had built. All the flowers Irene had planted the year before bloomed in full splendor. It was as if Irene was welcoming me home. The property was alive and buzzing with springtime energy. The sun was bright and the sky clear. I was happy to be back in our home, but I was stunned by feelings of loneliness and loss. A seesaw of emotions coursed through my heart and mind—so unbearable, and yet so necessary. There was no place for me to hide, nor any opportunity to deny that Irene was never going to be here with me in flesh and blood ever again. Irene's emptiness on the property made everything so meaningless.

Dropping my bags in the main house, I started up my VW pickup truck and went for a ride across the nearby Ashokan reservoir dam. It was a splendid place to be—so different from the surf and sun of southern California. The Catskill Mountains of New York State were Irene's hiking heaven. As I drove the truck I could hear faintly in my head a song Irene had made up while driving through the country in the truck with me: *"...driving around the bend with the turkeys in the field..."* I smiled and then grew terribly sad. I missed her so very much.

Once back in New York I contacted an old lawyer friend, and started the process of legally changing my name. "Ron Rubio" no longer resonated with me. I was different. I had always felt that my given name was not really me. It was a name given to me in a lurch. I was not even given a middle name. People had always liked the easy roll of my name, "Ron Rubio," but I wanted a name that represented my ethnicity and heritage. I wanted to be called "Vicente," my grandfather's name. I knew I was starting a new life, and the people who met me would now know me as "Vicente," not "Ron." My friends respected my name change and so it was.

In our house, I made a list of the immense work that needed to be done in order to get it ready for rent or sale. I was alone, but the girls had already done a great deal of packing on their own during the time I was on the West Coast. They had finished the hard part of packing up all their mom's stuff. I was grateful not to see Irene's things. As I went through our bedroom I opened her closet to see what was hanging up inside. The fragrance that struck my senses was Irene's. It brought me to my knees. I went inside the closet and closed the door. In the blackness of the closet I took deep breaths of her between my sobbing. *Irene! Take me away! Don't leave me behind!*

Being in the dark closet I wanted so badly to be transported to wherever Irene was in the Great Universe, to be with her in the place of light she now occupied. Opening the closet door I stumbled once again into reality and into what was once our bedroom. I felt so lonely. I lay on the bedroom floor for what seemed like hours. I remember noticing the late afternoon light filtering through the bedroom windows. *Irene will be finishing her last clients soon.* I fell asleep on the floor, and awoke in the cold darkness of the deep night. The next morning I started by first moving out of the main house and into the carriage house that was once Irene's office. Our bedroom was not "our" bedroom any longer. It now belonged to the spirits of two lost lovers. I would not sleep there ever again.

Irene kept me company with many timely visits. Big black crows greeted me in the morning. Eagles and hawks circled high above the property. Early one morning while eating breakfast on the deck off the dining room, lost in my thoughts of "us," I came out of my reverie, looked into the world around me, and was greeted by the presence of "Flash" the horse. We had known him for 18 years, during which time he was usually corralled next door.

As mysteriously as Flash appeared on the green lawn while I was not looking, he chose to leave when I turned to hear the sound of a bird behind me (see photos next page). Animals were connected to Irene. The horse had been her animal since she was a teenager. Seeing Flash free and grazing in the early morning light so near to me, I knew it was Irene who came to visit. Many dragonflies, creatures that symbolized transformation, appeared to me when I found myself in the gripping hold of deep grief. Their iridescent bodies hovered close to my face to remind me of the beauty of these ever-changing moments.

There was a lot of work to do on the property, and it kept me very busy. Besides the usual winter storm damage, there was the need to build storage space for all Irene's and the girls' belongings that had to be cleared from the main house. The work kept me busy during the day, but the nights were

Flash visits me. Author's photo, 2011.

lonely on the big property. Now that I was back in "our" home, the stark shock of the loss of Irene was so strong for me that at times the best I could do was stand in one place, rooted in silence. Then I would break down. Minutes and hours would pass by and I would not notice. Hunger and sleep came and went without my heeding their call. *So what? I am just a grey spirit here in this time and place...nothing matters.*

Things were brewing down south on Long Island. My sea captain friend told me the initial film shoot for the reality show PR package was going to happen on the first weekend of June, and he asked if could I get down to Point Lookout (on Long Island) for it. The reality TV show he wrote was about a sunken treasure he knew about, lying off Long Island. We were going to go after it. He had written me into the show as the crew's martial arts guru character, and I was also going to be trained as one of the divers that would go down for the treasure. My show nickname was "The Ninja." I said sure to my friend, and made my way down that weekend. It would be good to get away from the Shokan house for a couple of days.

Point Lookout is a small ocean community on a barrier island that faces both the mainland and the Atlantic Ocean. There were many wrecks off the coastline of Long Island. I met the rest of the crew at the Point Lookout docks. The crew consisted of my buddy, the experienced sea captain, and many other treasure divers. His first mate had tons of open sea experience and was a sure hand on any ship. The ship's photographer, who happened to be the ship captain's old girlfriend, was a former model and a gorgeous Lithuanian woman. *Romantic tension and drama.* An equally beautiful woman

Flash leaves me. Author's photo, 2011.

was a clairvoyant, and had been invited onto the crew to reveal any long forgotten memories the sunken treasure we would be pulling up might hold. Her "ghost hunter" assistant was also added. Then there was the ship's bard and musician who sang improvised songs on command, which would make the stern captain crack a grin during the dire times that lay ahead. On board was also the old mentor of the sea captain, who himself had seen it all and taught the sea captain everything he knew. He was a solid figure with a grizzly voice. Finally, there was me, The Ninja.

The show was shot on the open water off Long Island, and near another wreck the sea captain knew of. It was surreal experience for me. Since I had been solitary for several months, being around these new people was very exciting and stimulating. I did not know how to be around them, so I went into my Ninja character and had some fun. Smiling felt alien to my face, and the sound of my own laughter seemed to come from far away. I just allowed myself to flow with the moments.

The shoot went well and it was fun to be around people. The night of the last day of filming we all went out to the local bar. Everyone at the bar knew everyone, and I was introduced to the seafaring community. I drank shots of vodka for the first time in a long, long time. Soon the crew titled ourselves the "Samurai Pirates." We were pirates roaming the salty seas looking for sunken treasure and raising havoc in every port! I had morphed into the character I was given. I was a pirate of the salty seas!

That night we went back to the first mate's house and partied more. It was there that the sea siren seduced me. We danced and she came close, too close. I remember being very confused and trying to distance myself from her. She was a beautiful young woman, and a former model. The more I gently pushed myself from her, the louder her song of attraction became. She whispered in my ear that she was surprised by her own actions, and yet she could not help herself. During all the days of filming she had paid little attention to me. She had heard stories about me for years from her ex-boyfriend, the captain. I looked to my fellow pirate, the first mate, for clarification on what was happening. He said I could use his room that night...

Stop! What was happening? She was drunk, and I did not want to take advantage of the situation. This was all too crazy. But wait! We are pirates, for god's sake! This is *supposed* to be happening you fool! You are a pirate! The siren kissed me. My lips did not respond. It all felt too alien, though exciting. This was really happening. The siren kissed me again. I was led upstairs, and I awoke the next morning with a warm body next to mine. The sun shone brightly through the open windows. The smell of salt water and the sounds of seagulls quarreling were crisp and clear to my senses. I slowly disengaged myself from my still-sleeping companion. I lay there and wondered what had happened. My body felt warm again. I looked at this beautiful woman; she stirred and awoke. I touched my lips and they felt rich and full once again.

"You are so comfortable to sleep with..." the siren said to me as she awoke.

I did not know what to say for I had only known Irene's body for so many years. Is this what pirates really do? Drink hearty and romance by the sea? I was confused. *Flow with this.* Later, we went to the beach and talked. She told me about her life and I told her of mine.

"I live in Manhattan, come visit me."

"Sure."

I left that day and went back to Shokan to collect myself. I went over the facts of my few days in Point Lookout. The first mate said I could live at his house in Point Lookout, as the production for the TV show would pick up soon. Rent would be reasonable and I would be near the ocean, which was only five minutes away. Going into Manhattan by train would be easy, and I could start training in aikido again at the New York Aikikai. It all sounded good. My new female friend was inviting me to stay at her place in the city when I was there.

What was wrong with this picture? I was a widower of six months, and here I was offered many gifts to live again. It all seemed too good to be true. I checked in with Irene. In her living, Irene's connection to the animal world was awe-inspiring to me, and I was blessed with this connection as well. I had called upon her at Windansea Beach, and she answered me there by appearing as jet-black seals and big black crows; I would say her name here, to invite Irene to send me a sign of her presence. Signs of hawks and other power animals appeared. I also checked in with my friends. Irene's signs and my friends' words validated me and gave me support. I felt safe to continue keeping myself open, and yet I was wary because of the newness of it all.

"Hey, if a young, beautiful woman was offering herself to me, I would jump at the opportunity," one friend said.

"Yeah, well, you didn't just lose your wife."

"Ron, I mean, Vicente, life goes on. Do you think Irene would want you to stop living and be unhappy? You are a vibrant man. You look young and have the vibrancy of a young man. Get back into life."

"It is all so weird and surreal."

"Brother, Irene would want you to be happy and enjoy life. Flow with this. If you are uncomfortable then let it go. You are not obligated to anything or anyone. Your daughters are grown up and on their own. They have each other. You are on your own now."

I thought on this and made the call to the first mate in Point Lookout. I took up his offer to rent a room. I would have a small amount of funds coming in from the New York State property Irene and I bought and now sold. It would take care of rent and a little more. Life would be tight, but this was a start. I would live near the ocean and begin a new life in a place with no connection to my past. I planned to travel up to Shokan and work on the house when I could and take care of business. The TV show seemed promising. Maybe this was a turning point in my life. I had to try it. I wanted to live.

Soon I had set up my life in Point Lookout. I traveled into Manhattan by train and began my aikido training. I stayed at my friend's house in the city. The siren's watery New York City home was a shared one-bedroom in the "New" Harlem, where her bed was a foldout couch in the living room. By "New Harlem," I mean there was a infusion of young, white people living in cheap Harlem apartments—you would not have believed it possible back in the New York City of the 1970s and 1980s. She was working in the modeling department of a major clothing line downtown. She drew me into her life but kept me at a distance at the same time. She said to me that her mother back home in Lithuania did not approve of me. Hell! I could not help that I was a pirate! Whatever her mother thought about me did not seem to matter to the siren. I let myself go a little bit and felt some emotions for her, but it was strange. I was never one for just a physical relationship, and this was more true after Irene. Keeping my heart open for another woman was one thing; my body accepting another woman's body was going to be another thing.

This new intimate social experience was going to take some getting used to.

"Vicente, I told my mother about you. She feels that I should not get involved with you. You are very attractive to me, but I know I have to stay focused on my work," she said to me one night.

"I hear you. I enjoy your presence in my life. It is a beautiful thing and I understand your work and your life. I thank you for letting me get to know you." It was bewildering and sad to me. I did not understand this "dating dance."

In the coming days I started to back off from her and felt confused. It was nice to be in the presence of a woman again, but it was draining as well. Was this what Irene wanted for me? What am I being shown? This is all too confusing. My pirate mates told me to let it go. There will be other maidens in other ports. *YARR!* Most of the people in my new life saw me as a very powerful and magnetic personality. I was the exotic and dangerous Ninja. In fact, I was addressed as "Ninja" in Point Lookout, and Vicente was rarely used. I had lost one identity and gained another. I slowly took up the persona of The Ninja—handsome, mysterious, and deadly. I kept to the disciplined martial arts beach training I had started in San Diego. I was on the beach before sun up, training and writing every day. The days were hot and sunny. I looked for signs of Irene in Point Lookout, but there were none. We had never been here while she was alive. I was truly in a new land, and in a new time of my life. *Was it safe? Was I safe?*

With July 4th coming up I was invited to Vermont to the first mate's family home. It was on a beautiful lake he had inherited from his mother. His niece also came up the day before the fireworks and festivities. I had met her once before at a dinner party down on the Island. As everyone went out on a boat to waterski, I went up to the porch deck facing the lake and settled on an old couch in the shade with a book. I wanted to be alone. I heard the powerboat leave the dock, taking all my pirate friends away for some waterskiing. As I was closing my eyes to nap I heard the screen porch door open. I did not know that anyone was still in the house. I opened my eyes and it was the first mate's niece. She was beautiful with her flaming red hair. Silently, without a word, she sat at my feet, our skin touching. I felt odd and made room for her on the couch. She snuggled closer at my feet and legs. I could not make any more room on the couch. Finally she said to me she was tired from the drive up from the Long Island and wanted to be quiet for a little while. I was feeling strange at the closeness of this beautiful woman I did not know. Then, she got up slowly and laid herself next to me. I held my breath as I tried to make room for her on this couch we were on.

The couch was very narrow. She snuggled close to me. Face to face.

My book fell to the wooden porch. She wrapped her arms around me and held me quietly. I was floating. She was seducing me with her silence and soft warmness. *Who is this woman, and why? Irene! Is this supposed to be happening?* I smelled her hair and returned her embrace. She moaned softly, like a deep purr. The sun was warm. The silence between us was comforting. Then she got up, smiled, and thanked me. I fumbled and garbled a "thank you." She held me in her gaze. She was another siren from the great sea. I was taken by surprise. Then she was gone.

I did not pursue the opportunity to get to know her outright. The others returned and the Fourth of July partying started up. My model friend was there, and she was surprisingly involved with a man who had been part of the pirate circle for years. She was paying me little attention. I drank heartily, danced, and partied with my friends. Then I quietly excused myself to be alone. I went up to the sleeping alcove that I had chosen upon my arrival. As I was settling into my bed, the redheaded siren came upstairs and sat at the foot of my bed. We talked, and I did not know if she wanted to stay or what, but I did not offer. She got up and left.

That dark night in Vermont, I slept with owls hooting. In Shokan, we had owls as well; Irene could not hear them when they called in the night, but I could always hear them clearly. I missed Irene, and then I let her go. The next day I went up a waterfall with the first mate and his niece. She was drawn to me, and I was to her, but I tried to be as inconspicuous as possible. I did not want her uncle, the first mate, to get pissed at me. I called her the "Merwoman."

When it was time to leave and go back down to New York, I volunteered to ride with the Merwoman, who had driven up alone. On the way down I drove. We talked and it was very comfortable. Then she laid her head on my lap as I drove and I found myself stroking her thick red hair. I just flowed with this, but I felt uncomfortable as well. She said she was feeling so safe and comfortable with me, and then she sat up and laughed as she apologized for being such a distraction to my driving. We made it back to Point Lookout in one piece. She was too tired to drive to her home so she stayed at her uncle's house. I offered my room, and suggested I could sleep on the couch. She preferred the couch and I slept in my room. I thought nothing of it. I was not looking for anything else. She was too magical for me and I was too over-stimulated by the whole Fourth of July weekend's events.

That same weekend up in Vermont, something happened with my model friend and the man she was with, and it was very disturbing. He had taken advantage of her, or so the story was from her. It came out after we all got back from Vermont, and it was very uncomfortable for the circle of pirates because everyone knew him well. Later, she came to me, devastated by what had happened with this man. She said she had been raped by him. She told me she felt I should have protected her up in Vermont. This was confusing because while we were there, she had not spoken to me for some odd reason, and she seemed to be on real friendly terms with this man. None of this made sense to me. Here was a real social situation I did not comprehend at all—a chaotic pirate scenario. All she had to do if she wanted my help was to ask me—I would have done anything for her. I was open and relaxed while up in Vermont and I did not once sense she was in any danger. Strange! It felt like my feet did not touch the earth much while I was in Point Lookout. It was like living in a stimulating dream filled with colorful characters.

Irene, is this what you want for me? There is adventure around every corner. After one beautiful woman came and went from of my life, another beautiful woman is now there. They both came to me and seduced me. Am I not seeing this correctly? Have you chosen these women for me? Is the Merwoman for real? What am I to do?

The Merwoman was a young, vibrant woman who had her own business a couple of towns north of Point Lookout, also on Long Island. We started to hang out a little. We slept in the same bed together, but were not intimate. We hugged and that was it. We never kissed and I understood the boundaries of our relationship. I was fine with it. But she was so beautiful and had an extreme feminine appeal, and that made it challenging for me. I was grateful she lived in another town.

"I do not want to be in anything serious with you, Ninja. But you are very hard to resist. I am enjoying being around you. What I really want you to do is teach me aikido and the martial arts. I want you to be my teacher. Ninja, my uncle really doesn't like the idea that we are hanging out. He is very protective of me. I told him that you are hard to resist."

"Okay, that's fine," I said. "Listen, Merwoman, you are an adult woman and you make your own choices. I am fine with everything you say. Your uncle has to understand that you make your own choices."

"Look, Ninja, I also have work for you as a carpenter for the rental management business I run," she offered.

"Thank you, I could use the money."

It was in this way that we started to work together and be together. In my new headspace I was open to anything. I tried not to look at life too seriously so I would not get emotionally involved with the Merwoman or anyone else I met. I was relieved to be in the Point Lookout area, where there was no history or memories of "Irene and Ron." I liked that I was The Ninja, and that I could be anything I wanted to be. No one knew me. Being around a beautiful, full-bodied woman who was putting out energy and attention in my direction was very appealing, and her presence made me feel very alive. She said to me that she enjoyed being around me for the attention I drew everywhere we went. I was not aware of what she was talking about. When I was about the town with her, I did not concern myself with the attention of others. Because of my martial art training, I certainly would notice anyone in my periphery of awareness. But unless they registered as a threat, I paid no mind to others when out in public. What the Merwoman registered socially when we were out together I did not pick-up on, and in my processing life after Irene, I did not really care what other people thought anyway. The whole experience of being with the Merwoman was so different and surreal.

One night she asked if she could visit me out in the Point. Yes, sure. She arrived and we drank some wine in my room. She was making a birthday present for her mother from a ragged photo and bits of broken pieces of blue ceramic tiles. She was also going to add broken pieces of green glass and small jewelry objects. It was going to be a collage centered on a tattered photo of her great-grandmother she had found years ago.

"I like making art," she said as she worked at my desk, dry-assembling the broken pieces of green glass and blue tiles. I laid on my bed, tired and ready for sleep.

"This present is made up of broken things, like me. I like broken things." She had told me previously about the childhood abuse and trauma she had experienced at the hands of her father.

"I hear you, Merwoman. You and I were broken as children. We grew and became adults, and yet there remains something broken in us."

As the Merwoman continued to work on her art I fell asleep. I awoke to find her laying on top of me, looking into my eyes deeply. Silently, she drew her face to mine and kissed me. I did not understand what was happening since she did not want this to happen between us. She kissed me strongly. I became lost in my desires and we melted into each other. All that was restrained was now expressed. It was like a dream. It was like when the seafarers became enticed and lost in a siren's song. There was no way to deny the song of passion that came from the deep, dark seas. It was no wonder men had to be roped tightly to the mast in order to hear the song of the siren, or else be lost upon the jagged rocks.

Awakening the next morning, she was still next to me. It was not a dream. I had succumbed to the siren's song once again, and once again I was alive. I remembered that the last time I listened to the siren's song I had been battered and thrown into the dark waters. I looked at the Merwoman asleep next to me and wondered if that was to be my fate once again. For now I was alive. Moments alone and by the ocean reminded me that I was on a incredible journey. My life after Irene was so unreal for me in those early months after her passing. Accepting and moving in a direction of living by myself, for myself, and with myself kept me fresh and confused at the same time. Living in this haven for pirates as The Ninja had its strong points. The Ninja persona was exciting, unknown, and attractively mysterious. So I was going to stay bushy-tailed and wide-eyed, for life now was electrifying and dangerous.

Over the next few weeks stimulation was present in every moment of my life, but depression and grief were still all too real and with me constantly. The Merwoman kept me occupied with work and the opportunities to be with her. I was balancing my desire to seclude myself from her while still being open to anything that developed. Life in Point Lookout in the summer of 2011 was filled with parties and long nights. It was a lifestyle I hadn't lived for a very long time, and I was still not accustomed to being around a lot of people. It was a pirate's life of salty water, slamming down grog, and women. Certainly, other men in my position would enjoy the bachelor's life that was available to me. My life at "the Point" was a freedom from any social ideas I had ever had in my life as a husband, father, and mentor. It was a freedom, and I sadly reminded myself of "why" I was living a pirate's life in the first place...my baby had died. Crazy emotions. Happy–Sad? Thankful–Damned? No worries! I just flowed like the currents of the grey, cold Atlantic Ocean. My heart had been blasted to pieces and rendered to raw red. So, in this point of my grieving process, I continued to allow myself to just flow my experiences at Point Lookout. What did I have to lose? I had lost everything anyway. I was focusing more on "acceptance" over any questionings of "why?"

As July passed and August came, life on Point Lookout kept changing. The reality show gig was standing still, but the parties kept happening. The Merwoman and I were spending more time together and I was opening up to her. I was enjoying working with her and seeing her in her environment. I realized I always enjoyed seeing how the women I know live their everyday lives. I like how women set up their special places to hang their nice jewelry or favorite items. The Merwoman had beautiful tastes and style. It was a woman's or feminine touch that I appreciated. It resonated in me. Such simple soul comfort opened me up to her company. She was a dancer and studied a particular form of Indian dance. I was comfortable.

She invited me to stay at her home and it was a blessing in some ways. I allowed the whole scene with her to start creating a "we," though she was adamant that there was no "we." Her family was not too keen on me, and she would remind me there was no future between us. But, at the same time, she attracted me with invitations. I was getting more and more confused. Either I was not reading the situation correctly, or I was living in a very fluid environment that did not lend itself to stability. I started to think this was how younger people moved and developed an intimate relationship. Or, maybe I was being too heart-mushy sensitive and reading into the situation too much. *Do you want me or do you not? Was I asking too much of others?*

Then the Merwoman and I had an incident in the middle of August that made both of us seek shelter from each other. In trying to be helpful and courteous, I was perceived as being condescending and crossing boundaries. I did not know that opening doors for a woman would not be appreciated, or that asking if she needed a hand with something would mean she is not capable of handling it all by herself. In an incident along these lines, I had a meltdown in her car from feeling totally misunderstood in my generosity of assistance to her. I felt trapped, and I blew. My behavior surprised her and me equally. I was shocked to have the energy of anger rise from me. I thought I was doing well, and then this happened.

What happened between us was in line with what I had been experiencing the whole summer up that point—chaotic, highly stimulating energy was firing off, and creating even more chaotic, highly stimulating energy. I retreated back into myself, and she went back to her life. We saw each other still, but it was different. We were wary around each other, yet at the same time still attracted to each other. I started to stay at my place at the "Point" more. She did not kick me out, and I was still welcomed to stay with her. My desire for the Merwoman intensified while I was apart from her. My heart and sense of being were engulfed in a pain I was not ready for. I failed to recognize that I created a situation where I had been drawn into the energies of a "we." I had stepped into a boobytrap of my own creation. My feelings of desire, grief, loss, depression, and longing started to get mixed-up and indistinguishable from each other. My sleep began to get all whacked out.

It was about this time in late August that an incredible elemental force was growing in the expanse of the Great Atlantic Ocean. The annual hurricane season was stirring and the first hurricane was showing characteristics of abnormal strength and intensity. Weather experts were studying this unusually powerful hurricane—the first of the 2011 season—with great interest. It was the perfect hurricane as hurricanes go, except that it could be extremely dangerous to humans should it make landfall. A couple of years earlier, hurricane Katrina had devastated New Orleans and her destruction was extensive. This first hurricane of 2011 was predicted to be stronger than Katrina, and had an elemental potential far greater than anyone had seen in recent history. The first hurricane of the 2011 hurricane season of was named "Irene."

The winter sojourn was finally over. The cost had been high: a Matriarch lost in the high peaks, four warrior bulls killed protecting the herd in the lower valleys before they crossed the ragged mountains, one fourth of the young ones gone, and most of the elders perished, leaving six remaining.

With the coming of Spring, the gathered woolly mammoth herds settled once again into the security of the lush feeding grounds of the lower valleys—and into the jostling and preparations for the mating rituals that would soon follow. Deadly predators were as abundant as the prey they fed on, so with ease and relaxation came alertness and caution. Death was never too far away.

Woolly Mammoth Boy had seen many winters now, becoming one of three surviving senior bull mammoths. He had served under four Matriarchs and battled many of the herd's enemies. He had watched his cow mammoth die in an avalanche three moons prior, and his only calf— now a young bull himself—had been maimed in an attack by two saber-toothed tigers seven moons past.

I felt a tiredness in my weary bones. "Much suffering and so much loss..."

As I stood on a small hill overseeing the mammoth herds, I observed that all was safe. The security teams of young bull mammoths were in their sentry positions around the wide perimeter of the herd.

I saw a large, iridescent dragonfly darting in my direction.

"Young One, your watch is secured, will you not rest?" vibrated Thought-dragonfly as it drew near.

I continued to stare, saying, thinking, and feeling nothing. I was tired and silent. The dragonfly departed in a flurry of aerobatic patterns before my eyes, but I continued staring without seeing.

"Do you fade as your Man-boy-self fades?" chirped a tiny songbird that had perched on my long, curved ivory tusk. "Your heartbeat resonates with his...searching and uncaring. Do you fade as he is fading?"

I was frozen in thought, frozen in movement. I just stood and looked out onto the broad green valley teeming with abundant life. My bones became infused with the ancient ground on which I stood. I felt the upward pushing of young tendrils of green life deep below in the moist darkness. I heard the language of the soft, wet earthworms as they ate the red earth. I could smell the decay of creatures long gone to dust, mingling in the spring thaw below the surface. I saw in my mind's eye the center of the Universe in a single grain of dirt.

I saw my doom and was unafraid.

I blared a trumpeting call that vibrated the hearts of all the living creatures present in the vast valley plain below me.

All heard my thunderous call, froze momentarily, and then continued living.

42. Hurricane Irene: August 28, 2011

The great parade of woolly mammoths trod slowly along the narrow forest path, which was lined with thick undergrowth, to a clearing that opened up under the canopy of dense, ancient woods. Allowing only two or three of the great mammals to pass at a time, the matriarch led the way with the younger ones following in a long procession. The little newly born ones held tightly to the tails of their mothers so as not to get lost in the deep and immense woods. As the herd entered the clearing they began to spread out to form a large semicircle facing inward. Before them lay strewn a vast jumbled mass of white bones, bones of long-dead woolly mammoths—their ancestors. As the parade of mammoths stood in silence, the matriarch slowly moved with great care into the sea of brittle bones. She made her way gingerly to a particular set of white bones that had remnants of flesh and hide still attached, for these were of a recently deceased mammoth.

"Come close and offer grace to her," signaled the matriarch to the silent herd behind her. One by one they came forth and lovingly caressed and touched the bones with great reverence and tenderness. As she watched each and every one of her parade give respect to the bones of one of their own, the matriarch telegraphed to her gathered kindred, "Someday all of us will lay ourselves down here upon this sacred ground when our hearts beat their last. Then our bones will be so honored as we honor theirs now."

–Woolly Mammoth Boy Remembers

Hurricane Irene was due to make landfall in the next couple of days, and the whole eastern seaboard from Florida to Maine was preparing for the worst. There had not been a hurricane carrying such destructive force for a very long time.

Where would she make landfall? She was packing heavy wind and rain power. Hurricane Irene was breaking records. Seeing Irene's name on the TV, newspapers, and the internet every day was a constant reminder of how recent her passing from this mortal world had been. Equating this hurricane with Irene disturbed my daughter Josie. Josie thought I was foolish to think Irene would ever want to hurt anything. After all, Irene's name meant "Peace."

"Josie, as hurricanes go, Hurricane Irene is magnificent. Elemental forces of nature are without all the human emotional labeling we attach to them. Hurricane Irene is as beautiful as Irene was in her mortal life." Josie did not answer me. She thought I was losing my marbles, and I was.

Hurricanes had only rarely made landfall in the Northeastern United States since 1901. Hurricane Irene was breaking all models and patterns, and I saw the truth in the hurricane's coming. As the days drew nigh, plans were made to evacuate the coastal lands of New Jersey and New York. Merwoman suggested I stay with her during the hurricane. She did not want to leave her tenants alone and unassisted. I was thinking of my family home in Shokan as Hurricane Irene's movements became more unpredictable. Where she would go was a question no one could answer. Irene made landfall on August 27, and seemed to indicate that she would head up the East Coast. She was due in the New York City area by the 28th so I left on the 27th from Point Lookout and headed upstate to protect our Shokan home.

Hearing all the reports of Hurricane Irene made me miss Irene more than ever. It had only been eight months since her passing, and I had been through so much since then. My life in Point Lookout had been a

Hurricane Irene is coming!

seemingly endless cycle of exhilarating, confusing, and highly stimulating experiences. The romantic emotions and possibilities awakened in me by my summer relationships with two beautiful, young, and vibrant women left me bewildered and depressingly lost. I had been seduced and then pushed away. I had allowed myself to become close to another, and had opened my fragile heart in naïveté. I blamed myself for any pain I may have caused.

Was I meant to be with these women? Weren't these two women a gift from Irene, a sign from her, for me to move past her memory, and the memories of the life we had together? How was I supposed to find someone to be with? Am I meant to be alone? How can I go on?

Upon returning to Shokan I was a jumble of emotions and energy. I had always been sensitive to changes in the weather and barometric pressure, and Hurricane Irene was coming on strong. After "battening down the hatches" as best I could, I spoke to the clear, starry heavens that night: "Irene, my love...please be careful with the property...we have to sell the home for the kids."

Knowing I would lose power and electricity as soon as the hurricane hit, I went out and bought a case of wine to use as barter for food with friends I knew had diesel or gas generators to run their refrigerators. With candles bought and batteries ready, I sat back and waited. The afternoon of August 27, Hurricane Irene hit Long Island and New York City. Reports of flooding and minor damage came in. Then, Hurricane Irene changed course and headed inland—up the Hudson River.

Irene you are coming home...you are coming home to me...

The rain started as I went to bed on the night of August 27, and I fell asleep with dreams of Irene.

At 4 a.m. the next morning the rain was light, but turning heavy with gusts of wind. In the night, alone with the storm, something had been resolved in my heart. I had come to the conclusion that I had done my best to continue living after Irene died on December 29, eight months prior. I had sought to be around for my daughters, but they barely called or contacted me for months after Irene died. I understood. They were dealing with their own immense grief and loss. I also did not contact them because I did not know what to say. I did not want to burden them. Yet, I was so terribly lonely and feeling without any support. I took solace in the fact that they had each other, "The Three Lost Sisters." The girls also had adults and aunts who looked after and checked in on them. I do not know for sure...ask them. I understood their choices, but it had been so painful to be bereft of all that I knew—my wife, my daughters, our home.

I had tried to open my life to others and live a life of newness and vibrancy. It had been a disastrous experience. Trying to open my heart to new relationships in Point Lookout was the true indicator for me about moving forward. Allowing new experiences about living with others to be present in my life seemed to have backfired. It was the social indicator that was of value to me in moving on without Irene—not a career or money or a home to live in. It was the social component about living with others that mattered and was important to me. I was now a widower, alone and broken-hearted—was this to be me for the rest of my days? I felt I had tried, and judged myself a failure at it. I saw no chance for myself.

During the night's darkness and building elemental rage, my life played out in my sleepless mind's eye. I knew, and had accepted, that I was born with much to overcome. No one in my family saw much in my becoming anything. I was too sensitive and emotional. I was the compassionate, considerate, and loving person that people enjoyed to be around and confide in. Good guys finish last, I was told. I carried the dark curse of my father's rage and violence. Irene first thought I was bipolar and needed to be on medication. She then confirmed before passing what I thought was true: I was an undiagnosed person with Asperger syndrome. I was too complex with the damage and symptoms of post-traumatic stress disorder and traumatic brain injury to be around people. I imagined myself cursed. Who would want me? I could not stand myself.

In her time with me, Irene had helped me so much and taught me so much. *How was I to continue living without her? I was a liability to anyone and unpredictable for anyone to understand. Hell, my daughters didn't even call me. How could I continue to live without Irene?*

I awoke that morning on August 28 as Hurricane Irene arrived in Shokan with the conclusion that I would join Irene in death—as I should have done on the day she died eight months earlier.

"NO, NO WAIT!" A voice cried out in my heart, *"Seek help! Yes, seek help!"*

With the winds picking up strength and the rain coming down hard, I jumped in my truck and took off for my friend's house nearby. I was frantic and calm at the same time. Fallen trees blocked every street I tried to pass through. I was driving in circles, so I returned back the house. Hurricane Irene drove me back to our home. I tried to call out to my friends for help, but all lines were dead. Finally, I was able to reach my friend, the first-mate who was in Vermont, and talked a vague message of good-bye. I reached the Merwoman and I thanked her. I reached my sister-in-law, Irene's sister.

"Eve, it's Ron." I began to cry.

"Ron, are you okay?"

"Eve, thank you for everything you have done for Josie and me. Please take care of Josie."

"Ron. Are you okay? What are you doing?"

"Goodbye, Eve. Please take care of Josie and the girls." I hung up.

I prepared for my death. I was calm and determined to end this pain.

It was 5:00 a.m. I stripped down to my white *gi* pants and no shirt. I wrote a death poem to my blood daughter, Josie. *"Please understand. I am no good for anyone. You will be fine with your mother and your sisters..."*

I had no gun. I was not going to hang myself or bleed my self out, so I searched the house and found a full bottle of aspirin. By chance, I had an internet connection to search how much aspirin I needed to take myself out. I wanted to make sure I did not survive as a vegetable my daughters would have to care for. It took 36,400 mgs of aspirin to kill oneself. I had 864,600 mgs at hand. This would do the trick. Opening a bottle of red wine I guzzled a whole bottle in three minutes on an empty stomach. Not much of a drinker and my body clean, it hardly fazed me. I opened another. Hurricane Irene raged outside my window.

I opened the bottle of aspirin and started on the second bottle of red wine—*I liked red wine when I used to drink wine*—I laid the pile of aspirin next to my death poem.

I clearly saw myself taking the aspirin, and then laying myself out in the field of our property and allowing Hurricane Irene to wash me away. They would find me later. Then I heard noises behind me, steps, many steps. I turned around, and there were people in the room with me. Seven people in yellow rain gear—cops.

"Mr. Rubio, I am a Sergeant with Town of Olive police. You need help. We are here to bring you to the hospital."

How in the hell did they get here? I moved around the pool table creating distance between them and me.

"Don't come close to me." My head cleared in a flash of lighting. I saw six Department of Environmental Protection (DEP) cops and the sergeant. I eyed each and every one of them. I marked them for death.

"Mr. Rubio, we know you are a martial artist. I have with me six DEP officers, and more are coming. Please come with me," the sergeant said.

"Sarge, first, back off. Second, I am not going anywhere. I did not call you."

"Your sister-in-law called us." The sergeant was gauging the distance between him and me. "Mr. Rubio, I cannot imagine what you must feel losing your wife so recently. I am so sorry, but we have to take you in. You need help."

"Sarge, I am not going anywhere and I do not need your help. I did not call for you. Get off my property...NOW!" I was eyeing the group of cops and the sergeant. They are between me and the aspirin.

"Mr. Rubio, we know who you are. You have been helping kids in this area for years. Let us help you now," the sergeant said as he inched his way forward to me.

"Stop," I warned him and the others. "Please do not move."

"Mr. Rubio, I read your death poem. I saw the empty bottle of wine and the empty bottle of pills...let me help you."

"Sarge, you are now between me and my pills." I saw movement in the corner of my eyes from a nervous-looking cop. "Stop! And I mean it."

"Freeze everyone!" the sergeant ordered. "Look, Mr. Rubio, we know you can kick all our asses." He looked at the weapons rack filled with my wooden swords and staffs. "We only want to help you. I have these six officers here and more will arrive soon. We have to bring you to the hospital so you can get help. Please, it does not have to be hard."

"Sarge, it has to be this way. I did not call for your help, and I do not want your help." I slowly settled into a fighting stance and looked at each cop, one at a time. "I am not going anywhere. I am going to kill each and every single one of you in this room." I reached for the flick knife at my side. The six DEP cops threw back their yellow raincoats and reached for their sidearms. The sergeant did not move a inch.

I saw myself in a flurry of attack movements, cutting and slashing. Many cops go down. I am being shot numerous times. Suicide by cop.

"FREEZE! EVERYONE HOLD!" The sergeant commanded everyone in the room. I was eyeing the first one I would kill, a nervous jittery cop.

"Mr. Rubio..." The sergeant's voice was calm and deep. "In a short time the New York State Police will arrive and they will handle this very differently. They will use lethal force. Is this what you want for your daughter? I saw the poem you wrote to her."

I froze.

Josie...

"Sarge, get all these cops out of here and I will talk to you and you alone," I said.

"Everyone, stand down, and clear out right now." There was hesitancy in the six cops. "I said, EVERYONE STAND DOWN AND CLEAR OUT OF HERE RIGHT NOW." They backed down the stairs. The last one was looking at the sergeant, and not wanting to leave him alone with me. The sergeant glared at him, and then he also descended down the stairs.

Alone now, we looked at each other.

"Damn it Sarge...my wife is dead and life is shit...I have tried so hard to continue."

"Mr. Rubio, I cannot imagine the pain you must feel. I would not know how to handle it if my wife died. Please let me take you to the hospital. You need someone to take care of you. Your daughter needs you."

"I have three daughters, sergeant." I was very clear-minded.

"Look, Mr. Rubio, the State troopers just pulled up."

There were footsteps on the stairs, "Sergeant, you okay? The State Police are here," a faceless cop said.

"Yeah, I am fine, leave us alone. I am in control," the sergeant tells the DEP cop without taking his eyes of me.

"Well, what will it be, Mr. Rubio?" He asked looking at me with sadness in his eyes. He saw the death wish lingering in me. "Once I leave here the State Police take over."

"Sarge, I am not going to let anyone touch me. No one is strapping me down."

"Look, Mr. Rubio, I will ride down with you. Nothing will happen to you."

Slowly, I let out a long breath.

Josie, Annie, Zoë...

Irene, am I failing you again? I said I would go wherever you went. I am here and you are so far away.

"Mr. Rubio, please hand me your knife." He reached out to me with an open hand.

I won't harm this man, but I will take out others and be with you Irene...

I realized how much this man was risking. He had never cleared his jacket to get to his sidearm, and he was only one arm's length away from me. If I wanted to slice his throat it would be easy. With the sergeant watching my every move, I reached slowly to my side, flicked my blade open, and handed him the knife, handle first. This was to show him I was now at his mercy. The sergeant never flinched. He received the blade and closed it.

"Come on Mr. Rubio. You lead," he said in a quiet and calm voice.

As I walked out of the carriage house, I saw the driveway packed with DEP cops and a team of New York State Police. The road was jammed with cars. The hurricane was kicking ass. I was suddenly humbled by the manpower wasted on me. These guys should be available for other people's needs, not mine. I felt stupid.

"Everyone back off and clear out. I am going into the ambulance with him," the sergeant ordered. All personnel complied. Like the parting of the Red Sea, the sergeant led me through the throngs of officers to the ambulance.

The sergeant followed me into the ambulance. No one was talking, and all eyes were on him. "No one is strapping Mr. Rubio down. I am with him." I sat down on the gurney. I noticed the EMT looking at me. He was a young man in Army fatigues.

"I am going to take your vitals," the young EMT said to me smiling. "Do you know me?" he asked.

"No, young man I do not." I was tired now. My adrenaline was depleting.

"I am David Stoutenbergh, Sensei." The sergeant smiled at David and me. "I was your aikido student. Remember? You helped me and my brother Peter years ago."

"Yes, David. Yes, I do remember you."

"Don't you worry about a thing, Sensei. I will take care of you."

The ride to Kingston Hospital was tricky; fallen lines and trees were everywhere. I was numb and quiet. The sergeant was checking in on his com-set, and David was sitting next to me taking vitals and notes. As we pulled up to the hospital I saw security guards and two burly orderlies waiting. The ambulance doors opened, "Sensei, everything is going to be okay."

"Thank you, David. Please give my regards to your brother and family."

The two orderlies stepped up, flanked by the security guards.

"We got it from here, Sergeant," said the biggest orderly.

"I am walking him in," the sergeant said.

"Sergeant, that is not the hospital protocol. We got it from here, sir."

"I know." The sergeant was firm and calm. "This man is not going to be strapped down, and I am walking him in." He stared down the orderly.

The hospital guards and the orderlies did a silent check-in with each other. One of the guards talked into his com-set. No one was moving. The wind was howling and rain was drenching us all. The hospital security unit parted and the orderlies led the way in.

The sergeant walked me into the hospital with a gentle support on my left elbow. The hospital staff stood watching while the security unit backed off.

The orderly directed the sergeant to take me to the holding room. Once inside, I was told to sit on the gurney. The sergeant turned to me, "Look Mr. Rubio, you are okay now. Everything will be okay. Rest, and these people will take care of you."

I stood up and shook his hand. Our grip was firm and strong. We looked into each other's eyes.

"Thank you, Sarge," I said.

"You be well." Then he turned and was gone. There was a hurricane to attend to.

Once alone, I laid down on the gurney. The bright florescent light was glaring. I was tired. I was feeling that I had let Irene down again, but I was still alive.

Your daughters...Annie, Josie, and Zoë...hang on brother...

Hearing footsteps enter my room, I sat up.

"Mr. Rubio, I am the head nurse on this shift. I will be looking after you. You are safe and everything will be okay. I need to take your vitals and ask you some questions."

"Sure," I said. My voice was a long ways from my body.

I wanted to kill myself. I wanted those cops to shoot me dead.

"Your full name, Mr. Rubio?"

After the head nurse finished up her business, she paused and looked at me. "Do you remember me, Mr. Rubio?" *I heard this question before...where?*

"I am sorry nurse. I do not seem to recollect," I answered meekly.

"You helped my son, Joey, many years ago. You helped him so much in his life."

I felt like I was spiraling through the clouds. I had left my body hours ago. "Yes, I remember the name, Joey." My voice was coming from the other side of the universe.

"Mr. Rubio, I will take care of you. I am so sorry about what happened to you and your wife. I am so sorry. I will take care of you." She reached out and held my hand. As she did this I felt my inner eye refocus on my body sitting in that holding room and re-enter. I was feeling a warm hand on my hand, warm skin-on-skin.

I am alive!

Don't leave us! We need you!

"Can I get you anything to eat or drink?"

"Yes, tons of water and veggies. Anything green, please." I realized I was starving. I had come back from the dead.

"I will be right back."

I lay back down and closed my eyes. My body was humming. It was vibrating.

I am alive. What is my mission?

Footsteps. "There was no salad to be found. I brought some carrots and a few bottles of water." The head nurse was beaming at me. "I am glad you are here safe."

She quietly retreated from the room and I collapsed again. I fell asleep. I awoke to find the lights out and a blanket on me. I fell back asleep.

Later, I was awakened. The head nurse was back.

"Mr. Rubio, I am glad you have rested. The hospital therapist wants to interview you. They want to hold you for four days. That is mandatory for cases like yours." I looked at her with a puzzled look. "You tried to commit suicide. Four days is mandatory. They will want to give you medication."

"You know that is not going to happen to me," I said. "No one is putting anything into me."

"I know, Mr. Rubio. Look, talk to the therapist. She is waiting for you next door."

I got up and rinsed my mouth in the sink. I felt like I had come back from a long, dusty journey of darkness and death. The bright, cold hospital lights reminded me of when I took Irene to the emergency room back in December 2010 after coming back from Germany.

The interview with the therapist did not go well. The head nurse came back into the room.

"I heard that she wants to admit you to the Psych Ward."

"You know this is not going to go down easy." I looked at her with solidity in my being. I was quite alive again.

"Look, Mr. Rubio, I am on your side and I will take care of you. I will call the head psychiatrist on shift. I know him. I will talk to him." She got up and left.

Minutes went by and she returned. "He will be right over. He is seeing another case. I will put in a good word for you.

I laid back down and began my focusing on my breathing.

What was...was.

What will be...will be.

"Mr. Rubio, the doctor will see you now. I talked to him, and he seemed to know you." The head nurse smiled at me and led me into an interview room.

"Mr. Rubio, please come in." The head psychiatrist was a trim, slight man. "I know what the hospital protocol is with cases like yours. I know you have been under extreme stress, and the loss of your wife is extremely significant. I am sorry for your loss. Answer me this, Mr. Rubio, what would you intend to do if I let you leave here?"

"I would continue my training and keep moving forward. I know what I want to do," I answered.

"And what is that, Mr. Rubio?"

"To continue to help others, Doctor."

The doctor stared at me and looked at my folder. "I know of you and have heard of you for quite a while now." He looked at me, smiling. "I work with a couple of young men who had been your clients in the past. They speak very highly of you. I have heard of your work with young people in this area for a number of years. In fact, the head nurse on shift has spoken to me on your behalf."

"Thank you, Doctor."

"Look, Mr. Rubio, you do not belong up in the Psych Ward. Though hospital protocol dictates four days of medication and observation in cases like yours, I will not have you stay here. You need to go back to your training and doing your fine work with young men and people. I know you have gone through a lot this morning and today. I will not hold you here. I will sign the papers to release you. Is this clear to you, Mr. Rubio?"

"Yes, very clear. Thank you, Doctor. I appreciate your support and confidence in me."

"Very well. I'll get the papers set up and get you out of here." He stood up and faced me, extending his hand. I reached out and shook it. Our handgrip was firm and solid. "Mr. Rubio, be well and I know you will do fine. Keep up the good work. You are needed in this world." (He allowed me to go because he had heard the stories about me, the head nurse of the emergency ward gave me a great word of confidence, and the doctor saw that clarity in my heart and heard the truth of my integrity in my words. I guess being in a small community in which all knew me and trusted me goes a long ways.)

With that he left and the head nurse came back in. "I told you I would put in a good word." She came over and hugged me strongly. "Mr. Rubio, you will be fine. The papers will be ready and you can leave."

"Thank you so much for all that you have done for me today. Thank you," I said with sincere humbleness.

"Mr. Rubio, you really helped my Joey. You were a godsend to him and I will never forget what you did for my son."

After getting my papers I was released. I called my dear friend Stuart who came to pick me up. I left the hospital at 1915 hours (7:15 p.m.), and Hurricane Irene had moved northward up into Vermont. As I looked west toward the Catskill Mountains, the dark storm clouds were being scattered by high winds, revealing the setting sun which sent beams of light across the valley. The sun felt warm on my brow.

I understood clearly that I had been reborn through the devastation of my soul.

Irene Bell Brody died on December 29, 2010
Ronald Rubio died on August 28, 2011

Irene and Ron walking away together. Author's photo, 2007.

The huge, female woolly rhinoceros grunted heavily across the twenty-five paces that separated her from Woolly Mammoth Boy. Their battle was minutes old, and already both she and Woolly Mammoth Boy had sustained bloody injuries. With the woolly rhino holding her massive head downwards, snout to the ground, her four-foot-long single horn was aimed right at Woolly Mammoth Boy's exhausted heart.

Wandering unconsciously too close to the woolly rhinoceros while I was foraging, I had triggered a fight-response from the normally docile, yet easy to agitate rhinoceros.

"Danger! Awake! Defend!" called a mockingbird from a nearby tree, outside the battle circle in which I fought for my life.

As if on cue, the woolly rhinoceros charged. Gaining momentum quickly, she slammed into my hind flank. Her horn bit deeply.

I trumpeted a call of anger, swinging my massive head and smashing into the woolly rhino's exposed side with my steel-hard tusks. Crack! Crack! I heard several of the rhino's rib bones break. She was thrown backward and fell onto her forelegs.

My own rear leg had been rendered useless. I stood heavily on my other legs, trembling.

The fleeting thought crossed my mind: "I feel the death of me."

Unknown to Woolly Mammoth Boy, the rhino's horn had sliced open his femoral artery—he was slowly bleeding out. His mind slowly fogged as his blood loss became more acute.

A rustling startled him to focus as the rhino charged again. He looked up just in time to see her rushing toward his exposed side, under and behind his left foreleg. Woolly Mammoth Boy felt the hardened horn puncture his rib cage and pierce his massive heart. With one last effort, he swung his head and drove his tusks into the woolly rhino's chest, driving broken bones into her heart and lungs.

They both fell dead where they stood. Two massive creatures twitched in their death throes, and then were still.

Woolly Mammoth Boy's open, glazed eyes dried slowly in the spring sunshine, gleaming with life no longer. His heart had stopped. His blood *darkened the trampled and turned-up battleground where he had died.*

His body was now a gift for the buzzards and other scavengers. It would feed many. In time, his bones would be gathered by his kind, and brought to the place of his ancestors.

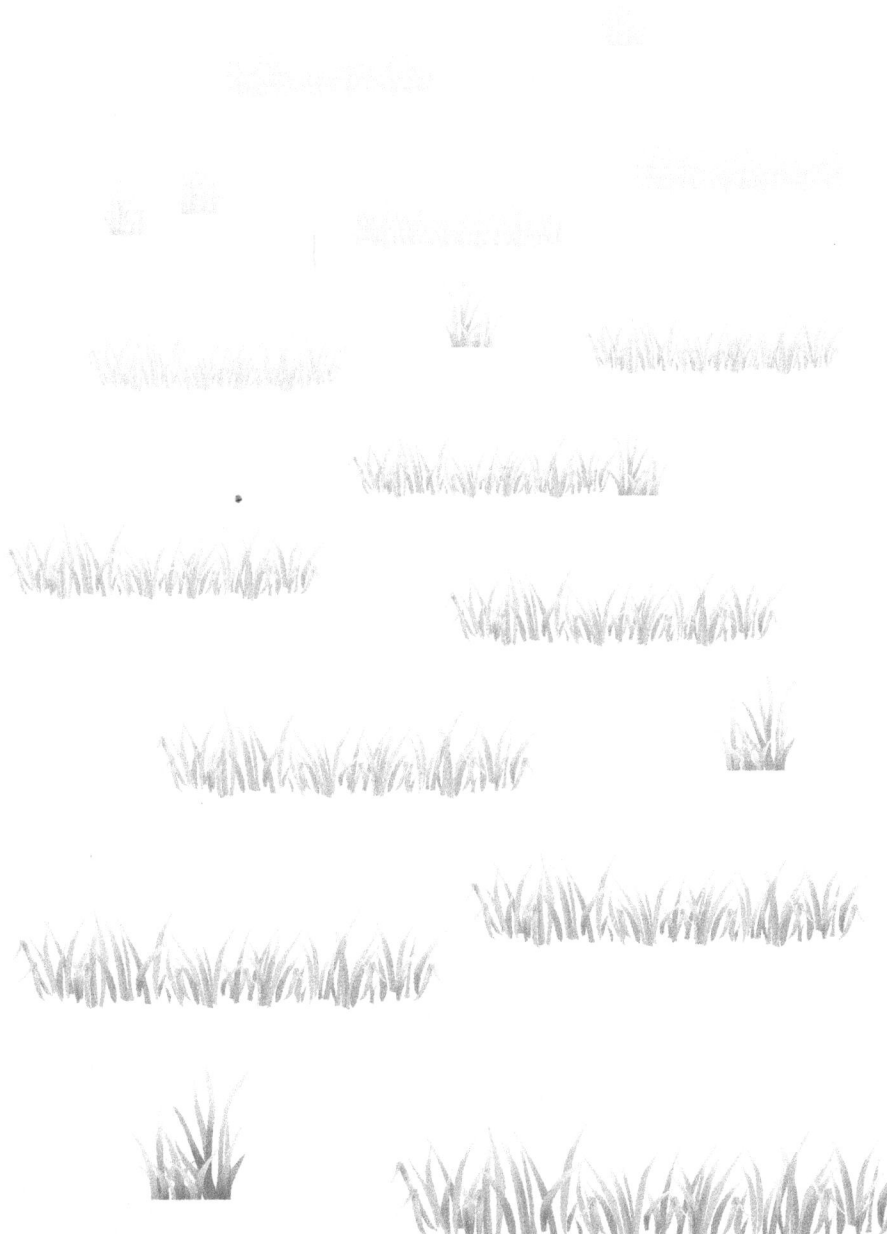

Part 8:
Shugyosha Samurai

43. Vicente

I floated in the vast void that is the boundless Universe. Here passed a hurtling mass of shooting stars, there a dying sun blasting into a zillion particles to fill the emptiness of what was. Battered and torn to pieces by saber-toothed tigers, pierced by hunter's spears, gnawed upon by a vulture's beak, I drifted alone in the darkness and the brilliance. A tiny whisper of my consciousness registered that my more recent human reincarnation had tried to destroy himself because of his grief and despair.

"So little one, what many adventures you have had!" A bodiless voice woke me from my slumber in the micro-universe of my mind.

"So, you are present to watch me drift as I am to be created," I said.

"Of course little one! This is the pleasure of the Universe!" Thought communicated to me.

I spoke of my intention, "Well, I am to be created without changing shape."

Thought was absent and then responded, "Well, little one, it seems that your time as a human being is not yet complete, though it is known to me that you have had the opportunity to evolve beyond the mortal boundaries from the karma of your past lives..." Thought paused in mid-sentence, and then continued, "You have decided to stay, to stay on and live, to continue a life in the circle of pain and suffering. I find this curious. Why continue to suffer?"

And as celestial stardust sprinkled upon my matted furry head, covering my long curved tusks, I answered, "I choose to stay for there is still much work to do.

There are so many who still suffer."

–Woolly Mammoth Boy Remembers

H URRICANE IRENE WAS LONG GONE. She had moved out to sea to dissolve after laying waste to nearby New York small villages and towns, and whole swaths of Vermont. I awoke on top of the portable, narrow massage table that had been set-up in the middle of my *sempai's* tiny living room. My martial arts *sempai* and close friend of many years, Stuart Allen had picked me up from the Kingston hospital the evening before. There was no power in his mobile home. I smelled of old wine and sweat, and still wore the same clothes I had when taken to the hospital. I had slept a deep sleep and hadn't moved all night as I recovered from my suicide attempt the day before. I felt like I was emerging from a chrysalis, wings wet and body vulnerable. My mouth felt like it had been dusted with dirt, dust, and bone ash.

I am alive. I had died, and now I am alive...

"Stuart, I want to get back to Shokan. I need to check out the house," I said with a brittle voice. I was still not quite in my body, which floated somewhere in the Great Universe. It had tried to find Irene out there.

"Sure, sure," Stuart looked at me without judgment and criticism. *I had tried to kill myself.* "I made some tea for you."

"Thanks, Brother. Stuart..." I looked at the floor. "I am sorry for what happened yesterday."

"Ron, I mean, Vicente, you did what you did. It's okay," he answered.

I could always rely on Stuart to be there for me. He, Irene, and I had been close.

"Yes, I am ready to get back to the house."

The drive back to Shokan from Kingston was hazardous, and filled with downed power lines and fallen tall trees all along the road. Upon arriving in Shokan, I saw the house was fine. Alone after Stuart left, I went into the carriage house where the lingering energy of what had happened a little more than 24 hours earlier was still vibrating. The open wine bottles were there, but the pile of aspirin was gone. I tore up my death poem to Josie and burned it. I opened the doors and windows and aired the place out. I let the death energy out.

I am alive and what was...was.

Later that day, news from my lawyer buddy came through that all the papers had been finalized in the courts. I was now legally "Ronaldo Vicente Rubio," and no longer "Ronald Rubio." I decided I would go by grandfather's name, "Vicente." I was no longer "Ron." He died and was no more.

A few days later I prepared to head back down to Point Lookout. I would have to face my circle of people there. Everyone had heard of the attempt on my life. How could The Ninja, the warrior, healer, and mentor to so many, try to take himself out? What a coward! How could he do this to his daughters? What was he thinking?

My life felt strangely ancient and very vast. The death of 18-year-old Derek in my arms in 2008, Irene's cancer in 2009, her death in 2010, and the death of 21-year-old Danny-Boy Kellogg from his cancer in March of 2011. (Danny Kellogg was a young man I met in Germany when Irene was there. He had 4th stage testicular cancer at the age of twenty years; we made friends and I kept up with him until he died from his cancer, in Manila in 2011.) Now my own death wish had left me empty and real. "Real" in the sense that I truly understood now what was "real" and "not real" for me, and what "loss" and "gain" was. It was all pointless and meaningless. I accepted now that things come and go. I had suffered from the desire of what I wanted, and then suffered when I lost it—the love forever. It all meant nothing now. *I was empty.*

I arrived in Point Lookout to find the town undamaged by the hurricane. My pirate friends were stunned by my suicide attempt. Mixed feelings. To some I was not to be forgiven, and then I realized it did not matter what they thought of me. In fact, it did not matter what anybody ever thought of me, or who I was, ever again. I was a different person in their eyes now. I realized I was going to stop trying to please others, and stop trying to figure things out about human psychology in the social world. I accepted that I was a unique human with autism, compounded by PTSD and TBI. It just did not matter what others thought of me any more. All that I once was died the day of Hurricane Irene. "Ron Rubio" had died. All I believed to be true died, and had turned to white ash and bones.

The question to myself was, *what am I to do with this new life I have been given?*

I reached out to the clairvoyant of the ship's crew, Tori Quisling, of nearby Port Washington. Throughout my former lifetimes I had resonated with the mysteries that existed, and of that which could not be explained by science and lab experiments. Though the original beliefs about our relationship to ourselves and the Universe were organic and life-inspired, I felt the religions of Man were too contrived and tailored for use over others. Guilt. Shame. "The Chosen Ones." Don't eat this. Don't wear that. Lots of rules. Lots of hypocrisy. The Philippines is a very strong Catholic nation, but at the same time there is a strong connection and respect for the world that could not be explained. At the core are indigenous beliefs in the powers and mysteries that could not be smothered by a Euro-centric religion originally enforced by the Spanish. I had this in my blood, and my psyche vibrated with such truths. I knew that Tori would be able to open some doors for me, so I called her.

"Vicente, I will help you. Come over and I will do a reading for you."

"Thank you, Tori."

Her office was a beautiful place filled with loving energy and light. I felt I had come home. The first session began and my truths were revealed.

"Vicente, you died that day. 'Ron Rubio' died that day, and he is no more. You are now this new person. You are now this 'Vicente.' You do know you did not have to return to this life. In your last lifetime you completed this 'Circle of Rebirth,' and yet you chose to come back. And all the trauma and hardships you faced in this lifetime prepared you for the work you are here to do—for the mission that you wanted and accepted, and that is to be here for others in need."

In following sessions I received insight from Irene and my Grandfather Vicente. Aspects of my life that I had no inkling about now made sense. My mission was clear to me.

"Vicente, your mission in this lifetime, a life you chose to come back to and the mission you asked for, is simple: You are to be present for others. Your presence alone is enough. You are here to raise the vibrations in others and, lastly, you are here to be a light for others. In all your former lives, you were always a warrior and a highly regarded one. You are now a healer and teacher, and you are best served if you remember this fact. You are a healer and teacher."

"Vicente, release all your worries and anxieties of this world, for all that you require will be provided to you because your mission takes precedence."

Much was revealed to me, and much was a reminder of what I knew in the core of myself. I felt I was ready to face what needed to be faced in this world. In the following month I realized I was being asked to leave the East Coast and start somewhere new. Was it to Germany to help Dr. Lentz and his cancer patients? Start completely new in the Philippines? Back to Oregon? California? I researched the Peace Corps and filled out my entrance papers. I was completely open to the world. I only knew I wanted to be of service to others. It did not matter where I was or what happened to me. I knew I was here to be available to others.

My older brother in California offered me work, and said he would set me up with my own place. It was challenging to be around people and I needed my own space, but my brother wanted to help out. I thought I would never move back to California, but that was when I was "Ron Rubio." I said "Okay." I packed up all my stuff from Shokan and had it all shipped to California. I should have sold it all. It was meaningless, but somehow still had meaning. I slowly started to say my farewells to a place where I had lived for many years.

A week before I was to move out to California, I got a call that our family dog Phoenix had died. I had to give all the animals away when Irene got sick in 2009. Two of my former students who got married, took our two dogs. I went to their home to see Phoenix before they buried her. She lay on the living room floor on her favorite rug she had chosen. She looked at peace. I knew she felt me leaving the area, and decided it was time for her to go as well. *Goodbye, Phoenix.*

One day in the middle of October 2011, as the leaves turned deep red and brown and the air grew cooler, I boarded a plane to Eugene, Oregon where I would pick up my car and drive down to California. My life on the East Coast was ending after 32 years. I came here a young man, and was now leaving a grown one.

I would be known as "Vicente" to all I would meet. My hair was growing back slowly. *One step at a time. One breath at a time.*

The blazing sun was bright upon the green glade. Dark, passing rain clouds allowed the sun only brief but brilliant appearances. The female woolly mammoth stood alone, trembling, not far from a half-circle of other females mammoths who attended her. The Matriarch watched as her younger sister prepared to give birth to the calf she had been carrying, heavily these last few weeks.

The Matriarch knew her herd was thinned by deaths from battle injuries, accidents, disease, and old age. The calf her younger sister carried added strength to herd. New blood. Survival. Continuation.

I stirred in the watery world of the womb. The building pressure pushed me downward through the birth canal. I could hear the pounding heart of the one who bore me.

Thump...thump-thump!

Thump...thump-thump!

Louder and stronger were the sounds of a heart beating and vibrating the liquid that I floated in. Slowly, my unopened eyes registered a change in the darkness. Light. Pressure. Pounding...the heart drumming loudly and strenuously.

Suddenly—blinding light! I surge out from the womb with a wash of bloody liquid and raw energy.

I was jarred by my fall. I lay motionless, registering my first breaths on the "outside." Hot air upon my wet, soft, hairless hide dried me quickly. I looked upward. I lay between the legs of a cow mammoth in a small pool of bloodied water, with my umbilical cord and part of my placenta still connecting me to her.

"Welcome, Woolly Mammoth Boy! Welcome back!" chirped a hummingbird as it darted to and fro. "You made it in one piece!"

I struggled to free myself from the remnants of the placenta that trailed out of the cow mammoth above me. A healthy shaking movement tore me free. I was now separate from my host of the last 22 months.

I lay and processed. Where am I? What am I?

I stood on my wobbly legs. I tested a flexible, short trunk that protruded from my face. I looked upward and around me, and saw a solid wall of woolly mammoth legs and chests, and huge mammoth heads with deep eyes that studied me.

One female woolly mammoth came forward and gathered my placenta, throwing it into the bush. The others gathered around me. They offered support to their sister who had just given birth.

"Does the sister accept her young?" the Matriarch asked from a deep rumble in her chest. The cow mammoth above my shaking, glistening body gingerly smelled me, nudged me around a bit, and then drew me closer to her. "Good. So it is! We acknowledge your acceptance and we will guard your little one with our lives."

With that, the Matriarch slowly, and with elegant deliberation, left her sisters to attend to other matters of the herd. Soon others wandered off as well, leaving me alone with the young cow.

"Welcome, Woolly Mammoth Boy! Welcome back!" shrilled the hummingbird as it swooped back down to me. "Welcome! You have returned!"

44. The Path of the Warrior

In the deep redwood forest, the pounding surf of the nearby salty ocean echoed in the hallowed ground where I stood alone. I am Woolly Mammoth Boy! I am the Universe incarnate. I am as imperfect as the most perfect of diamonds. I am as sane as the berserk madman who prowls the cremation grounds. I am Woolly Mammoth Boy! I have roamed the great icy blue glacial fields of the farthest north. I have dined on the sweet grass of Patagonia. I am well acquainted with Death held on the right and Life on the left. Ward! Be wary, for the saber-toothed tiger lurks; be cautioned, for all that appears permanent is as fleeting as the changing clouds in the vast heavens.

How do I know this? I am Woolly Mammoth Boy!

–Woolly Mammoth Boy Speaks

Her wedding ring lies in the nook of a giant redwood tree in a shady redwood grove in the far north in the borderlands between Oregon and California. Secluded off the beaten path—I was always good at finding those secret places when we were together—I placed her ring of white and yellow gold in the nook of this massive tree to be purified by the great Tree Goddess.

The coastal drive from Eugene to San Francisco was beautiful. I stopped at every redwood forest on my route. Irene would have liked the ride.

My new life, proposed by my brother in California, started differently than planned. That was okay. I had learned that life was constantly in flux, and nothing was guaranteed. My work with my brother involved maintaining this huge commercial building he owned, which included mopping and sweeping long, silent corridors with the hum of electricity constantly in the background like white noise. It was Zen work for me. I hardly spoke to anyone. I mopped and cleaned, for it was all that mattered. It was sacred work befitting a wandering warrior in constant practice. *Shugyo*—"constant practice."

I quickly found the local public rose garden and became a volunteer there. I piled the hours on as I had done at the San Diego rose garden the year before. Getting back into what I did as "Ron Rubio"—the mentoring—was challenging, and yet it was the service to others that was my life's mission. From my former life I remembered that I had a great private practice as a mentor to the autism youth population. So I hit the pavement,

Irene's wedding band placed in a redwood tree, 2011. Photo by author.

and went to all the agencies I could find with the book I had published on mind–body techniques in 2008 in hand. Within months I started to get responses.

"Hi, my name is Vicente..."

Living with my brother, his wife, and their three sons was a blessing and a challenge. I loved being with the family, but I needed my own space. I was still getting used to living again, and I was much more quiet and slower than my former self. Though I accepted my new path and new life, the vibrations and images of my former life, of Irene's sickness and her passing, would take my breath away at the most peculiar times. I felt that I needed to be wary of others since they did not understand what I was still going through. Instead of having my own place—as it was proposed to me—I slept in an 8-by-8-foot room I made in my brother's basement. It was okay—I had four walls and a sliding door.

One day the "dirt hit the fan" with my brother, and I knew I had to leave. It was just that brothers will be brothers, and Fred was still Fred. He loved me a bunch but he really did not have the slightest idea what I was going through and how fragile I was. If he did, he expressed it in a way I did not understand. I did not want to be an inconvenience to my brother and his family any more.

A few months earlier, I had started taking aikido classes with a sensei I had admired for years while I was living on the East Coast. His name was Frank Doran Sensei and his dojo, Aikido West, is located in Redwood City, California. Doran Sensei welcomed me with sincere warmth and friendship. His senior teachers were so warm and very gracious to me. I did have a shaky start with the members of the dojo, being a new guy from another dojo and fairly high ranked. I expressed my aikido, which was not familiar to the Aikido West crowd. Some felt I was too rough, too this or too that—to me I was doing the aikido that I have been doing for twenty-seven years. We each adapted to each other over time, though.

The morning after the blowout with my brother I walked into the dojo during morning class. Doran Sensei, seeing my gloom-and-doom demeanor, heard my tale of woe and offered me the opportunity to live in a small room in the dojo for free. Accessed by a ladder, it was above the dojo mats, and the room had a real door to close. The Aikido West dojo members welcomed me, and this is where I made my home for now.

When I first met Sensei I informed him of my life's situation, and he was most generous with his support. I was offered to teach at his dojo as a substitute teacher, and at the Stanford University Aikido club he had started thirty years prior. He recognized my 5th degree rank from my sensei, Yamada Sensei of New York Aikikai. After a while I decided I would best serve the Aikido West dojo by being a student rather than a teacher—that was the reason I came to the dojo in the first place, to be a student of Doran Sensei. I also needed to focus on getting back on my feet, and teaching would take up time. There would be a time I would teach aikido again, but not now.

Connections slowly opened for me. Some led to others, and others dispersed like the morning San Francisco fog before the warming sun. One job offer led me to a dance center to teach a children's dance class. The job did not pan out, but I was offered ballet classes for free. After almost 19 years of not putting on dance tights I was at a ballet barre once again, and my body was wondering what the hell I was doing! We thought we quit this stuff years ago! Nope. Once a dancer, always a dancer!

Being persistent, I was able to design, with my friend in San Diego, the director of the Autism Research Institute (ARI), a 16-day autism advocacy mission the Philippines. I lectured on "Mind–Body techniques for health and well being" and "Mentoring strategies" for the autistic youth population. It was a success. Returning to the Philippines awoke a desire to do more work there, and I went back three more times after this first initial mission in 2012. In October 2013, my newfound friends in the autism support community there invited me to present at the National Conference on Autism in Manila.

Each morning, I wake and give great thanks for my life's mission to serve others. I give great thanks for having a warm room to sleep in and hot water to cleanse myself. I allow myself to stay open in my heart and fearless in my spirit, for I understand that I go where I am sent—and I am sent where I am needed to raise the vibration in others, be a light for others, and be present for others. I do not question much because I do not have many questions to ask. I know my life's purpose, my mission, and I know I am provided for with all I require to accomplish what is asked of me. My life is very simplified and uncluttered by the material cravings, or by the superficially stimulated social world around me.

Each day my hair grows longer. Each day I shed my former life as a snake sheds its old skin by rubbing itself on a rock. My rock is the awareness that this is my life now.

What was…was.

What will be…will be.

All that is…is.

My mission is simple: to serve others, to protect and comfort others. This mission takes precedence in all that I do. And for this, I am blessed!

Woolly Mammoth Boy looked out upon the vastness of the celestial cornucopia of sparkling galaxies arrayed before him. He stood at the brink of blank nothingness. His mind was empty and his breath was deep in his belly. Motionless he stood, and stardust accumulated upon his head, gentling his furrowed brow. Visions and remembrances of past lives raced across his opened eyes. Unblinking, he stared directly into a blinding, white, exploding sun—his was vision was unscathed.

"You live on, my little one!" a song sang deep within my mind, echoing like a reverberating trumpet call in a deep, empty cave. "The Man-boy has been reincarnated as well—he too has come back."

I saw a male woolly mammoth calf appear in my deep awareness. I watched as the calf made its way toward a small, clear pool of water, near where his mother and other mammoths foraged and rested. Not more than a few months old, the calf had already survived one scrape with predators. His mother, and an alert sentry bull mammoth, had trampled his would-be killer to death, saving the calf's life.

As the calf neared the pool, a throaty toad-call rang out from the water lilies floating upon the surface. "Woolly Mammoth Boy! Woolly Mammoth Boy!"

I saw myself as the mammoth calf I was witnessing in my awareness. The woolly mammoth calf and I were one and the same.

"Yes, little one, the mammoth calf is you, and you are the mammoth calf. The Man-boy is you, and you are the Man-boy," Thought vibrated as a twinkling star.

I watched my long trunk drift ever so slightly between my long, generously curved, white tusks. As a blazing meteorite sped by me on its maddening race across the cosmos, another vision slowly came into my awareness: my Man-boy incarnate.

I saw something different about him almost immediately...he had changed. His face showed it, and his breathing validated the truth. The Man-boy was at peace. He finally was at peace.

Thought voiced joyfully, "You see truly, your human ward and self has grown. He is a 'Man-boy' no longer—he is a Man."

I raised my trunk and trumpeted a blaring call of declaration into the vastness of the Great Universe...

"I am!

We are!"

Epilogue

THE WARM HAWAIIAN WATERS BUOYED me up under the vast, open sky. I had waded offshore about a hundred meters into the endless waters, with the rich blue-green of the Pacific melding playfully into the upper reaches of the heavens.

I had come back to the Hawaiian Islands for a month of reflection, rejuvenation, and healing. My life on the mainland had taken incredible twists and turns. Having moved on from my stay and practice at the Aikido West dojo, I was debt-free with no place to call "home"; my mentoring work developing autism advocacy in the Philippines was building, and the whole world was open to me.

I knew one thing for certain—my mission to serve all living beings was a hot iron in my blood. Still, questions resonated inside me.

How can I best serve this world? Where am I to go? Where is my "home" on this earth?

As I waded in the warm, soothing Pacific, I called upon Irene to show me a sign. It was now almost three years since her passing and I checked in with her every day. Since being on the island I had had many "life signs" gifted to me already. I am awakened every morning by unseen doves that call my name loudly, "Vi-cen-te, Vi-cen-te!" Brown-skinned, black-haired Hawaiian people surround me and accept me easily as a local; there is a large population of Filipinos here with soul cooking that feeds my heart with joy. Plus, I have my only male cousin, my mother's brother's son, living on Oahu! Promising!

I called with great reverence, "Irene, Irene...*Irene.*"

Just then, no more than a hundred meters from me, a large sea turtle broke the calm ocean's surface—one of Irene's power animals in her mortal life! The hairs on the back of my neck and my arms rose...

Irene answered me!

I started to cry in the open water. As I looked for the sea turtle again, she was now only fifty meters from me...*she was swimming toward me.*

I closed my eyes in the face of the magic that was transpiring around me. As I opened them again, Irene Sea Turtle surfaced a mere arms-length distance from me! Her large turtle shell was green with algae and sea growth. Her head was as big as a football, and her golden eyes stared into mine. I silently sang her name, *"Irene Bell Blue Pele Old Turtle!"*

Slowly and elegantly, Irene Sea Turtle swam a tight circle around me... locking her eyes to mine as I rotated to stay with her. She was so close to me.

She answered me with her presence. I heard her in my heart, *"Yes, my love, stay here. I give you my blessings...."*

As Irene Sea Turtle finished her sacred, watery dance, still looking into my crying eyes, she slowly sank into the blue-green waters, and was gone.

Thank you, Irene, my love. I will serve this world from this paradise.

The very next day, I bought a one-way ticket to the Hawaiian Islands. After taking care of business on the mainland, I would be coming back to stay.

I have been gifted a new home here on earth, to ground me as I pursue my mission.

Mahalo.

About the Author

R. Vicente Rubio is a first-generation Filipino-American born in San Francisco in the late 1950s, and assessed with Asperger syndrome in 2010.

Vicente has enjoyed a full life as a professional dancer, musician, and artist. He is a mind–body specialist, having developed the holistic mind–body training practice of BodyKi in 1985. Under his former name, Ron Rubio, he is the author of the book *Mind/Body Techniques for Asperger's Syndrome* (Jessica Kingsley Publishers, London 2008).

A practicing martial artist, Vicente is a 5th degree black belt in aikido, and has studied capoeira, boxing, and the Filipino marital art Lapunti Arnis (of Cebu, Philippines), as well as various close-combat techniques.

He advocates for autism awareness and conducts parent training and professional teaching on successful healthy life skills and independent living for those on the autism spectrum. He has mentored and taught young people for more than thirty years.

Vicente is a grateful volunteer at the Inez Grant Parker Memorial Rose Garden of San Diego, and The San Jose Municipal Rose Garden, both in California.

He resides, gloriously happy, on the Hawaiian Islands.

Contact

woollymammothboy.com
woollymammothboy@gmail.com
pathfindermentoring.com